The Multilingual Turn in Languages Education

NEW PERSPECTIVES ON LANGUAGE AND EDUCATION

Series Editor: Professor Viv Edwards, *University of Reading, Reading, UK*

Two decades of research and development in language and literacy education have yielded a broad, multidisciplinary focus. Yet education systems face constant economic and technological change, with attendant issues of identity and power, community and culture. This series will feature critical and interpretive, disciplinary and multidisciplinary perspectives on teaching and learning, language and literacy in new times.

Full details of all the books in this series and of all our other publications can be found on http://www.multilingual-matters.com, or by writing to Multilingual Matters, St Nicholas House, 31–34 High Street, Bristol BS1 2AW, UK.

NEW PERSPECTIVES ON LANGUAGE AND EDUCATION: 40

The Multilingual Turn in Languages Education

Opportunities and Challenges

Edited by
Jean Conteh and Gabriela Meier

MULTILINGUAL MATTERS
Bristol • Buffalo • Toronto

Library of Congress Cataloging in Publication Data
The Multilingual Turn in Languages Education: Opportunities and Challenges/Edited by
Jean Conteh and Gabriela Meier.
New Perspectives on Language and Education: 40
Includes bibliographical references and index.
1. Language and languages—Study and teaching. 2. Multilingualism—Social aspects.
3. Multicultural education. 4. Education, Bilingual. I. Conteh, Jean, editor. II. Meier,
Gabriela, editor.
P53.45.M85 2014
418.007dc23 2014014812

British Library Cataloguing in Publication Data
A catalogue entry for this book is available from the British Library.

ISBN-13: 978-1-78309-223-9 (hbk)
ISBN-13: 978-1-78309-222-2 (pbk)

Multilingual Matters
UK: St Nicholas House, 31–34 High Street, Bristol BS1 2AW, UK.
USA: UTP, 2250 Military Road, Tonawanda, NY 14150, USA.
Canada: UTP, 5201 Dufferin Street, North York, Ontario M3H 5T8, Canada.

Website: www.multilingual-matters.com
Twitter: Multi_Ling_Mat
Facebook: https://www.facebook.com/multilingualmatters
Blog: www.channelviewpublications.wordpress.com

The policy of Multilingual Matters/Channel View Publications is to use papers that are
natural, renewable and recyclable products, made from wood grown in sustainable for-
ests. In the manufacturing process of our books, and to further support our policy, prefer-
ence is given to printers that have FSC and PEFC Chain of Custody certification. The FSC
and/or PEFC logos will appear on those books where full certification has been granted
to the printer concerned.

Typeset by Techset Composition India (P) Ltd., Bangalore and Chennai, India.
Printed and bound in Great Britain by the Lavenham Press Ltd.

Contents

Contributors

Joëlle Aden (joelle.aden@gmail.com) is full professor at Le Mans University (France) and a member of the INEDUM (Innovation in Education) research group within the CREN (Centre for Research in Education). She conducts research projects on the impact of empathy on language interaction and the role of embodiment in language learning and teaching. In her latest projects she analyses theatre activities from the point of view of the enaction theory (Varela) and paves the way for a new perspective on the potential role of arts education, namely drama/theatre, in developing empathetic skills, which she proposes to consider as part of transcultural competence. Doctoral theses under her supervision explore the links between the arts and SLE.

Jim Anderson (j.anderson@gold.ac.uk) is senior lecturer in languages in education at Goldsmiths, University of London. His work at Goldsmiths has built on his long experience of teaching languages in multilingual London secondary schools and it is here that he developed his interest in more integrated and inclusive approaches to language learning. Jim has led the development of the PGCE in Arabic, Bengali, Mandarin, Panjabi and Urdu at Goldsmiths and also leads a masters module on 'Teaching language in multilingual contexts'. His research interests lie in the areas of second language learning pedagogy and community/heritage languages.

A Mooznah Auleear Owodally (auleearo@uom.ac.mu) is senior lecturer at the University of Mauritius. Her studies in Newcastle and Durham made her conscious of the wealth of her language and literacy experiences, and she became interested in the challenges Mauritian children face as they join school. This interest came home with the arrival of her daughters; she thus started a PhD with the University of Cape Town investigating the emergent literacy practices of pre-school children in multilingual Mauritius. After her PhD, she developed a keen interest in religious literacy practices in multi-religious Mauritius. Her publications relate mainly to these two areas.

Shila Begum (mohammedansharali@yahoo.co.uk) arrived in England from Bangladesh in the 1980s at the age of five. Encouraged by her parents, she developed literacy skills in her heritage language. She holds a degree in childhood studies and a PGCE, and has four children, one of whom is autistic. She has worked in a range of roles including an early years teacher, interpreter and researcher. For the past 10 years, she has worked in the Bilingual Learning and Teaching Association, teaching complementary Saturday classes and working with families and mainstream teachers to promote the benefits of bilingualism and strategies to encourage bilingual learning with primary children.

Yu-chiao Chung (y.chung@gold.ac.uk) obtained her first degree in English and education. She was an English teacher at a secondary school in Taipei, Taiwan. She obtained a PGCE in teaching Mandarin as a second/foreign language from the National Taiwan University. After coming to the UK, she began to teach Mandarin to learners of different levels, both children and adults. She received an MA in English in education and an MRes in education and professional studies from Kings College, University of London. She obtained her PhD in education at Goldsmiths, University of London. This study was entitled 'Schools at home: parental support for learning Mandarin as a second or foreign language'. Yu-chiao's research interests include bilingualism and biculturalism, multilingualism and multiculturalism, creativity and e-learning in language teaching. She contributes to MA and CPD work in these areas at Goldsmiths.

Jean Conteh (J.Conteh@leeds.ac.uk) is senior lecturer in the School of Education at the University of Leeds, UK. Her interest in multilingualism and social justice came from her work as a primary teacher and teacher educator in multilingual contexts in different countries, and from the experiences of her own, dual-heritage children. She completed her PhD in 2001, investigating the factors which contributed to the success of pupils from minority ethnic backgrounds in multilingual primary schools in England. Since then, she has published many books, chapters and articles about the issues, and continues to work with primary teachers and students.

Fiona Copland (f.m.copland@aston.ac.uk) is senior lecturer in the School of Languages and Social Sciences at Aston University, Birmingham, UK. She taught English for many years in Nigeria, Hong Kong and Japan and also trained teachers in these countries. She is interested in how pedagogies for language teaching are developed and legitimised and whose interests these pedagogies serve. She particularly questions the belief held by many that EFL classes should be conducted in the 'target language' (i.e. English) as her experiences in classrooms round the world contradict this view. Her PhD focused on novice teacher talk in feedback conferences and she has published in this area.

Angela Creese (a.creese@bham.ac.uk) is professor of educational linguistics in the MOSAIC Centre for Research on Multilingualism, University of Birmingham, UK. She has been researching multilingual practices and pedagogies in school settings for over 20 years. She has worked in a number of multilingual ethnographic teams and is committed to describing the processes and benefits of researching multilingually across multiple research sites. She has published widely in the areas of language planning and policy, multilingualism and education, and linguistic ethnography.

Ken Cruickshank (Ken.Cruickshank@sydney.edu.au) is associate professor in education and lectures in TESOL, language, literacy and diversity to preservice teachers at Sydney University, Australia. He taught English, TESOL and languages in schools for many years and has been a tertiary educator since the 1990s. His doctoral study was on language and literacy practices in Arabic communities in Australia. His present research interests include community languages, internationally educated teachers and teaching-learning English as an additional language.

Laurent Gajo (laurent.gajo@unige.ch) is professor of linguistics at the Faculty of Humanities, University of Geneva, where he is the Head of the *École de Langue et de Civilisation Françaises*. He is a specialist of second language acquisition, multilingualism, bilingual education and language policy. He completed his PhD in 1999 and carried out several research projects on bilingual education. Through a qualitative approach to classroom interaction from the kindergarten to higher education, he continues to develop analytical tools to capture the integrated construction of linguistic and subject knowledge in different socio-institutional contexts. He is also involved in teacher training.

Ofelia García (ogarcia@gc.cuny.edu) is professor in the PhD program of urban education and of Hispanic literatures and languages at The Graduate Center, CUNY. She has been professor of bilingual education at Columbia University's Teachers College and dean of the School of Education at Long Island University. García's extensive publication record on bilingualism and the education of bilinguals is grounded in her life experience in New York City after leaving Cuba at the age of 11, teaching language minority students bilingually, and educating bilingual and ESL teachers. Among her best known books is *Bilingual Education in the 21st Century: A Global Perspective*. Her website is at http://www.ofeliagarcia.org.

Guangwei Hu (guangwei.hu@nie.edu.sg) is associate professor at the National Institute of Education, Nanyang Technological University, Singapore, where he teaches graduate courses in language assessment, language acquisition and research methodology in applied linguistics. Among his main research interests are bilingual education, family biliteracy practices, language-in-education policy and second language academic literacy. These research interests have arisen from his own experience of learning and teaching English as a foreign/second language. He has published extensively in these areas of interest.

Naomi Kano (kanotnj@kdn.biglobe.ne.jp) is assistant professor in the Graduate School of Humanities and Science at Ochanomizu University, Tokyo. She has taught English as a second/foreign language and Japanese as a foreign language extensively in international schools and universities in Tokyo and Singapore, including the United World College of Southeast Asia and the National University of Singapore. She received her doctorate and master of education from Columbia University, investigating the role of translanguaging in the literacy development of transnational Japanese youth. Her teaching experiences as well as her personal experiences as a member of a bilingual family in these multilingual contexts for more than two decades led her to work in the field of multilingualism and critical approaches to literacy education.

Sandra McKay (2sandra.mckay@gmail.com) is professor emeritus of San Francisco State University. Her main areas of interest are sociolinguistics with a focus on multilingualism, English as an international language and second language pedagogy, all areas in which she has published widely. Her interest in these areas developed from her work in international teacher education. Over the course of her career she has been fortunate enough to have worked in and travelled to over 100 countries.

Gabriela Meier (G.S.Meier@exeter.ac.uk) is lecturer in language education at the University of Exeter, UK. She speaks four languages and has always had a keen interest in languages, social cohesion and social justice. She started her career as an administrator, translator and language teacher and had many different jobs in different regions of Europe before she discovered her interest in academic work. She gained her PhD on the basis of an evaluation of a two-way immersion programme in Berlin, and she has recently conducted a study in a London bilingual project (funded by the Esmée Fairbairn Foundation), which resulted in the Bilingual Immersion Education Network (http://www.bien.org.uk). Her research led to a range of published work on social implications and language learning, above all in bi/multilingual programmes.

Enrica Piccardo (enricapiccardo@gmail.com) is assistant professor at the Ontario Institute for Studies in Education (OISE), University of Toronto. Her academic career has been under the sign of mutilingualism, and so has been the education of her trilingual children. She completed a binational PhD (Italy and France) in 2003, investigating the way creativity can foster computer-assisted language learning and teaching processes among secondary school students. The following year she was appointed *Maître de Conférences* (associate professor) at the University of Grenoble in France, where she worked on teacher education until 2009. She has published and presented extensively in several countries and in different languages in the old and the new continent.

Saiqa Riasat (blta2011@hotmail.co.uk) is one of the founders, project development worker and one of the teachers for the Bilingual Learning and Teaching Association (BLTA). Her degree in primary education enabled her to reflect on and question her own experiences and negative attitudes as an EAL learner in the British education system, and realise the academic and social benefits of being bilingual. She has worked in a variety of educational settings, delivering courses, inset training, workshops, seminars and parent courses, which aim to promote heritage language maintenance for EAL children, and promote true bilingualism. She played an important part in developing the multilingualism policy in Bradford.

Andrea Young (andrea.young@iufm.unistra.fr) grew up in Yorkshire, studied French in London and gained her PhD from Aston University for research into motivation and attitudes towards foreign language learning. After moving to Alsace to be with her French husband, she was appointed as a *Maître de Conférences* in the French university system and currently works in the Ecole Suéprieure du Professoriat et de l'Education at the University of Strasbourg. Living with her multilingual family in Alsace, a border region attracting significant numbers of migrants, Andrea experiences plurilingualism both professionally and personally on a daily basis. Her research and teaching interests include teacher language awareness, intercultural home–school partnerships and supporting second language acquisition. She has been involved in a number of European projects in these areas, notably with the European Centre for Modern Languages in Graz. For more information, see http://iufm-carel.unistra.fr/web.carel/web/en/andrea_young/tout.php.

Acknowledgments

We wish to thank the colleagues we called upon to review the draft chapters, some of them more than once. We appreciated their willingness to take on extra tasks in their already busy schedules and valued their feedback, which helped to shape the final content of the book: Jane Andrews, Adrian Blackledge, Clare Wardman, Eve Gregory, Charmian Kenner, Claudine Kirsch, Martin Lamb, Terry Lamb, Constant Leung, Katja Lochtmann, Vally Lytra, James Simpson, Raymonde Sneddon, Manka Varghese and Li Wei.

We acknowledge the work of all the authors who have contributed to this volume. We have enjoyed communicating with them, and meeting some of them on the way. We value their scholarship and have appreciated their collaborative responses as we felt our way towards the final version of the book.

We also wish to acknowledge Jackie Matthews for her intelligent and careful proofreading and compiling of the chapters for final submission as well as Peter Pool for checking the index.

Thanks are due to Professor Joe Lo Bianco for agreeing to write the Foreword on the strength of a conversation at a conference. We appreciate his enthusiasm for the project and the way he has captured the key messages of the book.

Finally, we are grateful to Professor Viv Edwards, Tommi Grover and the team of publishers at Multilingual Matters for their vision, commitment to publishing the books we need for multilingual futures and their pleasant and friendly working practices.

Jean Conteh and Gabriela Meier

Foreword

Naturalising the Multilingual Turn

We have often lived in social realities well before we can talk about them. Only slowly do we start to identify and name aspects of the settings we have inhabited, but as we do they take on the sharp edge of recognition that allows them to enter our consciousness. As concepts are named and distinguished we can then proceed to deepen, enrich, problematise and debate our social lives more fully.

While multilingualism has been a naturalised dimension of life for most people in the world, such as on the Indian subcontinent or in Africa – in parts of Europe, China, the Antipodes or in the Americas there have been political moves towards monolingualism at different times for different political ends. Today, however, through mass migration, economic globalisation, instantaneous communications and relative ease of travel, many nations have been transformed into self-consciously multilingual polities, now generating their own stocks of labels, names and discourses, treating multilingualism as a non-incidental, permanent fact of public life.

We can see the multilingual turn not only in the communication diversity of our societies. It is also evident in the concepts and discourses societies generate in order to accommodate multilingualism as an increasingly accepted feature of the public life of our communities, following periods during which personal multilingualism had often been relegated to private spheres. The global coverage of this book amply demonstrates these changes.

Multilingualism is entrenched in economic, educational and personal spheres of ordinary living. Like all change, however, there is resistance and hostility to combat. In this excellent new book, editors Jean Conteh and Gabriela Meier and the contributors help us to discuss, understand and normalise multilingualism, showing its pervasive presence in the lives of individuals and institutions across the world. While it becomes clear that this is not without its challenges, the authors suggest ways forward related to a number of these.

Education involves a series of selections. Curricula select from the wide variety of literacies that learners encounter naturally outside school only those which are allocated the prestige and privilege of counting for an academic standard education. Similarly, schools select from the multiplicity of languages that surround them only a small number to teach, or to teach about. The chapters of this volume coherently reinforce and extend our understanding of how schools' narrow selections can be broadened to be more representative of the lived worlds of learners, but also of teachers, curriculum writers and administrators. We all inhabit the interconnected public space that is the economic and social envelope of public education. In this vein, the book demonstrates that acknowledging multilingualism and multiliteracy throughout the academic and administrative operations of education can enhance the quality, seriousness and equity of education for all learners, not just for those who were brought up multilingually.

Joseph Lo Bianco
Professor of Language and Literacy Education
Graduate School of Education, University of Melbourne, Australia

Introduction

Jean Conteh and Gabriela Meier

The idea which developed into this book emerged in the concluding session of a BAAL conference at the University of Aston (UK) in July 2011,[1] where we, the editors of this book, participated in a group discussion that made us conclude that we might be witnessing 'the multilingual turn'. What seemed like a casual remark at the time led to an email exchange and ultimately the book you are holding in your hands now, which compiles contributions from 18 authors that all indicate in different ways that we may indeed be witnessing the multilingual turn in languages education.

This book aims to make a contribution to current thinking about multilingualism in education, reflecting the complexities of contemporary individual experiences in multi-layered communities. It is based on concerns that we feel are increasingly relevant for teachers, teacher educators and researchers, across the disciplines, not just specifically in language education, but for anyone with an interest in education. These concerns relate to how multilingual identities and competences can be valued in schools, how multilingualism can serve to construct a sense of belonging to one or more groups, and how, through multilingualism, social cohesion and justice for all can be promoted. Thus, we are interested in the language entitlement and education of all learners as social actors and global citizens in a complex world.

In this book, the authors examine the existence, possibilities, opportunities and potentials as well as the challenges of the multilingual turn. They present different perspectives on theories and classroom practices and thus, we hope, plenty of food for thought, so that readers can take these ideas further in their own work. In the following we outline the rationale for this book, define key terms, outline the three perspectives that flow through the three parts of this book, and outline the structure of the book.

Rationale: Why This Book at This Time?

We argue in this book that the multilingual turn is based on two important recent developments: the first in society and the second more related to education. The first concerns the recognition that in the globalised world, most societies are increasingly multilingual, and most people

1

are multilingual to a certain extent. Some argue that the 21st century could be seen as the post-national era (Hooghe & Marks, 2001), where 'the effects of globalisation and the diffusion of multiculturalism within nation states have given renewed emphasis to the question of language in diverse societies' (Castiglione & Longman, 2007, Preface). Over many years, in cities across Europe, successive waves of 'circular migration' (Vertovec, 2007), often following global events and trends, have led to the growth of contemporary, complex and multi-layered communities which Vertovec characterises as 'super-diverse'. This means that, increasingly, members of societies, including learners in classrooms, have – and develop – diverse language repertoires, which people use to 'actively construct their own patterns of language use, ethnicity, and social identity', often in 'strong contradiction to the fixed patterns and the reified ethnicities attributed' to them (Leung *et al.*, 1997: 544). Thus, individual identities, and group affiliations, do not fit neatly into monolingual national categories. Many people feel they neither belong to their country of residence nor the one their ancestors came from, as Lüdi and Py (2009: 160) argue:

> Numerous bilinguals do not feel fully accepted by either of the cultures in question. There again, the cause is often not bilingualism/biculturalism so much as 'monolingualist' and 'monoculturalist' ideologies dominant in one or both of the communities.

In this book we argue that in contemporary society monolingual conceptualisations and approaches which, as some argue (e.g. Makoni & Pennycook, 2007) have never been realistic, have become even less appropriate to think about language, language learning and pedagogy.

The second development concerns the tensions between diversity and inclusion in mainstream educational provision in relation to language diversity. In fact, the minority languages that children bring to school are often seen as a problem rather than a resource. Moreover, PISA[2] (for instance) has shown that language and socio-economic backgrounds are the two factors that determine school achievement most of all (Naumann, 2005; OECD, 2003; Stanat & Christensen, 2006). Children with minority language or indeed multilingual backgrounds are often marginalised and even to a certain extent excluded from unfolding their full potential for their individual progress and for the benefit of society. There is a growing body of literature that presents the arguments about language and education from social justice perspectives. For example, in terms of language diversity and bilingualism, Brock and Conteh (2011) argue the case for the rights of the bilingual child in education in England, and Meier (2010, 2013) argues that use of locally spoken languages in school can be associated with social inclusion and conflict resolution. In these ways, both editors of this volume have illustrated in their prior work the complex potential implications for individuals and perhaps also the wider society in understanding the role of language in educational achievement and success, as well as social development.

When we began discussing this book and the theoretical concepts that would underpin it, we found that another book was to appear within a short time of it, also with 'the multilingual turn' in the title (May, 2014). While the two books were conceived independently on opposite sides of the globe, they add strength to the argument that the multilingual turn may indeed be here. We expand on May's (2014) authoritative view of 'what a more critical multilingual perspective might mean for theory, pedagogy, and practice' to include the important strand of social cohesion and social justice as well as inclusion in the framework of ecologically informed perspectives on language learning and teaching. We include insights from continental Europe, UK, China, Mauritius, USA and Australia, which examine the opportunities and challenges of the multilingual turn, thus complementing and expanding on May's (2014) edited work.

Language and Multilingualism: Defining Key Terms

Before we turn to multilingualism in education, we need to clarify what we mean by language and multilingualism. There is a range of theoretical lenses that help us examine language and what it means to individuals and societies. In recent years, the myth of the monolingual nation of monolingual citizens has been challenged at several levels (see also May, 2014). For instance, it has been proposed that all language competences, even if only limited, should be recognised and celebrated as part of a person's plurilingual repertoire (COE, 2001). Thus, the focus has shifted from the native-speaker or deficit view to the bilingual or asset view (Hélot & De Mejía, 2008; Jenkins, 2006). The concept of a standard language has been further questioned, and language varieties have been (re)discovered, such as English language varieties and dialects (BBC, 2011), or world Englishes (Jenkins, 2006), with the implication that a language may be 'owned' by all who use it rather than just by those who acquired it as a first language (Ortega, 2014). This resonates with Blommaert and Backus's (2011) reconceptualisation of the familiar idea of language repertoire, moving it from relating closely to 'speech communities' to defining the language resources of individuals, as part of their 'indexical biographies', which change and grow (sometimes reducing) along their life journeys. Taking this view, all learners in classrooms have repertoires of languages and/or linguistic varieties, which could be activated as vehicles for learning and to foster language awareness and curiosity about their own languages and those of others.

You will have noticed that we have used both terms 'multilingual' and 'plurilingual' above. Which term is used depends largely on the tradition in which the literature was produced. Those who write in French tend to distinguish between the terms *multilinguisme*, which describes the existence of several languages in a given society, and *plurilinguisme*, which refers to the use of several languages by an individual (see chapters by Gajo and Piccardo & Aden, in this volume). There has not been such a distinction in English-language literature. More recently, however, the French term *plurilinguisme* has also found its way into English-language academic literature (e.g. Taylor & Snoddon, 2013). So you will find that authors in this volume use either one or the other, largely based on their backgrounds and/or the context of their work.

In the following three sections, we provide a brief outline of theoretical and conceptual perspectives related to language, learning and pedagogy that underpin the multilingual turn as presented in this book. We found that certain theoretical strands are threaded through the chapters, above all the common – albeit not always explicit – idea of the ecological perspective, which we will return to below.

Perspective I. Construction of Language: Ideologies, Socialisation and Identities

Clearly, languages do not exist in isolation; they are used in social contexts and in specific domains. Young people in schools are socialised 'through language' and socialised 'to use language' (Schieffelin & Ochs, 1986). However, decisions about which languages are taught, and through which languages content is taught, in schools are based on sociopolitical discourses and ideology. Woolard (1998: 3) argues that there is a relationship between language ideology and identity, based on:

> ...the very notion of person and the social group, as well as such fundamental social institutions as religious ritual, child socialization, gender relations, the nation-state, schooling, and law.

The languages we use and in what social contexts we use them shape our identities in that we constantly (re)organise a sense of who we are and how we relate to the social world through language (Norton, 2014; Norton Peirce, 1995: 16–17). Social engagement, however, depends on the goodwill of all participants, on the sides of both the newcomer and the established or more powerful group. If children have a limited command of the language of instruction, and of literacy, and no efforts are made to welcome them on their own terms, social stigma can be constructed, based on the 'implicit association between how well individuals express themselves and their intelligence' (Torres-Guzmán, 2002: 6). Clearly, this leads to disadvantages for some and advantages for others. Edwards (1998) provides practical ideas to make multilingualism visible in schools to signal to children and parents, as well as the whole school community, that they all are welcome as legitimate participants. But this is not enough to secure educational success. Some argue that it is a human right to learn through a language we understand (Skutnabb-Kangas, 1994); it is implicitly enshrined in a number of Human Rights Declarations, which outline the entitlement of education for all, regardless of their mother tongue. Moreover, as Edwards (2009: 46) points out, language rights not only concern those who speak a minority language; we also need to 'recognise that benefits also accrue to speakers of majority languages', and we argue here for the entitlement of all learners to reflect on and develop their language repertoires.

We do not claim that the above insights have been universally translated into practice, but we argue that in recent years researchers and teachers have increasingly problematised traditional models and definitions of language as part of the multilingual turn, as will be seen in this volume. Authors in this volume have questioned and examined current practice, and identified ideas, models and pedagogic interventions that could make positive contributions to changing practice by empowering all learners and teachers as legitimate participants, recognising and building on their diverse (linguistic) knowledge through various types of multilingual socialisation in educational settings.

Perspective II. Language Learning

There have been several 'turns' in the history of language learning theories. These describe paradigm shifts in how we, as researchers and teachers, have understood language learning, and they influence how languages are taught. Influential ones over the past 30 years have been the 'cognitive' turn (McLaughlin et al., 1983) and the 'social' turn (Block, 2003). In the first, in the psychological tradition, researchers argue that language learning should be viewed and understood as a cognitive activity where learners individually process incoming information. In the second, following the Vygotskyan tradition, language learning is understood as a socially mediated activity (Lantolf, 2000; Lantolf & Poehner, 2008), where learners construct meanings in interaction with others. Block (2003: 4) argued

> ... for a broader, socially informed and more sociolinguistically oriented SLA [second language acquisition] that does not exclude the more mainstream psycholinguistic one, but instead takes on board the complexity of context, the multi-layered nature of language and an expanded view of what acquisition entails.

This shares important understandings with ecological models of learning and development (Bronfenbrenner, 1979; Cole, 1996; van Lier, 2004), most notably that learning needs to be studied and understood as situated within specific social, cultural and historical contexts. Creese and Martin (2003: 161) explain how the very specific local experiences of individual participants in a classroom activity – both teachers and learners – are influenced by and influence in turn the more global outer layers of experience in school, community and the wider society.

We argue that it is important to consider the ways in which these previous 'turns' have contributed to our current understandings of the multilingual turn in languages education, leading to the key premise – encapsulated in the ecological model – that the processes of learning are both cognitive *and* social, as well as historical, cultural, emotional, kinaesthetic, interpersonal and moral (see chapters by Anderson & Yu-Chiao and Aden & Piccardo in this volume). Based on the fundamental idea that there is always a reciprocal relationship between classrooms and societies, embracing multilingualism in education will not only affect individuals and classrooms, but it can have wider societal implications, such as linking communities with each other, and linking schools, families and communities (see Chapter 8 by Meier and Chapter 9 by Conteh, Begum & Riasat in this volume). The contributions in the book show in different ways how this more holistic or ecological way of looking at language learning can be seen as one of the main foundations of the multilingual turn as we understand it.

Our construction of language learning in the multilingual turn also allows researchers and practitioners to recognise the agency of families and communities in their children's learning, and thus identify the contributions they make through the 'funds of knowledge' that children bring from home to their school learning, which González *et al.* (2005: 91–92) define as:

> ...those historically developed and accumulated strategies (skills, abilities, ideas, practices) or bodies of knowledge that are essential to a household's functioning and well-being.

Through providing children with 'ample opportunities to participate in activities with people they trust' (González *et al.*, 2005: 92), a key element of funds of knowledge in communities is their reciprocity, the ways they contribute cumulatively to enduring social relationships and thus to interdependence among community members. As children learn in this way, they develop a profound sense of belonging and of their own place in communities that are culturally and socially complex. And, as the authors point out, 'educational structures and practices often militate against such cultural identity', and this is why 'we should consider alternative policies' (González *et al.*, 2005: 48).

Perspective III. Language Pedagogies and Curricula

For historical reasons related to the influence of different educational traditions, the meanings brought to the word 'pedagogy' and 'curriculum' vary widely across different historical, social political contexts. Moreover, and as some chapters in this volume indicate, in some European traditions, the word 'didactics' is at times used interchangeably with pedagogy to indicate the body of knowledge related to the practice of teaching. As Alexander (2004: 10) suggests, the etymology of the words, along with recent political trends, has led to a limiting view of pedagogy/didactics becoming commonplace in policy documentation in England and other Anglophone settings, which – he argues – means that it is taken to refer to 'traditional direct instruction' and not much else. His global definition of pedagogy as 'the discourse which informs and justifies the act of teaching' indicates that there is more involved, as do the conceptualisations of language and learning that we have outlined above. Furthermore, as Trowler (2003: 96) argues, there is often a conflict between those who make policy and those who put it into practice. We argue that it is in the classroom activities and interactions constructed between teachers and learners that policy is enacted, and thus the need to see language pedagogies as dynamic and dialectical. Several chapters in this volume illustrate what this can mean for classroom practice (see chapters by Auleear Owodally; Conteh, Copland & Creese; and García & Kano in this volume).

Pennycook (2001: 115–116) further suggests that there may be a reciprocal influence between society and school; he argues that classrooms do not merely reflect the outside world but they are also social and cultural domains in their own right. Indeed, what happens in classrooms or schools may also influence the outside world to a certain extent. Alexander (2004: 11–12) continues his discussion of pedagogy in England by listing the three sets of 'domains of ideas and values' that – he argues – need to underpin the notion of pedagogy. His third set, which he suggests relates to the larger contexts of schools and policies, are culture (the 'values, ideas, institutions which inform, shape and explain a society's view of education'), self ('what it is to be a person . . . and how through education . . . selfhood is acquired') and history ('the indispensable tool for making sense of both education's present state and its future possibilities'). These are what – he suggests – 'anchor' pedagogy 'firmly to the questions of human identity and social purpose without which teaching makes little sense'. We suggest that these factors are vital to pedagogies that have the potential to bring the multilingual turn to life in classroom practice and this point is illustrated by a number of chapters in this volume.

A central domain of pedagogy is, of course, the curriculum. Curricula are largely determined by education ministries based on political decisions (Torres, 1998: 14), so we would expect perhaps that political ideologies rule what happens in schools. However, as we argue above and as can be seen in this volume, teachers and learners find and make spaces to interpret curricula in their own ways in the actions they take in their classrooms. Moreover, as discussed above, learning cannot simply be described as occurring within the mental processing of individuals, but needs to be thought of as taking place in the interactions that occur between them (Gibbons, 2000). As Gibbons suggests, an important implication of this is that both teachers and learners have agency in the processes of learning, albeit in unequal ways. Their roles are closely interrelated and co-constructed in the moment-by-moment interchange of classroom conversations. In this way learning can be seen as genuinely dialogic (Wolfe & Alexander, 2008). But, as Alexander (2010: 6) argues, dialogic teaching and learning is 'not the "speaking and listening" component of the teaching of national curriculum English under another name', but requires a repertoire of strategies and techniques which:

> ...harnesses the power of talk to stimulate and extend pupils' thinking and advance their learning and understanding. It helps the teacher more precisely to diagnose pupils' needs, frame their learning tasks and assess their progress. It empowers the student for lifelong learning and active citizenship.

Seeing learning as ecological and dialogic and pedagogy as dynamic and dialectical means that nothing is inevitable or predetermined; both learners and teachers are empowered to use the language and cultural resources at their disposal to 'learn without limits' (Hart et al., 2004). This is also – we argue – part of what is implied in the NACCCE (1999) report on 'creativity, culture and education', and the distinction it makes between 'teaching creatively' and 'teaching for creativity'. The four characteristics discussed by Jeffrey and Craft (2004) – relevance, ownership, control and innovation – have important implications for learning and, as illustrated in this book, also for the multilingual turn. Such constructions of teaching and learning open doors for the pedagogic opportunities of newly developing ways of conceptualising language use such as translanguaging (Baker, 2011: 208 ff.; García, 2009: 44 ff.) and of language learning as empathetic. The constraints of the mainstream system sometimes mean that such opportunities are not easy to realise, although there are exceptions (e.g. Meier, 2010, 2014). Such work begins to recognise the potential, and aligns well with the research carried out in complementary and other community-based learning initiatives (Blackledge & Creese, 2010; Conteh et al., 2007; Kenner & Ruby, 2012; Lytra & Martin, 2010). In several chapters in this volume, we show the importance of such existing research for the multilingual turn in its contributions to our understandings of pedagogy and the implications for curricula.

Positioning the Self: Editors' Personal Note

In this book there is much talk about the backgrounds of learners and teachers, their respective subjectivities, and the implications for their roles in the classroom. Clearly, this book was not conceived in a void, but based on viewpoints born out of the editors' own personal and professional backgrounds and experiences. We are aware that it is our life stories that shaped our interests in multilingualism in education. Indeed, we have found that our own different backgrounds and experiences of multilingualism have been a very positive factor in discussing and developing the ideas and arguments that underpin this book. They have afforded a real synergy, allowing us to bring together our different personal and professional experiences to develop new understandings about language, learning and the significance of the multilingual turn in languages education.

Gabriela Meier was brought up as a diglossic German speaker with a mentality that language learning is normal, albeit not automatic. Nearly all her Swiss relatives are bi- and multilingual; even her grandmother, who had no formal education beyond compulsory schooling, went to learn French in the French part of Switzerland as a young woman in the 1920s, and it was she who taught Gabriela her first words in French. Gabriela has carried on the tradition, and lived and worked in four different language regions in Europe, where she experienced herself what it can mean to be multilingual, to be a newcomer, and negotiate identity and a sense of belonging in the process. Jean Conteh grew up in a monolingual environment in the northeast of England. She only became aware that she had a 'Geordie' accent when she went to university – the first in her family to do so – in the south of England in the late 1960s, discovering in the process how this led to stereotypical judgements by others. Soon after, working as a volunteer teacher in West Africa, teaching English to students who often spoke three or four languages in their everyday lives, she was introduced to the complexities and fascinations of multilingualism. On her return to England in the mid-1980s, she took up a post in a multilingual primary school in West Yorkshire. Here the links between language, culture, achievement and attainment in the mainstream system soon became abundantly clear to her.

Structure of the Book

The book consists of three parts, which are framed by the present Introduction and the Conclusion at the end of the book. Each of the three parts has a short framing overview, which outlines what we deem is the key theme in each part. These are:

- construction of language and ideologies in the multilingual turn, socialisation and identity (Part 1);
- theorising the links between society and education, researchers' and teachers' perspectives on multilingual education and potential for social cohesion (Part 2);
- visions and innovations of the multilingual turn developed in practice (Part 3).

In the framing overviews, we also indicate the general implications for research of the chapters in the part. At the end of each framing overview, you will find two generic questions that are designed to focus attention on what we consider to be the overarching themes of each part.

In addition, there are three questions at the start of each chapter, which are designed to emphasise features that the authors suggest are important when reflecting on the multilingual turn. The questions alert your attention to specific aspects in each chapter, and invite you to consider any implications for practices elsewhere. At the end of the book we offer a conclusion, rounding off our interpretation of what can be learnt from this book in terms of the multilingual turn in languages education.

Part 1. Perspectives on the multilingual turn in constructions of language and ideologies, socialisation and identities

In Chapter 1, **Mooznah Auleear Owodally** examines the role of pre-school in developing children's multilingual repertoires, supported by official curriculum guidelines. Using a language socialisation theoretical framework and a discourse analysis methodology, she shows how languages are used or not used to socialise children, and to what extent these languages relate to their daily lives and their identities as Mauritians.

In Chapter 2, **Ken Cruickshank** presents a study conducted in four complementary schools in Australia, including diverse languages. He explores to what extent these school practices allow the students to reflect on the identities they choose for themselves, and those ascribed to them by others. He also discusses the extent to which complementary schools may influence mainstream education and what this means for learners.

In Chapter 3, **Guangwei Hu** and **Sandra McKay** present a critical analysis of a scheme of English language textbooks widely used with junior secondary pupils in China. They present an analytical framework, through which they examine how a multilingual society is represented both in the texts and in the societal discourses that have produced and are mediated in these textbooks.

In Chapter 4, **Andrea Young** presents her work in Alsace, a region of France where a variety of German and French are both spoken, besides other languages. She examines to what extent teachers are of the opinion that language is a right, a resource or a problem, and draws conclusions for teacher education.

Part 2. Perspectives on the multilingual turn in education

In Chapter 5, **Laurent Gajo** provides a review of social trends, language education research and changes in terminology, in order to theorise the move from multilingualism in society to multilingualism in pedagogy in Francophone contexts.

In Chapter 6, **Gabriela Meier** reviews proposals and concrete plans for integrated multilingual curricula in mainstream education that integrates language learning with language awareness. She identified 10 orientations that underlie these curricula.

In Chapter 7, **Jean Conteh, Fiona Copland** and **Angela Creese** present interview and classroom interaction data generated in three very different small-scale studies which bring together teachers' perspectives on their 'languaging' practices in multilingual classrooms in Greece and the UK. In this way, they raise questions about some of the commonly accepted notions that underpin language teaching and reveal possibilities for pedagogies to promote multilingualism.

In Chapter 8, **Gabriela Meier** reports on a large-scale questionnaire-based study carried out with 14–18-year-old students who were all participating in an established two-way immersion programme incorporating 10 languages in Berlin. Her findings begin to show the social benefits for the students who are learning in two languages.

Part 3. Visions of the multilingual turn in pedagogy and practice

In Chapter 9, **Jean Conteh, Shila Begum** and **Saiqa Riasat** present examples of activities for primary pupils in the north of England grounded in the 'funds of knowledge' (Gonzalez *et al.*, 2005) philosophy, which recognises the agency and expertise of families and communities in their children's learning. They argue for their potential for mainstream learning and the implications for the nature of classroom interaction to promote reciprocity and empowerment.

In Chapter 10, **Enrica Piccardo** and **Joëlle Aden** show the value of drama-based activities for language learning through empathy for young people from a diverse range of backgrounds in France.

In Chapter 11, **Ofelia García** and **Naomi Kano** present a case study of an intervention to develop translanguaging strategies in academic writing with bilingual Japanese American students preparing for a college entry exam in New York. Through the study, they call for educators' awareness toward the critical role that the multilinguals' natural communicative skills play in their literacy development.

In Chapter 12, **Jim Anderson** and **Yu-Chiao Chung** explore the contribution that arts-based creativity can make to building effective pedagogies for community and foreign language learning. They provide a rich range of creative activities to promote language learning linked with identity affirmation in four different educational settings in London.

Finally, a note about spelling. We decided to retain the spelling conventions adopted by the authors of each chapter for words where different versions are acceptable (e.g. socialise/socialize), in order to respect their choices and also to reflect the variety of English used in the specific contexts in which their chapter was written.

Notes

(1) Seventh British Association for Applied Linguistics (BAAL) Language Learning and Teaching SIG Conference. Theorising practice and practising theory: Developing local pedagogies in language teaching (7–8 July 2011).
(2) OECD Programme for International School Assessment. This assesses 15-year-old students in all OECD countries on a regular basis.

References

Alexander, R.J. (2004) Still no pedagogy? Principle, pragmatism and compliance in primary education. *Cambridge Journal of Education* 34 (1), 7–23.

Alexander, R.J. (2010) Speaking but not listening? Accountable talk in an unaccountable context. *Literacy* 44 (3), 103–111.

Baker, C. (2011) *Foundations of Bilingual Education and Bilingualism* (5th edn). Bristol: Multilingual Matters.

BBC (2011) *Voices*. See http://www.bbc.co.uk/voices/ (accessed 16 September 2013).

Blackledge, A. and Creese, A. (2010) *Multilingualism: Critical Perspectives*. London: Continuum.

Block, D. (2003) *The Social Turn in Second Language Acquisition*. Edinburgh: Edinburgh University Press.

Blommaert, J. and Backus, A. (2011) Repertoires revisited: 'Knowing language' in superdiversity. Working Paper in Urban Language and Literacies No. 67. Kings College, London. See http://www.kcl.ac.uk/sspp/departments/education/research/ldc/publications/workingpapers/67.pdf (accessed 28 September 2013).

Brock, A. and Conteh, J. (2011) Children's rights, identity and learning: The case for bilingualism. In P. Jones and G. Walker (eds) *Children's Rights in Practice* (pp. 124–139). London: Sage.

Bronfenbrenner, U. (1979) *The Ecology of Human Development*. Cambridge, MA: Harvard University Press.

Castiglione, D. and Longman, C. (2007) *The Language Question in Europe and Diverse Societies: Political, Legal and Social Perspectives*. Oxford: Hart Publishing.

Cole, M. (1996) *Cultural Psychology: A Once and Future Discipline*. Cambridge, MA: Harvard University Press.

COE (Council of Europe) (2001) *The Common European Framework of Reference for Languages (CEFR)*. Cambridge: Cambridge University Press.

Conteh, J., Martin, P. and Helavaara, R.L. (eds) (2007) *Multilingual Learning Stories in Schools and Communities in Britain*. Stoke-on-Trent: Trentham Books.

Creese, A. and Martin, P. (2003) Multilingual classroom ecologies: Inter-relationships, interactions and ideologies. *International Journal of Bilingual Education and Bilingualism* 6 (3/4), 161–167.

Edwards, V. (1998) *The Power of Babel: Teaching and Learning in Multilingual Classrooms*. London: Trentham Books.

Edwards, V. (2009) *Learning to be Literate: Multilingual Perspectives*. Bristol: Multilingual Matters.

García, O. (2009) *Bilingual Education in the 21st Century: A Global Perspective*. London: Wiley-Blackwell.

Gibbons, P. (2000) Teaching as mediation: Scaffolding second language learning through classroom interaction. Keynote address to the 8th NALDIC Conference. National Association for Language Development in the Curriculum, London.

González, N., Moll, L. and Amanti, C. (eds) (2005) *Funds of Knowledge: Theorising Practices in Households, Communities and Classrooms.* New York: Routledge.

Hart, S., Dixon, A., Drummond, M.J. and Mcintyre, D. (2004) *Learning Without Limits.* Milton Keynes: Open University Press.

Hélot, C. and De Mejía, A.-M. (eds) (2008) Introduction: Different spaces – different languages. Integrated perspectives on bilingual education in majority and minority settings. In C. Hélot and A.-M. De Mejía (eds) *Forging Multilingual Spaces: Integrated Perspectives on Majority and Minority Bilingual Education* (pp. 1–30). Bristol: Multilingual Matters.

Hooghe, L. and Marks, G. (2001) *Multi-level Governance and European Integration.* Lanham, MD: Rowman & Littlefield.

Jeffrey, B. and Craft, A. (2004) Teaching creatively and teaching for creativity: Distinctions and relationships. *Educational Studies* 30 (1), 77–87.

Jenkins, J. (2006) Points of view and blind spots: ELF and SLA. *International Journal of Applied Linguistics* 16 (2), 137–162; doi:10.1111/j.1473-4192.2006.00111.x.

Kenner, C. and Ruby, M. (2012) *Interconnecting Worlds: Teacher Partnerships for Bilingual Learning.* Stoke-on-Trent: Trentham Books.

Lantolf, J.P. (2000) Introducing sociocultural theory. In J.P. Lantolf (ed.) *Sociocultural Theory and Second Language Learning* (pp. 1–26). Oxford: Oxford University Press.

Lantolf, J.P. and Poehner, M.E. (2008) *Sociocultural Theory and the Teaching of Second Languages.* London: Equinox.

Leung, C., Harris, R. and Rampton, B. (1997) The idealised native speaker, reified ethnicities, and classroom realities. *TESOL Quarterly* 31 (3), 543–560.

Lüdi, G. and Py, B. (2009) To be or not to be ... a plurilingual speaker. *International Journal of Multilingualism* 6 (2), 154–167; doi:10.1080/14790710902846715.

Lytra, V. and Martin, P. (eds) (2010) *Sites of Multilingualism: Complementary Schools in Britain Today.* Stoke-on-Trent: Trentham Books.

Makoni, S. and Pennycook, A. (eds) (2007) *Disinventing and Reconstituting Languages.* Clevedon: Multilingual Matters.

May, S. (2014) *The Multilingual Turn. Implications for SLA, TESOL and Bilingual Education.* New York: Routledge.

McLaughlin, B., Rossman, T. and McLeod, B. (1983) Second language learning: An information processing perspective. *Language Learning* 33 (2), 135–158.

Meier, G. (2010) *Social and Intercultural Benefits of Bilingual Education: A Peace-linguistic Evaluation of Staatliche Europa-Schule Berlin (SESB), Vol. 12.* Frankfurt: Peter Lang.

Meier, G. (2014) 'Cette entraide et ce tutorat naturel qui s'organise entre eux: A research framework for two-way bilingual immersion programmes. In N. Mory, C. Kirsch, I. de Saint-Georges, G. Gertsd (eds) *Lernen und Lehren inmultilingualen kontexren: Zum umgang mit sprachlich-kultureller Diversitat im imklassencaum.* Frankfurt: Peter Lang.

NACCCE (National Advisory Committee on Creative and Cultural Education) (1999) *All Our Futures: Creativity, Culture and Education.* London: DfEE.

Naumann, J. (2005) Timss, Pisa, Pirls and low educational achievement in world society. *Prospects* 35 (2), 229–248.

Norton, B. (2014) Identity, literacy, and the multilingual classroom. In S. May (ed.) *The Multilingual Turn: Implications for SLA, TESOL and Bilingual Education* (pp. 103–122). New York: Routledge.

Norton Peirce, B. (1995) Social identity, investment, and language learning. *TESOL Quarterly* 29 (1), 9–31.

OECD (2003) *First Results from PISA 2003: Executive Summary*. Paris: Organisation for Economic Cooperation and Development.

Ortega, L. (2014) Ways forward for a bi-multilingual turn in SLA. In S. May (ed.) *The Multilingual Turn: Implications for SLA, TESOL and Bilingual Education* (pp. 147–166). New York: Routledge.

Pennycook, A. (2001) *Critical Applied Linguistics: A Critical Introduction*. London: Lawrence Erlbaum.

Schieffelin, B. and Ochs, E. (eds) (1986) *Language Socialization Across Cultures*. Cambridge: Cambridge University Press.

Skutnabb-Kangas, T. (1994) Mother tongue maintenance: The debate: Linguistic human rights and minority education. *TESOL Quarterly* (Special Topic Issue K-12) 28 (3), 625–628.

Stanat, P. and Christensen, G. (2006) *Where Immigrant Students Succeed: A Comparative Review of Performance and Engagement in PISA in 2003*. Paris: Organisation for Economic Cooperation and Development.

Taylor, S.K. and Snoddon, K. (2013) Special issue: Plurilingualism in TESOL. *TESOL Quarterly* 47 (3).

Torres, C.A. (1998) *Democracy, Education, and Multiculturalism: Dilemmas of Citizenship in a Global World*. Lanham, MD: Rowman & Littlefield.

Torres-Guzmán, M.E. (2002) Dual language programs: Key features and results. *National Clearinghouse for Bilingual Education: Directions in Language and Education* 14.

Trowler, P. (2003) *Education Policy* (2nd edn). London: Routledge.

van Lier, L. (2004) *The Ecology and Semiotics of Language Learning*. New York: Kluwer Academic Publishers.

Vertovec, S. (2007) Super-diversity and its implications. *Ethnic and Racial Studies* 30 (6), 1024–1054.

Wolfe, S. and Alexander, R.J. (2008) *Argumentation and Dialogic Teaching: Alternative Pedagogies for a Changing World*. See http://www.robinalexander.org.uk/wp-content/uploads/2012/05/wolfealexander.pdf (accessed 28 September 2013).

Woolard, K.A. (1998) Introduction: Language ideology as a field of inquiry. In B.B. Schieffelin, K.A. Woolard and P.A. Kroskrity (eds) *Language Ideologies: Practice and Theory* (pp. 3–47). New York: Oxford University Press.

Part 1

Societal Perspectives on the Multilingual Turn in Language(s) Education

Gabriela Meier

This part compiles studies from different sites that demonstrate different ways of tracing individual and societal multilingualism, language ideologies, language status and representations in schools, and what this may mean for learners and teachers. All authors look at societal and individual language ideologies, and how these are manifest in mainstream (Auleear Owodally) and complementary education (Cruickshank), in resources such as textbooks (Hu & McKay) and in beliefs that teachers hold about the place and uses of languages in schools (Young).

All contexts described in this chapter are presented as multilingual to a certain extent, even though some are politically constructed as monolingual, and in all contexts this multilingualism is represented in schools to varied degrees. The authors use different terms (home languages, oriental languages, official, foreign languages, etc.) to discuss the status of languages in society and in schools, indicating that some languages are related to religious practice and beliefs, ethnic identity or economic opportunities, and that some are seen as worthy to be used in schools and others less so.

The authors all highlight the importance of understanding classrooms as sites for the formation of social and cultural identity and ideological understandings, which are deeply embedded in local contexts. They stress how such ideologies can influence identities and belonging to social groups, and how teachers and learners in schools can adopt, resist or question such ideologies. One of the conclusions is that teacher education could play a role in providing opportunities for teachers to engage with research in this area, and reflect on their own beliefs and ideologies.

Methodologically, **Chapter 1** is a longitudinal case study of language socialization with a group of pre-schoolers in Mauritius. The dataset comprises video and audio recordings from the children's classrooms, along with field notes and stimulated recall interviews with their teachers. **Chapter 2** is an account of constructions of language and multilingualism in society from the perspectives of young people in three Australian schools. The data include interviews and observations as well as questionnaires and focus groups. **Chapter 3** examines one student's book from a widely used series to teach and learn English in secondary schools in China. This is a close-up analysis of one unit based on a detailed analytic framework, which the authors reproduce in their chapter. **Chapter 4** is based on interview data from 46 teachers in France, and gives an account of teachers' beliefs as to whether the languages that children bring to school are a right, a resource or a problem.

Generic questions for Part 1

- Is there a language hierarchy in place in the society where you live or work? Which groups speak these languages, and which languages do learners and teachers use in school and in other domains?
- To what extent is there a link between languages spoken outside class and those represented inside the classroom and in relevant resources?

1 Socialized into Multilingualism: A Case Study of a Mauritian Pre-school

A.M. Auleear Owodally

Guiding Questions

- To what extent does the Mauritian school context discussed here reflect language socialization outside school?
- What covert messages about language(s) are the school children in this context unconsciously exposed to?
- What are the opportunities and challenges associated with language socialization practices in multilingual contexts in Mauritius?

Introduction

Despite living on an island which boasts of its multilingualism, most Mauritian children spend the first few years of their lives in monolingual Kreol-speaking families where Kreol is the dominant language of the home and the environment. School is a major site where they are exposed to multilingualism – through the subjects taught (English, French and an optional ancestral language – one of the languages spoken or believed to have been spoken by migrants who came to Mauritius such as Hindi, Urdu, Tamil, Telugu, Marathi, Hakka, etc.), the written medium of instruction (English) and the oral media of communication (French and Kreol). In the context of this shift from home monolingualism to school-mediated multilingualism, one of the important language and literacy challenges that most children face is that they have to learn English and through English, given that English is the main language of literacy and the main written medium of instruction throughout the education system from the first year of primary schooling. Acting as the linguistic bridge between the home and the primary school, the pre-school is the first semi-formal institution where children are introduced to and exposed to English and multilingualism (Auleear Owodally, 2010).

In this chapter, I use a language socialization perspective to investigate the pre-school as a site where a group of children are socialized into English and, by extension, into local multilingualism. Focusing on daily routine activities (Duff, 2010; Ochs, 2000) in one government pre-school, I show how, through their language practices and language teaching practices, teachers socialize pre-schoolers into languages (their uses and functions), language learning and related ideologies.

I start with a brief overview of the local sociolinguistic situation, showing how the school system contributes to shaping and perpetuating Mauritian multilingualism. With respect to the ways children are socialized into English and local multilingualism, I describe some of the theoretical principles of language socialization which I then draw upon to frame my analysis of data obtained from a longitudinal study of a group of children in one government pre-school. After describing the research design and methodology, I present and discuss my findings.

Mauritian Education – Mauritian Multilingualism

Mauritius has been shaped by a history of voluntary and forced migration: French and British colonizers, African enslaved people, Indian indentured labourers and Chinese workers, all of whom brought along with them their diverse religious, cultural and language practices. These waves of migrants have constituted a richly multi-ethnic, multi-religious and multilingual population, with inhabitants cohabiting fairly peacefully in 'harmonious separatism' (Toth, 1995: 98). Although Mauritius is a secular state, it has developed a particular understanding and a particular performance of secularism (cf. Eisenlohr, 2006), with the religious often permeating secular institutions, sites and discourses. For instance, politicians regularly attend and participate in religious ceremonies, while religious images and practices often infiltrate ancestral language textbooks and classrooms in state schools (Auleear Owodally, 2012b). This point of contact between the religious and the secular is one of the many paradoxes of the local context.

The term 'multilingualism', used to qualify the present language situation in Mauritius, oversimplifies a more complicated language situation with different languages having different values and functions. Rajah-Carrim (2007) divides the languages used locally into three distinct categories: European languages (English and French), oriental/ancestral languages (Hindi, Urdu, Tamil, Telugu, Mandarin, Marathi, etc.) and local languages (Kreol and Bhojpuri). English is the de facto official language – the language of the parliament, the judiciary and education; however, it is socially rarely heard and seldom used. French, on the other hand, is a prestigious social language widely used in the spoken and written media and used as a home language among a small bourgeoisie. The oriental languages, which are often utilized in various in-group ethno-religious ceremonies, are seen as 'markers of ethnic and religious identity' (Rajah-Carrim, 2007: 52). The local languages, Kreol and Bhojpuri, are the most popularly used home languages, with the increased use of Kreol as the main home language in the past decades (the 2000 census data revealed that 69% of Mauritians claimed Kreol as the only home language, with this figure rising to 84% in 2011). However, Kreol has low social status for historical and economic reasons.

The education system has endeavoured to preserve and maintain individual and societal multilingualism. English is taught as a main language of literacy and used as the written medium throughout the education system, starting from the first year of primary education. French is taught as a quasi-compulsory subject until the fifth year of secondary education and the oriental languages are offered as optional subjects in primary schools. Paradoxically, Kreol has just recently (in January 2012) been introduced as an optional subject in the first year of primary schooling (cf. Auleear Owodally & Unjore, 2013).

The multilingual character of the primary and secondary school curricula has had a backwash effect on the pre-school. The pre-school curriculum guidelines state that pre-school children should be exposed to as many languages present in their environment as possible. The curriculum which was relevant at the time of data collection, the *2003 Pre-school Curriculum Guidelines*, further clearly stipulates that children must be introduced to English, given its essential role in the primary school curriculum: 'Since English is the official language throughout the education system, and English is the medium of instruction at a higher level of primary education, it is only logical through songs or poetry, a child will learn some English daily in relation to the theme being worked on' (Ministry of Education and Scientific Research, Mauritius, 2003: 42). The more recent 2008 curriculum, however, names no languages, preferring the vaguer term 'target language(s)' to refer to the languages found in the local context.

Despite the curriculum goal of introducing children to multilingualism in the pre-school, there is little research investigating how these pre-school guidelines get translated into practice. The few studies carried out in the Mauritian pre-school context (Auleear Owodally, 2008, 2010, 2012a, 2012b; Tirvassen, 2005) indicate that English and French are the two main languages that teachers introduce and teach. However, no study has yet focused on the ways in which children are socialized into the languages that form part of the local multilingual set-up. In this chapter, I focus on Mauritian pre-schoolers' socialization into English, and by extension, their socialization into multilingualism. The present study situates itself in the educationally oriented language socialization research in multilingual communities.

Conceptual Framework: Language Socialization

Language socialization, which is used to frame the present study, provides a sociocultural lens to analyse children's enculturation into local language practices at home and in educational settings in various contexts (Heath, 1983; Schieffelin & Ochs, 1996). Language socialization (henceforth LS) explores how 'communicative practices of experts and novices are organized by and organize cultural knowledge, understandings, beliefs and feelings' (Schieffelin & Ochs, 1996: 255). The notion of 'practices', central to this alternative approach to second language acquisition research, is conceptualized as 'meaningful actions that occur routinely in everyday life, [which] are widely shared by members of the groups, have developed over time, and carry normative expectations about the way things should be done' (Moore, 2006a).

With the increasing number of migrants in the UK and the US, much of the LS research has focused on the language socialization experiences of immigrants whose home culture/language differs from that of the host country. More recently, the LS framework has been extended to investigate language practices and language teaching practices in non-Western, postcolonial and multilingual contexts. For instance, Moore (2006b) has explored the teaching of French and Quoranic literacy in Cameroon, uncovering the complex ways in which children are socialized into bilingualism and biliteracy. However, Moore (2008) has highlighted the paucity of LS research in non-Western settings and has argued that such settings offer rich sites for exploring the sociocultural nature of language learning and teaching. The present study aims to add to the LS research in multilingual communities. It draws upon some of the basic principles of LS research to frame the investigation of the ways in which children are socialized into English (and multilingualism) in a pre-school in Mauritius, with the classroom as the focal point.

One of the basic tenets of the LS research is that language is an ever-changing and fluid social practice. Thus, scholars working with this perspective focus mostly on social interactions. They propose that through the use of language and in the use of language (Schieffelin & Ochs, 1996), language learners learn more than just language(s) or aspects of the linguistic code(s); they also learn other forms of knowledge (Duff & Talmy, 2011: 104–105; Garrett, 2005: 335). These other forms of knowledge include culture, social knowledge, ideologies, identities and subjectivities; these also affect values, beliefs, attitudes and world-views (Duff & Talmy, 2011: 95–96). For instance, in a study of first-grader learners of English as a second language in Hawaii, Emura (2006) shows how students, who are taught English are also taught the expected student behaviours in the classroom through the use of English and through classroom practices.

Extending the LS research base to Lx language contexts (Lx refers to language(s) other than the first language, cf. Pavlenko, 2006), scholars have foregrounded the classroom (teachers and learners, teaching and learning) as a key space for Lx language socialization. Classrooms (as micro-contexts) are viewed as being sociohistorically, socioculturally and sociopolitically situated and embedded in the larger localized macro context, reflecting as well as contributing to shaping or resisting recurrent, widespread and dominant language, social and cultural practices (cf. Baquedano-Lopèz & Kattan, 2010: 161; Blackledge & Creese, 2010: 17; Crago, 1992: 28).

In what ways are Lx learners socialized into communicative and cultural practices? According to Cook (1999: 1444), Duff (2010: 431), Ely *et al.* (2001: 358) and Kanagy (1999: 1468), in Lx language classrooms, language(s) and other forms of knowledge are transmitted explicitly (through direct and explicit teaching and discussion from experts), through modelling or implicitly (Cook, 1999: 1444; Duff, 2010: 431; Ely *et al.*, 2001: 358; Kanagy, 1999: 1468) as members take part in routines. As pointed out by Li (2008: 72), while explicit socialization is easily noticeable, implicit socialization is more frequent and often more pervasive because it is less obvious and thus harder to contest or contradict (Cook, 1999: 1444–1450). Many LS research studies have used an ethnographic approach and have focused on recurrent classroom activities (Ochs, 2000) such as classroom routines, (Cook, 1999; Kanagy, 1999), given that these are powerful organizers of teacher–student interaction in classrooms. Classroom routines, which often involve repetition (Moore, 2011), 'instantiate, in more or less explicit ways, important cultural categories, identities, norms and values' (Howard, 2009: 342, cited in Moore, 2011: 211).

Methodology

For the present chapter, I will draw upon a dataset collected as part of a longitudinal (January–October 2005) study of emergent literacy practices of a group of 13 children (aged between four and five) in a Mauritian pre-school (henceforth PSA). Although the pre-school consisted of some 40 children aged three to four and four to five, the focus of the research was the group of final-year students and their three female teachers. The teachers and the children are native speakers of Kreol. The children's responses to their teachers' questions in French indicate that they understand French; however, they always address their teachers and their peers in Kreol. Their passive understanding of French can be related to the fact that French is the lexifier of Kreol (lexically, French and Kreol share proximity) and that they are exposed to French in the environment, especially through the media (TV programmes and cartoons). The children also have minimal understanding, if any, of English, given it is hardly heard or used in the social environment.

Data were collected from the observed class, once a week over the whole school year, using video and audio recording devices. Field notes were also made during the observation period. Unstructured interviews, in the form of natural conversation, formed part of the data collection process. Often the stimulated recall technique was used, where the teachers were asked to explain why they had carried out an activity the way they had done. Data transcriptions and field notes constitute the major part of the corpus herewith referred to.

Following previous studies such as Kanagy (1999) and Ely *et al.* (2001), three routine activities are here examined for their social and linguistic organization (Ochs, 2000: 230) as follows:

- Circle time (9.30–10.00am): All the children are gathered together in a big circle; they say prayers, recall the day/month, talk about the weather, and discuss different topics of actuality, often including the theme they are working on.
- Language activity (10.15–10.45am): Each of the three teachers takes her group of children, separating the younger ones from the older ones. While the younger ones are given a colouring activity, the teachers and older children talk about the theme of the week, followed by a drawing activity.
- Mathematical activity (10.45–11.15am): During this activity, teachers teach numbers and mathematical concepts, followed by a mathematical activity/worksheet.

The transcribed data were analysed qualitatively, noting the verbal and non-verbal aspects of the conversations as teachers and learners participated in the classroom routines. Given the particular focus on English, the transcribed data and field notes were read and each time English was used, the English words and/or sentences were highlighted. Since all the incidents where English was used took place within the context of a switch from another language into English, I systematically noted down the context in which these oral English incidents were produced by italicizing the whole event. I used Auer's (1995: 116) working definition of code-alternation as 'a relationship of contiguous juxtaposition of semiotic systems' and a hyperonym for Brock-Utne and Holmarsdottir's (2003: 88) distinction between code-switching (an intersentential alteration of code) and code-mixing (an intrasentential change of code) to drive the data analysis. This is in line with Auer's (1995: 116) view that the meaning of code-alternation depends on its 'sequential environment', that is, the preceding and subsequent utterance(s).

An inductive approach to data analysis was used and pattern codes were allowed to emerge from the data. Analysis began with the first piece of transcribed data and continued in a recursive and iterative manner throughout the transcribed data (Patton, 1990). Re-readings of the transcriptions led to a more selective coding of the data (Strauss & Corbin, 1990). Codes were assigned and they were modified as the analysis of the transcriptions

Table 1.1 Codes and meta-codes

Broad categories	Pattern codes	Pattern meta-codes
Linguistic routines	➢ **Code 1**: Rituals: prayer time ➢ **Code 2**: Routines	
Strategies used to teach oral English	➢ **Code 1**: Code-alternation	✓ **Code 1.1**: Equivalence
		✓ **Code 1.2**: Eliciting equivalent terms in English
		✓ **Code 1.3**: Modelling by code-mixing technical/key vocabulary items

proceeded (Bogdan & Biklen, 1992). The constant comparison method (Glaser & Strauss, 1967; Lincoln & Guba, 1985, described in Hatch, 2002) helped in separating the data into distinct categories. In this chapter, I focus on the codes and meta-codes shown in Table 1.1.

When analysing the data, I use Gee's (2011) distinction between discourse and Discourse, concepts which acknowledge that micro contexts shape and are shaped by macro contextual factors such as the local sociolinguistic environment, the politics of languages, and the language teaching and learning environments. In this chapter, I provide data excerpts from several points in the school year to provide an overview of the (evolving) teaching practices and learning trajectories of this group of Mauritian subjects (teachers and learners).

Findings

The prayer-saying ritual: Socialized into the local model of secularism

Prayer time, carried out as a whole class activity every morning throughout 2005, follows a set pattern. The prayer routine typically consists of three main events, within which are embedded four interactional turns (cf. Kanagy, 1999: 1469). In the first event the PSA teachers, who themselves take the appropriate posture by standing straight and folding their hands, ask the children in French to keep quiet, to bow their heads, to fold their hands and to close their eyes (turn 1), before they actually start the prayer-saying session. The second event consists of the teacher reciting the prayer line by line in English (turn 2) and the children echoing the teacher's words in chorus (turn 3) – the same prayer is systematically recited throughout 2005. In the third and final event, the children sing a French song (turn 4).

Excerpt 1.1, which is representative of the prayer-saying event, indicates that English prayer reciting forms part of a ritual within a conversation, characterized by a moment of code-switching from French to English at the very moment when the prayer is recited.

Excerpt 1.1 Circle time, all teachers and children are gathered in a circle at the beginning of the school day (3 March 2005).		
T1:	Allez, joignez les mains ... (pause) fermez les yeux, baissez la tête ... (pause).	Come on, put your hands together ... (pause) close your eyes, bow your head ... (pause).
T2:	Viens on va faire la prière.	Come, we'll say the prayers.
T1:	O God (Ss) purify my heart (Ss) and help me (Ss) to fill it (Ss) with divine love (Ss) O God (Ss) purify my hands (Ss) and let them work (Ss) for humanity (Ss).	O God (Ss) purify my heart (Ss) and help me (Ss) to fill it (Ss) with divine love (Ss) O God (Ss) purify my hands (Ss) and let them work (Ss) for humanity (Ss).
T1:	Il faut pas crier ... qui crie? ... Il faut respecter la prière.	You must not shout ... Who is shouting? ... You have to respect the prayer.
Ss: *sing and mime*	Ma prière est faite, aussitot levé. Je fais ma toilette et je bois mon lait. Je pars pour l'école comme un bon enfant, disant la parole: au revoir, maman; au revoir, papa.	My prayers are said, as soon as I am up. I wash, and I drink my milk. I go to school like a good child, saying: good-bye, mother; good-bye, father.

The above event can be described in Moore's (2011: 214) term as 'guided repetition', where the teacher-directed repetition 'does not entail much or any allusion to or comprehension of literal meaning'. Given PSA children's limited proficiency in English at the beginning of the year, it is doubtful whether they actually understand the propositional meaning of the utterances. Yet, one could argue that during the prayer session, the children are active participants to the extent that they repeat after and echo the teacher, rather than remain passive silent recipients with no role in the classroom. In a similar way, Moore (2011) describes the use of guided repetition in Quranic schools in Cameroon, where children do not understand the Quranic Arabic texts that they recite. Moore (2011) says that the guided repetition emphasizes the teacher's authority, the importance of discipline and reverent renderings of bits of the sacred text. For Moore (2011), guided repetition socializes the children into developing ideologies related to Quranic Arabic, the language of the sacred text, as well as the language used in prayers, sermons and religious activities, hence contributing to shaping the children's identity as Muslims. In the case of prayer saying in English at PSA, the guided repetition, preceded by the cues for correct posture before the prayer recitation session, emphasizes the religious importance of the recited and repeated words and contributes to shaping the children's religious identity as secular Mauritians. The choice of English for this prayer session is, however, locally significant and symbolically loaded.

In the local multi-ethnic and multi-religious context where languages have social and religious indices, English is the only neutral language that has the potential to mediate a particular performance of secularism where the religious permeates secular institutions. I propose to use the term 'secular form of religiosity' to capture and describe this local religious paradox where a clear religious message is being expressed in a language that is not identified or identifiable with any specific local religious community. In Mauritius, prayers recited in French would connote Catholicism (French is the language of the Catholic Church); prayers in any of the oriental languages (for instance, Urdu/Arabic and Hindi) would be associated with the other religious groups (Muslims and Hindus, respectively); and prayers in Kreol might be seen as inappropriate because of its association with the Creoles, most of whom are Catholics. English is thus used as a resource by the teachers to include all the children, irrespective of their ethno-religious group, in the prayer-sharing session. Implicitly and through language choice (English), the teachers are socializing the children into this localized 'secular form of religious identity' at school. This English prayer reciting practice is also used throughout the education system in government schools, where exactly the same prayer is recited in English in primary and secondary schools at school assemblies. Conversely, in particular oriental language classrooms, prayers are sometimes recited in the respective oriental languages.

While in the pre-school, English is presented and used as a neutral language that can mediate a 'secular form of religious' identity, in their own private spheres – in their homes and in peripheral religious institutions (Auleear Owodally, 2012a; Rajah-Carrim, 2004, 2010) – children are exposed to the oriental languages as their own religious languages. This more personal religious identity is revealed when the children are asked to hold themselves properly at prayer time: some children fold their hands like their teachers, while others open their hands, reflecting the home environment in which the children are religiously educated and socialized.

Although it is clear that the children recited the English prayer without comprehending it, the longitudinal aspect of the study has demonstrated that regular repetition of the prayer by the children resulted in the children completely memorizing it after a few months. On 30 June 2005 (field notes), two of the PSA teachers were talking to each other, and T3 said the first sentence of the prayer and then got distracted by the conversation between

T1 and T2. At that moment, the children themselves started chanting the prayer, and completed it without making any 'mistake'. This episode, which indicates the enormous retentive capacity of the young learners, reveals that the learners have mastered the prayer script (cf. Kanagy, 1999: 1477) and shows that they have been successfully enculturated into the locally appropriate ways of being a religious Mauritian.

The analysis of the English prayer-recitation routine leads me to argue that at school – a secular educational institution in a secular state tolerant of diverse religious identities – teachers use English as a resource to develop a sense of religiosity that transcends in-group (religious) identities (those are often mediated by the oriental languages). Through English prayer saying at school, the children are socialized into cultivating the 'harmonious' aspect of the 'harmonious separatism' characteristic of Mauritius.

Routines: English as part of the morning show

Greetings and health questions, typically carried out in English, occur at the beginning of circle time, when the teachers gather all the PSA children in a circle in the middle of the classroom for the morning class assembly.

	Excerpt 1.2 Circle time, all children at the centre of the classroom (18 May 2005; same pattern observed on 31 May, 14 June, 26 August, 2 September 2005).	
T2:	Bonjour, les enfants.	Good morning, children
Ss:	Bonjour, Miss.	Good morning, Miss
T2:	Good morning, children.	Good morning, children.
Ss:	Good morning, Miss.	Good morning, Miss.
T2:	How are you children?	How are you children?
Ss:	I am very well thank you, Miss.	I am very well thank you, Miss.
T2:	Les enfants, on est bien. Tout le monde est bien?	Children, we are well? Everyone is well?
Ss:	Oui	Yes
T2:	Qui est malade? Qui est malade? Personne?	Who is ill? Who is ill? Nobody?
S:	Moi.	Me
T2:	Tu es malade. Qu'est ce que tu as?	You are ill? What do you have?
S:	*Silence*	***Silence***
T2:	Qu'est ce que tu as? (x2) Tu as la fièvre? Tu as la fièvre?	What do you have? (x2) You have fever? You have fever?
S:	Oui	Yes
T2:	Tu es malade. Quand on est malade, qu'est ce qu'il faut faire? Il faut apporter tricot!	You are ill. When you are ill, what must you do? You must bring your cardigan!
	T2 talks to T1.	

Excerpt 1.3 Circle time, conversation about the cold temperature (26 August 2005).	
T1:	Oui, c'est l'hiver. C'est pourquoi il fait froid. Tout le monde a mis tricot là?	Yes, it is winter. That's why it is cold. Everyone is wearing a cardigan?
Ss:	Oui	Yes
T1:	Très bien. Allez. <u>Good morning, children.</u>	Very good. Come on. <u>Good morning, children</u>
Ss:	<u>Good morning, Miss.</u>	<u>Good morning, Miss.</u>
T1:	Bonjour, les enfants.	Good morning, children.
Ss:	Bonjour, Miss.	Good morning, Miss.

While the children individually greet their teachers with a bright 'Bonjour, Miss' [*Good morning, Miss*] (French/Kreol) as soon as they reach school in the morning, at circle time they all participate in a collective greeting ceremony, revealing how the whole class activity is framed by this routine (cf. Kanagy, 1999: 1473).

Excerpts 1.2 and 1.3 illustrate how greetings are systematically and simultaneously performed in English and French using the concurrent translation technique, showing how highly scripted the text is in form and content (cf. Kanagy, 1999). Although this translation technique might clarify the meaning of 'good morning' at the beginning of the year, it underplays the communicative value of the greeting when utilized throughout the year in this ritualistic type of exchange. Moreover, the children reply in a mechanical manner, reciting the prefabricated responses (memorized utterances/ phrases: Krashen, 1988: 83), evidence of automatic habit formation where learners pick up chunks of language through habitual use while not necessarily understanding the meaning of individual words (Hamayan & Damico, 1991). It seems that these automatic replies achieve symbolical, rather than real, interactional functions (act of communicating) (Wray, 2000: 465). In fact, it can be suggested that the English greeting session often becomes a scene to be acted. For instance, in Excerpt 1.3, the use of the imperative form of the verb 'Allez' [*Come on*] prepares the children for starting the English act. This 'staging' practice socializes the children into seeing English as a language of show and performance, not particular to Mauritian (English) classes only (cf. Arthur, 1996 for Botswana and Arthur & Martin, 2006 for Botswana and Brunei schools). Chick (1996) refers to this staging as 'safe talk'.

English teaching strategies: Code-alternation

The analysis of the data indicates that code-alternation, within the teacher-led present-the-word-repeat-the-word English vocabulary teaching strategy, generally dominates classroom talk in the teacher-fronted and teacher-centred environment at PSA.

Providing equivalent terms in English

When the PSA teachers wish to expose the children to an English word or sentence, or even teach it to them, they often provide equivalent terms in English after having uttered the French word or sentence.

Excerpt 1.4 Small group maths activity (14 June 2005).		
T2:	(Holds a red object in her hands) Rouge. Madhav, c'est rouge. Rouge. Quelle couleur? Rouge. Regardez la table; la table est quelle couleur? Rouge. Regardez son tricot. Quelle couleur est son tricot? Rouge. Est-ce qu'il y a rouge sur toi? Ton tricot quelle couleur? C'est quelle couleur? Quelle couleur est ton tricot, Nilesh?	Red. Madhav, it is red. Red. What colour? Red. Look at the table; the table, what colour is it? Red. Look at her jumper. What colour is her jumper? Red. Are you wearing anything red? Your jumper? What colour? What colour is it? What colour is your jumper Nilesh?
S:	Rouge	Red
T2:	Rouge, <u>Red – Red.</u> C'est quelle couleur? <u>Red.</u> Je vais vous donner papier, vous allez dessiner un 0 pour moi. On peut dessiner ça. On dessine un cercle sur la table tous enfants. Allez dessiner. Allez dessine un cercle. Qui fait un cercle? Vous allez dessiner un cercle pour moi sur votre papier. On va colorier le cercle rouge. Quelle couleur? Rouge. Vous pouvez faire ça. Miss va vous donner papier là.	Red, <u>red – red.</u> What colour is it? <u>Red.</u> I will give you some paper, you will draw an 0 for me. We can draw that. We draw a circle on the table, all children. Come on, draw. Come, draw a circle. Who is making a circle? You will draw a circle for me on your sheet of paper. We will colour the circle red. What colour? Red. Can you do that? Miss will give you paper just now.

Excerpt 1.4 illustrates the use of direct translation (the use of words, phrases and/or sentences from two languages one after the other) as a language teaching strategy, with the direction of code-alternation being from French to English. While this reveals the PSA teachers' beliefs about the need to introduce the children to English, it also reveals their deeply ingrained belief that English should be taught via French or as a translation of French. This arguably socializes the children into perceiving English in relation to French or as a translation of French, rather than as an independent meaning-making mode. This also socializes the children into privileging French rather than English as the main meaning-carrying school language.

Eliciting equivalent terms in English

The PSA teachers also explicitly ask students for equivalent terms in English. For instance, the PSA teachers will use such phrases as: 'Comment on dit en anglais?' [*How do you say in English?*], 'Maintenant, en anglais!' [*Now, in English*], 'En anglais, on appelle ça ...' [*in English, we call this ...*], 'En anglais, on dit ...' [*In English, we say ...*], 'D'abord en français, et puis en anglais ...' [*First in French, and then in English ...*], to elicit specific English words.

Excerpt 1.5 Whole class activity (14 June 2005; similar teacher's reaction on 12 July 2005).		
T1:	What day is today?	What day is today?
S:	Mardi	Tuesday
T1:	J'ai demandé en anglais. What day is today?	I asked in English. What day is today?
S:	Tuesday.	Tuesday.
T1:	Très bien. Today is Tuesday. Kus, quand je pose la question en anglais, tu réponds en anglais.	Very good. Today is Tuesday. Kus, when I ask the question in English, you answer in English.

As illustrated in Excerpt 1.5, when the teacher asks a routine 'What is the day?' question in English, she expects the student to respond in English only. Here the teacher instructs the student to use the appropriate language, teaching him the expected school behaviours.

Sometimes, the PSA teachers also elicit the equivalent term in English without mentioning that it is the English term that they want. For instance, they will say: 'On dit ...' [*We say ...*], 'Comment on dit?' [*How do we say?*], 'Qu'est-ce que ça veut dire?' [*What does it mean?*], 'Qu'est ce qu'on a dit là?' [*What did we just say there?*], 'C'est quoi?' [*What is this?*].

Excerpt 1.6 Whole class language activity on the theme 'The House' (3 March 2005).		
T:	Le salon, on dit living room.	The living room, we say living room.
Ss:	Living room.	Living room.
T:	Comment on dit le salon?	How do we say living room?
Ss:	Living room.	Living room.

In Excerpt 1.6, the teacher starts by providing a word in French followed by its equivalent term in English, a word which she expects the student to repeat and echo after her (cf. Kanagy, 1999: 1489). She also urges the students to provide the English term by using the questioning strategy. Although the verbal cue, 'Comment on dit le salon?' does not unambiguously elicit the English word, the PSA students do provide the English equivalent as soon as they are prompted. It seems that both the previous experiences in the class and the context of the interaction indicate to the children that they should provide the English word. Through such echoic questions (Long & Sato, 1983, cited in Hendricks, 2003: 32), teachers require the repetition of an utterance as a confirmation that it has been properly understood or memorized. However, with this technique, teachers are developing mainly learners' short-term memory and testing it simultaneously. Such question-answer pattern-drill strategies, which have been noted in primary schools in Mauritius (Griffiths, 2000), as well as in primary and secondary schools in other African and Asian countries (Arthur, 1996; Bunyi, 1997; Chick, 1996; Fuller & Snyder, 1991; Martin, 2005; Rubagumya, 1994), socialize learners into being temporary learners and memorizers of words. In fact, the longitudinal data indicated that once a topic had been covered and words taught by the teacher, the children were not exposed to these English words again, hence undervaluing the importance of the words and the learning/memorizing of these words.

Modelling by code-alternating technical/key vocabulary items

Despite the fact that most of the mathematical terms have their equivalent forms in Kreol/French, the PSA teachers most frequently switch from French/Kreol to English for the technical mathematical vocabulary. The technical mathematical vocabulary taught at pre-school level is fairly limited and consists of: (1) numbers: *one* to *ten*; (2) shapes: *rectangle, square, circle, triangle, cube*; (3) colours: *red, blue, yellow, green*; (4) size: *big, small*; (5) specialized mathematical-technical vocabulary: *number, set(s), matching*; and (6) prepositions: *in, out, under*.

Excerpt 1.7 Small group maths activity (17 March 2001).
T1: Ki number **ki bizin** match **la? [What** number **must we** match **here?]**

Excerpt 1.8 Small group maths activity (3 May 2005).		
T2:	Allez on va faire number one ... number one, c'est combien? Comment on écrit number one maintenant?	So, we will write number one ... number one, how many is that? How do we write number one now?

Excerpt 1.9 Small group maths activity (2 September 2005).		
T2:	C'est quel number? ... Touchez number three	What number is this? ... Touch number three

An analysis of the PSA teachers' weekly plans reveals that they teach *colours*, *shapes* and *prepositions* on a fairly ad hoc basis; however, they teach *numbers* most regularly through the year (Excerpts 1.7–1.9). Teaching the numbers one to 10 seems to be high on the teachers' priority list and when they teach numbers, there is always the tendency to start counting from one, using repetition and scaffolding as the main teaching strategies. For example, when the PSA teachers teach a number, they make the children repeat the previous numbers, hence making them revise and memorize them, before building upon and adding to this knowledge. Furthermore, when the PSA teachers teach mathematical concepts, they use mostly English for all the mathematical terms, hence modelling the English terms through code-mixing; this contrasts with the translation method used to teach general English vocabulary items (see Excerpt 1.6). Consequently, when the PSA teachers ask the children questions in French or Kreol pertaining to mathematical concepts, the students instantly and intuitively reply in English.

Excerpt 1.10 Small group maths activity (5 April 2005).		
T:	Ca ki été ca?	What is this?
S:	Circle	Circle

Excerpt 1.11 Small group maths activity (11 May 2005).		
T1:	Là, combien il y a dedans?	Here, how many are there in it?
Ss:	One, One	One, One

The language choices made by the teachers for teaching mathematical vocabulary socialize the children into viewing English as a mathematical language, indexing English as a language which is serious and which is associated with formal mathematical vocabulary. As illustrated in Excerpts 1.10 and 1.11, the children's responses in English for mathematical words clearly indicate that they have internalized certain language behaviours and that they have consciously or unconsciously made the connection between mathematical terms and English.

In sum, these English language teaching strategies, which are used consistently throughout the year, raise students' awareness that they are in a formal language teaching and language learning environment where there are different languages distinguishable from each other by name. The children are also socialized into seeing English as a language that they learn through French and with respect to French, indexing French as the language of instruction and communication and English as a subject to learn (to name objects and to do maths).

Discussion

The aim of this chapter is to analyse a group of Mauritian pre-schoolers' socialization into English as the main language of education in Mauritius and, by extension, their socialization into local multilingualism. In this coming section, I discuss how the PSA children's socialization into language(s) and language function(s) are mediated by their teachers' language practices and language teaching practices, which reveal the latter's own ideologies of language and language learning (cf. Garrett, 2007: 235; Moore, 2008: 181). I use the term 'ideologies' to describe the abstract and often implicit belief systems which frame and influence language use and language behaviours and which are revealing of underlying language attitudes (cf. McGroarty, 2010: 11). I also discuss how the observed children are socialized into developing subjective (language) learner identities, before considering how the meaning of such terms as 'novice', 'experts' and 'norms' are socially and historically constructed and defined.

Socialized into linguistic hierarchies

In multilingual Mauritian pre-school classrooms such as PSA, teachers can draw from the local community's linguistic repertoire a 'set of resources for representing ideas, displaying stances, performing acts, engaging in activities, and building social personae' (Ochs, 2000: 231). PSA teachers' language practices and language teaching practices socialize the pre-schoolers into assigning different uses, functions and values to these languages.

In terms of language practices, PSA teachers could opt for either Kreol, their own home language and that of the pre-school children, or French, a language which is close to Kreol in terms of vocabulary and which is socially prestigious, or English which is the main language of education, although this would be less likely given that Mauritian children hardly have any proficiency in English when they join the pre-school and the PSA teachers themselves are not very fluent in it (cf. Auleear Owodally, 2012a). Their choice of embedding English within the extended French discourse socializes the children into assigning social and educational indexes to French and English. By contrast, their avoidance of Kreol for educational purposes and their use of Kreol to communicate with the children on social issues (like their health and what they are eating for lunch) socialize the children into tolerating Kreol, rather than using and valuing that language as an important educational linguistic resource. This language avoidance strategy might reveal the teacher's own negative attitudes towards Kreol as a potential language of education and these negative attitudes to Kreol reflect, reproduce and perpetuate local popular discourses of resistance towards Kreol as a school subject and a school language (Rajah-Carrim, 2007). Along similar lines, Rajah-Carrim (2007: 55) refers to some occasions in primary schools where students are asked not to speak Kreol; she suggests that 'the education system goes further than simply ignoring the existence of Kreol, it actively denigrates the language'.

In terms of language teaching practices, the PSA children are socialized into hearing French as the favoured pre-school language, used regularly and

communicatively in the classroom to put across social and academic information. As regards English, the way in which the children are taught to chorus
repeat after the teacher the daily prayer in English socializes them into perceiving English as a religiously neutral language used to start the day, and as
a language that carries no affective link with any particular ethno-religious
group. Furthermore, although the limited use of English in the classroom is
understandable in a macro-social context where English is seldom used, the
strategies used to teach discrete lexical items in English as translated versions
of French words foreground the communicative and meaning potential of
French while undermining that of English. Children are taught to name
objects and do maths in English, English thus being presented as an object of
serious study, and they are not exposed to the richer communicative value of
English, not even through simple storytelling appropriate for English language learners (cf. Cameron, 2001). The high degree of exposure to French and
the minimal formalized exposure to English, as part of the children's daily
routines, is likely to influence the learners' own beliefs about the potentials
of these languages, their knowledge of the language systems themselves
(cf. Ely *et al.*, 2001: 367), and by extension their future language behaviours.

Despite the official sanction of the use of multilingualism in pre-schools
through the 2003 *Pre-school Curriculum Guidelines*, PSA teachers make selective use of the available languages in their multilingual repertoire depending
on the purposes for which these are used, hence socializing the children, very
early in their lives, into assigning specific values to these languages. It can be
suggested that PSA teachers' language ideologies, which have been shaped by
their own language learning experience in a similar education context to that
of their students, are transmitted to their students through their language
practices and language teaching practices. This arguably contributes to the
reinforcement and internalization of existing local language ideologies and
the reproduction of Lx cultural and communicative practices (Duff & Talmy,
2011), where some languages are more used, foregrounded and privileged
than others in the educational arena. The data reveal that the pre-school is a
site where the legitimacy of certain languages and the existing linguistic
hierarchy are perpetuated, and that pre-school teachers act as important
mediators in this context.

Socialized as language learners

As social events, processes and practices (Cook, 1999: 1444; Duff, 2010),
language teaching and language learning are embedded in and shaped by
social, cultural and linguistic systems. At school, children, who are budding
(language) learners, are socialized into locally appropriate ways of learning
and appropriate ways of being students. Classroom teachers play a crucial
role in shaping the identity of the child as a subjective language learning student. Moore (2008: 181) and Garrett (2007: 235) refer to students' subjective

experiences as their particular and local ways of being in the social world which they inhabit.

At PSA, the children are socialized into local understandings of the role of the student within the structure of the educational institution. Being in a teacher-controlled and teacher-centred class, the pre-school children are trained to recognize and respond to their teachers' verbal and non-verbal cues (Garrett, 2007: 234). At circle time, as soon as the children are asked to take their positions, they know that the English prayer session will follow and they quietly and obediently repeat after the teacher. Students diligently repeat words after their teachers; they tend to answer questions in one-word utterances, and they often use the expected languages when responding to the teachers' prompts or questions. The students are thus positioned as repeaters of language chunks or vocabulary items and as speakers who are prompted to respond in a rote manner within very specific rehearsed scripts; they are disciplined into making linguistically appropriate choices at school. One could argue that despite being vocal in the recitation of prayers and using English words for mathematical concepts when asked specific questions by the PSA teachers, the language learners participate, in limited and constrained ways, in classroom discourse and English language learning moments, hence being socialized into fairly docile language learning subject positions (cf. Ohta, 1999: 1509). It is true that repetition can be an important learning resource for learners with limited linguistic resources in Lx, as it provides opportunities for them to observe and practise the language forms (cf. Moore, 2011: 217) for general and mathematical words in English. However, the downside to so much repetition is that it can hinder the children's development in the language being learnt. Such a language learning approach also develops ideologies of language learning as learning a compendium of vocabulary items – a subject – and this can negatively impact on students' motivation to learn languages.

In an era of communicative approaches to language teaching, learner autonomy, learner development and learner voice, such a traditional English language teaching approach, which emphasizes repetition, within the pre-school might appear alien to a Western readership. Crago (1992: 32) points out that in different cultures different communication skills are considered important and different language teaching approaches are valued with different people available for teaching the languages. Local phenomena must thus be understood and interpreted in the context of local realities and discourses. In Mauritius, it is clear that English is not a social language, but rather an educational language which is the passport to educational and professional mobility. Thus, the practices of repetition can be seen as reflecting larger practices and discourses, which create particular kinds of learners (Moore, 2011: 217). Research done by Griffiths (2000) in primary schools in Mauritius indicates that repetition is a common feature of language classrooms. Tirvassen (1999), on the other hand, talks of 'bachotage' or cramming in an education system that is extremely competitive and that values memorization. Furthermore, the educators are themselves products of and parts of a system that values certain aspects of English, the least of which is its value as a social language; the educators' role is thus 'culturally constrained and motivated' (Moore, 2008: 176; Poole, 1992: 611). The PSA teachers' teaching strategies, which arguably reflect their own language and language teaching ideologies, impact on the children's socialization as language learners. Finally, in Mauritius, where primary school classes usually consist of some 40 children, all of whom are learning a second and foreign language, as well as learning through a foreign language (English as a subject and as a written medium of instruction), there are time and space constraints that affect language teaching and language learning. That larger educational context might thus explain why learners are exposed to such language and language teaching practices and socialized into docile and repetitive language learner positions.

The ways in which the children are socialized into developing their identities as language learners is arguably strongly determined by local realities and local constraints.

The social construction of norms, experts and competence

Within the language socialization perspective, *novices* in different communities develop *linguistic and sociocultural competence* by observing and interacting with *experts or knowledgeable others* who represent the *norm* in their own contexts. For children acquiring their first language in a first language context, their caregivers and parents represent the norm; they are the experts. For language learners in a second language context, they are often in a context where they are exposed to native speakers who are the cultural carriers of the norm of the host country. For language learners in a multilingual context like Mauritius, such words as 'novice', 'linguistic and sociocultural competence', 'experts or knowledgeable others' and 'norm' become invested with local meanings and nuances.

PSA children are novice language learners and PSA teachers are the linguistic experts who act as language models. In Mauritius, where French is a second language and English is a foreign language, teachers themselves are often in a language learning situation. For instance, the PSA teachers' proficiency in English is limited; they also have limited opportunities to develop communicative competence and fluency in English, and maybe also in French. In the interviews, the PSA teachers said that they had secondary school level English (Cambridge School Certificate exam), a qualification that indicates their level of written proficiency but not necessarily their ability to use English fluently and communicatively. In fact, English language teaching in Mauritius (Mahadeo, 2006) exposes learners to a bookish type of language in an exam and competitive education system that does not provide maximal meaningful exposure to the language or maximal interaction in the language (Bissoonauth & Offord, 2001). The data can here be used to problematize the notion of teachers as knowledgeable others and linguistic experts. The role of the teachers as linguistic experts and language socializers is arguably constrained by the specificities of the local context.

In terms of sociocultural competence, the LS research indicates that language learners become socioculturally competent as a result of being socialized into local norms. PSA children's identity as language learners and potential language users is shaped by the specificities of the local context. The pre-school classroom is an important site where language learners are socialized into developing notions of what counts as language learning and what counts as successful language learners; hence, the pre-school is a site where teachers and learners perpetuate socially defined competencies and identities. These competencies and identities are further extended and reinforced in primary and secondary school, maintaining a traditional conception of language learners as passive learners. These language learners are not necessarily (orally) communicatively competent or fluent, and they also probably develop a localized version of sociocultural competence since English is not a social language in their context, but rather a language of education.

The data herewith presented illustrate some of the ways in which terms like 'competence' and 'norm' are socially and culturally shaped and constrained. Local contexts invest 'meaning' into these terms.

Conclusions

Taking Mauritian society as the locus for analysis, I have shown how, in their role as language learners in a multilingual context, the observed pre-school children are socialized into multiple community languages, language ideologies, learner identities and subjectivities, through their teachers' language practices and language teaching practices. The LS perspective has contributed to our understanding of (second and foreign) language learning in a pre-school in a complex multilingual context.

What are the pedagogical implications of a LS perspective on language practices and language teaching practices in the local context? It seems that a LS perspective raises awareness of the local boundaries within which the pre-school functions as a foundation LS site for local children. It also raises questions about the role of the pre-school in developing positive attitudes and language ideologies at the first stage of learning within the larger educational and professional trajectory of multilingual language learners and users in Mauritius. Since Mauritius has no natural resources, its main resource is its manpower and its main strength is its multilingualism. The emerging pillars of this island state, which now has to compete on a global, free and competitive market, value multilingual, communicative and sociocultural competencies. The data herewith presented raise questions about the extent to which local children are being richly enough socialized into multilingual language and language learning competencies so that they can explore and exploit those to their utmost educational and professional advantage in the years to come.

Appendix 1: Symbols Used in the Transcript

Abc (normal letters)	Discourse in French
Abc (bold letters)	Discourse in Kreol
<u>Abc</u> (underlined letters)	Discourse in English
[....]	Notes made by the Researcher at time of data collection
(S)	One student
(SS)	Students
(x2)	Repeated twice
(x3)	Repeated thrice

References

Arthur, J. (1996) Code switching and collusion: Classroom interaction in Botswana primary schools. *Linguistics and Education* 8, 17–33.

Arthur, J. and Martin, P. (2006) Accomplishing lessons in postcolonial classrooms: Comparative perspectives from Botswana and Brunei Darussalam. *Comparative Education* 42 (2), 177–202.

Auer, P. (1995) The pragmatics of code-switching: A sequential approach. In L. Milroy and P. Muysken (eds) *One Speaker, Two Languages: Cross-disciplinary Perspectives on Code-Switching* (pp. 115–135). Cambridge: Cambridge University Press.

Auleear Owodally, A.M. (2008) Building bridges to primary education in Mauritius? Emergent literacy experiences in a foreign language context: A case study of preschool children. PhD thesis, University of Cape Town.

Auleear Owodally, A.M. (2010) From home to school: Bridging the language gap in Mauritian preschools. *Language, Culture and Curriculum* 23 (1), 15–33.

Auleear Owodally, A.M. (2012a) Juggling languages: A case study of preschool teachers' language choices and practices in Mauritius. *International Journal of Multilingualism* 9 (3), 235–256.

Auleear Owodally, A.M. (2012b) Exposing preschoolers to the printed word: A case study of preschool teachers in Mauritius. *Journal of Early Childhood Literacy* 13 (1), 52–97.

Auleear Owodally, A.M. and Unjore, S. (2013) Kreol at school: A case study of Mauritian Muslims' language and literacy ideologies. *Journal of Multilingual and Multicultural Development* 34 (3), 213–230.

Baquedano-López, P. and Kattan, S. (2010) Language socialization in schools. In P.A. Duff and N.H. Hornberger (eds) *Encyclopedia of Language and Education, Vol. 8: Language Socialization* (2nd edn) (pp. 161–173). New York: Springer.

Bissoonauth, A. and Offord, M. (2001) Language use of Mauritian adolescents in education. *Journal of Multilingual and Multicultural Development* 22 (5), 381–400.

Blackledge, A. and Creese, A. (2010) *Multilingualism: A Critical Perspective*. London: Continuum.

Bogdan, R.C. and Biklen, S.K. (1992) *Qualitative Research for Education: An Introduction to Theory and Methods*. Boston, MA: Allyn & Bacon.

Brock-Utne, B. and Holmarsdottir, H.B. (2003) Language policies and practices in Africa – some preliminary results from a research project in Tanzania and South Africa. In B. Brock-Utne, Z. Desai and M. Qorro (eds) *The Language of Instruction in Tanzania and South Africa* (LOITASA). Dar es Salaam: E & D Publishers.

Bunyi, G.W. (1997) Multilingualism and discourse in primary mathematics in Kenya. *Language, Culture and Curriculum* 10 (1), 52–65.

Cameron, L. (2001) *Teaching Languages to Young Learners*. Cambridge: Cambridge University Press.

Central Statistics Office, Mauritius (2000) *Population and Housing Census*. See http://statsmauritius.gov.mu/English/Documents/Demogra/demofer.htm (accessed 10 July 2013).

Central Statistics Office, Mauritius (2011) *Population and Housing Census*. See http://statsmauritius.gov.mu/English/Pages/2011-Housing-and-Populations-.aspx (accessed 15 July 2013).

Chick, K. (1996) Safe-talk: Collusion in apartheid education. In H. Coleman (ed.) *Society and the Language Classroom* (pp. 21–39). Cambridge: Cambridge University Press.

Cook, H.M. (1999) Language socialization in Japanese elementary schools: Attentive listening and reaction turns. *Journal of Pragmatics* 31, 1443–1465.

Crago, M.B. (1992) Ethnography and language socialization: A cross-cultural perspective. *Topics in Language Disorders* 12 (3), 28–39.

Duff, P.A. (2010) Language socialization. In N.H. Hornberger and S.L. McKay (eds) *Sociolinguistics and Language Education* (pp. 427–454). Bristol: Multilingual Matters.

Duff, P. and Talmy, S. (2011) Language socialization approaches to second language acquisition. In D. Atkinson (ed.) *Alternative Approaches to Second Language Acquisition* (pp. 94–116). New York: Routledge.

Eisenlohr, P. (2006) The politics of diaspora and the morality of secularism: Muslim identities and Islamic authority in Mauritius. *Journal of the Royal Anthropological Institute* 12, 395–412.

Ely, R., Gleason, J.B., MacGibbon A. and Zaretsky, E. (2001) Attention to language: Lessons learned at the dinner table. *Social Development* 10 (3), 355–373. See http://www.stolaf.edu/people/huff/classes/Psych130S2012/Readings/Ely%20et%20al%20 2001%20dinner%20table%20talk.pdf (accessed 26 April 2014).

Emura, M. (2006) Language socialization in elementary school ESL: Multi-directional socialization processes. *Second Language Studies* 25 (1), 1–52.

Fuller, B. and Snyder, C.W. (1991) Vocal teachers, silent pupils! Life in Botswana classrooms. *Comparative Education Review* 35 (2), 274–294.

Garrett, P. (2005) What a language is good for: Language socialization, language shift, and the persistence of code-specific genres in St Lucia. *Language in Society* 34, 327–361.

Garrett, P. (2007) Language socialization and the (re)production of bilingual subjectivities. In M. Heller (ed.) *Bilingualism: A Social Approach* (pp. 233–256). Basingstoke: Palgrave Macmillan.

Gee, P. (2011) *An Introduction to Discourse Analysis: Theory and Method* (3rd edn). Oxford: Routledge.

Glaser, B.G. and Strauss, A.L. (1967) The *Discovery of Grounded Theory: Strategies for Qualitative Research*. Mill Valley, CA: Sociology Press.

Griffiths, M. (2000) Learning for all? Interrogating children's experiences of primary schooling in Mauritius. *Teaching and Teacher Education* 16, 785–800.

Hamayan, J.S. and Damico, E.V. (1991) Developing and using a second language. In E.V. Hamayan and J.S. Damico (eds) *Limiting Bias in the Assessments of Bilingual Students* (pp. 39–76). Austin, TX: Pro-Ed.

Hatch, J.A. (2002) *Doing Qualitative Research in Education Settings*. Albany, NY: University of New York Press.

Heath, S.B. (1983) *Ways with Words: Language, Life and Work in Communities and Classrooms*. New York: Cambridge University Press.

Hendricks, M. (2003) Classroom talk: 'There are more questions than answers'. *South African Linguistics and Applied Language Studies* 21 (1/2), 29–40.

Howard, K. (2009) Breaking in and spinning out: Repetition and decalibration in Thai children's play genres. *Language in Society* 38, 339–363.

Kanagy, R. (1999) Interactional routines as a mechanism for L2 acquisition and socialization in an immersion context. *Journal of Pragmatics* 31, 1467–1492.

Krashen, S. (1988) *Second Language Acquisition and Second Language Learning*. Upper Saddle River, NJ: Prentice Hall.

Li, D. (2008) Pragmatic socialization. In P.A. Duff and N.H. Hornberger (eds) *Encyclopaedia of Language and Education, Vol. 8: Language Socialization* (2nd edn) (pp. 71–83). New York: Springer.

Lincoln, Y.S. and Guba, E.G. (1985) *Naturalistic Inquiry*. Beverly Hills, CA: Sage.

Long, M. and Sato, C. (1983) Classroom foreigner talk discourse: Forms and functions of teachers' questions. In H. Seliger and M. Long (eds) *Classroom Oriented Research in SLA* (pp. 268–286). Rowley, MA: Newbury House.

Mahadeo, S.K. (2006) English language teaching in Mauritius: A need for clarity of vision regarding English language policy. *International Journal of Language, Culture and Society* 18. See http://www.educ.utas.edu.au/users/tle/journal/articles/2006/18-2.htm (accessed 10 July 2013).

Martin, P. (2005) 'Safe' language practices in two rural schools in Malaysia: Tensions between policy and practice. In A.M.Y. Lin and P.W. Martin (eds) *Decolonisation, Globalisation: Language-in-Education Policy and Practice* (pp. 74–97). Clevedon: Multilingual Matters.

McGroarty, M.E. (2010) Language and ideologies. In N.H. Hornberger and S.L. McKay (eds) *Sociolinguistics and Language Education* (pp. 3–39). Bristol: Multilingual Matters.

Ministry of Education and Scientific Research, Mauritius (2003) *Early Childhood Education. Preschool Programme Guidelines 3–5 Years*. Port Louis, Mauritius: Republic of Mauritius.

Moore, L. (2006a) Language socialization. Linguistic anthropology. See http://www.eolss.net/Sample-Chapters/C04/E6-20B-06-01.pdf (accessed 10 July 2013).

Moore, L. (2006b) Learning by heart in Quranic and public schools in a Fulbe community. *Studies in African Linguistics (Supplement)* 11, 176–187.

Moore, L. (2008) Language socialization and second/foreign language and multilingual education in non-Western settings. In P.A. Duff and N.H. Hornberger (eds) *Encyclopaedia of Language and Education, Vol. 8: Language Socialization* (2nd edn) (pp. 175–185). New York: Springer.

Moore, L. (2011) Language socialization and repetition. In A. Duranti, E. Ochs and B.B. Schieffelin (eds) *The Handbook of Language Socialization* (pp. 209–226). Oxford: Blackwell.

Ochs, E. (2000) Socialization. *Journal of Linguistic Anthropology* 9 (1), 230–233.

Ohta A.S. (1999) Interactional routines and the socialization of interactional style in adult learners of Japanese. *Journal of Pragmatics* 31 (11), 1493–1512.

Patton, M.Q. (1990) *Qualitative Research and Evaluation Methods*. Newbury Park, CA: Sage.

Pavlenko, A. (2006) *Emotions and Multilingualism*. Cambridge: Cambridge University Press.

Poole, D. (1992) Language socialization in the second language classroom. *Language Learning* 42, 593–616.

Rajah-Carrim, A. (2004) The role of Mauritian Creole in the religious practices of Mauritian Muslims. *Journal of Pidgin and Creole Languages* 19 (2), 363–375.

Rajah-Carrim, A. (2007) Mauritian Creole and language attitudes in the education system of multiethnic and multilingual Mauritius. *Journal of Multilingual and Multicultural Development* 28 (1), 51–71.

Rajah-Carrim, A. (2010) Mauritian Muslims: Negotiating changing identities through language. In T. Omoniyi (ed.) *The Sociology of Language and Religion* (pp. 29–44). Basingstoke: Palgrave Macmillan.

Rubagumya, C.M. (1994) Language values and bilingual classroom discourse in Tanzanian secondary schools. *Language, Culture and Curriculum* 7 (1), 41–53.

Schieffelin, B.B. and Ochs, E. (1996) The microgenesis of competence: Methodology in Language socialization. In D. Slobin, J. Gerhardt, A. Kyratzis and G. Jiansheng (eds) *Social Interaction, Social Context and Language: Essays in Honor of Susan Ervin-Tripp* (pp. 251–263). Lawrence Erlbaum Associates. See http://www.sscnet.ucla.edu/anthro/faculty/ochs/articles/The_Microgenesis_of_Comptenece-Methdology_in_Language_Socialization.pdf (accessed 26 April 2014).

Strauss, A.L. and Corbin, J. (1990) *Basics of Qualitative Research: Grounded Theory Procedures and Techniques*. Newbury Park, CA: Sage.

Tirvassen, R. (1999) La problématique du choix des langues d'enseignement dans des pays indépendants: l'anglais dans la politique de l'école mauricienne. *DiversCité Langues, Vol. IV.* See http://www.uquebec.ca/diverscite (accessed 10 July 2013).

Tirvassen, R. (2005) Les préalables à des propositions d'aménagement linguistique à l'école maternelle en milieu plurilingue. In F. Lallement, P. Martinez and V. Spaeth (eds) *Le Français dans le Monde, Français Langage d'Enseignement, vers une Didicatique Comparative (Numéro Spécial)*, January, 160–169.

Toth, A. (1995) Mauritius. In H. Metz (ed.) *Indian Ocean. Five Island Countries* (pp. 89–137). Washington, DC: Area Handbook Series.

Wray, A. (2000) Formulaic sequences in SL teaching. Principle and practice. *Applied Linguistics* 21 (4), 463–489.

2 Exploring the -lingual Between Bi and Mono: Young People and Their Languages in an Australian Context

Ken Cruickshank

Guiding Questions

- In what ways do government programmes and policies reflect the monolingual mindset of second language acquisition research in the context described here?
- In what ways does the 'messiness' of young people's multilingual practices present challenges for day and community schools?
- What are the opportunities and challenges of acknowledging local multilingual resources and practices in day and community school contexts in Australia?

Introduction

There have been some 67 language policies, reports and programmes produced in Australia in the past 40 years including the landmark *National Policy on Languages* which was heralded as bringing together the conflicting voices of ethnic/language groups and modern/foreign languages teachers (Lo Bianco, 1987; Lo Bianco & Gvodzenko, 2006). Australia also has a strength of linguistic resources: 25% of students in New South Wales (NSW), the largest state, come from bilingual/bicultural backgrounds; 30% of primary schools offer languages programmes; over 64 different languages are taught across education sectors (Lo Bianco, 2009). Policy initiatives foreground the promotion of languages for all students along with the maintenance and development of community languages.

In reality, the gap between policy and practice has never been greater. Less than 12% of students study a language in their final year of secondary school (down from 40% in the 1970s) compared with 40–50% in the US and UK (EC, 2012; Rhodes & Pufahl, 2009). Community languages programmes, funded initially in the 1980s, subsist in government primary and out-of-hours community languages schools, and modern languages such as French and Japanese continue strongly in elite government and non-government schools, but the picture is one of a desert with few oases (Kipp, 2008; Morgan *et al.*, 2013). A monolingual mindset seems to pervade government at Federal state and local levels: a focus on languages for trade has seen policy driven by economic imperatives, and concern over literacy levels has seen languages subsumed within English language literacy with a marginalised 'shell' of community languages (Kipp, 2008; Lo Bianco, 1999; Taylor & Henry, 2000).[1]

This chapter argues that the failure to halt the decline in languages study is, in part, due to the government failure to take into account the complex realities and resources of language practices and language learning at local levels. This is shown in the lack of consistent and coherent data collection and the lack of research into local language practices. There are few coherent accounts of any groups of young people in specific schools or areas and the skills, opportunities and experiences they have in terms of languages and language learning. This chapter, in an attempt to address this gap, draws on data from two studies in Sydney and Wollongong of young people in after-hours community languages schools learning Turkish, Chinese (Mandarin), Arabic and Cook Island Maori.

Background

This section explores the importance of contexts in research into multilingual practices, in this instance, the in-between sites represented by out-of-hours community languages schools. It looks at research into local multilingual practices and why these tend to be invisible to policymakers.

Top-down policy

Education and language policy in Australia have, with one or two notable exceptions, been 'top-down' Federal government initiatives. Funding has tended to support short-term programmes rather than structural change and language policy has had an over-focus on economic and trade goals and lack of building on existing resources (Kipp, 2008; Slaughter, 2009). Education, however, is divided between Federal and state governments, with the states responsible for the majority of funding, curriculum development, employing teachers and running schools. Languages programmes are delivered through state government schools (taking 75% of students), Catholic and independent sectors (25%) and after-hours community languages schools. There is a lack of any consistent and coherent cross-sectoral data collection, making it difficult for policy developers to design, monitor and evaluate programmes (Lo Bianco, 2009). It has been argued that Australia does much better in dealing with cultural than linguistic diversity – multiculturalism rather than multilingualism (Morgan et al., 2013).

Local resources

Internationally, there is a growing body of research into the complexity of multilingual experiences in local sites, including the work on urban multilingualism in Europe (Barni & Extra, 2008; Extra & Yagmur, 2004, 2011) and on linguistic landscapes or 'linguascapes' (Cenoz & Gorter, 2008; Shohamy & Gorter, 2009). These studies highlight the rich resources of languages in local environments, challenging accounts of multilingual contexts which rely only on aggregated macro-sociolinguistic data. They combine quantitative with a range of in-depth qualitative research strategies.

Situated practice

A common theme in many of these studies is that of situated practice: how speakers draw on all available linguistic resources in making meaning and how different contexts shape and are shaped by the multilingual language practices. Heller (2007) argues that concepts of 'context', 'site' and 'place' are central to making sense of people's affiliations and identity positions. Following work in linguistic anthropology, context can be characterised in terms of features such as the 'setting' that is the social and spatial framework in which encounters are situated; and the 'behavioural environment', the way that participants use their bodies and behaviour as a resource for framing and organising talk (Duranti & Goodwin, 1992).

In-between sites

Studies of bilingualism have tended to focus on day school, workplace or family/home contexts, drawing on sociological and ethnographic research traditions. The emphasis in research into day schools has often been on how minority languages and bilingual student 'funds of knowledge' are marginalised. Research into language in 'in-between' sites such as community places, technology-mediated interaction, media and community languages schools is much less common. These sites are places between mainstream and minority institutions and are places where issues of language choice, affiliations and identities are much less predetermined. They are often sites where 'second-generation rules' and issues of power and ideologies are much more in evidence. A focus on multilingual practices in in-between sites (between the constructs of mainstream and minority) can, in fact, serve 'to prise open powerful ideological positions which may often not be evident in other sites' (Hornberger, 2005: 606).

Community languages schools

Research into the after-hours community languages schools (called supplementary or complementary schools in the UK and heritage language schools in the US) run by parents and community members has burgeoned in the past decade with over 100 books, articles and reports (Blackledge & Creese, 2010; García *et al.*, 2013; Lytra & Martin, 2010). Many of the studies have found that although schools often have as their goal the passing on of cultural and linguistic heritage to subsequent generations and although they espouse policies of using only the community language in schools, the classroom reality is different. Young people negotiate, challenge and resist and their multilingual practices become the norm. Because these sites are much more dynamic, the socially constructed nature of terms such as 'community', 'language' and 'identity' are evident and there are fluid boundaries between language varieties indexing multiple identities (Heller, 2007). The use of complex language choices and code-switching as the unmarked form of language in these sites has been called flexible bilingualism (Blackledge & Creese, 2010), translanguaging (García, 2007) or heteroglossia (Bailey, 2007, drawing on Bakhtin). It is this notion of flexible bilingualism that makes it possible to focus on and normalise the perspectives of individual language learners, being able to access resources that enable them to learn or maintain one or more languages in their home, schools and local communities.

This chapter draws on data from two studies aiming to explore the nature of the linguistic resources on which young people in community languages schools draw. Specifically, it addresses the question of their self-reported use of and their attitudes to linguistic practices and resources. It uses these data to question categories of language, ethnicity and identity that are given as labels in policy documents. It argues that failure to take into account the multilingual practices in sites such as community languages schools is caused by a monolingual mindset in system-level policy and research.

Methodology

Community languages schools have been operating in Australia since 1859 and there are now over 100,000 young people across Australia learning one of 64 languages in over 1200 schools. Schools receive government funding and in NSW the majority of community schools have use of day school premises. The studies focused on two community languages schools in Wollongong, a regional city in New South Wales (NSW), and three schools in Sydney. The reason for the choice of schools and languages was to get a balance of city and regional schools, and of large, small and emerging languages.

The Arabic language school in Wollongong has been operating since the 1970s and now has over 100 students in classes on Saturdays in a local primary school. Arabic is the fourth most widely used community language in Australia but the community of some 1500 speakers in Wollongong is small and diverse. The families came from Lebanon, Egypt and Syria in the 1970s and 1980s to work in the steelworks and have a range of religious affiliations: Maronite Christian, Sunni and Shi'a Muslim, Druze and Orthodox. The school is the only remaining one of five Arabic schools in the area and draws students from across all religious affiliations.

The Chinese language school in Wollongong began in the backyard of Lin, the principal, in response to friends asking her to teach Chinese to their children. It grew to a school of 33 students within a few years and now operates from a day school on Friday afternoons. The students come from a range of backgrounds: Cantonese speaking, mixed marriages and some other backgrounds such as Korean, Malaysian and Anglo-Australian. Most families have little or no contact with each other and so the school acts as a connector. Apart from a few restaurants, there is little visible Chinese community presence in the city.

The Cook Island Maori language school was formed in 2007 and grew quickly to 50 students. Most are Australian- or New Zealand-born and many of the children come from mixed marriages. The school focuses on cultural activities along with teaching Rarotongan (Cook Island Maori) and operates on Saturday mornings in a day school in the inner west of Sydney. The teachers come from the main extended family groups and they see the school as the first institution to unite the families in a common effort; church affiliations are diverse, with families belonging to different denominations.

The Turkish community language school has been operating in the inner west of Sydney for some 25 years. Families from Cyprus and Turkey first settled in the 1970s and they now make up 10% of the total local population. Some 80 students attend the school in a local primary school.

The nearby Chinese community language school has 120 students. The families were mainly part of the migration in the 1980s from the People's Republic of China, but there are also families from Hong Kong, Taiwan, southeast Asia and numbers of children from mixed marriages. The school teaches Mandarin Chinese. Like 60% of all community languages schools, it is located in a local government primary school.[2]

Data collection and analysis

The first study involved the Cook Island Maori, Arabic and Wollongong Chinese schools. Eight focus group interviews with students aged 8–12 were conducted in the schools ($n = 38$) by three university researchers and three student research assistants.[3] There were also classroom observations in the Wollongong Arabic and Chinese schools. Observation schedules used lesson episodes and notes were taken on the types of activities, student participation and the use of English and target language by teachers and students. In addition, documentary evidence was collected from each of the schools. In-depth interviews were conducted with the three principals.

The second study, focusing on the Sydney Chinese and Turkish schools, involved a 19-question student survey administered in class ($n = 131$). The questions focused on the student's profile, language use, use with interlocutors, domains of language use, attitudes to learning languages, reasons for study, and use of media and technologies. There were also follow-up focus group interviews in each school ($n = 14$).

The topics in the focus group interviews were regarding the community language school (what they liked and disliked about it, why they attended), friends, family and extended family, day school (differences, likes/dislikes, interests), sport, weekend activities, and community and religious events. Incidents/findings from class observations were also discussed in focus group interviews. This general focus was taken because issues of language use and identity positioning are generally not conscious; whenever answers related to these, they were probed by interviewers. All focus group interviews were audio-recorded, logged and transcribed. Field notes were also taken from interviews. Analysis of interview data was firstly done by coding in terms of interview topics and themes identified from the research literature and then for common themes which were not part of the original analysis. Findings from documentary evidence, survey and notes were then cross-checked with focus group findings.

Findings

The following section gives the young people's accounts of their language practices and domains of uses, their self-reported language proficiency, their attitudes to and perceptions of their languages and the role these play in their identities. All of this is through the lens of their community language school.

Diversity in community languages schools

The Chinese school in Wollongong is typical of the changes in community languages schools. Two-thirds of the students were either from mixed marriages or non-Chinese background families. Lin, the principal, reported that many families send their children to the community languages school for Chinese language learning experiences they cannot get in the day schools. The prevalence of children from mixed marriages is also common in other schools. In both Chinese schools in Sydney and Wollongong, the backgrounds of the students were diverse: parents came from Taiwan, Hong Kong, China PRC, southeast Asia and elsewhere. Many spoke Cantonese and Hakka as their first language even though the schools were teaching Mandarin Chinese, which is now a high-status language in Australia because of government policy and economic factors.[4] An indicator of this is that many Chinese community languages schools have enrolments from Anglo-Australian families.

Students in the Wollongong Arabic school generally came from Arabic-background families but there was great diversity in countries of origin and religious affiliations. This was the same with the Turkish school in Sydney. The picture from aggregated data was that parents were largely overseas-born (88%) and students second generation (90%), but this belies the real diversity. The range of language experiences, affiliations and attitudes of the students varies – something which is evident in the findings about language use and fluency.

Using their languages

There was diversity in the young people's reported language use in all five schools. Young people in the Turkish, Chinese and Arabic schools reported a mix of English, community language and dialect being used in the home. The language used with parents was often the language/dialect in which the parents were stronger. There was much greater use of Chinese (Mandarin and Cantonese), Turkish and Arabic with grandparents, but much lower use with siblings, a finding confirmed in other studies (Rubino, 2010).[5] Language use in community contexts was complex. Students in the Turkish school, for example, communicated mainly in English at day school, community events and shopping; they used Turkish primarily in visiting relatives, with grandparents and at the mosque. Language choice tended to be strategic (Jørgenson, 2008): many reported using Turkish at day school on the sports field or playground with friends when they did not want others to understand them. They also used English in Turkish community classes in resistance to the teachers. Their amount of code-switching was influenced by their interlocutor (such as mother, father or siblings), by the context (at dinner/at community events) and also by the topic being talked about (such as sport, gossip, music).[6]

Survey data from the Chinese and Turkish schools in Sydney (Tables 2.1–2.4) indicated that 67% of Chinese students said they used a mix of English and Chinese words 'a lot' and similarly for 57% of Turkish students. The amount of word mixing and code-switching confirms other findings. The observations in Arabic and Chinese schools in Wollongong indicated that code-switching was common with friends, siblings and parents and also in class, despite the efforts of some teachers to enforce language use. This confirms the findings of Blackledge and Creese (2010). Interviewees are often unaware of code-switching and code-mixing simply because communication

Table 2.1 Language used by students to interlocutors (Chinese school, Sydney, $n = 54$)[a]

	Chinese/ Mandarin	Cantonese	English	Other[b]
Grandparents	31 (57%)	16 (30%)	2 (4%)	5 (9%)
Mother	23 (43%)	14 (26%)	12 (22%)	5 (9%)
Father	24 (44%)	12 (22%)	14 (26%)	4 (7%)
Brother and sister	5 (9%)	1 (2%)	33 (61%)	15 (28%)
Friends	1 (2%)	0 (0%)	52 (96%)	1 (2%)

Notes: [a]Students were asked what they 'usually speak to grandparents' and others, so that they could answer with more than one language/dialect. The diagram with 'speech bubbles' was adapted from that used in the Linguistic Minorities Project (Stubbs, 1985). The problems of self-reported language use are a limitation of these data.
[b]Other for 'Chinese' included other dialects such as Hakka, Hokkien and Teochew. For both Turkish and Chinese groups there were mixed marriages and in some cases it was the 'other' language of one spouse or grandparent. The question was an open one and some students responded 'Chinglish' for Chinese and English.

Table 2.2 Language used to students by interlocutors (Chinese school, Sydney, $n = 54$)

	Chinese/ Mandarin	Cantonese	English[a]	Other
Grandparents	30 (56%)	15 (28%)	4 (7%)	5 (9%)
Mother	29 (54%)	18 (33%)	5 (9%)	2 (4%)
Father	25 (46%)	14 (26%)	12 (22%)	3 (6%)
Brother and sister	5 (9%)	1 (2%)	31 (57%)	17 (31%)
Friends	1 (2%)	0 (0%)	52 (96%)	1 (2%)

[a]Students reported four grandparents speaking English whereas only two reported using English to grandparents. There are many possible reasons for this. Children may have overestimated grandparents' fluency; in other studies (Cruickshank 2006) parents and grandparents reported using English instead of the home language to children when they really wanted them to understand. English tended to be used when asserting authority.

Table 2.3 Language used by students to interlocutors (Turkish school, Sydney, $n = 60$)

	Turkish	English	Other
Grandparents	53 (88%)	2 (3%)	5 (8%)
Mother	27 (45%)	30 (50%)	3 (5%)
Father	23 (38%)	30 (50%)	7 (12%)
Brother and sister	3 (5%)	54 (90%)	3 (5%)
Friends	1 (2%)	55 (92%)	4 (7%)

Table 2.4 Language used to students by interlocutors (Turkish school, Sydney, *n* = 60)

	Turkish	English	Other
Grandparents	55 (92%)	1 (2%)	4 (7%)
Mother	33 (55%)	22 (37%)	5 (8%)
Father	25 (42%)	26 (43%)	9 (15%)
Brother and sister	4 (7%)	54 (90%)	2 (3%)
Friends	1 (0%)	56 (93%)	3 (5%)

in multilingual contexts involves drawing on all resources available. It was only in focus groups when the bilingual research assistants described their own use of languages that students then began reporting their own code-switching and code-mixing.

Emerging domains of use

The importance of travel and the notion of a transnational family were important findings. All 21 students interviewed in the Wollongong Arabic school had visited relatives in parents' countries of origin, with stays of up to six months. Nearly all the young people in the Turkish school reported spending time overseas in the parents' countries of origin. Accounts of visits from relatives were also common. The notion of 'family' was one that crossed national boundaries. For students in the Cook Island Maori school the construct of 'family' included extended family in New Zealand, Australia and the Cook Islands. Visiting relatives increased community language use in the home.

> Before when, like, my aunty stayed, my aunty speaks in Islander, and I just didn't know what they were saying and I was just going like that (shrugs) because that's what I always do if I don't understand. I just keep doing that (shrugs) if I didn't understand. (Toni)

With relatives, such as Toni's aunty, who spoke little English, the home conversations switched to Cook Island Maori and it was impolite for children to shift the language of interaction. She had to follow conversations in Cook Island Maori and eventually became a participant. There were many comments about how the young people accepted correction in conversation with relatives. Peter reported, in the excerpt below, how he had self-corrected his answer in Cook Island Maori to his nan.

> My nan said to me one time, 'Are you not happy that I am here?' in Cook Island and I didn't know what she said I just said, 'Yes'. And she said, 'You are not happy?' and I said, 'I mean I AM happy'. (Peter)

Fatima, in the Arabic school, commented on the change in her language caused by her visit to Lebanon. She spent three months there attending school. Her first memory in shifting from English to Arabic was the physical effects of speaking in Arabic all day. She reported that by the end of the time there she spoke, thought and even dreamed in Arabic.

> In Lebanon my jaw used to hurt at the end of every day – it was getting my mouth around the Arabic sounds. They are so different to English. (Fatima)

The second emerging domain was that of language use in technology and media. Students in the Turkish school in Sydney reported regular use of Turkish on Facebook and mobile phones. Fifty-eight percent used Turkish on the iPhone and 42% sometimes or a lot on Facebook. Most students in the Turkish and Chinese schools also reported sometimes/a lot watching TV from overseas (93% of Turkish and 79% of Chinese students). The most popular kinds of television programmes Chinese families liked to watch at home included drama, followed by news, and to a much lesser extent sport and documentaries. For Turkish families, however, soaps, drama and news were the most popular, followed by sport, documentaries and concerts. The students reported listening to/watching music DVDs (86% Turkish and 62% Chinese sometimes/a lot). Internet use in the community language emerged as common practice in the focus group interviews. The technology and media domains fitted into existing cultural patterns. For the Chinese background families, historical dramas were important; for the Turkish background families, family dramas and Turkish music played key roles. Turkish background families tended to have family members still in Turkey or Cyprus and so technology-mediated communication and following Turkish news were more common. Some of the Turkish background young people were allowed to spend time in shopping centres/malls after school as long as they kept in touch with their mothers via mobile phone. This emerging domain for community languages from the development of global media is an important finding.

Reasons for language learning

At first glance the reasons for studying in the community languages schools were similar: parental decisions/pressures and cultural/linguistic heritage. Most young people expressed positive attitudes to their language although responses were mixed regarding attending the community languages school. Meeting and socialising with friends from different day schools was a key reason for liking the school. There were, however, marked differences between languages and young people in the reasons for learning at the community language school.

Students in both Chinese schools stressed linguistic reasons for attending the schools. The two main reasons were because of their background (80% agree or strongly agree) and because parents wanted them to study (64% strongly agree/agree). Additional comments from students in both Chinese schools focused on language and family communication rather than cultural reasons.

It is my background language. (S [student] 2)
I want to learn my parents' language. (S 7)
I could understand my grandma. (S 21)
I can talk to my dad in that language. (S 28)
Many people speak that language and I want to understand what they were talking about. (S 31)

Instrumental reasons also came through strongly. The mixed nature of the Wollongong Chinese school also meant that the focus was more on Chinese as a global language rather than heritage reasons.

It's important to learn Chinese. My brother is doing the HSC [Higher School Certificate – Year 12] and you can get good marks. (James)

In an interview, Lin, the principal, stressed the language teaching role of the school.

We don't spend that much time on Chinese New Year and cultural things. Some of the families go to Sydney for the festivals; there isn't much going on in Wollongong. We focus more on the language side of things.

This foregrounding of language over cultural reasons confirms the findings from Archer *et al.* (2010) that discourses of culture for Chinese were constructed around language issues. The higher cultural capital of Mandarin Chinese compared to Arabic and Turkish and studying it for the final Year 12 exam was perhaps another reason behind this. Language, more than shared cultural backgrounds, was also a unifying feature of the Chinese schools; cultural background was more an assumed 'Chineseness' underlying the work of the school.

For young people in the Turkish and Arabic schools, the reasons were more related to family and heritage. Among the main reasons for studying Arabic were travel overseas and communicating with relatives, their heritage, liking the teacher, and parents wanting them to study. Ninety percent (strongly agree/agree) of Turkish background students gave as the reason that they wanted to travel to/visit Turkey and 83% (strongly agree/agree) that it was because of their background. To a lesser extent, the theme of general satisfaction derived from knowing another language was also evident. Typical comments included:

> It's fun and I am learning to talk to my family in Turkish. (S 58)
> My background is very important. (S 62)
> It is my language and I learn more. (S 78)

The situation for students of the Cook Island Maori school was different. They came from families where parents had often been forced through schooling to lose their language: the school had been established to help revive the language. This was being done through cultural activities such as dance, singing, games and the building of vocabulary in the language. The four young people interviewed had a strong sense of the learning and cultural heritage gained from the community language school. This was not just through the classes but associated sports, musical activities and performances. They expressed strong solidarity with the teachers. One reason for this could have been that many of the teachers were in the same position as the students themselves in gaining fluency in Rarotongan and they were also parents of many of the children in the school. There was a strong sense of cultural maintenance through dancing, drumming and songs.

> (We learn) Like so our culture and, like, the language doesn't die out. (Peter)
> I'm proud to learn it while I still can ... so that our culture can keep going and get larger. (Alice)

The sense of urgency in cultural and linguistic heritage and maintenance permeated the reports from teachers and students.

Interviewer:	Why do you think it is important?
S 1 Peter:	So the language doesn't die out.
S 2 Alice:	So you don't like say that oh like we'll just all speak English and the whole world will speak it.
S 1 Peter:	Yeah and everybody will just speak English.
S 2 Alice:	Yeah and if like we die no one else will speak it there will just be all English and there will be no Cook Islands.

Ascribing reasons and attitudes to any single factor is not possible. In many ways attitudes were constructed in the school sites themselves. This emerged in the ways participants in Arabic and Cook Island Maori schools described the language they were learning.

What counts as language?

There was no common term that students in the Cook Island Maori school used for their language. Most commonly they used the term 'the language' or 'language'. Two of the students used the term 'Cook Island'. One used 'Islander' which is interesting as it is a term of abuse in New Zealand where the word Pasifika is used.

> my aunty speaks in Islander. (Toni)

In the Arabic language school, the term 'Arabic'[7] was constructed by the young people as the 'proper' language, something external to them:

> (In Lebanon) they speak the real Arabic – different Arabic we learn here. (Bilal)
> My dad wants me to learn Arabic because when I go to Lebanon could speak proper with my grandparents and that. (Ahmed)

In contrast to this, there were few terms that they used to refer to their own language at home. Some used the term 'dialect'; one used 'Lebanese'. They discussed code-mixing and switching with the interviewer, Maryam, who was from one of the families in the school. There was no sense of this being other than an 'unmarked' language of family communication. Arabic is commonly characterised as a diglossic language with the formal spoken/written variety and a range of regional dialects. In the diaspora the *al fus'ha*, the high form, tends to be quickly replaced by English except in the religious domain. For the young people in this school there was a clear division between their Arabic of family interaction and the 'proper' Arabic of school and visiting relatives overseas. On the other hand, they used the term 'Arabic' as a cultural marker for themselves and their friends. This marker of identity had been promoted by the school and is discussed in a later section. Constructs of language were being established through interaction in the schools, through the representation of the language by the teachers, constructions in the diaspora and agency by the students themselves. In addition, the reasons for and attitudes to the language study related to the attitudes to language and culture that were played out in the schools and thus varied according to social, historical linguistic and religious factors. This finding aligns with findings in UK studies that the schools are sites where notions of language and culture, community and family are constructed and contested (Blackledge & Creese, 2010).

Self-reported language proficiency

Students were asked to rate themselves on their ability to understand, speak, read and write Chinese or Turkish and English. The results showed high levels of confidence in their spoken language abilities. Seventy-four percent of Chinese background students rated their ability to speak and understand Chinese as good although only 24% rated their literacy in Chinese highly. Eighty percent of Turkish background students rated their ability to understand and speak Turkish highly and 68% rated their literacy skills as high. The differences could be due to many factors such as language codification (Turkish is written in Roman script), pedagogy and teacher expectations (teachers in the Turkish school were second generation themselves).[8] Although self-reporting data are limited, the confidence that students expressed in their abilities is interesting. Almost half of the Chinese students reported that they intended to study Chinese to Year 12 but only 12% of the Turkish students did so. This difference could be due to the different status of the languages and perceived utility value. Attitudes to language study were conflicting. Young people across schools commented that the language learning was 'hard'. Many commented that they would not keep attending if their parents did not force them to go and yet in answer to questions about themselves as parents, nearly all commented that they would send their children to community languages schools, for family, cultural and religious reasons.

> (We go) Because it's our language and we have to learn it. (Aysa)

These responses did not seem to be conflicting but, rather, indicative of the range of attitudes to language and language learning. The reality is, however, that most stop attending the community languages schools by secondary school level. Schools report high attrition rates in community languages school at the end of grades five and six moving on to secondary school.

Senses of family and identities: Arabic language school

Data from interviews with the students in the Arabic school indicated that notions of family grouping were central to their understandings of their language and cultural affiliations. It was in the context of the community school that the young people made friends with others beyond their extended family grouping and they used the term 'family' to describe this. Students' sense of 'community' was one of extended family groups. Extended family activities and weekend sport linked to day school and the wider community figured large in their lives. For the students, the sense of linguistic and cultural identity afforded by the school was built on notions of 'family'. Although the students indicated in interview data that they were aware of the backgrounds of the other students, there were only one or two references to others being 'Christian' or 'Muslim'. This socialising with young people from different day schools but similar backgrounds was the most common reason for attending the school. Many commented on the time they spent in the playground during recess as the best part of the school.

> ... people here are more like family members ... so you feel more related to them than the others and like we've known them for a long time. (Fouad)
> I like recess here. We get to meet friends you haven't met yet. (John)

In terms of markers of self-identification, the students tended to use the term 'Arabic' much more than 'Lebanese' or 'Muslim'. 'Arabic' was a marker of people's backgrounds as well as a term for language. This differs from other studies of Arabic-background young people in Sydney, where the group markers of 'Lebanese' and more recently 'Muslim' predominate (Poynting & Noble, 2004). This could indicate the greater emphasis on 'Arabic' rather than 'Muslim' or other markers in principals' and teachers' interactions with students. There are also fewer Arabic-speaking students in Wollongong day schools and less of a visible presence of regional and religious organisations.

> That's because they are Arabic and they have the same culture and every-thing. (Fouad)

Markers of identity varied according to contexts being described with little sense of contradiction. The majority of participants reported friendship groups at the day school that tended to consist of other students of Arabic background and students of Macedonian, Turkish and other minority back-grounds: they reported three loose groupings in day schools of 'Aussies', 'Asians' and the 'rest' (which included themselves). Several of the students, particularly boys, reported shifting between friendship groups of 'Aussies' and others in their day schools. For the young people, the term 'Aussie' was one realised in family contexts in Australia and overseas.

> I feel more Aussie (in Lebanon) because like sometimes they laugh at you because you don't speak proper Arabic or you don't understand them. (Ali)

The identity positioning or affordances relate to the contexts in which the young people were operating; they were both self- and other-defined.

Identity and different contexts: Cook Island Maori language school

The data from the Cook Island Maori school gave a strong sense of nego-tiating cultural and language identities in the community language and the impact of this on their day school selves. The four young people interviewed all reported three groups in their day schools: Aussies (English-speaking backgrounds), Asians/Chinese and 'multiculturals' (including Greek, Turkish and Pasifika students). They reported shifting between groups.

Peter: Nah my friends are multicultural.
Toni: Mostly yeah.
Alice: Yeah.

Joe: I've got lots of Indian friends, Chinese friends and everything like that.

Interviewer: Do any of your other friends ... do they go to a language school?

Toni: Ah my friend she is Lebanese she goes to language school and they teach their culture there.

Alice: Oh some. Like my Turkish friend he goes to Turkish language.

The students reported that initially others in their day school had no awareness of their Cook Island identity; it was something they kept hidden. Students and parents both reported on the changes in interviews. The affiliations with 'Cook Island Maori' they developed in the community language school impacted upon their day school interactions.

Toni: I told my friends at day school I was from the Cook Islands and all the people in my class don't know where the Cook Islands are.

Peter: Sometimes they don't really talk about it at all. Like when I said at school I am 'Cook Island' they were like, 'what?' They didn't even know what it was. It's not like everyone in the world knows. We went to this Aboriginal thing and there were some people who were taping us and they said, 'What country are you from?' And we said, 'the Cook Islands' and they just looked at us like, 'What?'

Alice: That's the same at my school cause heaps of people they think coming from the Cook Islands is heaps original and all that 'cause my school is heaps multicultural.

A common theme emerging from interviews with parents/teachers was the feeling that their language and culture has been suppressed or lost. There were feelings of sadness at this generational loss and the aim of the school was very much one of pride in visible cultural activities. Jane, Peter's mother and deputy principal at the school, recounted how Peter had spoken at a day school assembly.

No one at the school knew he was Cook Island Maori. I was there the day at assembly. He got up in front of the teachers, in front of the school and he said he was Cook Island Maori and then he spoke in the language. I had tears in my eyes. I never thought I would see the day that this happened. (Jane)

She saw the school as doing something that individual families did not have the resources to do, building what Blackledge and Creese (2008) call a 'heritage identity position'. The school initiated a marker of being 'Cook Island Maori'; this was one affiliation which was not available in the home/family or day school. The marker did not show in the data as equivalent to

'Australian' and the idea of double-barrelled nomenclature did not emerge in these or other interviews. 'Cook Island Maori' was a sense of belonging which had emerged in the community language school and drew on their combining notions of family, church, language, shared values and heritage as expressed through cultural practices and events which in part had been legitimised by the mainstream school assembly.

Australian in an Asian body: Wollongong Chinese school

Seven of the younger students in the Chinese school all attended different day schools and their reasons for liking coming to the community school related to opportunities for seeing their friends. Typical comments here included:

> It's fun and I meet different people. (Joshua)
> I can meet new people and learn new things. (Aidan)

There was less of a sense of the school being an extension of family. Attending the community school was seen more in the order of out-of-school commitments such as sports, music and coaching classes. The main difference was that they got to meet up with friends of similar backgrounds in the Chinese school.

Six of the seven reported being in friendship groups of Chinese and other 'Asian' backgrounds in the day schools. These friendship groups included students of Korean and Japanese backgrounds. They spoke about school friendship groups in terms of 'Chinese' and 'Australians' or 'Westerners'. In their responses the term 'Chinese' was used both as a language and identity marker.

> I like being with Chinese people because of my looks – at (day) school they call me slanty eyes. (Kam)
> I prefer Chinese friends. The other kids make fun of me at school. (James)

All seven young people reported feelings of exclusion and incidents of racism in the range of day schools that they attended. This topic was raised by the participants themselves not in response to any question. There was not the same sense of being able to shift between groups as the young people in the other schools reported. The incidents they reported at school did not impact on their liking for school: they expressed positive comments on their teachers and school and reported being academically successful. In this group, affiliation with Chinese heritage was strong. Their families celebrated Chinese New Year and they reported viewing of Chinese movies.

Two students in the class, Katie and Jackie, insisted on being interviewed separately, apart from the young students, by one of our researchers. Katie, an adoptee from Taiwan, and her friend Jackie, of Malaysian (non-Chinese) background are aged 13 and are placed in the same Level 3 (older learners) class. They are therefore three to four years older than the others but have much lower levels of proficiency. Katie's parents have been sending her to the Chinese school for three years in the hope that she would learn some Chinese for when the family visits Taiwan. Jackie's parents want her to learn Chinese for its prestige. Both girls identify strongly as 'Australian' and attend Anglo-Australian English-speaking schools. They met at the Chinese school and share an opposition to and determination not to learn Chinese. Both of them self-defined as 'Australian' which they saw as oppositional to 'Asian', used when describing their classmates in the Chinese community school. They identified 'Asians' as those with noticeable non-English accents. They sit at the back of the class.

> I don't know because they are all Asian here and they speak it to the teacher and everything. At (day) school they all just speak English and you don't feel any different. (Katie)

> I am Australian person stuck in an Asian body, which is a good way of putting it. You've grown up around Australians your whole life so you are just in an Asian body. I know it's weird. (Katie)

> There are, like, two little Asian kids at my school but they are in primary and the first year I came they called me their names by mistake and there is one other girl who is in Year 12. She is a family friend, from Sri Lanka. (Jackie)

Lin commented that when the school was in her garage, Katie was positive about her learning. As the school had grown, she and Jackie had to be placed in a separate beginner class with children four or five years younger. This had a negative effect on their learning and they had 'gone backwards'. Both Katie and Jackie used the term 'Asian' not 'Chinese' to describe the identity they are choosing to reject. This marker, coming from the day school context, is a pejorative term used for those of Korean, Chinese and Vietnamese backgrounds, a term which homogenises the 'other'. The use of this term by Katie rather than the specific term 'Chinese' indicates that she was adopting a majority position against those choices offered through the community language school.

For both girls, identity options in the school were marginalising. Their sense of belonging was to the majority group in their day schools; their parents had for different reasons made the decision for them to learn Chinese and this categorised them as 'Asians', a label they saw as being overseas born with accents in English (Blackledge & Creese, 2010). It was the specific Level 3 class context which exacerbated this opposition; the other two classes of young children were majority non-Chinese background. For the other students in the class, the school created affordances for a 'Chinese' identity which was not possible in the day school or the community.

Discussion and Conclusions

Diversity of young people

One key finding from the data here is the diversity of the learners. In this study, over 80% of learners were Australian born and over 80% of parents were born overseas, a profile typical of their communities; superficially the young people would be described as 'heritage' language learners. Within this broad statistic lies a complex set of differences: Chinese-speaking parents spoke a range of Chinese dialects such as Cantonese; several came from the diaspora in southeast Asia. Students born in Australia had spent varying times visiting parents' countries of origin. In each of the class groups there was a range of proficiencies. Terms of 'heritage' and 'background' are enshrined in NSW languages syllabuses but are, in fact, what Lo Bianco (2009) labels a 'simplified set of categorisations' describing complex phenomena.

The complexity and dynamism of the young people's identities defy any simplistic labelling. The young people were actively constructing notions of family, community language and multilingual identities in community school contexts. Their attitudes to their language learning were generally positive. Attitudes to their languages skills were complex, with many rating their proficiencies highly although this did not always equate with attachment to continued learning at the schools. It is likely during their secondary school years that they will stop attending the community language school and distance themselves and be distanced from the study of their home language and culture.

This snapshot of the young people in the community languages schools, however, shows a diversity where multilingual practices and identities are the norm.

Diversity of language practices

The learners reported complex patterns of languages use in many domains: the importance of grandparents as a source of language maintenance is confirmed here as in other studies and is something which does not emerge in census data where the question of language 'used at home' is asked (Borland, 2006; Lambert, 2008). The young people seemed to use the language with parents in which the parents were stronger. Although the language used with friends and siblings was overwhelmingly English, code-switching was reported as a regular feature of most interactions.

The growing role of the global media and IT domains on diasporic languages is a finding which aligns with other studies (Karim, 1998; Lam, 2006; Tsagarousianou, 2004). Social media contact and interactions with interlocutors in Australia, in other diasporic contexts and in the countries of origin using Skype, Facebook and Twitter, along with the input of 24-hour up-to-date satellite TV and DVDs in the community language are all having significant impacts on the perceptions and use of the language/s in the home.

Implications for day schools

The implication of 'flexible bilingualism' as the norm for interactions challenges day school and community school constructions of the young people: at day school they are often seen as monolingual English speakers but with bicultural backgrounds: they are labelled as 'Lebanese' or 'Asian/Chinese' but little space is given to their bilingualism. In community schools, they tend to be judged as dialect or low-level speakers of the community language when the actual language practices in the community schools reflect the notions of flexible bilingualism.

There existed also an enormous disconnect between their day schools and their community languages and home experiences and lives. It is 'surreal' that the day schools often have no knowledge of which of their students are learning in community languages schools or of the language practices and cultural knowledge they have acquired and use in contexts outside day school, a finding which also resonates with other studies (Morgan *et al.*, 2013).

Their accounts of day schools revealed ways in which the growing segmented schooling system is reflected in divisions between groups of students based on other-ascribed labels. The question also arises as to the extent day schools are aware of the divisions and how they are being replicated. The shifting of identifications between community schools and day schools is interesting. Young people in the Cook Island Maori and Arabic language schools were able to shift identifications formed in the community school site to day schools. Two of the students in the Chinese school had internalised 'Asian' ascriptions from the day school and many others reported other-ascribed identities from there.

Their day schools reported in this study seem to have found it much easier to deal with 'multiculturalism' in broad brushstroke terms rather than the complexity and challenges of 'multilingualism' and the changes happening in communities. It still seems the case that if an Anglo-background student has access to travel and study overseas and has access to gaining language practices in other languages this would be construed as of benefit to school learning; for young people of bilingual/bicultural backgrounds these skills and experiences are constructed problematically or ignored.

The ways to overcome this disconnect lie in the collection of data and the development of research. Data on student learning across contexts and sectors need to be collected and research into in-between sites such as community languages schools needs to be linked with research into day school sites. The question arises of how any sense can be made of young people's languages, ethnicities and identities unless the many contexts in their daily lives are taken into account in all their messiness and complexity. There are spaces beyond the monolingual mindset of government policy – the multilingual turn?

Acknowledgments

The author acknowledges the work of co-researchers Dr Honglin Chen, Dr Valerie Harwood, Dr Liam Morgan, Dr Linda Tsung and Danielle White in the research projects on which this chapter is based.

Notes

(1) *Australia's Language: the Australian Language and Literacy Policy* (1991) heralded the subsumption of ESL and other programmes being subsumed under English language literacy. This led to a division between heritage/community languages and modern/foreign languages. Community languages were framed in terms of equity programmes; languages programmes were framed in terms of economic rationalism and the trade benefits. The focus has shifted from Japanese to Chinese and now recently to Hindi. At present the key languages are Chinese, Japanese, Korean and Indonesian. Curriculum documents now label students in terms of 'beginner' or 'background' learner rather than language proficiency.

(2) The NSW government provides free accommodation for community languages schools in government day schools if principals agree. This has given schools increased status although access to resources and storage space are often problematic. Schools have also received government funding since 1980. In NSW this means AUD $120 per student per year, establishment grants for schools and funding for professional development.

(3) Two of the university researchers spoke Arabic and Mandarin Chinese. The student research assistants were bilingual in Arabic and Mandarin and worked in pairs with the tertiary researchers; they were closer in age and known to the students. The researcher in the Cook Island Maori school was doing her study as part of an undergraduate honours thesis supervised by one of the researchers.

(4) The traditional Chinese community in Australia was Cantonese speaking; with recent immigration, Mandarin speakers constitute 1.7% of the population and Cantonese-speakers 1.3% (Census data, 2011). Cantonese community languages schools now generally also teach Mandarin Chinese.

(5) Census data asks about home language and so community language use is underreported because use in grandparents' homes is not counted. Students reported using the dialect/language of the grandparents rather than 'standard' forms.

(6) The collection of authentic interactional data was beyond the scope of this study, but would be needed for any conclusions to be made about language choice and code-switching.

(7) The use of the term 'Arabic' in Australia seems to be different from usage in the UK. The teachers and young people used it to refer to language and although religion was a key reason for Muslim background students learning the language the term itself was not used in these data to refer to identity or religion. The majority of the

Arabic-speaking immigrants in Australia have come from Lebanon and Egypt and just under half of the Australian Arabic-background population are of Christian background. This may be one reason why the term is seen more as a marker of heritage and cultural belonging.

(8) In other words, teachers' expectations may have been lower or more realistic in terms of Turkish reading and writing. The families had been in Australia for longer and literacy in English would tend to have replaced Turkish literacy. As day school teachers and/or second generation they would tend to construct the children as second language learners of Turkish rather than inadequate first language learners.

References

Archer, L., Francis, B. and Mau, A. (2010) The culture project: Diasporic negotiations of ethnicity, identity and culture among teachers, pupils and parents in Chinese language schools. *Oxford Review of Education* 36 (4), 407–426.

Bailey, B. (2007) Heteroglossia and boundaries. In M. Heller (ed.) *Bilingualism: A Social Approach* (pp. 257–274). Basingstoke: Palgrave Macmillan.

Barni, M. and Extra, G. (eds) (2008) *Mapping Linguistic Diversity in Multicultural Contexts.* Berlin: Mouton de Gruyter.

Blackledge, A. and Creese, A. (2008) Contesting 'language' as 'heritage': Negotiation of identities in late modernity. *Applied Linguistics* 29 (4), 533–554.

Blackledge, A. and Creese, A. (2010) *Multilingualism: A Critical Perspective.* London: Continuum.

Borland, H. (2006) Intergenerational language transmission in an established Australian migrant community: What makes the difference? *International Journal of the Sociology of Language* 180, 23–41.

Cenoz, J. and Gorter, D. (2008) Multilingualism. In J. Simpson (ed.) *The Routledge Handbook of Applied Linguistics* (pp. 401–412). Oxford: Routledge.

Cruikshank, K. (2006) *Teenagers, Literacy and School: Researching in Multilingual Context.* Abingdon: Routledge.

Duranti, A. and Goodwin, C. (eds) (1992) *Rethinking Context: Language as an Interactive Phenomenon.* Cambridge: Cambridge University Press.

EC (2012) *Key Data on Teaching Languages at School in Europe* (2012 edn). Brussels: Education, Audiovisual and Culture Executive Agency, European Commission.

Extra, G. and Yagmur, K. (eds) (2004) *Urban Multilingualism in Europe: Immigrant Minority Languages at Home and School.* Clevedon: Multilingual Matters.

Extra, G. and Yagmur, K. (2011) Urban multilingualism in Europe: Mapping linguistic diversity in multicultural cities. *Journal of Pragmatics* 43 (5), 1173–1184.

García, O. (2007) Foreword. In S. Makoni and A. Pennycook (eds) *Disinventing and Reconstituting Languages* (pp. xi–xv). Bristol: Multilingual Matters.

García, O., Zakharia, Z. and Otcu, B. (eds) (2013) *Bilingual Community Education and Multilingualism: Beyond Heritage Languages in a Global City.* Bristol: Multilingual Matters.

Heller, M. (ed.) (2007) *Bilingualism: A Social Approach.* Basingstoke: Palgrave Macmillan.

Hornberger, N. (2005) Opening and filling up implementational and ideological spaces in heritage language education. *Modern Language Journal* 89, 605–609.

Jørgensen, J.N. (2008) Polylingual languaging around and among children and adolescents. *International Journal of Multilingualism* 5 (3), 161–176.

Karim, K. (1998) From ethnic media to global media: Transnational communication networks among diasporic communities. International Comparative Research Group Strategic Research and Analysis Working Papers. See http://www.transcomm.ox.ac.uk/working%20papers/karim.pdf (accessed 30 September 2013).

Kipp, S. (2008) Community languages in Australia. In M. Barni and G. Extra (eds) (2008) *Mapping Linguistic Diversity in Multicultural Contexts* (pp. 293–310). Berlin: Mouton de Gruyter.

Lam, W.S.E. (2006) Re-envisioning language, literacy and the immigrant subject in new mediascapes. *Pedagogies: An International Journal* 1 (3), 171–195.

Lambert, B. (2008) *Family Language Transmission: Actors, Issues, Outcomes*. Frankfurt: Peter Lang.

Lo Bianco, J. (1987) *National Policy on Languages*. Canberra: AGPS.

Lo Bianco, J. (1999) Policy words: Talking bilingual education and ESL into literacy education. *Prospect* 14 (2) 40–51.

Lo Bianco, J. (2009) *Second Languages and Australian Schooling*. Australian Education Review, No. 54. Camberwell: Australian Council for Educational Research.

Lo Bianco, J. and Gvozdenko, I. (2006) *Collaboration and Innovation in the Provision of Languages Other than English in Australian Universities*. Melbourne: University of Melbourne.

Lytra, V. and Martin, P. (2010) *Sites of Multilingualism: Complementary Schools in Britain Today*. Stoke-on-Trent: Trentham Books.

Morgan, L., Chodkiewicz, A., Cruickshank, K. and Tsung, L. (2013) *Mapping Language Study in NSW Schools: A Local Area Case Study*. Sydney: University of Technology Sydney.

Poynting, S. and Noble, G. (2004) *Living with Racism: The Experience and Reporting of Arab and Muslim Australians of Discrimination, Abuse and Violence since 11th September 2001*. Sydney: University of Western Sydney.

Rhodes, N. and Pufahl, I. (2009) *Foreign Language Teaching in US Schools: Results of a National Survey*. Washington, DC: Center for Applied Linguistics.

Rubino, A. (2010) Multilingualism in Australia: Reflections on current and future research trends. *Australian Review of Applied Linguistics* 33 (2), 17.1–17.21.

Shohamy, E. and Gorter, D. (2009) *Linguistic Landscape: Expanding the Scenery*. Oxford: Routledge.

Slaughter, Y. (2009) Money and policy make languages go round: Language programs in Australia after NALSAS. *Australian Federation of Modern Language Teachers Association* 43 (2).

Stubbs, M. (1985) *The Other Languages of England: Linguistic Minorities Project*. London: Routledge.

Taylor, S. and Henry, M. (2000) Challenges for equity policy in changing contexts. *Australian Education Researcher* 27 (3), 1–15.

Tsagarousianou, R. (2004) Rethinking the concept of diaspora: Mobility, connectivity and communication in a globalized world. *Westminster Papers in Communication* 1, 52–65. See https://www.westminster.ac.uk/_data/assets/pdf_file/0014/20219/005WPCC-Vol1-No1-Roza_Tsagarousianou.pdf.

3 Multilingualism as Portrayed in a Chinese English Textbook

Guangwei Hu and Sandra Lee McKay

Guiding Questions

- To what extent does the textbook for the study of English as a second/additional language examined here promote multilingual/multicultural diversity more generally, and how does this represent the students' own backgrounds or that of envisaged communication partners?
- What are the opportunities and challenges of connecting English language study with certain cultures and not others?
- To what extent do the communication and accommodation strategies identified in the textbook reflect realistic communication opportunities, and what are the opportunities and challenges of including such strategies in textbooks, or indeed in language lessons?

Introduction

A multilingual turn is evident today in China, where in 2001 the Ministry of Education (MOE) mandated that public primary schools start formal English education beginning in Primary three and continue this instruction through secondary school. In addition, in the same year, the MOE issued a directive that within three years at least 5–10% of undergraduate university courses be conducted in English or other foreign languages (Hu & McKay, 2012). Hence, there is tremendous support today for developing a bilingual/multilingual population in China (Wei & Su, 2012), with most young Chinese studying English to add to their competence in

Putonghua (i.e. the standard variety of Mandarin designated as the official language of the People's Republic of China) and, in some cases, one or more varieties of Chinese or an ethnic minority language (Hu & Alsagoff, 2010). As a multi-ethnic country, China is home to 56 autochthonous ethnic groups. The Han majority, accounting for 91.59% of the population in China, mostly speak Putonghua and/or some varieties of Chinese (e.g. Cantonese and Shanghainese), whereas the 55 ethnic minority groups, with a population of 106 million, speak some 80 languages (National Bureau of Statistics of China, 2001; Zhou & Sun, 2004). A multilingual turn, of course, suggests more than just the acquisition of another language in a foreign language classroom, particularly one that is mandated by the MOE. Often, particularly in the case of English, a ministry mandates the learning of a language for political and economic purposes, which is clearly the case in China today (Bolton & Graddol, 2012). However, if a multilingual turn is to have any benefits for the society and its citizens, the acquisition of English as an international language (EIL) needs to be accompanied by increased respect for and understanding of those who speak English and by the use of English to promote cross-cultural understanding (Baker, 2009).

Language textbooks are powerful tools not just in developing knowledge of a language but, more importantly for our purposes, in promoting a particular view of what it means to be a multilingual/multicultural individual, particularly in the present era of globalization (Gray, 2012; Orton, 2009b). The goal of this chapter is to examine one of China's most widely used junior secondary English textbook series – *Go for It!* – approved by the MOE and published by the People's Education Press (2007), in order to ascertain how it portrays multilingualism and multiculturalism. Our aim is to determine to what extent this textbook, in its representation of multilingualism and multiculturalism, promotes respect for diversity and cross-cultural understanding. We begin by discussing previous work that has informed our investigation of how multilingualism and multiculturalism are portrayed in the textbook series. Specifically, we review literature on EIL, focusing on its role as a lingua franca, its bias toward native-speakerism and its cultural basis. Next we examine aspects of the current Chinese context that have influenced both an emphasis on English language teaching (ELT) and the approach being promoted to deal with cultural and ideological differences. Within this sociocultural context, we discuss the factors that have given rise to the *Go for It!* textbook series and its pedagogical underpinnings. We then describe our methodology, focusing on the development of a comprehensive analytic rubric for scrutinizing the textbook. Finally, we present our critical analysis of how *Go for It!* deals with globalization, the spread of English, new definitions of English ownership, varieties of English, topics and patterns of cross-cultural communication and cultural issues in the learning and use of English.

English Language Textbooks

English in its global role: Implications for English textbook development

Several features of English in its global role are relevant for a critical analysis of any current English language textbook. These include the widespread use of English as a lingua franca, the dominance of a native-speaker bias and the cultural goals in teaching EIL.

English as a lingua franca

It is widely agreed that today there are more second language (L2) speakers of English than speakers of English as a first language (L1). Currently it is estimated that over 1 billion people are learning English worldwide and according to the British Council, 750 million of these learners are English as a foreign language (EFL) speakers, while approximately 375 million are English as a second language (ESL) speakers (Beare, 2010). Hence, most English learners today are adding English to their linguistic repertoire, not replacing their first language with English, as is often the case with ESL immigrant learners. Instead, they are using English alongside their first language, often for specific purposes. Given the fact that today there are more L2 than L1 speakers of English, the former, particularly those living in EFL countries, are more likely to use English with other L2 speakers of English than with L1 English speakers (McKay, 2012). Since the majority of English interactions today are between L2 speakers of English, ELT needs to prepare students for cross-cultural exchanges that do not involve members of the Inner Circle, that is, those Anglophone countries that traditionally claimed ownership over English (Kachru, 1992). To this end, it is essential for English textbooks to provide models of effective EIL interactions, raise students' awareness of linguistic and cultural diversity, and develop their ability to negotiate multilingual or translingual practices (Canagarajah, 2007).

The native-speaker bias

The vast geographical distribution of English use today has resulted in English being embedded in many different social contexts, leading Widdowson (1994) over 25 years ago to argue that English belongs not only to those who speak it as an L1 but also to those who use it as an additional language. Hence, while in a sense English has become de-nationalized (Smith, 1976), no longer belonging to speakers of the Inner Circle, it has become re-nationalized or embedded in many countries where it serves an intranational and/or international purpose. This suggests that today many speakers do not necessarily aspire to a native-speaker target but rather want to become intelligible speakers of English who can use English in cross-cultural exchanges to serve specific ends (Canagarajah, 2007; Seidlhofer, 2004).

L2 pedagogy and research, however, have traditionally been dominated by the assumption that the goal of bilingual users of English is to achieve native-like competence in English. As Kumaravadivelu (2012: 15) points out:

> A good example of an enduring episteme in the field of teaching EIL, in spite of its conceptual and definitional ambiguities, is that of the *native-speaker* and its benevolent twin, *native-speaker competence*. We may have only an unreal (or, to use a more familiar terminology, idealized) version of who a native-speaker is or what constitutes native-speaker competence. But, that has not prevented us from letting the episteme take an all-encompassing hold on the knowledge systems governing almost all aspects of English language learning and teaching. The episteme symbolizes West-oriented, Center-based knowledge systems that EIL practitioners in the periphery countries almost totally depend on.

English textbooks are not immune from this native-speaker episteme. It is evident in the almost exclusive linking of English to Anglo-American countries and the privileging of native speakers in discourse and visuals (Matsuda, 2002).

However, for those individuals who use English essentially as a language of wider communication alongside one or more other languages they speak, achieving native-like competence is often not necessary or desired. Rather than relying any longer on the native-speaker model, what is needed is greater understanding of the language use patterns of speech communities that use English alongside other languages (Sharifian, 2011). Graddol (1997: 12) aptly summarizes the issue in the following manner:

> But a full understanding of the role of English in a world where the majority of its speakers are not first-language speakers requires an understanding of how English relates to the other languages which are used alongside it. The European concept of bilingualism reflects an idea that each language has a natural geographical 'home' and that a bilingual speaker is therefore someone who can converse with monolingual speakers from more than one country. The ideal bilingual speaker is thus imagined to be someone who is like a monolingual in two languages at once. But many of the world's bilingual or multilingual speakers interact with other multilinguals and use each of their languages for different purposes....

English textbooks, depending on how they frame multilingual communication, can play a significant role in promoting sensitivity to translingual practices and catering to the needs of L2 learners of English who do not desire to be assimilated into a monolingual English-speaking culture but often have specific communicative goals in learning English.

Yet research on the content of current ELT textbooks shows that a native-speaker bias is pervasive (Sárdi, 2002; Shin et al., 2011; Yuen, 2011). Matsuda (2002), for example, in her analysis of Japanese seventh-grade English textbooks, found that non-Japanese characters in the books were predominantly native speakers from English-speaking countries and that these characters played a more significant role in the dialogues, speaking more words than their Japanese counterparts. The number of speakers from non-English speaking countries constituted only 10% of the characters and the number of exchanges between L2 and L2 speakers was very limited, even though in reality these are the most frequent type of interactions in EIL exchanges. Similarly, and of greater relevance to the present study, Orton's (2009b) analysis of a current set of English textbooks published by the People's Education Press for senior secondary students in China revealed a predominant focus on the land, history and cultural practices of Anglo-American societies in the Inner Circle. A prominent new feature of this textbook series was reported to be 'direct and sustained Chinese–native English speaker contact, which is managed in English' (Orton, 2009b: 150).

Cultural goals in teaching EIL

In terms of EIL, in which English is used largely in cross-cultural encounters, Kramsch's (1993) concept of developing a *sphere of interculturality* in L2 classrooms is particularly relevant. Kramsch argues that addressing cultural differences in a language classroom should involve more than just the transfer of information about a specific culture. Rather, learning about another culture should require that one considers one's own culture in relation to another. Hence, the process of learning about another culture entails a reflection on one's own culture as well as the foreign culture. In the Chinese context, textbooks can encourage this perspective by presenting information about other cultures as a basis for Chinese students to compare cultures and reflect on their own culture in relation to others to establish a sphere of interculturality.

Such efforts to promote interculturality, however, are largely missing from many contemporary ELT textbooks. Instead, cultural values and ideological beliefs that are 'West-oriented, Center-based' (Kumaravadivelu, 2012: 15) predominate in these textbooks (Xiong, 2012; Yuen, 2011). For example, Gray (2012: 87) demonstrates convincingly that current ELT textbooks illustrate a pervasive use of celebrities, drawing on images of 'personal and professional success, celebrity lifestyles, cosmopolitanism and travel'. All these factors center on the value of individualism and economic status and are associated with a middle-class lifestyle in Western societies. At the heart of much of the attention to celebrities, both in textbooks and in society at large, is a belief in the individual and his/her ability to become a celebrity. This belief, as Gray points out, is central to the ideology of new capitalism and the self-made man that is the bedrock of Western social systems. Thus, many

ELT textbooks subtly promote deep-seated Western cultural values rather than fostering critical reflections on cultural beliefs and practices from an intercultural perspective.

The Chinese social context for English learning

Any critical assessment of a textbook must, of course, be based on the context for which it is intended. Hence, it is necessary to consider the role of English today in China, as well as the ideological functions of education in society. China's rise as a world power has been accompanied by an increasing 'penetration [of English] into the institutional life of China', leading to 'a historically unprecedented level of linguistic accommodation and appropriation' (Lo Bianco, 2009a: 23). Since the late Qing Dynasty's defeat by the Western powers in the two Opium Wars, English has been viewed as a vehicle for accessing Western scientific knowledge and technological skills, exploring/repudiating Western ideology, interacting with the West and/or modernizing China (Gao, 2009; Orton, 2009a). China's intensive English language planning and massive investment in ELT, however, did not start until its opening up to the outside world in the late 1970s (Gao, 2009). Since then, educational policy makers and other government officials have encouraged the mass acquisition of English because it is seen as beneficial to China's development, facilitative of cross-cultural exchange between China and the rest of the world, and capable of broadening Chinese people's horizons (Lo Bianco, 2009b). Chinese society at large has also embraced the language enthusiastically (Gao, 2012). This general societal interest in English has been motivated by the perceived benefits that accrue to proficiency in the language, such as greater educational opportunities, better employment prospects and other opportunities for upward social mobility (Gao, 2009; Lo Bianco, 2009b). As a result, 'the scale of the spread of English in China in recent decades has taken most observers by surprise' (Bolton & Graddol, 2012: 4).

Not all people, however, are positive about mass English education in China. This is because, as Lo Bianco (2009a) points out, serious language learning implicates intercultural encounters that revolve around deep questions of cultural practice, personal meaning and identity formation. Thus, some netizens (i.e. those who make regular use of online communication) complain in internet forums that 'English learning reduces the national self-esteem of the Chinese' and 'reveals a Chinese national characteristic of self-despising' (Gao, 2009: 69). A sizeable proportion of university teachers in a survey study reported in Lo Bianco (2009b) expressed concerns about loss of national identity, culture and tradition as a result of the massive growth of English learning in China. Whether these concerns are or will turn into reality, of course, depends on how culture is conceptualized, framed and taught in English classrooms, especially those for young learners, across China.

While the officially perceived overarching aim of English textbooks in China is to promote the acquisition of English, the educational authorities are well aware that the English curriculum also serves an ideological and moral purpose because 'language is the vehicle for culture, and foreign cultures will have certain influence on students' life-views, world-views and values' (MOE, 2001: 48). The MOE specifically acknowledges an awareness of the cultural and ideological dimensions of English language textbooks, stating that 'English teaching materials should perform the function of moral and ideological inculcation, and facilitate students' formation of correct life-views and values' (MOE, 2001: 48). Thus, instead of endorsing acceptance of cultural and ideological differences (Lo Bianco, 2009b; Orton, 2009a), the MOE suggests that students develop their cultural 'discerning ability' (i.e. the ability to tell the good from the bad).

The statements above reflect a Chinese quest for knowledge accessible in English to 'protect China physically and culturally' and project English proficiency 'as part of the social capital of China's 21st-century modern citizen, someone still thoroughly patriotic, but also internationally competent' (Orton, 2009a: 85). However, they do not envision English learning to be used to develop what Kramsch (1993) calls a sphere of interculturality in which students examine a foreign culture as a way of critically reflecting on their own culture. It is also important to mention at this point that although China has taken a multilingual turn by promoting the learning of English, in many ways China still fosters a dominant monolingual habitus. For example, the Han (the ethnic majority in China) often ignore the fact that the 55 officially recognized autochthonous ethnic minority groups, largely concentrated in the rural and mountainous regions of western inland China and accounting for 8.41% of the total population in China, speak more than 80 languages and that bilingualism and trilingualism are common among these ethnic minorities (Beckett & Postiglione, 2012). In the MOE English curriculum document cited above, neither the languages of the ethnic minority groups nor their cultural practices are seen to have a part to play in developing students' cultural 'discerning ability', even though this would demonstrate a true multilingual turn in the sense we are using the term. Given this overall context of English teaching in China, to further contextualize our investigation, we provide below background information on the textbook we have chosen to examine.

Background Information: The *Go for It!* Textbook Series

Before the mid-1980s, production of English textbooks for the basic education sector in mainland China was centrally controlled by the MOE through its publishing arm, the People's Education Press (Hu, 2002a; Orton,

2009b). However, widening sociocultural and economic differences between the eastern coast and the western inland since China's reform and opening-up endeavors in the late 1970s precipitated the central government's educational overhaul in 1985 to suit the country's development and modernization agenda (Hu, 2003). Central to the educational overhaul was the adoption of an educational decentralization policy which allowed socio-economically more advantaged provinces/municipalities to develop their own English language curricula for basic education and publish their own English language textbooks for use in their schools (Hu, 2002b). Production of English language textbooks for schools located in the less advantaged regions, however, remained an undertaking of the People's Education Press (Hu, 2003). As a result, the People's Education Press had the lion's share of the school English textbook market at the turn of the 21st century. Its *Junior English for China*, a textbook series published in collaboration with Longman, was adopted in about 70% of junior secondary schools nationwide (Hu, 2002a).

To comply with the English curriculum standards for compulsory education (MOE, 2001) and to fend off growing competition from other textbook publishers in China (Zhang, 2008), the People's Educational Press and Thomson Learning (renamed as Cengage Learning in 2007) started to develop a new basal English textbook series for use at junior secondary school (i.e. Grades 7–9) in China in 2000 (Cengage Learning, 2005). To this end, the international textbook series – *Go for It!* (Nunan, 1998–1999) published by Heinle & Heinle – was chosen and adapted to the Chinese context by a team of experienced Chinese and overseas English textbook writers. The resultant Chinese edition of *Go for It!* was unveiled and piloted in junior secondary schools in Beijing in 2001. The textbook series was then formally released in 2003 for use by junior secondary schools across mainland China (Xiong, 2012). In only two years, 50 million copies were adopted by schools in 29 of the 31 provinces/municipalities/autonomous regions in mainland China, and during the first five months in 2005 alone, 15 million copies were sold (Cengage Learning, 2005). Because of its huge market share and the centrality of textbooks in the Chinese education system (Hu, 2002c), the textbook series has been an important shaping influence on the formation of language ideology and cross-cultural understanding in millions of Chinese youth (Xiong, 2012). This is the main reason why we have chosen this textbook series for a critical examination of how multilingualism and multiculturalism are represented in learning materials for Chinese learners of English.

The Chinese edition of the *Go for It!* series we focus on in this chapter is the latest edition jointly produced by the Curriculum and Teaching Materials Research Institute, the Center of Research on English Curriculum and Teaching Materials Development, and Cengage Learning Asia (People's Education Press, 2007). The whole textbook series consists of five sets: Sets 1 and 2 for use at Grade 7, Sets 3 and 4 at Grade 8 and Set 5 at Grade 9. Each set consists of a student's book, a teacher's book, a workbook, a test and games package, audio cassettes and wall charts. The textbook series has been hailed as making an important contribution to 'the transformation of the traditional English teaching and learning methods in China to modern communicative methods' and 'mov[ing] teaching in China away from a grammar-based, teacher-centered traditional approach to a learner-centered approach' (Cengage Learning, 2005, para. 4). Specifically, the textbook series is characterized by a combination of communicative and structural curricular orientations, organized by a variety of thematic topics (e.g. environmental protection, vacations and volunteering) and realized in a task-based and learner-centered pedagogical approach (Xiong, 2012; Zhang, 2008). To facilitate an in-depth analysis, we have decided to concentrate on the student's book for Grade 9. We have chosen the student's book for the highest junior secondary grade level because it provides opportunities for the textbook writers to give a more comprehensive treatment of issues of multilingualism and multiculturalism, given that the learners are expected to possess broader language knowledge, higher English proficiency and greater intercultural awareness in comparison to their junior counterparts.

The chosen student's book consists of 15 instructional units and three review units. Each instructional unit is made up of: (a) an opening section (i.e. Section A) which introduces the unit's target vocabulary and grammar focus through several listening, oral and reading tasks; (b) a consolidating section (i.e. Section B) which expands and reinforces the vocabulary and grammar knowledge introduced in Section A by providing a number of tasks that allow students to use their newly learnt knowledge in an integrated manner (i.e. involving the four macro language skills of listening, speaking, reading and writing); (c) a 'self-check' section which allows students to self-evaluate their mastery of the learning targets; and (d) a reading section which contains several pre-, during- and post-reading tasks centered on a reading passage, providing an extended treatment of the unit topic and introducing a learning strategy. Our analysis covers all the four sections of the 15 instructional units but excludes the three review units, which repeat, to a considerable extent, the language and topical content of the instructional units. It is important to point out that our analysis does not address in what ways the original *Go for It!* and its adapted Chinese edition are different. A comparison between the two would be irrelevant because the aim of our study is to unveil to what extent and how multilingualism and multiculturalism are represented in the Chinese edition of the textbook rather than the original one.

Methodology

Informed by the points discussed above in our review of the relevant literature, we set out to examine the representation of multilingualism and multiculturalism in the focal English textbook from both a quantitative and a qualitative perspective. To facilitate the quantitative survey, we began by developing an analytic scheme that defined a number of key dimensions on which multilingualism and multiculturalism can be represented, promoted or ignored in a textbook. Guided by the insights discussed earlier, we drew on published discussions of the role of materials in teaching EIL (e.g. Gray, 2010; Matsuda, 2002, 2012; Matsuda & Friedrich, 2011; McKay, 2012; Orton, 2009b) and our own discussions with doctoral students from EFL countries to identify these dimensions for integrating multilingual and multicultural practices, together with the various manifestations and omissions of such practices in English language learning materials. The initial analytic scheme was tested on units of the focal textbook and refined iteratively until further coding of the textbook units yielded no further changes to the analytic scheme. Such iterative refining was necessary to develop a sensitive and well-fitted analytic scheme to allow dimensions of multilingual and multicultural representation to establish prevalence or absence. The finalized scheme is presented in Table 3.1. For the sake of space, the analytic scheme will be explained in the following section, where the quantitative results generated by its application are presented.

One of us used the finalized analytic scheme to code each of the four sections of the 15 units in the students' book for Grade 9 described above. The other one then reviewed the coding results independently to identify omissions, redundancies and points of disagreement. We resolved all the issues raised and discrepancies identified through discussion so that we

Table 3.1 Analytic scheme

Dimensions	Manifestations
Pedagogical orientation	(1) Are Anglo-American pedagogical practices adopted in the textbook? (a) Pair/group work (b) Individual work (c) Oracy skills (d) Literacy skills (e) Opinion/debate (f) Fact/evidence
Topics	(2) Does the textbook cover topics from a wide range of cultures and promote cross-cultural awareness? (a) Anglo-American contexts (b) Other Western contexts (i.e. non-Anglophone ones) (c) Chinese contexts (general/mainstream) (d) Chinese contexts (ethnic minorities) (e) Chinese contexts (local cultures) (f) Other/unspecified contexts

(Continued)

Table 3.1 (*Continued*)

Dimensions	Manifestations
People/places/events	(3) Is there a dominant Western presence? (a) Western names, places, events (b) Chinese names, places, events (c) Names, places, events from other contexts (d) Western inventions (e) Chinese inventions (f) Inventions of other societies
Patterns of communication	(4) What patterns of communication are found in the textbook? (a) L1–L1 communication (b) L1–L2 communication (c) L2–L2 communication (d) L2–Chinese communication (e) L1–Chinese communication (f) Chinese–Chinese communication
Content of cross-cultural communication	(5) Does the textbook cover topics that learners frequently encounter in cross-cultural communication? (a) Topics about learners' own countries (b) Topics about personal interests/experiences (c) Topics about popular culture
Multiculturality as a learning goal	(6) Does the textbook promote multiculturality rather than mere knowledge of Anglo-American/Western cultures as a learning goal? (a) Anglo-American/Western cultures (b) Chinese culture (c) Other cultures
Cross-cultural communication skills/strategies	(7) Does the textbook address communication and accommodation strategies for cross-cultural communication? (a) Dos (b) Don'ts
Multilingualism in school and society	(8) Does the textbook represent and promote multilingualism? (a) Use/learning of specific languages other than English (b) General references to unspecified languages
English in local life-worlds	(9) Does the textbook encourage learners to explore their own local life-worlds in which English has gained entry? (a) Use of English for sociocultural purposes (b) Use of English at work (c) Use of English in local educational contexts

Table 3.1 (*Continued*)

Dimensions	Manifestations
Language ideology	(10) What language ideology is promoted? (a) Native-speakerism (b) Code-switching (c) Varieties of English (d) English knowledge as cultural/symbolic capital
Critical framing of English learning and teaching	(11) Does the textbook offer topics and discussions that frame English and ELT critically? (a) Inequalities in access to English (b) Language-related social injustice/oppression (c) Sociocultural impact of English learning (d) Linguistic globalization

reached complete consensus regarding the coding results reported in this chapter. In the process of coding the textbook units, we also aimed to identify one or two units that would best exemplify the textbook's general approach to representing multilingual and multicultural issues. Further qualitative analysis of these units would provide a close-up view of how multilingualism and multiculturalism are portrayed in the textbook. To this end, we converged on two units independently. Because of space constraints, we decided to focus on Unit 7 in our in-depth analysis. Apart from the aforementioned reasons, Unit 7 was selected also because of its potential for a balance of Chinese culture and other cultures, hence allowing for a view of EIL, an inclusion of both L1 and L2 speakers of English, and cultural comparisons. We went through our coding notes, consolidated our understandings of the various issues arising in our close scrutiny of the unit, and identified the missed opportunities to promote multilingualism and multiculturalism.

Findings and Discussion

In this section, we report the quantitative patterns identified with our analytic scheme before presenting an in-depth analysis of Unit 7 in order to offer a more robust understanding of how the various dimensions of the analytic scheme are enacted in the textbook.

Quantitative patterns

Recent reviews (e.g. Butler, 2011; Hu & McKay, 2012; Orton, 2009a) of ELT in Asian countries, including China, point to an intensifying trend toward top-down promotion of Anglo-American pedagogical practices. By

Anglo-American pedagogical practices, we mean teaching methodologies such as communicative language teaching (CLT) and task-based language teaching (TBLT) that originated in or are typically associated with Anglo-American contexts and have spread to other contexts. Such Anglo-American methodologies are characterized by extensive use of pair/group work that values oracy skills over literacy and involves learners in understanding, expressing and debating opinions rather than factual information. Active promotion of these exonormative methodologies can produce a homogenizing effect on pedagogical practices and conflict with culturally based local values (Butler, 2011; Hu, 2002c). Consequently, one dimension of our analytic framework focuses on the extent to which Anglo-American pedagogical practices are adopted in the textbook. As summarized in Table 3.2, over one-third of the tasks require pair/group work, more than half of the tasks target oracy skills, and the input/output for about 30% of the tasks is opinion-based. These figures represent marked increases from the previous textbook series (i.e. *Junior English for China*), reflecting a stronger presence of CLT and TBLT practices.

As we have pointed out earlier, the world today has witnessed significant changes in the users and uses of English. These changing demographics of English language learners and users as well as the diverse contexts of English uses mean that contemporary English-medium communication occurs routinely across various boundaries – cultural, ethnic, linguistic, national and/or societal (Matsuda & Matsuda, 2011). Therefore, an important dimension of the representation of multilingualism and multiculturalism in a textbook is whether the topics covered reflect the sociolinguistic reality of English use. Our analysis makes a distinction, where feasible, between Anglo-American contexts (i.e. Anglophone countries in the Inner Circle) and other Western

Table 3.2 Pedagogical orientations adopted in the textbook

Category	No. of tasks	Average per unit	% total no. of tasks	Ratio
Type of task				
Pair/group work	138	9.20	34.50	
Individual work	272	18.13	68.00	1:1.97
Target language skills				
Oracy skills	210	14.0	52.50	
Literacy skills	327	21.80	81.75	1:1.56
Input/output for tasks				
Opinion/debate	121	8.07	30.25	
Fact/evidence	279	18.60	69.75	1:2.31

Note: Percentages do not add up to 100% because a task may belong to two categories.

Table 3.3 Topics featured in the textbook

Topic and context	Total no. of topics	Average per unit	% of total no. of topics
Anglo-American contexts	50	3.33	39.06
Other Western contexts (non-Anglophone ones)	4	0.27	3.13
Chinese contexts (general/mainstream)	26	1.73	20.31
Chinese contexts (ethnic minorities)	0	0	0
Chinese contexts (local cultures)	11	0.73	8.59
Other/unspecified contexts	37	2.47	28.91

contexts (i.e. non-Anglophone Western countries such as France and Germany). This distinction is motivated by previous research (Widdowson, 1994) on the widespread but anachronistic perceptions of the ownership of English by the Anglophone countries. As can be seen from Table 3.3, topics covering Anglo-American and other Western contexts top the list, followed distantly by an equal split of topics between Chinese and other/unspecified contexts. Notably, none of the topics covers ethnic minorities in Chinese contexts, contributing to a 'myth of linguistic and cultural homogeneity' (Matsuda & Matsuda, 2011: 183) in China. The Anglo-American and Western presence becomes even more dominant in terms of people, places, events and inventions introduced or mentioned in the textbook. Table 3.4 shows that over 57% of the names, places and events are Western ones and that an overwhelming 81.25% of the inventions mentioned originated in Western contexts.

To determine whether the textbook reflects the changing demographics of English users and uses, it is also instructive to examine the patterns of communication portrayed and/or imagined therein. As summarized in

Table 3.4 Names, places, events and interventions introduced in the textbook

Category	Total no.	Average per unit	% of total no.
Western names, places, events	130	8.67	57.27
Chinese names, places, events	72[a]	4.80	31.72
Names, places, events from other contexts	25	1.67	11.01
Western inventions	26	1.73	81.25
Chinese inventions	6	0.40	18.75
Inventions of other societies	0	0	0

[a]Four names are Chinese Americans or Chinese Canadians.

Table 3.5 Patterns of communication portrayed in the textbook

Category	Total no. of communications	Average per unit	% of total no. of communications
L1–L1 communication	28	1.87	47.46
L1–L2 communication	4	0.27	6.78
L2–L2 communication	1	0.07	1.69
L2–Chinese communication	4	0.27	6.78
L1–Chinese communication	11	0.73	18.64
Chinese–Chinese communication	11	0.73	18.64

Table 3.5, over 47% of the communicative events presented in the textbook involve communication among L1 speakers of English from Inner Circle countries such as the UK and the USA. In addition, a sizeable proportion of the communications are portrayed to occur between English L1 speakers and Chinese L2 speakers of English or L2 speakers of English from other societies. Thus, L1 speakers of English feature in 72.88% of all the communicative events, which reflects a strong native-speaker bias.

To determine the content of cross-cultural communication depicted in the textbook, we took a closer look at the topics covered in the textbook. Our examination reveals that more than half of the topics (about 58%) involve cross-cultural communication directly or are likely to feature in cross-cultural encounters. Of this subset of topics, the majority have to do with personal interests and experiences, and about a quarter deal with popular culture, including such topics as pop music, sports, tourism and diet (see Table 3.6). The remaining ones involve sharing information about one's own country and culture, such as interesting places in China and Chinese language etiquette (i.e. how to talk politely in Chinese). Except for Unit 12, whose theme is 'customs', students seldom have an opportunity to reflect on cultural values, discuss cultural activities and share cross-cultural experiences. Overall, the content of cross-cultural communication focuses largely on the transfer of information about national culture, invites only limited reflection on the students' own culture and rarely encourages the deep cross-cultural comparisons that are necessary to create a sphere of interculturality (Kramsch, 1993).

Table 3.6 Content of cross-cultural communication

Category	Total no. of topics	Average per unit	% of total no. of topics
Topics about own country	11	0.73	14.86
Topics about personal interests/experiences	44	2.93	59.46
Topics about popular culture	19	1.27	25.68

Table 3.7 Learning about different cultures

Category	Total no. of episodes	Average per unit	% of total no. of episodes
Anglo-American/Western cultures	9	0.60	36.00
Chinese culture	4	0.27	16.00
Other cultures	12	0.80	48.00

To determine whether multiculturality is promoted as a learning goal, we analyzed those episodes in the textbook where cultural information is presented explicitly for cultural learning. Table 3.7 summarizes the results of our analysis. A total of 12 episodes concern cultural practices (e.g. attitudes toward punctuality, table manners and what people do when they meet for the first time) in Brazil, Colombia, Japan, Korea, Mexico, Peru, Singapore and Switzerland. Notably, all these episodes appear in a single unit (i.e. Unit 12) that addresses customs in different countries from what may be described as a tourist's perspective. By contrast, the nine episodes about Anglo-American/ Western cultures are spread out over seven units. These episodes depict, among other things, April Fools' Day pranks in the UK and the USA, cultural attractions in Paris, Anglo-American linguistic etiquette, and giving and receiving gifts in England. Surprisingly, there are only four episodes related to Chinese culture, discussing linguistic etiquette in Chinese, gift giving and receiving in China, a Chinese music band and things that Chinese teenagers are and are not allowed to do. On balance, cultural practices of the Anglo-American/Western societies that are represented as predominantly monolingual and white enjoy greater prominence in the textbook, and there is a lack of both depth and breadth of cultural content in the textbook.

Although recent scholarship on EIL (e.g. Canagarajah, 2007; Hu, 2012; McKay, 2012) well recognizes the importance of developing learners' capacity to use various pragmatic strategies to enhance communicative intelligibility and negotiate cross-cultural communication, only three units of the textbook give some attention to communication and accommodation strategies for cross-cultural communication. This takes the form of advice on what (not) to do in cross-cultural encounters, for example, the importance of considering relationship and situation when making requests, the need to avoid sounding rude in requests, and the 'mistakes' that an exchange student makes at 'an American friend's house'. More often than not, these dos and don'ts are based on Anglo-American norms.

Despite accelerating transnational flows of people and a sizeable population of ethnic minorities in China, the textbook does not incorporate sufficient recognition of the widespread multilingualism in contemporary China and other societies (Hu & Alsagoff, 2010). There are only sporadic mentions of the learning and use of specific languages other than English: four mentions of French and three mentions of Chinese. In addition, there are three general references to unspecified languages in the context of: (a) asking learners to write about what has helped them most in learning another language; (b) discussing how learning about language etiquette can help one 'become better at English, or any other language' (p. 93); and (c) asking learners to find examples of language etiquette from movies or books.

The textbook's lack of recognition of multilingualism is also reflected in its sparse attention to the use of English in students' own sociocultural contexts. Ironically, although the textbook is produced for millions of Chinese students to learn English, it provides them with rather limited opportunities to explore the role of English in their life-worlds or to use the language for ostensibly communicative purposes (rather than mere language practice). As can be seen from Table 3.8, there are only 14 episodes involving the communicative use of English in students' own educational contexts, for example, interviewing students from another school in English, writing an English article for a school magazine and writing a letter to the editor of an English school newsletter to express one's own opinion. There are even fewer episodes concerning the use of English for sociocultural purposes, for example, writing an English guide to one's own city and sharing with visitors to China a list of things they are supposed to do in a variety of situations. There is only a single mention of English for vocational purposes: mastery of English can lend one a good job (p. 107). Together with the dominant patterns of cross-cultural communication presented earlier, the limited use of English in students' local life-worlds portrayed by the textbook is likely to reinforce the belief that English is learned primarily for communication with L1 speakers of English in/from the Inner Circle.

This leads us to an examination of the language ideologies promoted in the textbook. As pointed out earlier, the dominant language ideology permeating the textbook is native-speakerism. This ideology is conveyed in multiple ways – in a learner's complaint that native speakers talk too quickly, in the complete absence of code-switching from language samples provided, in the total lack of attention to varieties of English spoken in different parts of the world, and in the claim that 'the culture of a nation is in its language' (p. 92), which accompanies a passage on making polite requests in English and thus links English to Anglo-American cultures. The absence of

Table 3.8 English in students' life-worlds

Category	Total no. episodes	Average per unit	% of total no. of episodes
Use of English for sociocultural purposes	9	0.60	37.50
Use of English at work	1	0.07	4.17
Use of English in local educational contexts	14	0.93	58.33

code-switching examples in the textbook is particularly noteworthy for two reasons. First, since the majority of English speakers today are bi/multilingual and often live in contexts where English is used on a daily basis, code-switching is a natural part of their language use. Second, given the current widespread endorsement of teaching English exclusively through English with its complete negation of the value of a discretionary use of the L1 in English classrooms, there is a need to model the value of carefully designed code-switching in language classrooms. Another language ideology promoted in the textbook is the belief that English competence is a most valorized form of cultural/symbolic capital. This is evident in Xu Zheng (a character in the textbook) winning 'a prize for his essay about the importance of English' (p. 7) as well as in claims like 'English is used around the world' (p. 7) and 'Working hard at English can lead to a good job' (p. 107).

Finally, one omission is starkly evident in the textbook and epitomizes its ideological stance toward fundamental issues surrounding English and its relation to multilingualism and multiculturalism; that is, there is a conspicuous lack of effort to critically frame the teaching and learning of English. The textbook includes no topics, texts or tasks that invite learners to consider such important issues as inequalities in English education, language-based social injustice/oppression and the spread of Western values through ELT. Nor does it encourage learners to critically examine the dominance of English, the sociocultural impact of English learning and the implications of linguistic globalization for contemporary life.

A close-up analysis of Unit 7

The opening section (section A) introduces the topic of travel by asking, 'Where would you like to visit?'. The text has a line drawing of two characters (Sam and Gina) viewing two travel posters, one for Florida and the other for Brazil with the words, 'Take it easy on a Florida Beach' and 'Trek through the Amazon Jungle' (p. 52). In the Florida poster there is a line drawing of a man lying on a beach chair with sunglasses, a cold drink and a shade umbrella. In the Amazon poster, there is a man with a backpack, a trekking hat and a machete in his hand. Nothing is done with the line drawing in terms of analyzing it for its semiotic value, even though the choice of destinations clearly would be unrealistic for most students from China. Underneath the line drawing is a listening activity that asks students individually to listen to a dialogue between Sam and Gina and fill out a chart that asks where each character would like to go and why. This is followed by a pair-work activity that asks students to look at the posters and practice a conversation with their partner about where they would like to go.

Then there is another listening task where students listen to a dialogue between a girl and two boys (they are not given a name, an age, nor any information about their relationship) talking about taking a vacation together and where they would like to visit. Their preferences include Hawaii, Mexico and Niagara Falls, but in each case one of the characters offers an objection to the suggested location. The girl finally suggests they go to San Francisco together, and one boy agrees if the girl pays for it. Students need to use this information to order statements in a chart. This is followed by an individual listening task that asks students to match the place (Hawaii, Mexico and Niagara Falls) with the reason for not visiting the place. Once again the activities present non-Asian locations supporting a Western orientation. In addition, the locations would be expensive and unrealistic for most students to visit.

Next there is a short reading text entitled 'Travel Spotlight: Paris' with a picture of the Eiffel Tower. The text suggests that the reader consider visiting Paris, arguing that although it does not have beaches or mountains it has 'fantastic sights' like the Eiffel Tower and Notre Dame Cathedral. It states that, although France is expensive, a tourist can use the underground trains that are inexpensive and adds, 'One thing that is not expensive in France, however, is wine!' (p. 54). The reading ends with the following generalization: 'Most people in France have learned English. But many people don't like to speak English especially in Paris. So unless you speak French yourself, it's best to travel with someone who can translate things for you' (p. 54). This is a surprisingly stereotypical statement to include in a text that would hopefully promote cross-cultural understanding.

Section A ends with two pair-work activities. The first provides the following model dialogue and asks students to make a similar dialogue about Hong Kong, Mexico City, New York and Sydney, providing them with information about each location.

A: Where would you like to go, Kathy?
B: I'd like to visit Kunming.
A: Isn't it supposed to be very hot?
B: Yes it is. I'm only going to pack light clothes. Kunming is also beautiful and has lots of wonderful sights. (p. 54)

The second activity asks students to identify a city and list things they like and don't like about it. Both activities target aural/oral skills and are opinion-based.

The theme of Section A, 'Where would you like to visit?' clearly holds the potential for Chinese learners to find out about other countries and cultures through cross-cultural exchanges. However, the visuals, topics, dialogues and activities do not live up to that potential. The visuals are mainly Western. The poster line drawing has two Caucasian-looking characters (Sam and Gina). There are photos of the Eiffel Tower, and four backpackers in an unidentified city. It is difficult to tell the backpackers' ethnicity since their backs are toward the camera and the dialogue (one girl and two boys) that accompanies the photo does not specify who the speakers are.

An examination of the topics also shows a Western and middle-class bias. All of the locations mentioned are outside of China except for Kunming and Hong Kong. An overwhelming majority of these locations are Western. All of the foreign locations for travel assume that the Chinese student comes from a wealthy background in which it is possible to travel to places like Florida, Brazil, Hawaii, Mexico, Niagara Falls, San Francisco, New York or Sydney, supporting Gray's (2012) contention that ELT textbooks have a middle-class bias. The dialogues appear to occur only between L1 speakers of English (i.e. Gina and Sam; the one girl and two boys). There is nothing in either dialogue to suggest that they are anything other than L1 speakers of English, reinforcing a native-speaker bias.

The tasks include both individual and pair work. Pair work is a typical feature of CLT and TBLT, which encourage oral communication among learners. These pair-work tasks can be productive learning activities when they are well structured. However, some of the directions for these tasks give students little motivation to interact with their classmates. For example, the first pair-work activity asks the following:

> Look at the vacation posters in 1a. Practice conversations with your part-ner. Then tell which place you would like to visit and why. (p. 62)

Given the directions, students would likely repeat the two-line dialogue in the line drawing with the two posters (i.e. 'Where would you like to go on vacation, Sam?'; 'I'd like to trek through the jungle because I like exciting vacations.'), followed by a dialogue of their own making. It is then a rather mechanical exchange based on expressing opinions and having a model that suggests students would select a remote place largely inaccessible to them.

Perhaps the most disappointing aspect of this section is its inability to promote a sphere of interculturality in which students are encouraged to compare their own culture with other cultures, to become aware of the diversity existing within all cultures, and to be provided with models of English as a lingua franca.

Section B opens with a listening task in which a travel agent, Jeff, from ACE Travel answers questions from three customers on the phone about places they would like to go to. One wants a warm place, one a nature tour and another a place for kids. Jeff recommends Hawaii, a whale watch tour and Los Angeles/Hollywood, respectively. This is followed by an email from S.T. Zhang requesting some information about taking a trip to eastern China. Zhang wants to know about a place for his/her family of three that has out-door activities where they could stay in an inexpensive hotel or apartment with a kitchen and a big pool. Students are then asked to write an email mes-sage to S.T. Zhang suggesting where to go and where to stay. This is followed by group work in which students need to survey three students on an ideal place for a school trip. The possibilities are Qufu (Confucius's hometown), the Great Wall and the Stone Forest (a tourist attraction in Yunnan, China).

Unlike Section A, this section provides more coverage of the Chinese context and includes Chinese characters. Attention to the Chinese context provides a nice balance with Section A's focus on Western places and names. However, apart from S.T. Zhang, all the other speakers in the section appear to be L1 speakers, and nothing is done to encourage students to make cross-cultural comparisons. Finally, once again there is a middle-class bias. Such a bias is evident in the recommended leisure activities of a holiday in Hawaii, a whale watch tour and a Hollywood visit. It is also evident in the task in the 'self-check' section that follows. The task asks students to consider which of the following places they would like to visit and write an article about why they would like to go there. The visuals provide four choices – the San Francisco Golden Gate Bridge, the Sydney Opera House, London's Big Ben and the Eiffel Tower. All of them are Western locations that would be expensive to visit from China.

The final reading section focuses on students' hopes and dreams. The section includes a reading entitled 'I'd love to sail across the Pacific', followed by activities that encourage students to read with a focus. The reading starts by asserting that everyone dreams about things they want to do and hope to achieve in the future. It then summarizes a survey of 'thousands of students across China'. Whether the survey is real is not clear since there is no source for the reading. According to the survey, after finishing their education, some students want to start work right away to help their parents while others hope to go on to a university. Most want to make money, but they want a job they like to do, the most popular being computer programming. The students' dreams are quite varied, ranging from working as a volunteer at the 2008 Olympics to going to the moon. In keeping with Gray's contention of the class bias in ELT materials and their attention to celebrities, quite a few students dream of 'becoming famous, perhaps famous sportspeople or singers' (p. 58).

Unit 7 ends with three open-ended discussion questions and an activity that asks students to write down a dream they have, share it with a friend, and together work out the steps needed to achieve the dream. The discussion questions are as follows:

(1) Is there anyone in the world who does not hope or dream?
(2) Might the dreams of Chinese teenagers be different from Western teenagers?
(3) Can dreams come true?

Question 2 is unusual in a textbook that rarely encourages students to make cross-cultural comparisons. The example given for the writing task consists of a dream to have one's own company some day and the following steps to achieving it: (a) 'working hard at school to learn as much as I can'; (b) 'finding out how successful people did it'; (c) 'choosing to study the right subjects at university'; and (d) 'having a 'winner's attitude: I can do this!'. Such input clearly valorizes neoliberal values – distinction, commitment, passion and choice in the fulfillment of the self – widely associated with the new capitalism that dominates in Anglo-American societies (Gray, 2010). Thus, students are 'interpellated in these materials to the subject position of white-collar individualism in which the world of work is overwhelmingly seen as a privileged means for the full and intense realization of the self along lines determined largely by personal choice' (Gray, 2010: 714).

Conclusions

Our quantitative and qualitative analyses of the focal textbook reveal its clear pedagogical leaning toward such Western language teaching methodologies as CLT and TBLT. There is a diversity of task types and skill focus; however, a great majority of these are based on content removed from most students' life-worlds and provide little opportunity for students to examine the semiotic value of visuals. As regards its stance on multiculturalism, the textbook displays a stark imbalance in its representation of particular cultures. As in other studies of English textbooks (e.g. Gray, 2010, 2012; Matsuda, 2002; Matsuda & Matsuda, 2011; Yuen, 2011), Western contexts, characters, events and places predominate. Although many topics are situated in cross-cultural communication contexts or are likely to appear in such contexts, little opportunity is provided to encourage students to reflect on cultural experiences and make cross-cultural comparisons for the development of a sphere of interculturality. Anglo-American and Western cultural practices are represented more prominently than both Chinese cultural practices and those of other societies. Thus, the textbook is lacking in both breadth and depth of cultural teaching.

A multilingual turn is not encouraged in the textbook either. There are very few occasions in which the use of languages other than English is mentioned, much less dealt with in terms of their value and significance. The dominant patterns of communication represented in the textbook involve either the use of English among L1 speakers or interactions between L1 and L2 speakers, failing to reflect the sociolinguistic reality of EIL (Matsuda & Friedrich, 2011; McKay, 2012). Pragmatic strategies for cross-cultural understanding receive only sporadic attention. Furthermore, there are few occasions in which the use of English in students' own life-worlds is explored. In terms of the overall ideology of the textbook, there is a general Western bias, a support of native-speakerism, a view of English knowledge as the most valorized cultural capital, and a conspicuous lack of attention to varieties of

English or code-switching among multilingual speakers as a common phenomenon. Last but not least, the textbook makes no attempt to deal critically with the spread of English, linguistic globalization and the negative effects it can have, including inequalities in English learning and the Western and middle-class bias that permeates many English textbooks.

Because this study is based on a textual analysis that focuses on the textbook representation of multiculturalism and multilingualism, we do not know how the focal textbook impacts upon students' language and cultural learning in the classroom, that is, their actual language and cultural practices. As Matsuda and Matsuda (2011: 173–174) point out, 'an analysis of textbooks can provide only a partial picture of the classroom reality' and individual teachers may make their own 'efforts to supplement what the textbooks do not provide'. This, however, does not exonerate textbook writers from biased and misleading representation of the multilingual and multicultural reality of the contemporary world. For, as Gray (2010) rightly points out, textbooks not only mediate subject knowledge but also reproduce ideologies.

References

Baker, W. (2009) The cultures of English as a lingua franca. *TESOL Quarterly* 43, 567–592.

Beare, K. (2010) *How Many People Learn English Globally?* About.com. See http://esl.about.com/od/englishlearningresources/f/f_eslmarket.htm (accessed 20 August 2014).

Beckett, G.H. and Postiglione, G.A. (eds) (2012) *China's Assimilationist Language Policy: The Impact on Indigenous/Minority Literacy and Social Harmony*. London: Routledge.

Blommaert, J. (2010) *The Sociolinguistics of Globalization*. Cambridge: Cambridge University Press.

Bolton, K. and Graddol, D. (2012) English in China today. *English Today* 28 (3), 3–9.

Butler, Y.K. (2011) The implementation of communicative and task-based language teaching in the Asia-Pacific region. *Annual Review of Applied Linguistics* 31, 36–57.

Canagarajah, S. (2007) Lingua franca English, multilingual communities, and language acquisition. *Modern Language Journal* 91, 923–939.

Cengage Learning (2005) *Thomson Learning Asia and PEP Press Reaches 50 Million Copy Milestone*. Cengage Learning. See http://news.cengage.com/corporate/thomson-learning-asia-and-pep-press-reaches-50-million-copy-milestone/ (accessed 20 August 2014).

Gao, S. (2012) The biggest English corner in China. *English Today* 28 (3), 34–39.

Gao, Y. (2009) Sociocultural contexts and English in China: Retaining and reforming the cultural habitus. In J. Lo Bianco, J. Orton and Y. Gao (eds) *China and English: Globalisation and the Dilemmas of Identity* (pp. 56–78). Bristol: Multilingual Matters.

Graddol, D. (1997) *The Future of English*. London: British Council.

Gray, J. (2010) The branding of English and the culture of the new capitalism: Representations of the world of work in English language textbooks. *Applied Linguistics* 31, 714–733.

Gray, J. (2012) Neoliberalism, celebrity and 'aspirational content' in English language teaching textbooks for the global market. In D. Block, J. Gray and M. Holborow (eds) *Neoliberalism and Applied Linguistics* (pp. 86–113). New York: Routledge.

Hu, G. (2002a) English language teaching in the People's Republic of China. In R.E. Silver, G. Hu and M. Iino (eds) *English Language Education in China, Japan, and Singapore* (pp. 1–77). Singapore: National Institute of Education.

Hu, G. (2002b) Recent important developments in secondary English-language teaching in the People's Republic of China. *Language, Culture and Curriculum* 15, 30–49.

Hu, G. (2002c) Potential cultural resistance to pedagogical imports: The case of communicative language teaching in China. *Language, Culture and Curriculum* 15, 93–105.

Hu, G. (2003) English language teaching in China: Regional differences and contributing factors. *Journal of Multilingual and Multicultural Development* 24, 290–318.

Hu, G. (2012) Assessing English as an international language. In L. Alsagoff, S. McKay, G.W. Hu and W. Renanyda (eds) *Principles and Practices for Teaching English as an International Language* (pp. 123–143). New York: Routledge.

Hu, G. and Alsagoff, L. (2010) A public policy perspective on English medium instruction in China. *Journal of Multilingual and Multicultural Development* 31, 365–382.

Hu, G. and McKay, S. (2012) English language education in East Asia: Some recent developments. *Journal of Multilingual and Multicultural Development* 33, 345–362.

Kachru, B.B. (ed.) (1992) *The Other Tongue*. Chicago, IL: University of Illinois Press.

Kramsch, C. (1993) *Context and Culture in Language Teaching*. Oxford: Oxford University Press.

Kumaravadivelu, B. (2012) Individual identity, cultural globalization, and teaching English as an international language: The case for an epistemic break. In L. Alsagoff, S. McKay, G.W. Hu and W. Renanyda (eds) *Principles and Practices for Teaching English as an International Language* (pp. 9–27). New York: Routledge.

Lo Bianco, J. (2009a) Intercultural encounters and deep cultural beliefs. In J. Lo Bianco, J. Orton and Y. Gao (eds) *China and English: Globalisation and the Dilemmas of Identity* (pp. 23–55). Bristol: Multilingual Matters.

Lo Bianco, J. (2009b) Being Chinese, speaking English. In J. Lo Bianco, J. Orton and Y. Gao (eds) *China and English: Globalisation and the Dilemmas of Identity* (pp. 294–309). Bristol: Multilingual Matters.

Matsuda, A. (2002) Representation of users and uses of English in beginning Japanese EFL textbooks. *JALT Journal* 24 (2), 80–98.

Matsuda, A. (2012) Teaching materials in EIL. In L. Alsagoff, S. McKay, G. Hu and W. Renanyda (eds) *Principles and Practices for Teaching English as an International Language* (pp. 168–185). New York: Routledge.

Matsuda, A. and Friedrich, P. (2011) English as an international language: A curriculum blueprint. *World Englishes* 30, 332–344.

Matsuda, A. and Matsuda, P.K. (2011) Globalizing writing studies: The case of US technical communication textbooks. *Written Communication* 28, 172–192.

McKay, S.L. (2012) Principles of teaching English as an international language. In L. Alsagoff, S. McKay, G. Hu and W. Renanyda (eds) *Principles and Practices for Teaching English as an International Language* (pp. 28–46). New York: Routledge.

MOE (2001) *Quanrizhi Yiwu Jiaoyu Putong Gaoji Zhongxue Yingyu Kecheng Biaozhun [English Curriculum Standards for Compulsory Education and Senior Secondary Education]*. Beijing: Ministry of Education.

National Bureau of Statistics of China (2001) 2000 *Nian Diwuci Quanguo Renkou Pucha Zhuyao Shuju Gongbao [Communiqué on the Fifth Population Census in 2000]*. See http://www.stats.gov.cn/tjsj/ndsj/renkoupucha/2000pucha/html/append21.htm (accessed 20 August 2014).

Nunan, D. (1998–1999) *Go For It!* (Student Books 1–4). Boston, MA: Heinle & Heinle.

Orton, J. (2009a) English and the Chinese quest. In J. Lo Bianco, J. Orton and Y. Gao (eds) *China and English: Globalisation and the Dilemmas of Identity* (pp. 79–97). Bristol: Multilingual Matters.

Orton, J. (2009b) 'Just a tool': The role of English in the curriculum. In J. Lo Bianco, J. Orton and Y. Gao (eds) *China and English: Globalisation and the Dilemmas of Identity* (pp. 137–154). Bristol: Multilingual Matters.

People's Education Press (2007) *Go for It!* Produced jointly by the Curriculum and Teaching Materials Research Institute, Center of Research on English Curriculum and

Teaching Materials Development, and Cengage Learning Asia. Beijing: People's Education Press and Cengage Learning Asia.

Sárdi, C. (2002) On the relationship between culture and ELT. *Kalbu Studijos* 3, 101–107.

Seidlhofer, B. (2004) Research perspectives on teaching English as a lingua franca. *Annual Review of Applied Linguistics* 24, 209–239.

Sharifian, F. (2011) *Cultural Conceptualisations and Language.* Amsterdam: John Benjamins.

Shin, J., Eslami, Z.R. and Chen, W.-C. (2011) Presentation of local and international culture in current international English-language teaching textbooks. *Language, Culture and Curriculum* 24, 253–268.

Smith, L. (1976) English as an international auxiliary language. *RELC Journal* 7 (2), 38–43.

Wei, R. and Su, J. (2012) The statistics of English in China. *English Today* 28 (3), 10–14.

Widdowson, H.G. (1994) The ownership of English. *TESOL Quarterly* 28, 377–388.

Xiong, T. (2012) Essence or practice? Conflicting cultural values in Chinese EFL textbooks: A discourse approach. *Discourse: Studies in the Cultural Politics of Education* 33, 499–516.

Yuen, K.-M. (2011) The representation of foreign cultures in English textbooks. *ELT Journal* 65, 458–466.

Zhang, Y. (2008) *Yiwu jiaoyu kecheng biaozhun shiyan jiaokeshu yinyu (xin mubiao) jiaocai jieshao* [Introducing the *Go for It!* textbook series]. Beijing: People's Education Press. See http://www.pep.com.cn/ce/czyy/tbjxzy/jcjj/jianjie/201009/t20100908_887025.htm (accessed 20 August 2014).

Zhou, M. and Sun. K. (eds) (2004) *Language Policy in the People's Republic of China: Theory and Practice Since 1949.* Boston, MA: Kluwer Academic Publishers.

4 Looking Through the Language Lens: Monolingual Taint or Plurilingual Tint?

Andrea Young

Guiding Questions

- To what extent are local languages reflected in the schools described in this chapter, and what are the opportunities and challenges associated with this?
- What is the predominant view of diverse languages according to the teachers interviewed: a right, a resource or a problem?
- What are the opportunities and challenges identified with regard to teacher beliefs in multilingual contexts such as in Alsace?

Introduction

In a bid to better understand the challenges and complexities facing teachers in linguistically diverse classrooms, interviews with head teachers ($n = 46$) were conducted in the Alsace region of eastern France during 2011. Through listening to teachers' voices and analysing their discourse we reveal anxieties and questions concerning language development, learning and citizenship and explore beliefs about bilingualism.

In this chapter we first present and analyse the context in which the research was undertaken, firmly believing in the power of local contextual factors and national institutional structures to influence and constrain teachers' beliefs and pedagogical practices. Secondly, we report on teachers' views on the use and support of pupils' heritage languages at school. A thematic analysis of the data looks at language through three lenses: language as a right, language as a problem and language as a resource (Ruiz, 1984, in Harrison, 2007). Our aim is to uncover overt and covert language practices and policies within the school context and to understand the ideologies upon which they are founded.

The Monolingual Nation State Inheritance: Language Policies and Education in the French Context

Since revolutionary times, when the French language was identified as one of the pillars of the *République*, the use of languages other than French on French territory has aroused passionate reactions. The campaign to mould the population into French citizens, 'one language, one people, one nation' (Charaudeau, 2001), has operated on many levels, notably in the domains of legislation and education (Albertini, 1992). The French language is enshrined within the Constitution: 'la langue de la République est le français' (Article 2 of the Constitution, National Assembly, 1958). This article effectively legitimises a linguistic norm for the nation, inasmuch as the French language is regarded as the cement of the nation and mastery of this 'one' official, unifying language is viewed as an act of citizenship.

With the introduction of free, compulsory and secular education (Law no. 11-696 of 28 March 1882), French became the sole language of instruction in France, and republican ideals and values were reinforced through this medium to the exclusion of all other linguistic varieties, often referred to as *patois* or *dialectes*, spoken by pupils. This monolingual ideology, rooted in French political history, not only places the standard literary French language of the governing elite on a pedestal, towering over all other modes of expression at school, but frequently it simultaneously seeks to restrict or even ban other languages which can be perceived as a threat to the dominance of French.

In addition to promoting French citizenship through the sole medium of French, schools were invested with the responsibility of providing equal access to education for all citizens, regardless of their family backgrounds. These two ideas of citizenship and equal access to education through French are combined in the following statement to be found on the ministerial website for education professionals, EDUSCOL:

> La langue française est l'outil premier de l'égalité des chances, de la liberté du citoyen et de la civilité: elle permet de communiquer à l'oral comme à l'écrit, dans diverses situations; elle permet de comprendre et d'exprimer ses droits et ses devoirs.

> *The French language is the primary tool of equal opportunities, freedom of the citizen and civility: it facilitates both oral and written communication, in various situations, and allows citizens to understand and express their rights and duties.* (EDUSCOL, 2012a, our translation)

That a person needs to be able to function in the language(s) of the country in which s/he resides is not under question. However, that the language of education should be envisaged by education professionals as the sole mode of expression and unique legitimate form of communication in which a person should function (outside the designated foreign language learning hours) is not only out of step with the evolution of our globalised societies, but is detrimental to the wellbeing and learning of bi/plurilingual children (Couëtoux-Jungman *et al.*, 2010; Moro, 2004). Children for whom the language of education is the only language habitually used at home may also suffer from such a restricted vision of language and languages, inasmuch as their tolerance of otherness and their openness and curiosity to learn (about) new languages may be adversely affected. Official rhetoric which continues to ignore the role of home languages in learning only serves to reinforce a monolingual nation-state ideology in contradiction with the multilingual reality of many schools and the plurilingual aspirations of European language policy (Cavalli *et al.*, 2009). Equality is consequently all too often equated with uniformity and equal treatment, rather than with equity and equal opportunity. This often leads education professionals in France to teach and treat all children, regardless of their linguistic and cultural heritage, in the same way. Differentiation with respect to an individual child's linguistic repertoire is rare and teachers are reluctant to ask about children's home languages and hesitate to adapt their teaching to bi/plurilingual pupils' needs.

This reticence to take an inclusive approach to home languages is complex and multifaceted. A contributing factor could also be teachers' fears, especially in their role as civil servants who owe allegiance to the state (Article 28 of Law no. 83-634 of 13 July 1983), of failing to respect the law which states that no statistical data relating to ethnicity must be collected (EDUSCOL, Ministère de l'Education Nationale, 2007: Article 8 of law no. 78-17 of 6 January 1978 relating to computer databases and civil liberties). Some teachers may associate, albeit incorrectly, ethnicity with language, which would explain their reluctance to ask which languages are spoken at home by pupils and their families. No doubt insufficient information about the relevance of a child's home language to learning is also an important factor. It could also be for many teachers, whose only foreign language learning experience has been within the school environment and who live and work in an officially monolingual state where language policies to promote and protect French abound, that the idea of considering any languages other than those officially endorsed by the institution, either as the national language of instruction or a foreign language taught as a subject, as of significance, simply does not occur to them.

The legacy of monolingual, nation-state language policies designed to promote and protect the French language in the public sphere, while confining other languages to private spaces, still pervades modern-day France. For example, radio stations have broadcasting quotas for French music; television stations dub rather than subtitle programmes, films, interviews, etc. in French; all foreign words used in advertisements must be translated into French; and for the benefit of any French-speaking participants at an international conference held in France written abstracts must be provided in French for each presentation (Law no. 94-665 of 4 August 1994 relating to the use of the French language). These regulations are for the most part aimed at limiting the linguistic hegemony of English, a language which is paradoxically viewed as a necessity for international communication, but also as a threat to the supremacy of the French language. The belief that French, a defining element of the French citizen and nation, needs to be protected and promoted persists, leading many sections of French society to sideline, reject or ignore other languages present in French society.

Ager, in his book *Identity, Insecurity and Image: France and Language* (1999), writes about mainstream society's fear of certain social groups whose linguistic and cultural practices, they believe, could lead to the disintegration of the nation state as they know it, through the rejection of shared values, beliefs and norms. Ager argues that such fears nurture the myth of inclusion which still persists in France today: 'The idea of the all-inclusive, cohesive society ... ignoring all those who do not accept the guiding principles and are not prepared to lose their group or community culture in order to absorb that of the greater unit.' He also sounds an ominous warning note, namely that this vision 'seems less and less to respond to the conditions of modern society: mass immigration...' (Ager, 1999: 86–87). Over a decade has passed since Ager published his analysis and we are now in an age of super-diversity (Vertovec, 2010). Yet, in this 21st-century world of global communication and closer political and economic cooperation, monolingual myths about language, inclusion and identity still abound. Unsurprisingly, tensions between monolingual ideologies and increasingly complex multilingual realities are surfacing and the language lens of the 19th-century nation state is beginning to crack.

When Nation-State Language Ideologies Meet Linguistic Diversity at School

Within the French educational context, schools, especially nursery and primary schools, are traditionally and indeed officially viewed as guarantors of the quality and dominance of French. It is here that children are first required to learn about and through the French language. Other languages are taught at school, but within defined timetabled slots, and very few schools embark upon language awareness projects such as the one carried out in Didenheim (Young & Hélot, 2003, 2007). Although theoretically it is possible to learn one of eight languages (Arabic, Chinese, English, German, Italian, Portuguese, Russian or Spanish) at primary school, the hegemony of English is reflected in the figures, with 91% (RERS, 2012) of 7–11 year-old children learning English as a foreign language at primary school for 54 hours per year (EDUSCOL, 2012b). This trend continues in secondary and higher education.

In Alsace, a region of France bordering Germany and German-speaking Switzerland, the linguistic situation is quite different. The local language policy promotes the learning of German at school; thus eight out of 10 children (Académie de Strasbourg, 2012a) aged between three and 12 learn German as a foreign language at school in Alsace. A further specificity of Alsace is the bilingual programme (French/German) which allows pupils from nursery school age (three upwards) to be taught through French and German in equal proportion if their parents so choose (see Huck *et al.*, 2005). It should also be noted that regional varieties of German, known as Alsatian, are still spoken by many people in Alsace (Huck *et al.*, 2005), albeit by an aging population. Alsatian speakers frequently do not choose to pass on this linguistic variety to their children and grandchildren, believing it to be worthless and stigmatising. Indeed in the past, most recently after WWII, many children were punished for using Alsatian at school and parents were advised to speak French with their children in the interest of their educational achievement and future careers.

Another particularity of Alsace is its history of immigration (Frey, 2009). The Strasbourg education authority hosts the fifth highest number of foreign national pupils in secondary education, after French Guyana, Corsica, Paris and Créteil in the Paris suburbs (RERS, 2011). According to the 2007 census (ORIV, 2011), the proportion of immigrants in Alsace (10.1% of the population) is higher than the national average (8.3%), with a greater number of Europeans, a lower proportion of immigrants from North Africa and a comparatively high number of migrants from countries such as Turkey (ORIV, 2011). The high number of migrant families and the turbulent linguistic heritage of this border region, whose inhabitants have changed nationality four times over the past 100 years, have led to a wide range and higher-than-average degree of linguistic and cultural diversity in this region.

It has been acknowledged that as a direct consequence of our increasingly globalised world, many school populations now include a greater number of pupils with a wider variety of home languages which are not languages of instruction (OECD, 2010). This places additional strain on teachers, who very often have received little or no training to prepare them to support these pupils (Cajkler & Hall, 2012; Murakami, 2008; Wiley, 2008). France is no exception to this situation. Data compiled from official birth registration in France (INSEE, 2010) indicate that 27.2% of children born in France in 2010 had at least one parent of foreign nationality. While nationality does not always equate with linguistic competence in a given language, these figures do give us an indication of the linguistic and cultural diversity present in schools. Whether families speak a language other than French at home and whether parents are in a position to choose to pass on their language(s) to their children is another matter. Social pressure to conform to the norm, which is to speak French only, abounds. Even well-meaning, but misinformed teachers and other education professionals may advise parents to speak to their children in French, believing this to aid the acquisition of French. Parents listen to professionals and naturally want what is best for their children. Those that can speak French well enough may try and comply with this advice; those that cannot may feel powerless to help their children, forced into adopting a new identity, unauthorised to pass on their linguistic and cultural heritage to the next generation (Couëtoux-Jungman et al., 2010; Moro, 2004).

Those parents who may wish their children to grow up as bilinguals may find that nurturing a family language in an environment where the dominant language is omnipresent and which may even be hostile to their home language, can also be quite an arduous task. With the event of satellite TV and the internet, access to media in the home language is nowadays much easier than it was a generation ago. If there is a local minority-language speaking community, this will also support language transmission and development. But providing a child with a language-rich, textual environment where s/he can also develop literacy skills in the home language is not always a simple affair. Community/complementary schools or classes may exist in some towns and cities, but not for all languages and not always within easy access for the families concerned. Parents may have other priorities or restrictions on their time and do not necessarily possess the pedagogical skills and knowledge to teach literacy in their home language themselves.

In the French context, the Ministry of Education set up so-called ELCO classes (enseignement des langues et cultures d'origine) in the 1970s to encourage the maintenance of heritage languages for migrant pupils. Bilateral agreements between France and the countries concerned (Algeria, Croatia, Italy, Morocco, Portugal, Serbia, Spain, Tunisia and Turkey) provide teachers from the countries of origin. Classes (one and a half to three hours per week) are provided free of charge to families on school premises and are usually held outside school hours. In the Strasbourg area during the school year 2009–2010, out of a total of 4799 primary school pupils enrolled in ELCO classes, 2612 were learning Turkish, 1981 Arabic (Algerian, Moroccan and Tunisian varieties), 128 Portuguese, 59 Spanish and 20 Serbian (Académie de Strasbourg, 2012b). The peripatetic teachers of these classes rarely have the opportunity to exchange with their French mainstream counterparts, many of whom know little about the content and objectives of these classes.

If education professionals do not fully understand the complex, plurilingual situations which many of their pupils and families are now experiencing and the issues they raise, how can they advise parents appropriately? Furthermore, how can they meet their own professional objectives, which require all children to be given equal access to learning through the language of instruction, if they are not equipped with a greater understanding and knowledge about language, how languages are acquired, how they interrelate and how language development can be supported?

Teachers working in the French context are doubly challenged; not only do they need to be better informed, but they are also working within a context which is still dominated by a monolingual mindset, where high-status, international languages such as English are viewed as a threat to French, and low-status language varieties such as the languages of immigration and regional languages are dismissed as at best useless and at worst a handicap. At the interface between the institutional language of instruction (French) and the languages spoken by pupils and their families, teachers have to deal with increasingly complex linguistic and cultural situations, the fruit of super-diversity, for which they have scant training. Tensions between the monolingual ideologies underlying school language policies and the manifest learning needs of pupils trouble the mind of the caring professional, leaving her/him with a multitude of questions to which they can only guess at appropriate responses. Yet, on account of the close, regular, personal contact which s/he has with pupils and their families, the teacher is in a privileged position of power with respect to the languages authorised, valued or prohibited at school.

Professional Perspectives, Powers and Practised Policies

Although teachers are subject to national and/or regional education policies, required to follow a curriculum and expected to attain certain targets for their pupils, within the context of the school and especially within their own classrooms, it is within the teachers' power to adapt pedagogy to the needs of their learners. This means that sometimes, in spite of national directives and/or public opinion, they will choose an innovative, lesser trod path if they think it will ultimately aid learning. As alternatives to the monolingual vision, visions of multilingual, interculturally competent cosmopolitan citizens of the world (Banks, 2011; Starkey, 2011) have been proposed by researchers in the field of education (García et al., 2006; Lemaire, 2009) and are supported by organisations such as the Council of Europe (Beacco & Byram, 2007), the OECD (2010) and UNESCO (2011). However, if teachers are to act appropriately in the interests of their pupils' wellbeing and academic progress, they need to understand the complex issues relating to plurilingual learners. Given that the majority of teachers in France are not from a migration background (Charles & Legendre, 2006) and have only a school-based experience of languages, how are they supposed to understand complex issues such as bilingualism, biliteracy, multiple identities and inter-cultural communication with little personal experience and training? They may well have internalised the dominant monolingual perspective and their language lenses could be de facto monolingually biased. Perhaps they are themselves products of a school system rooted in 19th-century language ideologies which they in turn perpetuate. Or could they be key actors in the evolution of the language lens through which pupils' languages are ignored or acknowledged, judged as an asset or as a deficit, supported or outlawed?

We have previously reported on innovative teacher education modules which allow teachers and future teachers to explore the multiple dimensions of linguistic and cultural awareness (Mary & Young, 2010). In this chapter, we explore teacher discourse relating to pupils' home and school languages and their role in learning. More specifically, we report on head teachers' views on the use and support of pupils' heritage languages at school. The data were collected through interviews conducted in 2011 with head teachers (*n* = 46) in a variety of schools (nursery, primary and secondary) and reported by undergraduate students on school observation placements as part of an awareness-raising module focusing on overt and covert language practices and policies within the French school context, in the Alsace region. A series of questions was posed during the interviews, including:

- Y-a-t-il des règles dans l'école concernant l'utilisation des langues des élèves? Pourquoi? [*Are there any rules at school concerning the use of the pupils' languages? Why?*]
- Pensez-vous qu'il serait utile d'encourager le plurilinguisme dans les écoles? Pourquoi? [*Do you think it would be useful to encourage plurilingualism in schools? Why?*]

The reported data from these two questions reveal a range of practised policies, underpinned by a variety of beliefs, ideologies and conventions (Hornberger & McKay, 2010). We have chosen to analyse the data looking at language through three language lenses: language as a right, language as a problem and language as a resource (Ruiz, 1984, in Harrison, 2007).

It is our belief that through listening to teachers' voices and analysing their discourse we can identify beliefs and underlying ideologies which will in turn help us to better understand the challenges and complexities facing teachers in linguistically diverse classrooms. We hope that by exposing teachers' anxieties and questions concerning language development, learning and citizenship we will be able to adapt teacher education programmes to include these concerns, and to link individual perspectives with the broader sociolinguistic context within which teachers work.

Pupils' Heritage Languages at School: Right, Resource or Problem?

The respondents in our sample did not all supply consistent responses relating to pupils' heritage languages. Eight teachers (17%) saw home languages as both a right and a resource, six (13%) saw them as a resource but a problem and three (7%) saw them as a problem but a right. However, the majority of the sample was roughly split down the middle with 20 teachers (43%) generally considering home languages as a resource and 19 (41%) as a problem. Fifteen teachers (33%) spoke of pupils' rights to use their home language in the playground, but only four of them (9%) said they allowed home languages to be used in the classroom. The other 11 out of the 15 teachers who mentioned language rights, although accepting the use of home languages in the playground, were categorical about the necessity of keeping to a French-only policy in class. We will discuss their remarks in greater detail below.

Language as a right

Four teachers (9%) claimed that bi/plurilingual pupils in their schools were free to use the language of their choice. One of them even referred to 'leur droit de parler leur langue maternelle et qu'il serait injuste d'être contre ce droit' [*their right to speak their mother tongue and that it would be unfair to be against this right*]. Another said 'cela fait parti de l'enfant donc il est autorisé à parler sa langue d'origine s'il en a besoin' [*it is part of the child so he is allowed to speak his home language if he needs to*]. These comments reveal both an empathetic understanding of what it means to learn through a language other than the one spoken at home and a concern for social justice and equity. Language is an integral part of our identity, a cultural and linguistic heritage passed down through generations by close family members. Our home language is therefore emotionally charged and intrinsic to motivation and consequently learning. Refusing to authorise a child to use her/his home language as a cognitive tool for learning is effectively an act of discrimination. UNESCO underlines language as a human right, stating that the integration of migrant 'children should be facilitated by teaching the language in use in the school system' and that 'opportunities should be created for teaching children their own language and culture' (UNESCO, 2003: 16–17). UNICEF (2007) proposes five reasons as to why minority language children should develop their home language including maintaining communication between grandparents, parents and children, promoting a positive self-image and supporting the learning of the second language.

The remaining two teachers who viewed home language use at school as a right talk of pupils being 'libre' [*free*] and 'liberté d'expression' [*freedom of speech*]. This is, let us not forget, another tenet of republican ideology (liberté, égalité, fraternité).

A further 11 teachers (24%) claim to allow children to use their home languages in the playground, but that a French-only rule applies in the classroom. One teacher explains 'il n'est pas de notre droit de décider quelle langue est employée en dehors des cours' [*it is not our right to decide which language is used outside the classroom*]. The justification for a French-only in the classroom rule include: 'ils sont dans une école française' [*they are in a French school*]; 'il est normal de parler français' [*it is normal to speak French*]; 'les cours sont en français et la scolarité postérieure à la notre l'est également, donc ils se doivent de parler bien le français. La seule manière est de le pratiquer en classe' [*lessons are in French, as is school education after ours, so they owe it to themselves to speak French well. The only way is to use it in class*]; 'c'est la langue du pays où ils vivent et celle parlée par tous' [*it's the language of the country where they live and the one spoken by everybody*].

The idea of what is 'normal' and acceptable or unacceptable, 'anormal', is also mentioned by another teacher. 'Il semblerait anormal que des élèves scolarisés en France puisse parler l'arabe, l'espagnol ou même le wolof en cours de français' [*it would appear abnormal for children schooled in France to be allowed to speak Arabic, Spanish or even Wolof in French class*]. These teachers are probably right; it is unusual for children to be invited to use a language other than French in a French school. So much so, that when they are asked, for whatever reason, they often view this with suspicion and surprise. The children involved in the languages and culture project in Didenheim (Hélot & Young, 2002, 2006) were initially reluctant and often embarrassed when first asked to share their knowledge with the rest of the class, and the participating Turkish parents were amazed that the school was interested in their language. However, does the fact that it does not currently happen very often mean that it is of no educational value and should be prohibited? Learning is more effective when we can link what we already know to what we are learning (Hedegaard, 2005). If bi/plurilingual children are not allowed to make these links between what has been learnt and encoded in the home language and culture and what is being taught at school, then their learning may not be as successful.

It would appear from the data elicited from initial questions that no distinction is made between different linguistic varieties. One head teacher says that *dialecte*, meaning Alsatian, is not permitted in class, and another mentions the European language Spanish in the same breath as Arabic and Wolof (both spoken in Africa). However, upon examining the responses to further questions, it becomes apparent that German benefits from a different status in the classroom – that of a legitimate foreign language to be learnt at school – but is nevertheless usually confined to timetabled slots. The bilingual education system (French/German) in operation in Alsace also strictly separates the two languages, with a different teacher for each language, teaching at different times/on different days and different subjects taught through each language. This strict separation of languages, with different, distinct spaces for different languages reveals, we believe, a monolingual, uninformed vision of how bilinguals function, namely that languages should occupy two separate spaces and must be kept apart so that there is no mixing, no confusion. Such a vision does not take into account the numerous studies (August & Shanahan, 2006; Bialystok, 2001; Cummins, 2008; Genesee *et al.*, 2006) which have shown that an individual's languages are inextricably linked, that there is an underlying language competence (Cummins *et al.*, 2001) which nurtures both languages and which allows information and skills learnt through one of them to be encoded into the other (provided that the vocabulary to be able to do so has been supplied).

The teachers who adhere to this separate spaces for different languages policy usually believe that by banishing all languages except the language of instruction, the national language in this instance, from the classroom, they are helping the bi/plurilingual children to acquire the majority language. They believe that they will best acquire French by only speaking, hearing and referring to French, which is of course, usually, also the home language of the teacher. They fear that by allowing another language to be used in the classroom the language of instruction will no longer occupy prime position in the languages hierarchy. This fear is completely unfounded. Do children in bilingual sections and schools fail to acquire the language(s) of the school and the surrounding environment in which they live? Yet here we are not even evoking the possibility of bilingual education, but simply the right to speak one's home language in the classroom in order to make connections between the different languages in one's repertoire.

These unfounded fears and beliefs are undoubtedly deep rooted in a monolingual ideology inherited from bygone days of 19th-century nation-state building when citizens were forced to leave behind their regional languages and embrace the single official language of the République. Education was at that time used to develop the national language, outlaw the regional ones and produce future monolingual French citizens. Teachers were responsible as civil servants for ensuring that French was used as the sole language of instruction. It would appear that this responsibility is still felt.

Traces of a monolingual ideology which links language policy with nation building, allegiance to the state and integration into the dominant group are apparent in much of the discourse employed by a number of these teachers. Do teachers feel duty bound as civil servants and representatives of the state to promote the French language to the exclusion of all other languages? Operating within a covert linguistic hierarchy which positions French firmly at the top of the pyramid and the heritage languages of the pupils squarely at the foot of it undoubtedly influences their attitudes and constrains their actions. Could it be that those who still adhere to the belief that 'protection of the language is protection of the nation' (Ager, 1999: 88) view languages other than French as a threat or a problem?

Language as a problem

As previously stated, 19 out of the 46 head teachers interviewed (41%) consistently viewed pupils' home languages as problematic. A majority of 10 out of the 19 viewed use of the home language as being in opposition to mastery of the language of instruction. That is to say, they appeared to believe that use of the home language would detract from competence in French. One teacher distinctly disagreed with the idea of developing plurilingualism at school, arguing that the children were already learning German and 'les enseignantes ont déjà du mal à leur enseigner le français' [*the teachers already have difficulties teaching them French*]. The beliefs that children cannot cope with more than one language at a time and that coming into contact with several languages will confuse them are well known 'bilingual myths' (Grosjean, 2013). It is clear from the discourse of many teachers that they believe the national language to be in some way threatened by the presence of other languages: 'il faut avant tout encourager et tout mettre en œuvre pour que chaque élève ait une bonne maîtrise de notre langue, à savoir le français' [*above all else everything should be encouraged and put into place so that each pupil masters our language, that is to say French, well*]. Another head teacher working in a rural location where some of his pupils speak Alsatian at home maintained:

> il ne faut pas aller trop vite dans l'apprentissage des langues. La première mission de l'Ecole est l'apprentissage de la langue nationale; base de tous les apprentissages ... Le directeur pense donc qu'il serait utile d'encourager le plurilinguisme dans l'école, mais qu'il ne faut pas commencer trop tôt. Les enfants doivent prioritairement assimiler la complexité de leur langue nationale.
>
> [*Learning languages should not be entered into too hastily. Schools' main priority is the teaching of the national language; basis for all learning ...The head teacher thinks therefore that it would be useful to encourage plurilingualism in the school, but that it should not be started too early. The children must assimilate the complexity of their national language as a priority.*]

This head teacher is concerned that other languages may in some way interfere with the learning of the national language, which is central to the primary curriculum.

The reasons which lie behind this preoccupation are linked to the fear that if minority language pupils do not acquire the national language to a sufficient degree, they will fail to integrate/assimilate into mainstream society: 'puisque une majorité d'élèves est d'origine étrangère et ne parle pas encore couramment le français, ils préfèrent les encourager à parler bien le français pour pouvoir bien s'intégrer' [*since a majority of pupils is of foreign origin and do not yet speak French fluently, they prefer to encourage them to speak French well so they can integrate well*]. Another teacher, while maintaining that plurilingualism is a laudable goal and that it can be a positive addition to a curriculum vitae, underlines her reservations thus: 'seulement si nous ne maîtrisons pas la langue du pays dans lequel on vit, on a plus de difficultés à s'y intégrer, car tout le monde sait que la langue est la clé de l'intégration' [*yet if we do not master the language of the country in which we are living, it is more difficult to integrate, because everyone knows that language is the key to integration*]. No-one would advocate the idea that children do not need to learn the language of the country in which they are living. They obviously need to learn this language and learn it quickly if they are to catch up their peers and access learning. However, what is surprising in these statements is the teachers' either/or vision. They appear to believe that either a child maintains her/his home language and therefore will learn the language of instruction less successfully or they will set aside their home language and therefore acquire the language of the school more efficiently. We know from research that this is just not true (August & Shanahan, 2006; Cummins, 2008). Children learn by building on what they already know. It does not make any educational sense to require them to leave their prior knowledge and skills encoded in their home language at the door of the school. As one teacher was quoted as saying 'bien maîtriser une langue permet de mieux apprendre d'autres langues' [*mastering a language well is beneficial for the learning of other languages*].

Unfortunately, this teacher was referring to the mastery of French before any other language. S/he was viewing plurilingualism through a monolingual lens and from her/his own perspective as a native French speaker. Evidence pointing to the ability to decentre and view plurilingualism from a different perspective, a plurilingual one, that of the minority language speaker, is predictably not very common among the teachers who view home languages as a problem. This is also apparent in the way in which these teachers name and talk about languages:

> Certains enfants arrivent en première année de maternelle en pratiquant peu le français car ils n'entendent que parler alsacien dans leur entourage. On ne peut donc pas leur demander d'apprendre une nouvelle langue trop tôt, il faut tout d'abord qu'ils maîtrisent leur langue maternelle. D'après lui on peut commencer à leur faire entendre une autre langue à partir du CP, puis progresser au fur et à mesure des années.

> [*Some children arrive in the first year of nursery with very little French because they only hear Alsatian spoken around them. We can't ask them to learn a new language too early on; they first have to master their mother tongue. According to him, listening to another language can be introduced as from the first year of primary school, then progress as they move up the years.*]

If these children speak Alsatian at home, does this not make Alsatian their 'mother tongue'? For this teacher French is automatically assumed as the mother tongue, his/her own mother tongue perhaps? If the children were to wait until the first grade of primary school to learn a 'new language' (French), it would be considered as outrageous. This may simply be a slip of the tongue, but nevertheless it is a revealing one and not the only one contained in the data which may reveal the teachers' own monolingual perspectives.

Conflicting discourses according to which languages are being discussed is another feature of the data. If the subject of discussion is home languages and the acquisition of French as a second language, the teachers who view them as a problem invariably underline the necessity of guaranteeing successful acquisition of French through sidelining the home language and this as early as possible. If the subject of discussion is the learning of German as a second language through the bilingual (French/German) schooling system in operation in Alsace, quite different arguments are put forward:

> selon elle, l'enfant, à trois ans, serait trop jeune pour lui faire intégrer une seconde langue, d'autant plus si elle lui est complètement étrangère et si l'enfant n'a jamais été à l'école. Selon elle il faudrait attendre que l'enfant ait au moins fait une année scolaire au préalable avant de le mettre en classe bilingue. La directrice m'a également dit que le bilinguisme ou le plurilinguisme ne peut qu'être bénéfique pour l'enfant s'il maîtrise au préalable sa langue maternelle, quelle qu'elle soit. Se serait le facteur déterminant la réussite ou non de l'enfant dans l'apprentissage d'une langue étrangère. Et enfin, elle nuance également les atouts et avantages du plurilinguisme par la critique suivante: 《on aurait tendance à en attendre de trop de la part de ces enfants et à leur mettre une pression supplémentaire par rapport aux autres enfants》.

> [according to her, the three-year-old child is probably too young to integrate a second language, all the more so if it is completely foreign and if the child has never been to school before. According to her it would be better to wait until the child has been at school for at least a year before placing him/her in a bilingual class. The head teacher also told me that bilingualism or plurilingualism can only be beneficial for the child if he masters his mother tongue first, whatever that may be. It would be the factor which conditions the success or not of the child in learning a foreign language. Finally she qualifies the benefits and advantages of plurilingualism with the following comment: 'we probably expect too much from these children and place extra pressure on them compared to other children'.]

Here it would appear that the head teacher believes that children as young as three cannot acquire a second language easily, that they should first acquire their mother tongue before attempting to learn a second language, that professional and perhaps parental expectations are too high and that they need more time to acquire a second language. Much of what this teacher maintains is borne out by the research (Bialystok, 2001; Cummins *et al.*, 2001). It is not an easy feat for anyone to acquire a second language. It requires a great deal of cognitive activity and a considerable amount of time. However, this neither means that it is an impossible endeavour nor that it necessarily has to be a painful one. Concerning whether it is better to learn languages simultaneously or sequentially, allowing the stronger language to develop before a second one is introduced, there is no clear-cut answer. There are benefits from both approaches. However, what we can say from the research is that all the languages in a child's linguistic repertoire should be allowed to contribute to the learning of a new language and no one language should be banned from the classroom and the learning process (García *et al.*, 2006; Genesee *et al.*, 2006). The question of expectations and allowing the child the necessary time to develop his/her languages is a crucial one. If teachers could adjust their expectations in these respects not only with regards to the learning of a second language in a bilingual school programme, but also with respect to the learning of the national language as a second language as in the case of minority language speakers, learning a second language could be a much more pleasant experience and most probably a more efficient one too.

Language as a resource

Yet, there is evidence to suggest that some teachers are adjusting their ideologies in an attempt to adapt to the multilingual reality of current situations in schools in Alsace. Some teachers are beginning to acknowledge the bilingualism of these children and to practise policies of inclusion (Bonacina, 2010) as opposed to ignoring pupils' plurilingual repertoires and characterising them as linguistically deficient. Twenty out of the 46 teachers in our study (43%) viewed the home languages of their pupils as a resource for the minority language pupil and/or the whole class.

With respect to the minority-language speaking pupils, seven teachers out of the whole sample of 46 (15%) spoke of valuing and maintaining linguistic and cultural heritage. Teachers talked of ELCO teaching in positive terms, explaining that it not only allowed these pupils to learn their heritage language but also to acquire accreditation through examinations. Teachers also mentioned the importance of preserving a cultural heritage, 'connaître ses racines' [*knowing one's roots*] 'un lien avec leur culture d'origine' [*a link with their heritage culture*] and facilitating intergenerational communication between non-French speaking family members, notably grandparents. This same teacher also spoke of creating a link between the heritage culture and school, and between families and school, adding that 'ce lien est indispensable pour que l'élève réussisse au mieux' [*this link is essential for pupils to succeed to the best of their abilities*]. One teacher talked about valuing heritage languages and encouraging 'un bilinguisme autre que français/allemande ou français/anglais' [*other forms of bilingualism than French/German or French/English*].

Similar concerns about language maintenance were voiced with respect to regional languages. Head teachers spoke of 'préserver le dialecte' [*preserving the dialect*], 'un enrichissement à la fois historique et linguistique ... sauvegarder ce dialecte qui tend à disparaître au fil des générations, ce qui selon lui est regrettable' [*both a historical and linguistic enrichment ... safeguarding this dialect which tends to disappear with the passing of generations, which according to him is regrettable*], 'une valorisation du patrimoine ... faire vivre les langues régionales, de moins en moins d'élèves parlent le dialecte, parle l'alsacien. Encourager, favoriser le plurilinguisme permettrait de faire perdurer ces langues régionales' [*a valuing of heritage ... support for regional languages, fewer and fewer pupils speak dialect, speak Alsatian. Encouraging plurilingualism would allow these regional languages to endure.*]

Eight head teachers out of the total sample of 46 (17%) spoke of language and cultural awareness raising activities for the benefit of the whole class/school which could be put in place as a result of the linguistic and cultural diversity present at the school. Several teachers supplied specific examples such as exchanging vocabulary in different languages, an annual cultural celebration where parents bring in specialities to taste and decorate the school, a Russian child talking about his old Russian school and Russian culture to the other pupils, teaching new words to friends in heritage languages, or inviting pupils to contribute knowledge acquired outside school during geography classes when the Arab-Muslim world is discussed. Other teachers talked of 'sensibiliser les enfants à la diversité de cultures' [*sensitising children about cultural diversity*], 'découvrir la diversité des origines des unes et des autres' [*discovering the diversity of each other's origins*], 'de découvrir une autre culture et de comprendre leur façon de faire ... d'échanger et de faire partager' [*discovering another culture and understanding their way of doing things ... exchanging and sharing*]. One teacher explained that more than half of the pupils in the school were of foreign origin and as a result 'le plurilingualisme est déjà très présent dans cette école' [*plurilingualism is already very present in this school*] and that as a result the 'contact entre les enfants de divers origines sont enrichissants car cela permet aux enfants de découvrir des cultures différentes de la leur' [*contact between children of diverse origins is enriching as it allows children to discover cultures different from their own*].

Five out of the total sample of 46 head teachers (11%) made reference to heritage languages as a future professional resource for pupils. Speaking several languages, it was thought, would afford greater opportunities in the job market, especially in areas such as tourism and business and would look good on a CV. The languages mentioned by these teachers were European languages (English, German, Spanish), with an emphasis placed on German by several head teachers who referred to the border location of Alsace with Germany. One head teacher said that he encouraged plurilingualism 'mais uniquement pour la langue allemande' [*but only for the German language*]. Only one teacher mentioned heritage languages other than European ones, adding that alongside another modern foreign language such as English or Spanish, they could be 'un atout indéniable dans le travail à l'échelle international' [*an indisputable advantage in an international working environment*].

Five head teachers (11%) also made references to the relationship between the multilingual/multicultural world and school. They talked of plurilingualism as allowing pupils to be 'plus ouvert au monde et aux autres cultures' [*more open to the world and to other cultures*], of countries being 'en constant interaction' [*constantly interacting*], of heritage language teaching contributing to intercultural education, of language learning which 'ouvre la porte sur le monde' [*opens the door onto the world*] and languages representing 'un pont entre les hommes et les cultures' [*a bridge between people and cultures*], creating 'compréhension réciproque' [reciprocal comprehension] and meaning 'entendre les autres peuples et leur manière de penser, de vivre' [*listening to other peoples and their way of thinking and of living*], 'une véritable ouverture au monde' [*a veritable opening up to the world*]. This last head teacher also talked of pupils learning to decentre through learning about other countries, cultures, traditions and ways of life. Another spoke of anti-racist education, maintaining that plurilingualism could help pupils to understand otherness, 'faire taire le racisme et le rejet de certaines minorités. En effet, les enfants pourraient comprendre que chacun est différent avec sa culture et son identité, mais que finalement on se ressemble tous' [*silence racism and the rejection of certain minorities. Indeed, children could understand that everyone is different with their culture and identity, but that at the end of the day we are similar*]. One teacher raised the issue of self-esteem and feeling proud of one's heritage, and effectively argued that heritage language teaching, contrary to some beliefs, does not encourage cultural segregation and entrenchment but 'leur permet de se découvrir et de se créer une identité propre au sein de la France' [*allows them to discover themselves and to create their own identities within France*].

However, one head teacher analyses the challenges currently facing schools with respect to plurilingualism thus:

> ... le plurilinguisme est un atout scolaire, du moins pour les langues européennes. C'est vrai qu'à l'école, on ne prend pas en compte des différentes langues qui peuvent être parlées dans la classe. Je pense que peut-être il faudrait mettre en place un système qui favorise ses différents parlés et qui peuvent même apporter des points aux élèves. Mais, cela doit être difficile à établir puisque l'école se fait en français exclusivement et non dans une autre langue. Pour répondre à votre question, je pense qu'effectivement il faut encourager le plurilinguisme, comment je ne sais pas puisque cela semble être difficile en France. Nous avons déjà des cours de langue vivante à partir de la maternelle dans certain établissement, que faire de plus? Et puis les autres langues étrangères ne sont pas admises en classe ... Alors oui il faut encourager le plurilinguisme en

France mais il faut aussi alors trouver des façons de le faire, ce qui me semble plus difficile.

[... *plurilingualism is an advantage at school, at least for European languages. It's true to say that at school we do not take into consideration the different languages which may be spoken in class. I think that perhaps it would be a good idea to set up a system which fosters these different spoken varieties and which could even give pupils extra points. But that must be difficult to set up because school is conducted exclusively in French and not in another language. To reply to your question, I think that indeed plurilingualism should be encouraged, how I don't know since it appears to be difficult in France. We already have foreign language classes from nursery school age in some schools, what more can we do? And then the other foreign languages are not allowed in class.... So yes plurilingualism should be encouraged in France, but ways have to be found to do it, which seems to me more difficult.*]

In his response he acknowledges the difficulties in any endeavour to break down barriers between languages and to attempt to redress the balance so that all the language varieties used by pupils receive the same respect and are regarded as important factors in the education of a pupil.

Only one teacher in the sample mentioned the cognitive benefits of bilingualism. Interestingly, this was also the only head teacher who referred to research findings.

Seeing Through New Lenses, Changing Perspectives

It is interesting to note traces of conflicting discourses within the data, inasmuch as while many teachers openly and positively acknowledge plurilingual competence, they also question the value and/or legitimacy of their pupils' home languages at school. Is this a case of elite, prestigious bilingualism in dominant European languages versus the bilingualism of the migration masses? As we suggested earlier in this chapter, perhaps, having internalised the dominant monolingual perspective, the teachers' language lenses are monolingually biased. It could be that as products themselves of a school system rooted in the 19th century language ideologies, they are in turn reproducing the monolingual norm. We believe that teachers could be key actors in the evolution of the language lens through which pupils' languages are ignored or acknowledged, judged as an asset or as a deficit, supported or outlawed. Teachers can and should play a key role in bridging the gap between home and school, be these linguistic and/or cultural bridges. Super-diversity is a reality for an increasing number of schools. We cannot continue to work in schools of the 21st century looking through language lenses inherited from a bygone age and hope to make progress. Our 21st-century pupils need informed professionals to help them make sense of an increasingly complex and interlinked world.

Findings underline the need for teacher educators to develop courses which adopt a critical language awareness approach (Alim, 2010), allowing teachers to uncover, analyse and question language ideologies, to become aware of their own positions in the world, to address and negotiate tensions and empowering them with knowledge and pedagogies so that they may become agents of change in the multilingual classroom (Hélot & Ó Laoire, 2011). Exploring teacher attitudes and ideologies about languages may lead us to a deeper understanding of what Borg terms 'teacher cognition ... what teachers know, believe and think' (Borg, 2003: 81). Teacher cognition pertaining to the rights, resources and needs of heritage language pupils is an appropriate starting point upon which teacher education programmes seeking to raise language awareness can build. Looking through teachers' languages lenses, be they monolingually tainted or plurilingually tinted, may contribute to rendering such courses more relevant to participants. Courses designed to incorporate complex issues about which participants may hold strong opinions and opening them up to debate and critical examination among educators through a problem-based learning and/or collaborative approach (Mary & Young, 2010) may contribute to an evolution in the way educators think about languages in the interests of equity and social justice for all their pupils.

References

Académie de Strasbourg (2012a) *L'académie de Strasbourg les chiffres clé. Année scolaire 2011–2012 et rentrée 2012.* Strasbourg: L'Académie de Strasbourg.

Académie de Strasbourg (2012b) *Nombre de nationalités présentes dans le dispositif ELCO 67. Année scolaire 2009–2010.* Strasbourg: L' Académie de Strasbourg.

Ager, D.E. (1999) *Identity, Insecurity and Image: France and Language.* Clevedon: Multilingual Matters.

Albertini, P. (1992) *Les Ecoles en France IXX aux XX siècles.* Paris: Hachette.

Alim, H.S. (2010) Critical language awareness. In N.H. Hornberger and S.L. McKay (eds) *Sociolinguistics and Language Education* (pp. 205–231). Bristol: Multilingual Matters.

August, D. and Shanahan, T. (eds) (2006) *Developing Literacy in Second-language Learners: Report of the National Literacy Panel on Language Minority Children and Youth.* Mahwah, NJ: Lawrence Erlbaum.

Banks, J.A. (2011) Educating citizens in diverse societies. *Intercultural Education* 22 (4), 243–251.

Beacco, J.-C. and Byram, M. (2007) *Guide for the Development of Language Education Policies in Europe* (final version). Strasbourg: Council of Europe.

Bialystok, E. (2001) *Bilingualism in Development: Language, Literacy, and Cognition.* Cambridge: Cambridge University Press.

Bonacina, F. (2010) A conversation analytic approach to practiced language policies: The example of an induction classroom for newly-arrived immigrant children in France. PhD thesis, University of Edinburgh.

Borg, S. (2003) Teacher cognition in language teaching: A review of research on what language teachers think, know, believe, and do [Review article]. *Language Teaching* 36 (2), 81–109.

Cajkler, W. and Hall, B. (2012) Multilingual primary classrooms: An investigation of first year teachers' learning and responsive teaching. *European Journal of Teacher Education* 35 (2), 213–228.

Cavalli, M., Coste, D., Crisan, A. and van de Ven, P.-H. (2009) *Plurilingual and Intercultural Education as a Project*. Strasbourg: Language Policy Division, Council of Europe. See www.coe.int/t/dg4/Linguistic/Source/LE_texts_Source/EducPlurInter-Projet_en.doc (accessed 20 August 2014).

Charaudeau, P. (2001) Langue, discours et identité culturelle. *Ela – Etudes de linguistique appliquée* 123–124 (3/4), 341–348.

Charles, F. and Legendre, F. (2006) *Les enseignants issus des immigrations: Modalités d'accès au groupe professionnel, représentations du métier et de l'école*. Paris: Sudel.

Couëtoux-Jungman, F., Wendland, J., Aidane, E., Rabain, D., Plaza, M. and Lécuyer, R. (2010) Bilinguisme, plurilinguisme et petite enfance: Intérêt de la prise en compte du contexte linguistique de l'enfant dans l'évaluation et le soin des difficultés de développement précoce. *Devenir* 22 (4), 293–307.

Cummins, J. (2008) Teaching for transfer: Challenging the two solitudes assumption in bilingual education. In J. Cummins and N.H. Hornberger (eds) *Encyclopedia of Language and Education, Vol. 5* (pp. 65–76). New York: Springer.

Cummins, J., Baker, C. and Hornberger, N.H. (2001) *An Introductory Reader to the Writings of Jim Cummins*. Clevedon: Multilingual Matters.

EDUSCOL (2012a) *Maîtrise de la langue française*. See http://eduscol.education.fr/pid26179/c-maitrise-langue-francaise.html (accessed 20 August 2014).

EDUSCOL (2012b) *Enseigner les langues vivantes à l'école élémentaire*. See http://eduscol.education.fr/cid45718/enseigner-les-langues-a-l-ecole.html (accessed 20 August 2014).

Frey, Y. (2009) *Ces Alsaciens venus d'ailleurs. Cent cinquante ans d'immigration en Alsace*. Nancy: Edition Place Stanislas.

García, O., Skutnabb-Kangas, T. and Torres-Guzmán, M.E. (eds) (2006) *Imagining Multilingual Schools: Languages in Education and Glocalization*. Clevedon: Multilingual Matters.

Genesee, F., Lindholm-Leary, K., Saunders, W.L. and Christian, D. (2006) *Educating English Language Learners: A Synthesis of Research Evidence*. Cambridge: Cambridge University Press.

Grosjean, F. (2013) *Myths About Bilingualism*. See http://www.francoisgrosjean.ch/myths_en.html (accessed 20 August 2014).

Harrison, G. (2007) Language as a problem, a right or a resource? *Journal of Social Work* 7 (1), 71–92.

Hedegaard, M. (2005) The zone of proximal development as a basis for instruction. In H. Daniels (ed.) *An Introduction to Vygotsky* (pp. 227–252). London: Routledge.

Hélot, C. and Ó Laoire, M. (2011) *Language Policy for the Multilingual Classroom Pedagogy of the Possible*. Bristol: Multilingual Matters.

Hélot, C. and Young, A. (2002) Bilingualism and language education in French primary schools: Why and how should migrant languages be valued? *International Journal of Bilingual Education and Bilingualism* 5 (2), 96–112.

Hélot, C. and Young, A.S. (2006) Imagining multilingual education in France: A language and cultural awareness project at primary level. In T. Skutnabb-Kangas, O. García and M.E. Torres Guzman (eds) *Imagining Multilingual Schools: Languages in Education and Glocalization* (pp. 69–90). Clevedon: Multilingual Matters.

Hornberger, N.H. and McKay, S.L. (eds) (2010) *Sociolinguistics and Language Education*. Bristol: Multilingual Matters.

Huck, D., Bothorel-Witz, A. and Geiger-Jaillet, A. (2005) *Rapport sur la situation linguistique en Alsace (France)*. Project 'Language Bridges', a sub-theme working group of the Interreg IIIC project 'Change on Borders'. See http://ala.u-strasbg.fr/documents/Publication-L'Alsace et ses langues.pdf (accessed 20 August 2014)

INSEE (2010) *Naissances selon le pays de naissance des parents*. Institut national de la statistique et des études économiques. See http://www.insee.fr/fr/themes/tableau. asp?reg_id=0&ref_id=NAISLIEUNAISPAR (accessed 20 August 2014).

Lemaire, E. (2009) Education, integration, and citizenship in France. In J.A. Banks (ed.) *The Routledge International Companion to Multicultural Education* (pp. 323–333). London: Routledge.

Mary, L. and Young, A. (2010) Preparing teachers for the multilingual classroom: Nurturing reflective, critical awareness. In S.H. Ehrhart, C. Hélot and A. Le Nevez (eds) *Plurilinguisme et formation des enseignants: Une approche critique/Plurilingualism and Teacher Education: A Critical Approach* (pp. 195–219). Frankfurt: Peter Lang.

Moro, M.-R. (2004) *Enfants d'ici venus d'ailleurs: naître et grandir en France*. Paris: Hachette.

Murakami, C. (2008) 'Everybody is just fumbling along': An investigation of views regarding EAL training and support provisions in a rural area. *Language and Education* 22 (4), 265–282.

OECD (2010) *OECD Reviews of Migrant Education – Closing the Gap for Immigrant Students: Policies, Practice and Performance*. Paris: Organisation for Economic Cooperation and Development.

ORIV (2011) Actualités sur … l'intégration, la promotion de l'égalité et la ville. *Bulletin d'information de l'observatoire régionale de l'intégration et de la ville* 63.

RERS (2011) *Repères et références statistiques sur les enseignements, la formation et la recherche*. See http://media.education.gouv.fr/file/2011/01/4/DEPP-RERS-2011_190014.pdf (accessed 20 August 2014)

RERS (2012) *Repères et références statistiques sur les enseignements, la formation et la recherche*. See http://cache.media.education.gouv.fr/file/2012/36/9/DEPP-RERS-2012_223369.pdf (accessed 20 August 2014)

Ruiz, R. (1984) Orientations in language planning. *NABE: Journal for the National Association for Bilingual Education* 8 (2), 15–34.

Starkey, H. (2011) Citizenship, education and global spaces. *Language and Intercultural Communication* 11 (2), 75–79.

UNESCO (2003) *Education in a Multilingual World*. UNESCO Education Position Paper. Paris: UNESCO.

UNESCO (2011) *Enhancing Learning of Children from Diverse Language Backgrounds: Mother Tongue-based Bilingual or Multilingual Education in the Early Years*. Paris: UNESCO. See http://unesdoc.unesco.org/images/0021/002122/212270e.pdf (accessed 20 August 2014).

UNICEF (2007) *Education Rights and Minorities*. Florence: Minority rights group international. See http://www.unicef-irc.org/publications/pdf/minorities_rights.pdf (accessed 20 August 2014).

Vertovec, S. (2010) Towards post-multiculturalism? Changing communities, conditions and contexts of diversity. *International Social Science Journal* 61 (199), 83–95.

Wiley, T. (2008) Language policy and teacher education. In S. May and N.H. Hornberger (eds) *Encyclopedia of Language Education, Vol. 1* (pp. 229–241). New York: Springer.

Young, A. and Hélot, C. (2003) Language awareness and/or language learning in French primary schools today. *Language Awareness* 12 (3/4), 234–246.

Young, A.S. and Hélot, C. (2007) Parent power: Parents as a linguistic and cultural resource at school. In A. Camilleri Grima (ed.) *Ensemble: Promoting Linguistic Diversity and Whole-School Development* (pp. 17–32). Strasbourg and Graz: Council of Europe and European Centre for Modern Languages.

Part 2

Perspectives on the Multilingual Turn in Education

Jean Conteh

Following the broader societal perspectives on the multilingual turn which were discussed in Part 1, in Part 2 of the book we move closer to classrooms and to the complexities of teaching and learning. The chapters in this part all consider how education systems in different social, historical and political contexts make sense of the multilingual turn, and the implications for languages education. The first two chapters focus on policy and curriculum and the second two focus on teaching and learning. In this way, we begin to see how the multilingual turn has been and can be conceptualized in particular school structures and curricula, both from the perspectives of the individuals within them and more widely. As in Part 1, the chapters raise issues about the implications of the multilingual turn for all members of society, not just those who may be categorized as 'multilingual'. Readers are invited to consider the relevance of the chapters and the implications for the educational contexts that are most familiar to them.

The four chapters offer different approaches to and perspectives on understanding the multilingual turn: the first two from the outer layers of society, policy and curriculum development, and the second two from the inner layers of particular schools, classrooms and the experiences of their participants. **Chapter 5** (Gajo) and **Chapter 6** (Meier) provide theoretical and pedagogic perspectives on the issues from more global viewpoints, developed by researchers taking – arguably – 'outsider' stances, while **Chapter 7** (Conteh, Copland & Creese) and **Chapter 8** (Meier) provide important evidence from the 'insiders' – that is, the teachers and learners – in a range of contexts.

The chapters also offer examples of different approaches to researching the multilingual turn. Chapters 5 and 6 review the development of theory, policy documentation and – in Chapter 6 – curriculum materials through critically analysing the existing research, policy and pedagogic literature. They also identify the implications for other contexts. A key message here is the need to understand how the multilingual turn needs to be understood, situated in particular social, historical and political contexts. Chapters 7 and 8 are more directly empirical, presenting findings from different research studies and showing the contributions that can be made in the field by different kinds of research. Chapter 7 reports from three, very different, small-scale, detailed classroom-based studies, and Chapter 8 from broader survey research. Both chapters add to our understanding of the multilingual turn and the benefits for individuals and societies. In this way, we show how the issues need to be – and perhaps can only be – understood from different kinds of evidence generated using a wide range of research methodologies and data collection strategies.

Generic questions for Part 2

- What kinds of research approaches and questions offer the most productive ways of understanding the reciprocal links between society and education?
- What do you think 'multilingual pedagogies' need to include?

5 From Normalization to Didactization of Multilingualism: European and Francophone Research at the Crossroads Between Linguistics and Didactics

Laurent Gajo

Guiding Questions

- To what extent is the didactics of plurilingualism not only a new trend within L2 didactics but a new paradigm in education?
- Is research on multilingualism a means to develop a new understanding of what a language is?
- What are the issues of language alternation in the curriculum and in classroom interaction?

Introduction

This chapter does not intend to analyze data gathered in a specific 'terrain', but will examine the conditions under which the notion of the *didactics of plurilingualism* emerged in the European social and scientific context.

The increasing intensity of Francophone research on multilingualism is measured, including the abundance of terms, well exceeding the opposition between *plurilingualism* and *multilingualism*, highlighting at the same time both the diversity of points of view and the complexity of the field. This Francophone creativity is also reflected in the terminology within the so-called didactics of plurilingualism, an expression that is struggling to find an English equivalent. Moreover, the problem of terminology is also linked to the non-specificity and metaphorical character of given terms (e.g. *immersion*).

The progress of Francophone and European research between 1982 and 2012 seems to be articulated in two main phases: a phase of the standardization/recognition (normalization) of plurilingualism and a phase of its didactization. The first one grew widely in the 1980s. In the 1990s and beyond it revisits gradually the notions of language and communication skills in order to propose new notions, such as bilingual speech and plurilingual competence or even plurilingual resources. The didactization phase starts to develop in the late 1990s to be deployed mainly in the following decade, through the notions of the didactics of plurilingualism or pluralistic approaches to languages and cultures. In the course of these developments, the need to ponder the role of social representations in the definition and didactization of plurilingualism becomes clear. In all these areas (recognition of plurilingualism, social representations and plurilingual teaching), linguistics plays a major role, in relation to sociolinguistics, social psychology and, above all, didactics, while North American research is generally anchored in the field of education.

These trends should not, however, hide the heterogeneity and tensions within the Francophone research on plurilingualism. Both the level of acceptability and meanings of plurilingualism vary and the contextual effects are central. Thus, the didactics of plurilingualism can be promoted in order to reject, in an acceptable way, a given language, or to value another one, or even to develop an alternative in language education. Talking about *plurilingualismS* (in the plural form) is therefore very useful, as is the fact of documenting actual teaching practices.

After tracing the main steps of Francophone and European research on plurilingualism and 'its' didactics, we will focus on the case of bilingual education. More specifically, we will show how a tool developed in linguistic theories, that of code-switching (language alternation), can be enriched by a didactic perspective in order to allow a reasoned and nuanced articulation between language practices, teaching strategies and socio-educational contexts. Before concluding, we intend to emphasize, through the notion of social representation, the ideological dimension of 'talking about multilingualism'. In the conclusion, we will make the argument for the contextualized didactics of plurilingualism and for a theoretical perspective balanced between reification and contextualization.

Terminological issues

Talking about languages in contact is not so easy and requires the use of a wide range of terms which tend to relate to specific concepts, theories or research traditions. First, it should be noticed that the terms themselves are given various connotations according to the context or to the period in which they are used. For example, the Latin word 'bilinguis' not only refers to 'bilingualism' but also to 'unreliability' (Colin, 2004; Py & Gajo, 2013). This negative perspective could probably explain some major orientations in the research on bilingualism until the first part of the 20th century (Baker, 1988, talks about a period of negative effects of bilingualism). Nowadays, even if bilingualism has developed as a strong field of research with its own tools, the connotation effects are still important and the current period of positive effects is seen by certain scholars as 'ideology-driven'.

Nevertheless, scientific creativity takes advantage of the Latin and Greek derivation to propose slight differences in the research field on languages in contact. The well-known opposition between 'bilingualism' and 'diglossia' is nowadays widespread and shared among international researchers. Other terms, more hybrid in their composition, are less used but still very interesting. This is the case for the French notion of 'polylectalisme', proposed by Berrendonner *et al.* (1983) in order to focus on the intralinguistic variation (registers). Thanks to the terminology, intralinguistic variation can thus be put in parallel with interlinguistic variation, both being considered as two degrees of the same phenomenon. This helps in the process involving the normalization and didactization of multilingualism, as we will see below.

In the European tradition, the main terminological difference concerns the use of 'multilingualism' and 'plurilingualism' (Beacco *et al.*, 2010; CoE, 2001; Moore & Gajo, 2009), the latter being much more common in the Francophone scientific community. The former refers to the societal level, whereas the latter refers to the individual. Such a distinction helps our understanding of the specific issues concerning languages in contact at both levels. In Europe, applied research on multilingualism became more intensive after WWII and supported European construction as a pacified and unified body. Hence, the problem has to be considered primarily at the societal level. Alongside this process there is the decolonization process which particularly affects the French-speaking world. Maintaining the position of the French language can also occur only with a strong reflection on linguistic diversity at the geopolitical level. Nevertheless, individual plurilingualism remains an important issue for the 'Francophony' as well as for the European perspective, since it is at the same time the condition for, and the consequence of, societal multilingualism.

Languages in Contact: Three Levels of Comprehension

Beyond terminology, research dealing with languages in contact has produced evidence of the useful distinction between societal and individual levels. Moreover, a third level of investigation progressively evolves, namely that of institutions. We can therefore argue for a three-level organization of research on multilingualism:

- *macro-level* (societal): issues are conceived of in terms of language diversity; even if a rate of diversity can be measured and a territory declared as more or less multilingual, diversity is the norm;
- *meso-level* (institutional): issues are conceived of in terms of diversification; this process comprises strategies of recognition of social diversity; it can be undertaken by schools, administrations, media, companies, etc.;
- *micro-level* (individual): issues are conceived of in terms of identity and resources; languages in contact question the individual in two main directions, his or her values (the feeling of 'otherness') and his or her ability to communicate (the plurilingual repertoire).

The institutional level is crucial to implementing a language policy. For example, increasing individual plurilingualism through schooling necessitates, at the very first stage, raising awareness of diversity by making languages and cultures just visible, in the social environment and in the classroom. Such a visibility is the initial condition for recognizing multilingualism as a fact, then as a value and, finally, as a possible added value.

In the following section, before going back to the meso-level and the 'didactization' of plurilingualism, we intend to describe the process of its normalization at the crossroads of macro- and micro-levels.

Towards the Normalization of Plurilingualism

The phase of normalization lies in an in-depth description of plurilingual practices in their social context and took place in the 1980s and the 1990s. There are three main dimensions of the research which support this process (Lüdi, 2011):

(a) The variationist perspective is developing in opposition to a (mono-)normative scientific heritage.
(b) The holistic perspective creates a new point of view on plurilingualism, usually seen as an addition of monolingual skills (isolationist perspective).
(c) The interactionist perspective focuses on plurilingualism as resulting from situated practices and departs from a decontextualized perspective.

The variationist perspective (a) allows for a better understanding of the actual language practices of a speech community (Coseriu, 1973/1966; Labov, 1976). Sociolinguistic research is conducted in different areas and stimulates a critical analysis of the social norms. In the Francophone field, large-scale inquiries are carried out and notions such as 'polycentric norms' or 'plurinormalistic processing' (Marcellesi *et al.*, 1985) are proposed. Slight differences between 'unity' and 'unicity' contribute to a new perspective on language description, keeping together the language as a coherent entity (unity) and its varieties as equally important components. The French notion of *polylectalisme* (see above) fits into this perspective. The variationist point of view is not, however, sufficient to capture the very nature of plurilingualism, as it takes for granted the boundaries of a speech community (Lüdi, 2011), whose definition often relies on a top-down perspective. Furthermore, if these communities are heterogeneous in terms of language varieties, they are oriented towards a common language. Consequently, a more fine-grained analysis should take place in order to understand better the speaker's practices and his or her possible experiences not only with language varieties but also with a variety of languages.

The holistic perspective (b) tends to describe the speaker's territory in its complexity and heterogeneity. Languages are coming into contact in given speech communities through the plurilingual experiences of their members. Various theoretical fields are of help in identifying a new perspective on multilingual communities and plurilingual social practices. First, based on Weinreich's (1953) work on language contact, a new trend is progressively developing in sociolinguistics (see the recent research of Borel, 2012, on languages in contact and in contrast). Particular features of bilingual communities are pointed out. For example, Ladmiral (1982) proposes the notion of *communauté di-linguistique*, which is composed of three speakers' groups: monolinguals in one language, monolinguals in another language, and bilinguals. Second, in the early 1980s, strong research and various experiments were carried out by psycholinguists on the bilingual speaker (see, in particular, Grosjean, 1982 and, for recent developments, Grosjean, 2010). In this area, Grosjean's work contributed to developing a specific point of view (bilingual point of view) on bilingual practices, which are not considered as resulting from an addition of monolingual practices (monolingual point of view). The bilingual speaker is able to switch from a bilingual to a monolingual mode of communication in relation to the task being conducted. Third, in the same decade the field of applied linguistics began to focus on bilingualism as a specific issue to be linked, on the one hand, to second language acquisition and, on the other hand, to the description of bilingual discourse. Swiss linguists Lüdi and Py initiated different research projects in this area (Lüdi, 1987; Lüdi & Py, 1984, 1986, 2003). Notions such as 'bilingual speech' ('parler bilingue') and 'transcodic marks' ('marques transcodiques') were developed to show how the bilingual speakers actually behave in communication and to normalize their specific discourse marks. These marks are given different functions according to the communicative setting. In order to differentiate clearly situations where speakers are learning a second language (L2) and others where they are sharing the same bilingual repertoire as their partners, an important distinction is elaborated between exolingual (Porquier, 1984) and bilingual situations (the model is more complex, with two axes: endolingual/exolingual and unilingual/bilingual; see De Pietro, 1988; Lüdi, 1993; Py, 1991). Such descriptions contribute to a departure from a normative view of language as a stable and impenetrable system, and instead legitimate the speaker's practices as being part of a complex and coherent linguistic repertoire.

The interactionist perspective (c) considers language as an activity that takes place and makes sense in social contexts and interpersonal communi-cation. As a 'situated practice', language is seen not only as a linguistic com-petence but also as a communicative one (see Hymes, 1972, and Hymes, 1984 for the French version) or, in other terms, as a practice rather than as a struc-ture (Lüdi, 2011). The notion of 'contextualization' becomes central and goes beyond the one of context (Gajo & Mondada, 2000; Porquier & Py, 2004), which can refer either to the social situation (macro-context) or to the com-municative task being interactively conducted (micro-context). At the indi-vidual level, extending the 'situationist' perspective (macro-context) to the interactionist one (micro-context) means adopting terms such as 'partici-pant', 'social actor', 'agent' or, in the French tradition, *(co-)énonciateur*. Therefore, grasping language as a process requires new descriptive tools, and the same occurs with bilingual speech. In this perspective, the notion of 'languaging', recently adapted to bilingual communication as 'translanguag-ing' (Baker, 2001; García, 2008) or 'multilanguaging' (Lüdi, 2011) is greatly of assistance. García's definition of 'translanguaging' might be situated at the crossroads between the interactionist and the holistic perspective:

> For us, translanguaging includes but extends what others have called language use and language contact among bilinguals. Rather than focus-ing on the language itself and how one or the other might relate to the way in which a monolingual standard is used and has been described, the concept of translanguaging makes obvious that there are no clear-cut boundaries between the language of bilinguals. (García, 2008: 47)

In the current decade, such a perspective on plurilingualism is shared by a growing number of researchers, who propose and develop such notions as 'poly-lingual languaging' (Jørgensen, 2008) or 'metrolingualism' (Otsuji & Pennycook, 2010). This shift raises very interesting terminological issues and shows that terms such as 'bilingualism' are still anchored in a monolingual and normative view on language, whereas the situated perspective argues for 'languaging' as a practice resulting from interactional choices and using communicative tools beyond the usual boundaries of a given language. Nevertheless, this context-bound perspective on language is mostly related to everyday or 'street' language (see, for example, the paradigm of urban sociolinguistics) – and to the negotia-tion of complex identities – and does not necessarily capture the specific features and constraints of institutional contexts, in which actors are supposed to use given codes and are considered as more or less competent. Moreover, taking into account not only the practices but also the social representations (see below) could reveal that 'normativity' (versus 'norm') still is a complex problem to deal with in plurilingual communication.

The notion of resource probably offers a possible way to articulate situated choices and social determinations (expectations), as in the following statement:

> The plurilingual speaker is comprehended as a social actor who develops a repertoire made up of various languages and varieties of languages, and different forms of knowledge. These resources constitute linguistic and cultural capital and multiple forms of investment. They can take contrasting values in different contexts, and they involve intentions that cannot be reduced to regulating norms. (Moore & Gajo, 2009: 142)

Variationist, holistic and interactionist perspectives together help in the grounding of bilingualism (and, by extension, multi- and plurilingualism) as a specific but interconnected field in social sciences, triggering the articulation between individuals and social contexts. Key notions such as 'plurilingual repertoire' (Coste & Simon, 2009), 'plurilingual resources' (Lüdi & Py, 2009) and, above all, 'plurilingual competence' (Castellotti & Moore, 2011, for a recent discussion) are developed:

> Plurilingual and pluricultural competence refers to the ability to use languages for the purposes of communication and to take part in intercultural interaction, where a person, viewed as a social agent has proficiency, of varying degrees, in several languages and experience of several cultures. This is not seen as the superposition or juxtaposition of distinct competences, but rather as the existence of a complex or even composite competence on which the user may draw. (CoE, 2001: 168)

All these notions are discussed as a common set of theoretical tools among researchers, but they are also considered to be critical issues in political and educational actions. Although multilingualism is progressively regarded as a new norm in social organization, individuals are usually building up their plurilingual competence by dealing with various monolingual communicative tasks through complex trajectories. If a certain degree of separation between languages helps to stimulate plurilingual repertoires, a global view of the speaker's trajectory (Coste, 2006) is needed in order not to cancel any recognition of the plurilingual competence as an issue per se. Precisely at this level enters the role of education, operating at the intersection between social and individual issues. In this respect, recent European work (Beacco et al., 2010) has shown the opportunity to integrate the concept of the school curriculum into the wider perspective of an experiential curriculum, which takes into account all social experiences that are potentially oriented to learning. This is particularly relevant to languages education, as language often is the principal medium of learning episodes and, in many cases, is an issue in itself.

Towards the Didactization of Plurilingualism

After having explained the main lines of the changing perspective on language diversity and, thus, on language in general, we would now like to analyze the conditions under which the descriptive tools developed in that new perspective can be 'didactized' in order to fit into the educational system. As envisaged above, plurilingualism does not correspond to a stable state, and even less so to the final outcome of an acquisition process. Plurilingual practices vary and configure scalable language learning resources. If these basic assumptions are important to orient the didactization process, understanding the mechanism of plurilingualism also assumes a link with the conditions of its acquisition and its placement, notably in educational settings.

European research has progressively developed in the last two decades the notion of the 'didactics of plurilingualism', primarily supported by French-speaking and German-speaking networks (see the paradigm of 'Mehrsprachigkeitsdidaktik' and its links to the theories of L3 acquisition and language transfer; Candelier, 2008). This is a bottom-up movement, which first tends to grasp the specific features of new educational trends that cannot be analyzed as being part of the field of second language theories and practices. Such a perspective, from a Francophone standpoint, can be anchored in earlier research conducted under a variationist and social paradigm, be it monolingual or bilingual. For example, Marcellesi et al. (1985), proposed to develop a 'language-variation pedagogy' ('pédagogie de la variation langagière'): 'Il s'agit donc de passer d'une politique hégémonique de la langue, fondée sur une pédagogie de l'unicité, à une dialectique de l'un et du multiple, du commun et de la variation' [It is thus necessary to depart from a hegemonic perspective on language, based on a pedagogy of homogeneity, in order to adopt a dialectic of the one and the multiple, of the standard and the variation] (Marcellesi et al., 1985: 1, our translation). Other researchers focus their work on languages in contact within migrant communities and propose to integrate a social dimension into the field of second languages education by elaborating a 'languages sociodidactics' ('sociodidactique des langues'; Dabène, 1994).

The didactics of plurilingualism: Basic principles

Today, the notion of the 'didactics of plurilingualism', recently called by Blanchet and Coste (2010) the *didactique de la pluralité linguistique* (Billiez, 1998;

Gajo, 2009; Moore, 2006) appears to be an umbrella term for various 'pluralistic approaches' (see Candelier, 2008). Before briefly presenting these approaches, we would like to identify some common basic principles:

- *integration of language contact into the didactic model*: languages are considered to be naturally in contact, socially and/or according to L2 learning processes; this contact cannot be consigned to the periphery of linguistic curricula, and cannot be defined in isolation from the latter;
- *plurilingualism as an end and a means*: if the command of a plural repertoire remains a fundamental goal in language didactics, the didactics of plurilingualism afford plurilingualism the status of 'competence under construction', quickly determining successive learning and reinforced around the clock;
- *accounting for L2 as a taught and as a teaching language in contact*: if L2 continues to function as a taught subject, it has to be envisaged in terms of how it relates to the other languages present in the school curriculum and in the students' repertoires; furthermore, in given cases, L2 also steps in as a teaching language for different subjects and scholastic tasks (bilingual education) and thus raises new issues.

These characteristics help us to understand to what extent the emerging approaches related to them cannot be simply embedded within L2 pedagogy. Such approaches could be organized into two main categories: education for plurilingualism and plurilingual education. This distinction was used by Beacco *et al.* (2010) and then abandoned. As it is an important heuristic opposition for us, we intend to keep it and to rephrase the two categories as 'teaching plurilingualism' and 'plurilingual teaching'. The first aims, above all, for the emergence of a favourable attitude towards languages, cultures and their diversity. Education hopes to create citizens who are not just linguistically competent but also tolerant and open; as such, this homes in on attitudes and social representations – a construction of a specific vision of bilingualism, breaking with conceptualizations of languages which are purely cumulative. The second aims for the development of a student's plural repertoire by the situating of resources; it works on practices. Plurilingual teaching and teaching plurilingualism both account for language contact, but in the first it is employed in an upfront manner, as it were, with contact predisposed, while the second theorizes contact and directly rests on the notion of contact. On the contrary, in a 'traditional' L2 pedagogy, contact remains virtual, not integrated into didactic theory and sometimes even avoided. In relation to contact phenomena, the approach is situated down the line, so to speak. Like L2 pedagogy, plurilingual teaching concerns the development of communicative competence. Nevertheless, like teaching plurilingualism, it involves a global and joined-up perspective on languages, seen within the framework of the plural repertoire.

The didactics of plurilingualism: Main approaches

Languages in contact can be approached in different ways:

- working *towards* languages in contact: it refers to 'teaching plurilingualism' and involves approaches like intercultural pedagogy or language awareness;
- working *on* and *with* languages in contact: it refers to 'plurilingual teaching' and involves intercomprehension between closely related languages and integrated pedagogy;
- working *in* or *through* languages in contact: it concerns content-based teaching or, more specifically, bilingual education (content and language integrated learning, CLIL).

Intercultural pedagogy traditionally deals with migrant languages. However, it results from a fairly large category bringing together methods which aim to work *from* and *on* the social representations of diverse cultural and/or linguistic groups. Intercultural pedagogy envisions plurilingualism as a value to be understood primarily from the point of view of its social reality, and often intertwines with ethical considerations; it aims for a sensitization, an awareness, which can be separated from the effective development of linguistic resources.

While based on portrayals and eulogizing an open attitude towards diversity, *language awareness* (Candelier, 2003, on the European EVLANG project; Perregaux *et al.*, 2003, on the Swiss EOLE project) focuses more on languages themselves and prepares for practice by the stimulation of the linguistic consciousness (notably, the tracking of language learning mechanisms by language comparison). As such, it is not just sensitization which is aimed for, but also basic linguistic education, proposing a form of integration into the didactic model of language contact.

Based on the development of intercomprehension facilitated between languages of the same family (such as Romance languages), *intercomprehension* or *neighbouring language didactics* (Escudé & Janin, 2010) deals first and foremost with practices and, in particular, with comprehension, written and/or spoken. This approach contributes to the development of interlinguistic learning strategies and facilitates some saving of time in the simultaneous or consecutive learning of several languages.

Primarily understood as an approach combining L1 and L2 (Roulet, 1980), *integrated pedagogy* is today expanded to an approach common to the different languages of a given curriculum (Brohy & Rezgui, 2008). It results principally from L2 didactics, but is realigned by a simultaneous recognition of multiple linguistic curricula. It can perhaps be understood, more widely, as coordinated didactics, dealing not only with the plurality of languages but also with the plurality of approaches within the curriculum; in this case, it could be considered as a synonym for the didactics of plurilingualism.

Finally, *bilingual education* consists of using an L2 as a teaching language in one or more disciplines within the curriculum, such as mathematics, history or biology (García, 2008). Principally centred on the development of multilingual practices, it puts the issue of bilingualism at the heart of the school subjects, a setting thought to favour the use and learning of languages and, at the same time, to benefit from the diversity of linguistic tools/filters.

Bilingual Education and Language Alternation

This approach is not necessarily considered as a 'pluralistic approach' by some researchers (see, for example, Candelier, 2008), since the principle of language alternation (code-switching), often central in bilingual education, does not characterize all the approaches. In our view, this perspective reduces the field of plurilingual practices in education and does not help to capture the role of languages throughout the school subjects. Furthermore, it fails to grasp the role played by language alternation in three directions: plurilingual communication, language/content acquisition and curriculum organization. Before coming back to language alternation, we briefly focus on the notion of bilingual education and its European declinations.

Among the pluralistic approaches, bilingual education is the only one to be fundamentally 'action-oriented' and based on bi-/plurilingual practices, in the sense that students have to deal with different languages in the accomplishment of several tasks in the everyday life of the school. Bilingual education could be defined as the total or partial use of an L2 for teaching one or more non-linguistic subjects (NLS). Languages are thus envisaged in their contact and in their usage – implication in the subject matter (Gajo, 2008, proposes the notion of 'multi-integrated pedagogy'). Research on bilingual education has become intensive in the last two decades over the world, with more and more synergies between American, European and Asian traditions (So & Jones, 2002). These synergies show differences in the theoretical tools referred to by researchers to investigate bilingual education. Indeed, if research can focus on a wide range of dimensions (curriculum, teacher education, classroom interaction, students' representations, and so on), the focus on the same dimension can be made through different paradigms. In the European Francophone tradition, for example, research on classroom interaction is mainly conducted by (applied) linguists – and not by educationists – and is considered as central to many investigations. An important contribution is made by discourse and interaction analysis, with original investigation lines of the following topics: the notion of integration, the notion of NLS, the notion of language alternation.

The process of *integration* is central to bilingual education and appears in the umbrella term 'CLIL' (Coyle *et al.*, 2010; Nikula & Marsh, 1998). The

French acronym 'EMILE' (Enseignement d'une matière par l'intégration d'une langue étrangère; Baetens Beardsmore, 1999) also puts the emphasis on the concept of integration but with a focus on the subject rather than on the language and on teaching rather than on learning. Our own research tries to understand better the linguistic issues *in*, *of* and *from* the subject matter:

> With regard to the process of integration between the subject matter and the L2 knowledge, we favour the study of the articulation between the negotiation of form and that of meaning, which are often considered as separate procedures. More precisely, our research has investigated the links between subject meaning, its linguistic forms and second language competence in order to, first, address specific subject problems, and secondly find out to what extent the highlighted linguistic forms share discourse elements and/or structures. (Gajo, 2007: 563)

Under these conditions, bilingual education makes more visible the linguistic nature of the content knowledge and of teaching a subject. Indeed, the construction and transmission of knowledge are mainly verbal and interactional. This argues for a critical perspective on the notion of NLS, since all subjects are language-related. For this reason, Gajo (2009) recently proposed the notion of 'DdNL' ('discipline dite non linguistique' [*so-called non-linguistic subject*]). Moreover, it has to be noted that NLS are not only linguistically relevant but also 'naturally' embedded in language diversity. If scientific developments are historically due to the confrontation of ideas shaped in different cultural traditions and conveyed through a variety of languages, plurilingual interaction in the classroom creates a stimulating framework and brings in new tools for the construction of knowledge.

Implementing – or just recognizing – plurilingualism in classroom interaction means dealing with the notion of language alternation, which is one of the most important transcodic marks (see above). This notion has been extensively described in linguistics, notably in the field of sociolinguistics and of discourse and interaction analysis, but a strong didactic perspective on it is missing. Moving from a strictly descriptive perspective to a didactic one requires new theoretical tools. In the case of language alternation, a first distinction between a micro-level and a macro-level is needed. The former corresponds to the well-known code-switching that occurs in discourse elaboration. This *micro-alternation* is nevertheless contextualized in relation to *macro-alternation* phenomena, which permit, at the didactic level, the creation of chains of monolingual tasks alternating between L1 and L2; the placement of bilingual resources by/for essentially monolingual tasks, as is often the case in the socioprofessional world, is therefore key here. The macro-level concerns the curriculum organization, where L1 and L2 are given particular areas (subjects, parts of subjects, period, etc.). An in-depth analysis of classroom interaction allows for further understanding and the identification of a meso-level of language alternation. This *meso-alternation* occurs when code-switching is encouraged at transitional points between particular didactic tasks (for example, explanation in L2 and summary in L1). More or less planned ahead of interactional practices, this kind of alternation is linked to teachers' strategies or to explicit methodological approaches. There is a similarity between meso-alternation and the notion of *translanguaging*, defined as a 'pedagogical practice which switches the language mode in bilingual classroom – for example, reading is done in one language, and writing in another' (García, 2008: 45). Also referring to Auer's (1984, 1995) work, Gajo *et al.* (2013) state that:

> meso-alternation is, in a way, similar to *discourse-related code-switching* (Auer, 1984), but its description does not rely solely on conversational analysis but also refers to ethnographic or psychosocial dimensions (Auer, 1995). In the case of meso-alternation, both linguistic contexts [L1 and L2] are potentially activated and produce therefore, together with micro-alternation, a plurilingual mode in interaction.

In order to understand better the role of plurilingualism within the classroom and the curriculum, it is important to build up a theoretical model which could at the same time distinguish and articulate the three levels of alternation, 'students and teachers changing the language from one subject to another, from one task to another and from one word to another' (Auer, 1984).

Language Alternation, the Didactics of Plurilingualism and Social Representations

All three levels of language alternation are not given the same degree of attention in practice. Normalizing macro-alternation seems to be easier than recognizing micro-alternation. For example, in many cases, bilingual schools try to organize their curriculum through the principle of 'one person/one language' (known as the principle of Ronjat-Grammont; Hagège, 1996). In doing so, they promote a kind of separation between languages and aim at avoiding as much as possible code-switching in classroom communication. The explanation can certainly be found in the dynamics of social representations, still largely anchored in a monolingual view of plurilingualism. Such representations are widely shared among school authorities, which tend to maintain some confusion between total immersion (based on an L2 didactics) and submersion (using an L2 as it were an L1), for example, or to give more value to exchange programmes (two monolingual spaces) than to bilingual teaching (one bilingual space). Plurilingualism is seen as a goal of education but not clearly as a means to achieving that goal, contrary to the principles presented above. Furthermore, bilingual programmes can be promoted as a transitional means of going from one monolingualism to another. This has been the case in some Baltic countries, where bilingual education was supposed to be the better way to push back the Russian language.

Consequently, social representations play an important role in the multilingual turn in education. Plurilingualism is not only a matter of curriculum or of practices to be technically implemented, but is also linked to the question of *acceptability*. Some representations are widely discussed, whereas others are taken for granted and remain implicit, even if the practices have changed. Since the mid-1990s, Francophone research in sociolinguistics and applied linguistics has been very active on the topic of social representations in language education (Gajo, 2000; Matthey, 1997; Moore, 2001; Py, 2004; Stratilaki, 2011). Principally based on previous investigations in social psychology, this Francophone trend develops through three main issues: an analysis of the discursive dimension of representations; an analysis of the typology of arguments on plurilingualism; and an analysis of the dynamics linking representations, teaching and learning.

Major results show that discourse and social interaction is at the same time a setting for the reification and the negotiation of social representations. Even in bilingual communities, the monolingual point of view remains important when people try to talk about their own practices (Cavalli *et al.*, 2003). This monolingual heritage is also visible in pupils' drawings: 'primary school children asked to draw "what goes on in the head of someone who speaks more than one language" usually portray plurilinguists by contrasting them with monolinguists, who remain the yardstick for what is normal' (Castellotti & Moore, 2002: 13). Therefore, researchers raise the question of how to incorporate the notion of social representation into teaching approaches. Going back to the pluralistic approaches mentioned above, we can link this question with the developments of awareness-raising approaches or, to a lesser extent, with comparative methods (Castellotti & Moore, 2002). But it is by no means certain that a plurilingual toolkit in education would be sufficient to overpass a technical comparative work in order to stimulate an in-depth questioning on the boundaries of languages. Such a process has to deal with the social tensions between languages and behind multilingual situations. Thus, a sociodidactics of plurilingualism should address a new set of questions: can multilingualism be understood without reference to specific languages? Is multilingualism 'per se' an issue of power? Even if the social dimension of languages comes into question, is there a place for multilingualism in itself?

These questions are important today and raise two main issues: the relevance of the social context in languages education, and the ideological dimension of multi/plurilingualism. The first issue is supported by the development of a *contextualized sociodidactics* of languages and of plurilingualism (Blanchet & Chardenet, 2011; Blanchet *et al.*, 2009; Castellotti & Nishiyama,

2011), which tends, for example, to confront the new European models of languages education – mainly based on the Common European Framework of Reference for Languages and on the notion of plurilingual competence – with Asian or African contexts and works on notions like methodological adaptation or the culture of education. The second issue is addressed by *critical sociolinguistics* (Heller, 2003), which considers the power behind education systems and actors, and even in the dynamics of research. In this way, a kind of hermeneutics of discourse on multi/plurilingualism has recently begun to develop (de Robillard, 2010; Canut & Duchêne, 2011–2012; Maurer, 2011) and tries to grasp the ideological dimension underlying statements on language diversity and plurilingualism in education. Both the contextualized and critical perspectives give particular attention to the *historicity* of multilingualism and to the discourse on multilingualism. At the European level, it is indeed necessary to remember that research on multilingualism is closely linked with the construction of the EU and also partially funded by this body and, on the education side, strongly supported by the Council of Europe. Nevertheless, recalling these circumstances should not be a reason to question the value of European research but, on the contrary, to maintain an awareness of the fact that the social problems addressed by this research are still important for Europe and relevant to non-European situations. Plurilingualism as a tool for communication, knowledge construction and, after (before!) all, for peace remains a central issue, which need not be diluted along with a strong and serious applied linguistics.

Conclusion: Towards a Contextualized Didactics of Plurilingualism

In this chapter, we have tried to describe the conditions under which plurilingual practices can be first normalized and then didactized. The contribution of European and Francophone research to this process is significant, notably thanks to the synergies between different fields of language theory and education. For example, the early intersection of theories on multilingualism and theories on second language acquisition has been of help in initiating at the same time a specific stand on multilingualism and a renewed perspective on language in general, being considered in its fundamental variation. This fruitful intersection has recently produced the notion of *plurilingual acquisition competence* ('compétence d'appropriation plurilingue', Castellotti & Moore, 2011). Furthermore, through some investigations in multilingual settings, several researchers have emphasized the link between language practices and social representations. Indeed, language learning phenomena exist and evolve largely within the dynamic of social portrayals, these being fuelled, communicated and re-discussed in the classroom.

As such, the question of linguistic diversity muscles in more and more on pedagogical approaches. The examination of languages which are present in and outside of the classroom, and of their contact, is easier when undertaken from a 'non-isolationist' perspective; this touches not only on second language didactics, but also on first language didactics (which may be second or third for migrant students; the notion of 'language of instruction' would be more appropriate). Consequently, languages which are *in* and *for* education can be better captured through the paradigm of the didactics of plurilingualism. This paradigm is derived from new approaches which have been undertaken in the field of language education and which were identified as:

- different enough from 'traditional' approaches, mostly focused on one language at a time;
- close enough to each other to be integrated into a common didactic paradigm.

Under these conditions, it becomes clear that the didactics of plurilingualism is built up from a bottom-up perspective and has to be envisaged as promoting a contextualized perspective of language education. The basic assumption is that languages are *in context* and *in contact*.

Nevertheless, contextualization is a process and, as such, embraces various degrees. Linguistic and didactic tools have to be elaborated and stabilized in a complex tension between reification and contextualization. The notion of plurilingualism results from a kind of reification, as does the notion of language itself. But, these notions are powerful and useful enough for both theory and practice. Even social representations are stretched between reification and contextualization. The main issue is to elaborate sufficient and appropriate words to talk about plurilingualism and its didactics in order to allow some fruitful tension and transfer between theory, practice and social representations. But there is a *behind* and a *beyond*.

Behind a given term sometimes occurs a wide range of meanings and of social projects. For example, some programmes of bilingual education can be intended as two monolingual programmes in parallel with no connections to each other and no extension to other languages inside and outside the classroom. This is linked not only to the fact that pedagogical orientations vary, but also to the social hierarchy of languages. In this way, by implementing CLIL, some European educational systems are mainly concerned with innovative and effective ways to teach widely used languages, mostly English. Lesser used languages, when they come into consideration, are often valued through other pluralistic approaches, for example language awareness.

Beyond the choice of the right words, adopting the plural form for 'plurilingualism' – *plurilinguismes* (Moore, 2006) – corresponds to a significant step forward in the Francophone research.

References

Auer, P. (1984) *Bilingual Conversation*. Amsterdam: John Benjamins.

Auer, P. (1995) The pragmatics of code-switching: A sequential approach. In L. Milroy and P. Muysken (eds) *One Speaker, Two Languages. Cross-disciplinary Perspectives on Code-switching* (pp. 115–135). Cambridge: Cambridge University Press.

Baetens Beardsmore, H. (1999) Consolidating experience in plurilingual education. In D. Marsh and B. Marsland (eds) *CLIL Initiatives for the Millennium* (pp. 24–30). Jyväskylä: Continuing Education Centre, University of Jyväskylä.

Baker, C. (1988) *Key Issues in Bilingualism and Bilingual Education*. Clevedon: Multilingual Matters.

Baker, C. (2001) *Foundations of Bilingual Education and Bilingualism* (3rd edn). Clevedon: Multilingual Matters.

Beacco, J.-C. and Byram, M. (2003) *Guide pour l'élaboration des politiques linguistiques éducatives en Europe – de la diversité linguistique à l'éducation plurilingue*. Strasbourg: Language Policy Unit, Council of Europe.

Beacco, J.-C., Byram, M., Cavalli, M., Coste, D., Egli Cuenat, M., Goullier, F. and Panthier, J. (2010) *Guide pour le développement et la mise en œuvre de curriculums pour une éducation plurilingue et interculturelle*. Strasbourg: Council of Europe.

Berrendonner, A., Le Guern, M. and Puech, G. (1983) *Principes de grammaire polylectale*. Lyon: Presses universitaires de Lyon.

Billiez, J. (ed.) (1998) *De la didactique des langues à la didactique du plurilinguisme. Hommage à Louise Dabène*. Grenoble: CDL-LIDILEM.

Blanchet, Ph. and Chardenet, P. (eds) (2011) *Guide pour la recherche en didactique des langues et des cultures. Approches contextualisées*. Paris: Editions des archives contemporaines.

Blanchet, Ph. and Coste, D. (eds) (2010) *Regards critiques sur la notion d'' interculturalité'. Pour une didactique de la pluralité linguistique et culturelle*. Paris: L'Harmattan.

Blanchet, Ph., Moore, D. and Asselah Rahal, S. (eds) (2009) *Perspectives pour une didactique des langues contextualisée*. Paris: AUF/Editions des archives contemporaines.

Borel, S. (2012) *Langues en contact – langues en contraste. Typologie, plurilinguismes et apprentissages*. Berne: Peter Lang.

Brohy, C. and Rezgui, S. (eds) (2008) La didactique intégrée des langues: expériences et applications. *Babylonia* 1.

Candelier, M. (ed.) (2003) *Evlang – l'éveil aux langues à l'école primaire. Bilan d'une innovation européenne*. Brussels: De Boeck Duculot.

Candelier, M. (2008) Approches plurielles, didactiques du plurilinguisme: le même et l'autre. *Cahiers de l'ACEDLE* 5 (1), 65–90.

Canut, C. and Duchêne, A. (2011–2012) Introduction. Instrumentalisations politiques et économiques des langues: le plurilinguisme en question. *Langage et société* 136, 5–12.

Castellotti, V. and Moore, D. (2002) *Social Representations of Languages and Teaching. Guide for the Development of Language Education Policies in Europe. From Linguistic Diversity to Plurilingual Education*. Strasbourg: Council of Europe.

Castellotti, V. and Moore, D. (2011) La compétence plurilingue et pluriculturelle. Genèses et évolutions. In Ph. Blanchet and P. Chardenet (eds) *Guide pour la recherche en didactique des langues et des cultures. Approches contextualisées*. Paris: Editions des archives contemporaines.

Castellotti, V. and Nishiyama, N.J. (eds) (2011) Contextualisations du CECR. Le cas de l'Asie du Sud-Est. *Le Français dans le monde; Recherches et applications, No. 50*. Paris: CLE International.

Cavalli, M., Colletta, D., Gajo, L., Matthey, M. and Serra, C. (2003) *Langues, bilinguisme et représentations sociales au Val d'Aoste*. Aosta: IRRE-VDA.

CoE (Council of Europe) (2001) *Common European Framework of Reference for Languages: Learning, Teaching, Assessment (CEFR)*. Language Policy Unit. Cambridge: Cambridge University Press.

Colin, J.-P. (2004) (Co)existence d'une ou plusieurs langues dans un pays ou un individu: un tour d'horizon terminologico-historique. In G. Holtzer (ed.) *Voies vers le plurilinguisme*. Besançon: Presses universitaires de Franche-Comté.

Coseriu. E. (1973/1966) *Probleme der romanischen Semantik*. Tübingen: Narr.

Coste, D. (2006) Pluralité des langues, diversité des contextes: Quels enjeux pour le français? In V. Castellotti and H. Chalabi (eds) *Le français langue étrangère et seconde. Des paysages didactiques en contexte* (pp. 11–25). Paris: L'Harmattan.

Coste, D. and Simon, D.-L. (2009) The plurilingual social actor. Language, citizenship and education. *International Journal of Multilingualism* 6 (2), 168–185.

Coyle, D., Hood, Ph. and Marsh, D. (2010) *CLIL: Content and Language Integrated Learning*. Cambridge: Cambridge University Press.

Dabène, L. (1994) *Repères sociolinguistiques pour l'enseignement des langues*. Vanves: Hachette.

De Pietro, J.-F. (1988) Vers une typologie des situations de contacts linguistiques. *Langage et société* 43, 65–89.

De Robillard, D. (2010) Réponse à Anne-Claude Berthoud. Dylan, un exemple parmi d'autres des coûts et difficultés du travail de la diversité: naît-on ou devient-on divers? *Les Cahiers de l'Acedle* 7 (1), 35–61.

Escudé, P. and Janin, P. (2010) *Le point sur l'intercompréhension, clé du plurilinguisme*. Paris: CLE International.

Gajo, L. (2000) Disponibilité sociale des représentations: Approche linguistique. *TRANEL (Travaux neuchâtelois de linguistique)* 32.

Gajo, L. (2007) Linguistic knowledge and subject knowledge: How does bilingualism contribute to subject development? *International Journal of Bilingual Education and Bilingualism* 10 (5), 563–581.

Gajo, L. (2008) L'intercompréhension entre didactique intégrée et enseignement bilingue. In V. Conti and F. Grin (eds) *S'entendre entre langues voisines: Vers l'intercompréhension* (pp. 131–150). Geneva: Georg.

Gajo, L. (2009) De la DNL à la DdNL: Principes de classe et formation des enseignants. *Les langues modernes* 4, 15–24.

Gajo, L. and Mondada, L. (2000) *Interactions et acquisitions en contexte. Appropriation de compétences discursives plurilingues par de jeunes immigrés*. Fribourg: Editions universitaires.

Gajo, L., Grobet, A., Serra, C., Steffen, G., Müller, G. and Berthoud, A.-C. (2013) Plurilingualisms and knowledge construction in higher education. In A.-C. Berthoud, F. Grin and G. Lüdi (eds) *Exploring the Dynamics of Multilingualism* (pp. 287–308). *The Dylan Project*. Amsterdam: John Benjamins.

García, O. (2008) *Bilingual Education in the 21st Century. A Global Perspective*. Oxford: Wiley-Blackwell.

Grosjean, F. (1982) *Life with Two Languages: An Introduction to Bilingualism*. Cambridge, MA and London: Harvard University Press.

Grosjean, F. (2010) *Bilingual. Life and Reality*. Cambridge, MA and London: Harvard University Press.

Hagège, C. (1996) *L'enfant aux deux langues*. Paris: Odile Jacob.

Heller, M. (2003) *Eléments pour une sociolinguistique critique*. Paris: Didier.

Hymes, D.H. (1972) On communicative competence. In J.B. Pride and J. Holmes (eds) *Sociolinguistics: Selected Readings* (pp. 269–293). Harmondsworth: Penguin.

Hymes, D.H. (1984) *Vers la compétence de communication*. Paris: Hatier-Crédif.

Jørgensen, J.N. (ed.) (2008) Polylingual languaging around and among children and adolescents. *International Journal of Multilingualism* 5 (3).

Labov, W. (1976) *Sociolinguistique [Sociolinguistic patterns]*. Paris: Minuit.

Ladmiral, J.-R. (1982) Problèmes psychosociologiques de la traduction. In J. Caudmont (Hrsg.) *Sprachen in Kontakt – Langues en contact* (pp. 129–142). Tübinger Beiträge zur Linguistik 185. Tübingen: Narr.

Lüdi, G. (1987) Les marques transcodiques: Regards nouveaux sur le bilinguisme. In G. Lüdi (ed.) *Devenir bilingue – parler bilingue* (pp. 1–21). Tübingen: Niemeyer.

Lüdi, G. (1993) Statuts et fonctions des marques transcodiques en conversation exolingue. In G. Hilty (ed.) *Actes du XXe Congrès international de linguistique et philologie romanes. Université de Zürich 6–11 avril 1992* (pp. 123–136). Tübingen and Basel: Francke.

Lüdi, G. (2011) Vers de nouvelles approches théoriques du langage et du plurilinguisme. *Travaux neuchâtelois de linguistique* 53, 47–64.

Lüdi, G. and Py, B. (1984) *Zweisprachig durch Migration. Einführung in die Erforschung der Mehrsprachigkeit am Beispiel zweier Zuwanderergruppen in Neuenburg (Schweiz).* Tübingen: Niemeyer.

Lüdi, G. and Py, B. (1986, 2003) *Être bilingue.* Berne: Peter Lang.

Lüdi, G. and Py, B. (2009) To be or not to be ... a plurilingual speaker. *International Journal of Multilingualism* 6 (2), 154–167.

Marcellesi, Ch., Romian, H. and Treignier, J. (1985) Quelques concepts et notions opératoires pour une pédagogie de la variation langagière. *Repères* 67, 23–31.

Matthey, M. (ed.) (1997) *Les langues et leurs images.* Neuchâtel, Perros-Guirrec and Lausanne: IRDP, TILV and LEP.

Maurer, B. (2011) *Enseignement des langues et construction européenne. Le plurilinguisme, nouvelle idéologie dominante.* Paris: Éditions des archives contemporaines.

Moore, D. (ed.) (2001) *Les représentations des langues et de leur apprentissage: Références, modèles, données et méthodes.* Paris: Didier.

Moore, D. (2006) *Plurilinguismes et Ecole.* Paris: Didier.

Moore, D. and Gajo, L. (2009) Introduction – French voices on plurilingualism and pluriculturalism: Theory, significance and perspectives. *International Journal of Multilingualism* 6 (2), 137–153.

Nikula, T. and Marsh, D. (1998) Terminological considerations regarding content and language integrated learning. *Bulletin VALS-ASLA* 67, 13–18.

Otsuji, E. and Pennycook, A. (2010) Metrolingualism: Fixity, fluidity and language in flux. *International Journal of Multilingualism* 7 (3), 240–254.

Perregaux, C., de Goumoëns, Cl., Jeannot, D. and de Pietro, J.-F. (ed.) (2003) *Education au langage et Ouverture aux langues à l'école (EOLE)* (2 vols). Neuchâtel: Secrétariat général de la CIIP.

Porquier, R. (1984) Communication exolingue et apprentissage des langues. In B. Py (ed.) *Acquisition d'une langue étrangère III* (pp. 17–47). Paris and Neuchâtel: Presses Universitaires de Vincennes and Centre de linguistique appliquée.

Porquier, R. and Py, B. (2004) *Apprentissage d'une langue étrangère. Contextes et discours.* Paris: Didier.

Py, B. (1991) Bilinguisme, exolinguisme et acquisition: rôle de L1 dans l'acquisition de L2. *Travaux neuchâtelois de linguistique* 17, 147–161.

Py, B. (2004) Pour une approche linguistique des représentations sociales. *Langages* 154, 6–19.

Py, B. and Gajo, L. (2013) Bilinguisme et plurilinguisme. In J. Simonin and S. Wharton (eds) *Sociolinguistique du contact, modèles, théories. Dictionnaire encyclopédique des termes et concepts.* Lyon: ENS Editions.

Roulet, E. (1980) *Langue maternelle et langues secondes: vers une pédagogie intégrée.* Paris: Hatier-Crédif.

So, D.W.C. and Jones, G.M. (eds) (2002) *Education and Society in Plurilingual Contexts.* Brussels: Brussels University Press (VUB).

Stratilaki, S. (2011) *Discours et représentations du plurilinguisme.* Frankfurt: Peter Lang.

Weinreich, U. (1953) *Languages in Contact: Findings and Problems.* New York: Linguistic Circle of New York.

6 Our Mother Tongue is Plurilingualism[1]: A Framework of Orientations for Integrated Multilingual Curricula

Gabriela Meier

Guiding Questions

- How can learning a second (or further) language for all learners in a classroom be combined with recognising other languages which students may bring to the classroom?
- What are the main orientations that underlie integrated multilingual curricula, and to what extent do they resonate with curricula in other contexts?
- To what extent could the framework of orientations presented here be useful for curriculum development in other contexts?

Introduction

This chapter is concerned with curriculum development in the framework of the multilingual turn. Based on a review of documents on multilingual education, with a focus on integrated multilingual curricula, it offers a framework of orientations that may provide some guidelines for curriculum development in multilingual contexts.

Integrated multilingual curricula are based on the idea of *multilingual education*. The latter is based on the idea that learners and teachers use more than one language to access learning of languages and/or content in formal educational contexts. Thus models of multilingual education can include bilingual, trilingual or multilingual education, but they normally do not include traditional successive and separate language education, such as traditional modern foreign language lessons, where one language is studied exclusively. Different terms have been used to describe pedagogic approaches using more than one language. In German language publications the terms *Mehrsprachigkeitsdidaktik* or *Mehrsprachendidaktik* have been used, while in English-language writing the term *bi- or multilingual education* and in French-language literature (see Gajo, this volume) *didactique du plurilinguisme* are often used. However, Candelier (2008) has shown that *Mehrsprachigkeitsdidaktik* and *didactique du plurilinguisme* are both used in an imprecise way and can refer to different things, such as intercomprehension, third-language education, content and language integrated learning (CLIL) and language awareness, concepts which I will describe in the next section. In terms of terminology, it has to be noted that there is a difference between German/French and English language use: *didactique* in French or *Didaktik* in German traditionally refer to 'the instructional process' (Kansanen, 2002: 427), while in English the term pedagogy is often used in its stead.

Integrated multilingual curricula, which are the focus of this chapter, are programmes that integrate multilingual education approaches such as language learning and language awareness activities. They focus on the development of high-level competence in at least two languages, while they recognise and encourage the use of other languages. In Europe, there have been interesting proposals (Candelier, 2008; Coyle *et al.*, 2009; Hufeisen, 2011; Kleppin, 2004; Reich & Krumm, 2013), and concrete plans in Switzerland (Passepartout, 2008, 2009) and in Luxembourg (Berg & Weis, 2007) for such curricula, but in practice such programmes are still the exception, at least in European mainstream education. As I will argue in this chapter, integrated multilingual curricula may well be one way of translating the multilingual turn into practice in mainstream education, potentially benefitting all learners. The review comprises documents outlining proposals for multilingual integrated curricula, and plans which are actually being implemented at the time of writing in mainstream education in Switzerland and in Luxemburg.

Curriculum-specific considerations frame this chapter. Richards (2007) claims that a curriculum should be designed on the basis of a needs analysis, including learner needs and situational needs. According to Linse (in Hudelson, 1993: 46), learner needs include the consideration of:

cultural, political, and personal characteristics of students [...] in order to plan activities and objectives that are realistic and purposeful. [...] It is the school's responsibility to provide equal access to school opportunities and to validate the experiences of all students, regardless of their political and/or cultural backgrounds.

Situational needs include 'political, social, economic, or institutional' factors (Richards, 2007: 91). Based on this, themes that are important for my documentary review are concepts related to main actors (learners), pedagogic activities and objectives, situational parameters and equal opportunities.

McKernan (2008: 26) argues that the conception of a curriculum is based on 'a defined orientation, or values, embedded in a curriculum perspective, which characterizes the most prized virtues connected with a curriculum style or practice'. Thus, a curriculum is based on values, ideologies, perspectives and other dispositions, and I will refer to these underlying forces as orientations. I feel the term orientations is appropriate, since this chapter is not about establishing a predictive framework, but it is about proposing ideas, or indeed ways of thinking, that curriculum developers may want to consider when negotiating, designing and adapting curricula in multilingual contexts. McKernan (2008: 14) points out that '[w]ho, when, why and how become key questions that need to be answered in negotiating and implementing a curriculum'. Thus, questions like these guided the review and informed the framework of orientations offered in this chapter.

The chapter consists of five parts. Following this introduction, I will provide a brief overview of multilingual educational approaches, and the concept of integrated multilingual curricula as ideas and as actual plans for implementation. The fourth section will show the results of my review and outline 10 orientations that can be identified in the documents. In the final section, I draw the strands together and discuss potential implications for curriculum development and research.

Types of Multilingual Education: The Building Blocks

This section provides an overview of approaches that could be considered the building blocks of integrated multilingual curricula. All multilingual models are based on the understanding that learners have linguistic knowledge and experiences that can be activated for language learning and that learners can draw on their wider linguistic repertoires for learning.

Intercomprehension

Intercomprehension, championed above all by Meißner (2005) in Germany (see also Bär, 2010; Carrasco Perea, 2010), seems of importance predominantly in university departments, such as in Romance languages institutes, and also as an extension in departments for Germanic or Slavic studies (Klein, 2007). This is based on the idea that learners use knowledge of closely related other languages to receptively engage with a new language that has previously been unknown. Concepts such as *savoir* or declarative knowledge (vocabulary, grammar, etc., or knowing what) and *savoir-faire* or procedural knowledge (skills and strategies, or knowing how) are seen as central (Meißner & Reinfried, 1998). Resources activated to help individual *savoir* and *savoir-faire* are: parallel texts, categorising practice (*Idenfikationsübungen*), dictionaries and grammar books, categorisation of translingual phenomena (*Serienbildungen*), and error prophylaxis (false friends, attention to transfer risks) (Meißner, 2003). This resonates with Cummins' (2008) interdependence hypothesis or Jessner's (2008) metalinguistic awareness. In order to make learners become conscious of their intercomprehension strategies, Meißner (2003) suggests think-aloud protocols (*Lautdenkprotokolle*), where learners are invited to think about the strategies they apply to access meaning and form of a spoken or written text. This is an approach firmly based on the conception of learning as a cognitive activity (Meißner, 2003).

Third-language education

Third-language education is often based on the assumption that students (often) add English as a second language to their first language, and then add further languages to their language repertoires as they continue in education or in their professional lives (Bahr *et al.*, 1996; Cenoz, 2012; Hufeisen, 2003; Lutjeharms, 2003). It is based on the idea that learners learn languages successively, and thus can build on previous language learning experiences, for instance, German after English. Learners in today's classrooms each have different language and life experiences; it may therefore not always be appropriate to expect that all learners in a class have learned languages in a clearly defined and predictable order, and to a similar level, as would be expected in a third-language model. This may be suitable for adult learning for which groups self-select, but perhaps not for (heterogeneous) mainstream school contexts.

Content and language integrated learning (CLIL)

CLIL is increasingly popular in Europe. This is usually described as a one-way immersion model (Baker, 2006), as it uses an additional/second language to teach content (e.g. geography, arts) by immersing students in this language during the lesson. In the one-way model it is assumed that the learners do not speak the immersion language as their first language, in contrast to two-way immersion education (see Meier, Chapter 8, this volume). The term CLIL is commonly associated with educational programmes such as bilingual education, immersion education, plurilingual education, content-based language teaching or language across the curriculum (Coyle *et al.*, 2009; Mehisto *et al.*, 2008). CLIL often builds on previously gained competences in a modern foreign language. Thus, it assumes some basic language competence at the outset (Lasagabaster & Sierra, 2010). Major countries to adopt CLIL-style education on a large scale are Germany (Breidbach *et al.*, 2012) and Spain (Consejería de Educacíon, 2005; Dobson *et al.*, 2010). While Germany applies CLIL predominantly at secondary level, and for more able students, Spain predominantly takes a whole school approach starting at primary level.

I have come across two issues with CLIL-type education. First, from speaking to teachers who teach French through CLIL in London, I know that CLIL models sometimes attract families who speak the language of content instruction at home, in this case French. However, these teachers struggle sometimes to accommodate those learners who speak French fluently already, since CLIL is not designed for this. Second, CLIL or other so-called bilingual programmes often separate the languages, i.e. the one-teacher one-language model (Hélot & De Mejía, 2008) that is sometimes referred to as parallel monolingualism, or two solitudes (Cummins, 2008). In contrast to the methods described above, CLIL and other bilingual models may not make full use of opportunities to link to other languages, and develop multilingual, rather than two separate monolingual, competences.

Language awareness

The idea of language awareness is centred on educational initiatives from the 1980s in the UK, based on Eric Hawkins' (1984) ideas. This is aimed at addressing both English as an additional language and foreign-language learning while challenging cultural stereotypes. Labercane *et al.* (1998: 91) suggest that the underlying philosophy is to activate learners' curiosity and 'to challenge students to ask questions about language'. Similar to methods discussed above, this approach aims at activating previous language knowledge to build greater language awareness. Language awareness acknowledges that 'the knowledge, interest and contributions of pupils with foreign mother tongues present many opportunities for thinking about language in the classroom' (Oomen-Welke & Karagiannakis, 1998: 12). Thus, the discourse based on Hawkins' work in the UK put language awareness, and thus minority languages, on the agenda (i.e. people talk about it even if no action follows) perhaps earlier than in other contexts, such as Germany, France, Switzerland or other European regions, where initiatives such as *Eveil aux langues* in France and Switzerland (see Moore, 1995) or *Ouverture aux langues à l'école in Luxembourg* (Tonnar, 2010) emerged from the 1990s onwards.

Translanguaging

More recently the idea of translanguaging has been increasingly used and developed (see García & Kano, this volume). This concept, established by Williams in Wales (1994), has been defined by García (2009) to describe discursive practices of bilingual students. The students in the US context that García and colleagues describe may be predominantly bilingual, but translanguaging, as I see it, should also include practices of (potential) multilingual learners. Thus, I adapted the following quote:

> Translanguaging is the act performed by bilinguals [and multilinguals] of accessing different linguistic features of various modes of what are described as autonomous languages, in order to maximize communicative potential. It is an approach to bilingualism [and multilingualism] that is centered, not on languages as has often been the case, but on the practices of bilinguals [and multilinguals] that are readily observable in order to make sense of their multilingual worlds. (García, 2009: 140)

In 2011 García and Sylvan defined it as 'the process by which bilingual [or multilingual] students and teachers engage in complex discursive practices in order to "make sense" of, and communicate in, multilingual classrooms' (García & Sylvan, 2011: 389). These practices include translation and code-switching, but go beyond these in that these approaches are used in in all activities, including 'reading, writing, taking notes, discussing, signing and so on'. Translanguaging, as defined by García and Sylvan (2011: 389), is also related to *transculturación*, which 'refers to the complex and multidirectional process in cultural transformation, as well as to the questioning of the epistemological purity of disciplines and of the knowing subject'. In other words, it refers to recognising diverse linguistic and other knowledges that are not normally valorised in schools and that enable learning for all. Thus, translanguaging is a pedagogic approach that has multilingual practices at its heart, which additionally enables cross-cultural exchange and identity development.

This concept is increasingly used in European literature (see Gajo, this volume), but there is no translation into German or French as it seems. Lüdi (2013), for instance, observed that it is now used for what used to be referred to as *parler plurilingue* but, as can be seen from the above, translanguaging involves more than just speaking multilingually.

Integrated Multilingual Curricula

In recent years many practitioners and authorities have recognised that their learners are multilingual and have experimented with multilingual approaches on a small scale or in pilot projects, which sometimes attracted the attention or collaboration of researchers, as is evident from this book (see particularly Part 3). However, these have remained the exception and there have been very few integrated multilingual efforts in mainstream education. In this section, I focus on exactly such things, namely on proposals and plans for the mainstream sector. This section has three parts: first I outline documents relating to proposals, and secondly I introduce documents relating to concrete plans for the implementation of integrated multilingual curricula in Switzerland and Luxemburg. At the end of this section, I additionally mention a model from the USA, which is not mainstream but may nevertheless offer relevant insights since it can look back on many years of experience.

Proposals for integrated multilingual curricula

Four proposals or prototypes were identified among the literature reviewed that relate to integrated multilingual curricula (Candelier, 2008; Coyle *et al.*, 2009; Hufeisen, 2011; Kleppin, 2004; Reich & Krumm, 2013), which will be introduced in chronological order.

Kleppin (2004) bases her ideas for an integrated multilingual curriculum on third-language acquisition and intercomprehension models. She argues that first languages should be taken into consideration when learning and teaching new languages at school, and that the three following points should form part of an integrated multilingual concept (Kleppin, 2004: 89–91): language learning is dynamic and multilingual, intercultural understanding must be at its core, and language awareness should form part of it.

Candelier (2008) refers to so-called pluralistic approaches, which according to him consist of four different types: (1) intercultural approach(es); (2) integrated languages education; (3) intercomprehension between related languages; and (4) language awareness. Based on this, he elaborates the framework for a pluralistic approach (FREPA), or CARAP (*cadre de référence pour les approches plurielles*) (CARAP, 2007a). Candelier questions the French term, which is often used when referring to language awareness, namely *éveil aux langues*, which can be translated as 'awakening to languages'. He shows that language awareness can be continued throughout primary school and, clearly, it should not just be about becoming aware but about continuing to build increasing language awareness (Candelier, 2008). In Switzerland they have, presumably for this reason, combined *Eveil aux langues* + <u>Language Awareness</u> + <u>BE</u>*gegnung mit Sprachen und Kulturen* (language awakening, language awareness and contact with languages and cultures) in the ELBE project (Degen & Stadelmann, 2007).

Coyle *et al.* (2009: 12) propose an integrated multilingual curriculum that includes four dimensions (4 Cs) to form a conceptual framework, 'which connects content, cognition, communication and culture. Culture and intercultural understanding lie at the core of the conceptual framework, offering the key to deeper learning and promoting social cohesion'.

Hufeisen (2011) proposes a comprehensive language curriculum (*Gesamtsprachencurriculum*) based on CLIL with additional language awareness features, similar to Coyle *et al.* (2009). However, it goes beyond the latter, in that the proposed curriculum aims to address the promotion and recognition of the personal multilingualism of learners more explicitly and comprehensively.

Reich and Krumm (2013) produced a comprehensive and authoritative guide, in the first instance, for the implementation of a multilingual integrated curriculum in Austria, but with important insights that are potentially applicable to other educational contexts. This includes clear and useful guidelines not only for compulsory schooling, but also for vocational courses and teacher education. In their book, they propose that language awareness and language learning strategies should permeate all stages and types of education, whereas in the first four years of schooling, additionally, knowledge about languages should be emphasised and from Year 5 onwards this topic should be widened in a systematic manner to comprise language comparison and links between languages, society and culture.

Concrete plans for integrated multilingual curricula

This section brings in two sets of documents, relating to recent initiatives in Switzerland and in Luxembourg. It is perhaps not surprising that it is officially multilingual countries like these that are at the forefront of promoting integrated multilingual curricula in the mainstream school sector. I will introduce the situation in each country by first providing a brief introduction to education policy related to language learning before I describe the documents related to the respective integrated multilingual curricula.

In Switzerland, which has four official languages, the education and language acquisition policy is decided by each of the 26 cantons (regional authority). Normally, a second language is studied from Year 3 or 5 (age 10 or 12) through to the end of compulsory education at 16, and often beyond in vocational or upper secondary contexts. In many cantons the 'second' language introduced is English, but in some it is French or German. A third language is often introduced at lower secondary level (Year 7–9, aged 14–16). Switzerland has a relatively high proportion of families with migrant histories; thus many learners bring diverse languages to school: on average one in five children speaks a language other than the school language at home (Truniger, 2003).

Passepartout (2007, 2008, 2009) is the name of a first-time collaboration of six cantons which have jointly reorganised 'second' language education (*Fremdsprachen*) in mainstream schools; some but not all of the six cantons are officially bilingual German and French. This includes a series of documents, available in two languages, relating to this language education reform. I review the core document on pedagogic principles (Passepartout, 2008), and that on definitions (Sauer & Saudan, 2008). Unlike many other cantons that have opted for English as their first additional language, these cantons have opted for French in Year 3 and English in Year 5, in their German-speaking regions. However, they have gone further and their aims for practice are that:

- The core principles of pedagogy and multilingualism are known and shared by all.

- The aims and content of the lessons in different languages are coordinated.
- Teachers are familiar with all learning and teaching materials used in their school to teach different languages.
- Competences, learning strategies and techniques are developed in an integrated way.
- The same evaluation criteria are used.

The project description (Passepartout, 2007) lists the building blocks that form part of their integrated multilingual curriculum: ELBE (éveil aux langues, language awareness and contact of languages and cultures), language exchange projects and CLIL/immersion. Passepartout is work in progress and only the textbook for French exists so far (at the time of writing); the trial teacher materials for this will be presented next. Further materials are to follow and the project should meet its objectives fully in 2020.

Grossenbacher et al. (2012) have elaborated a visionary and practical handbook for teachers of French working in the Passepartout cantons on the internal border between German- and French-speaking parts of Switzerland. This handbook supports the teaching materials Mille Feuilles (which literally means 1000 sheets, but is also a name for a sweet) for French as a second/other language. The authors state that the materials aim to promote the development of communicative competences in the French language (as a second/additional language) as well as the development of multilingual competences (Grossenbacher et al., 2012: 8), based on other languages, which the learners study at school and/or that they bring to school from family contexts. My review of the actual student and teacher materials of Mille Feuilles (Bertschy et al., 2010a, 2010b) show, however, that French is integrated with English and German, but only marginal references are made to the integration of home languages, and no concrete activities can be found.

As can be seen below, this approach nevertheless integrates diverse languages, insofar as it at least makes links between the languages taught at school. The core principles are bilingual/immersive content learning; as well as exchange and contact. These are framed by three overarching perspectives: (1) content and action orientation; (2) awareness of languages and cultures; and (3) cross-linguistic instruction (Grossenbacher et al., 2012: 8). The interesting point about the Swiss model is that it is being rolled out widely over an entire region in the mainstream sector, and that it views language learning as a multilingual integrated activity. One of the weaker points, in the context of an integrated multilingual pedagogy, is that there is a discrepancy between the teacher guidelines (emphasis on inclusion of family languages) and the classroom materials (no concrete ideas of how to include these). Thus the initiative discussed next may be insightful in this respect. The work with Mille Feuilles started in 2009 and was evaluated in 2010 and 2011 by the Institute de recherches et development (IRDP). The evaluation was generally positive; many teachers and children liked the concept. Challenges were found with reference to parents, who did not understand the new approach, and teachers found it hard to get used to the new approach (Elmiger, 2011; IRDP, 2010). It needs to be noted that the evaluation is based on interviews with teachers and classroom observations, and thus is largely based on teacher experiences and estimations.

The school system in Luxembourg is trilingual (German, French and Lëtzebuergesch), and school children are expected to learn these languages, which all have official status. The languages are taught consecutively. German is used for core and Lëtzebuergesch for enrichment subjects from Year 1, French is introduced as a subject in Year 2. The learners are particularly diverse: only just over half (55.66%) of the learners speak Lëtzebuergesch at home, while 21.9% speak Portuguese and 22.6% speak other languages.

The Luxemburg education ministry commissioned an action plan for the readjustment of language education, which contains 66 action points towards an integrated curriculum, founded on the idea that the mother tongue of the Luxemburg people is *le plurilinguisme* (Berg & Weis, 2007), the idea that inspired the title of this chapter. They add that *plurilinguisme* can obviously not be considered a language, but it aims to make visible the often complex linguistic repertoires of individuals, who cannot be ascribed one mother tongue. The aims outlined are 'to achieve a high-level plurilingualism for the future generation, and to counter any exclusion produced through the education system, specifically language education' (Berg & Weis, 2007: 12, my translation). While Passepartout was only to cover a part of Switzerland, this action plan covers the whole Grand Duchy.

The document entitled *Ouverture aux languages à l'école: Vers des competences plurilingues et pluriculturelles* [Openness Towards Languages in School: Toward Plurilingual and Pluricultural Competences] is a teacher guide based on the action plan described above (Berg & Weis, 2007). The guide *Ouverture aux langues*, which is designed to complement the wider curriculum by starting with what children bring to school, points out that children each have their own history and future trajectory. This guide refers to Eric Hawkins' ideas about language awareness and pluralistic approaches as framed by Candelier (2008). The idea is that this approach can be used in all subjects, for which it offers practical activities applicable to a range of subjects. The activities, which are available online, comprise ice breakers, and activities dealing with linguistic identity, language contact, vocabulary, loan words, intercomprehension, natural science and humanities, cultural expressions and a section on Lëtzebuergesch.

This constitutes a collection of ideas rather than a comprehensive teacher textbook or step-by-step guide. Therefore, it must be understood as a first step towards achieving the goals of the action plan. However, personal communication with a teacher educator in Luxemburg indicated that *Ouverture aux langues* is not (yet) used widely or consistently; however, she uses the resource in her teacher education course. While it may not yet be implemented fully, it provides ideas that could potentially be implemented in many other contexts, or may develop awareness in teachers and learners to see opportunities when they occur.

Dynamic plurilingual pedagogy

As becomes clear in this section, there may not be many integrated multilingual curricula in the mainstream sector but there are a number of non-mainstream initiatives. The Internationals High Schools Network, examined by García and Sylvan (2011) is one such example of an interesting non-mainstream model from the USA. This is mentioned here for two reasons: first, it could be described as being based on an integrated multilingual curriculum, since it uses building blocks of learning of English through content-based instruction combined with translanguaging, based on a 'dynamic plurilingual pedagogy' (García & Sylvan, 2011); and secondly, because it builds on many years of experience and may provide insights that are useful for the purpose of this chapter, that are not available from the more recent initiatives reviewed here.

The Internationals High Schools Network was founded in 1985 as a not-for-profit network, which in 2011 comprised 13 schools. This programme was set up to support young people with migration histories in the USA, and to facilitate access to further education. Based on García and Sylvan's (2011: 394) analysis, their pedagogy is based on 'dynamic plurilingual pedagogy', which means that students' languages and their language practices are at the core of the curriculum and learning is based on 'dialogical action' (García & Sylvan, 2011: 391) between students and students as well as between students and teachers that promotes understanding. The authors examined how students and teachers in this programme built plurilingual abilities, and found that they did this based on principles such as learner difference, collaboration, learner-centred pedagogy, language and content integration, language use from the students up (based on their language practices), experiential learning and local sensitivity. I bore these findings in mind as possible starting points when examining orientations underlying the documents introduced above.

Orientations Underlying Integrated Multilingual Curricula

I explored to what extent there are shared and overlapping orientations that underlie these different curricula, as expressed in the documents reviewed. In this section I present the results of this review, which are

Table 6.1 Orientations identified in documents reviewed

Type of document	Documents reviewed	Orientations									
		(1) Language learning	(2) Competence	(3) Learner	(4) Language awareness	(5) Content	(6) Intercultural	(7) Collaboration	(8) Action	(9) Evaluation	(10) Local
Proposals	Kleppin (2004)	X	X	X	X		X	X	X	X	
	Candelier (2008)	X	X	X	X		X	X	X	X	X
	Coyle et al. (2009); CARAP (2007a)	X	X	X	X	X	X	X	X	X	
	Hufeisen (2011)	X	X		X	X	X	X	X		
	Reich and Krumm (2013)	X	X	X	X	X	X	X	X	X	X
Plan	Berg and Weis (2007) Luxembourg	X	X	X	X	X	X	X	X	X	X
Teacher guide	Tonnar (2010) Ouverture aux langues	X	X		X	X	X	X		X	
Plan	Passepartout (2007, 2008, 2009) Switzerland	X	X		X	X	X	X	X	X	
Textbook for French	Grossenbacher et al. (2012) Mille Feuilles	X	X	X	X	X	X	X	X	X	
US model	García and Sylvan (2011)	X		X	X	X		X	X		X

summarised in Table 6.1. As will be seen in the following discussion, some of these orientations overlap, but these themes, or indeed orientations, can be identified as individual topics in the documents.

As can be seen from Table 6.1, the orientations consistently found in all documents relating to integrated multilingual curricula were language learning, language awareness and collaboration orientations. Additionally, the orientations consistently mentioned in all European documents were competence orientation and intercultural orientation. The 10 orientations identified, which are discussed in this section, can offer possible answers to McKernan's (2008) questions as follows:

> *Why* do we need an integrated multilingual curriculum?
>   (1) Language learning
>   (2) Competence
> *Who* is this for?
>   (3) Learner
> *What* should this include?
>   (4) Language awareness
>   (5) Content
>   (6) Intercultural
> *How* should this be taught?
>   (7) Collaborative
>   (8) Action
>   (9) Evaluation
> *Where* should this be situated?
>   (10) Local

(1) Language learning orientation

All documents have highlighted this orientation. Authors generally agree with the idea that languages are not studied or acquired in isolation from one another but that language learning is a plurilingual and pluricultural activity, as proposed by the much cited Common European Framework of Reference (CEFR), which referred to the 'existence of a complex or even composite [linguistic] competence on which the user may draw' (CoE, 2001: 168). Tonnar suggests intercomprehension can help learners build confidence to use 'their (partial) linguistic knowledge to communicate, and to get them used to mobilise this knowledge in their language learning and in other subjects' (Tonnar, 2010: 14, my translation). It follows that intercomprehension could be one tool in the toolbox of an integrated multilingual classroom, but it may not always be available to all learners. This would depend on their *savoirs* or individual language repertoires. However, the *savoir faire* as a strategy to access unknown languages may be a useful strategy that could be taught to all learners. In Luxembourg, there are intercomprehension opportunities between German and Lëtzebuergesch (and English), as well as between French and Portuguese, for instance. Grossenbacher *et al.* (2012) introduce the concept of 'cross-linguistic instruction', through which they suggest that links are established between L2, L1 and L3 and other languages, based on the idea of transfer between languages, awareness of similarities and differences between languages (comparison), as well as utilisation of language (learning) experiences, with the aim of making language learning more effective. Coyle *et al.* (2009: 15) introduce the idea that 'appropriate code-switching between languages, particularly in EAL (English as an additional language) and home language contexts, enriches understanding and encourages the development of pluriliteracy across the curriculum'. From this follows that intercomprehension would also come under the umbrella of translanguaging. Viewing language learning as conceptualised by translanguaging may indeed be likely to result in what Coyle *et al.* (2009: 26) hope their curricular idea may be able to deliver, namely that learners 'become genuinely pluriliterate, building knowledge, skills and understanding through using more than one language in the curriculum and in the wider world'.

(2) Competence orientation

This was referred to in all documents reviewed, but not explicitly in García and Sylvan's article. Many of the reviewed authors, not surprisingly perhaps, focus on *individual, cognitive development* including language awareness in the sense of becoming aware of different language features (Kleppin; Candelier; Coyle *et al.*; Reich & Krumm), and constructivist views of learning based on developing personal plurilingual competences (Kleppin; Candelier; Coyle *et al.*; Reich & Krumm) and strategies (Kleppin; Coyle *et al.*; Hufeisen; Reich & Krumm). Furthermore, skills development is also seen as important, such as intercomprehension skills (Kleppin; Candelier), as well as other functional and transferable skills (Coyle *et al.*), or language learning strategy instruction (Reich & Krumm). Hufeisen sees as an objective that learners achieve basic interpersonal communication skills (BICS) and cognitive academic language proficiency (CALP) (see Cummins, 2000) in two languages as a basis for all further language learning. In order to achieve this, she suggests that the learners should be provided with support for both languages throughout their schooling if necessary. Communication skills (Kleppin; Coyle *et al.*) were also mentioned. García and Sylvan also emphasise as an objective the development of English language and literacy that enables students to access US universities and hence participate in society. They seem to emphasise the idea of learning how to be a multilingual learner in a new language environment and in the wider society.

(3) Learner orientation

This is mentioned in all documents, except in Hufeisen, Tonnar and in the Passepartout base documents. In their literature review, Reich and Krumm identified a tendency to emphasise cognitive learning aims, which is in line with Grossenbacher *et al.*'s cognitive understanding of learning based on learner schemata, or activation of previous knowledge. However, Grossenbacher *et al.* combine cognitive and sociocultural perspectives that: learners develop knowledge based on their previous learning; each person develops their own understanding of the world based on their own individual background knowledge (schemata); and learners construct meaning in interaction with other people, based on Vygotsky's theories. The latter emphasises the social component as crucial for constructing meaning and thus learning. As the Swiss authors point out, the orientation that all knowledge is subjective and that each learner develops a different type of knowledge (radical constructivism) (von Glasersfeld, 1987), may serve as a philosophical foundation for the understanding of learning, but would be difficult to translate into teaching materials (Grossenbacher *et al.*, 2012: 16). However, the socioconstructivist approach, combining psychological and sociocultural theories, may indeed be helpful as a theoretical basis for teaching and reflects current calls that advocate a combined or integrated paradigm (Larsen-Freeman, 2007; Watson-Gegeo, 2004). García and Sylvan go beyond the linguistic experiences and suggest that students, especially where high numbers of learners with migration in their biographies are present, have usually diverse previous lives, and varied academic, linguistic and life experiences; thus they have diverse and very individual *schemata*. In any case, whether previous life or language experiences are more or less heterogeneous in a classroom, schemata have to be assumed to be heterogeneous – and, according to García and Sylvan this should be a starting point when adopting a more integrated multilingual pedagogy.

(4) Language awareness orientation

This is one of the core building blocks of an integrated multilingual curriculum in all documents reviewed. Passepartout in Switzerland have adopted the ELBE principle (*éveil aux language* + language awareness + contact with languages and cultures) (Sauer & Saudan, 2008: 8). Reich and Krumm found that there are two ideological approaches: one is to generate links between a limited and selected number of languages, and the other is a general openness to all languages. The former is in line with those models that aim to create links between languages taught at school, and the latter includes the languages learners bring to school. Thus the language awareness orientation can activate learners' knowledge about and curiosity towards language and interest in comparing languages, and it can legitimise other languages, such as minority languages and their speakers by recognising all languages as valuable for learning. Thus, it can have a constructive (see above) as well as a critical theoretical underpinning. As Norton and Toohey (2004: 1) argue, 'advocates of critical approaches to second language teaching are interested in relationships between language learning and social change'. Thus, language awareness can address individual learning in the classroom and at the same time take into consideration the wider societal context and power relations that influence who we are and what we do outside educational institutions.

(5) Content orientation

Content orientation is mentioned by all, except Kleppin and Candelier. It is considered a core part of integrated multilingual curricula by Hufeisen, Coyle *et al.* and Grossenbacher *et al.*, who emphasise content as the main vehicle for language learning. Thus, CLIL is widely suggested as a building block for an integrated multilingual curriculum, however, not alone, and Reich and Krumm point out that there are only few CLIL models that integrate multilingual approaches. Some authors also mention cross-curricular links as important (Coyle *et al.*; Grossenbacher *et al.*; Reich & Krumm). Reich and Krumm propose that there is not just one way of incorporating multilingualism into the curriculum. They propose it either as a discrete subject, which is similar to Eric Hawkins' initial ideas, which runs the risk of isolating it from other content subjects, or as a cross-curricular (horizontally) linked activity, incorporated in a series of subjects, which seems to be the preferred option. Content orientation is also mentioned as a main tenet by García and Sylvan (2011: 396), who see 'content as the driver', while they stress that 'systematic support for students who are developing additional language' is required. In the model they describe (García & Sylvan, 2011: 397) 'content is rigorous and expressed in authentic and rich language that is scaffolded by collaborative structures that allow for peer mediation and teacher support'. Scaffolding and peer mediation, borrowed from sociocultural theory, are also important concepts in CLIL (Moate, 2010). The cross-curricular aspect of this could also be seen as based in the *constructivist* tradition, where learners build on what they know already.

(6) Intercultural orientation

This orientation has been mentioned by all, but not specifically by García and Sylvan. The literature showed that there was a strong focus on intercultural competence and understanding (Kleppin; Candelier; Coyle *et al.*; Hufeisen), awareness of languages and cultures (Grossenbacher *et al.*), plurilingual and intercultural education (CARAP, 2007a), and social cohesion (Coyle *et al.*). According to Grossenbacher *et al.* (2012: 12) the cultural component has three dimensions: (1) to recognise commonalities between cultures; (2) to gain awareness of French-speaking cultures (in the Swiss context) as part of the target language instruction; and (3) comparison of the target cultures with the learners' own cultures. Kleppin argues that intercultural competence should be an inherent component of language education, as well as the development of empathy and cooperative abilities. While the Swiss authors are concerned with connecting learners across language boundaries, among other intergroup contacts, the US authors make the important point of experiential learning (discussed further below), which incorporates language use and cultural learning within the community, and may well be conducive to opportunities for intercultural learning.

(7) Collaborative orientation

This orientation plays a role in all documents to a greater or lesser extent. The documents mention various levels of collaboration: student–student (all documents, bar Reich and Krumm), student–teacher (García & Sylvan), teacher–teacher (García & Sylvan; Reich and Krumm), teacher–parent (Tonnar), teacher–staff (García & Sylvan) and school stakeholders (Hufeisen, García & Sylvan). Grossenbacher *et al.* (2012) and Tonnar (2010) provide teaching materials, which include many task-based activities that are designed to promote collaboration among peers. This resonates with García and Sylvan's (2011) emphasis on collaboration between learners with very diverse backgrounds and levels of English. They see this as an integral part of the design of a dynamic plurilingual pedagogy, where 'students are able to share their different perspectives, experiences, and talents' (García & Sylvan, 2011: 395), while they build communities in which both more able and less able students are challenged in 'creative projects because students of different levels work together to accomplish a final product they would not be able to do on their own' (García & Sylvan, 2011: 395). García and Sylvan (2011), who argue that the traditional conceptualisation of the teacher as bearer of knowledge providing 'target' language input, as suggested by Krashen's (1985) input hypothesis, is unlikely to work in a heterogeneous classroom, such as the ones they describe. They point out that 'collaborative dialogue is very important in the development of an additional language'. Thus, the collaborative and group-work model is considered more conducive to learning. From their writing, it follows that the teacher's role is that of a facilitator who spends little time in front of the class, but much time supporting individuals and groups, thus foregrounding and valuing student knowledges and abilities. Teacher collaboration, according to García and Sylvan (2011), should mirror that expected of students, in that teachers are also conceptualised as a diverse group with different strengths and weaknesses. They suggest that cross-curricular teacher teams 'focus on the design of their curricula and their pedagogies, their challenges and successes, and their students' progress' (García & Sylvan, 2011: 396). The main tenet here is that teachers, like students, can learn much from each other. Tonnar (2010) suggests collaboration between teachers and parents, which can enrich the teachers' knowledge about the languages of their learners, especially where the teacher has no knowledge of the respective languages. An important point made by Hufeisen (2011), is the importance of informing stakeholders about the objectives of new initiatives. García and Sylvan (2011) agree that the activity of learning and teaching should be supported by the administrative staff and the wider community. This requires close collaborative networks between all people involved.

(8) Action orientation

This orientation is mentioned in all except in Tonnar's *Ouverture aux Langues*. Thus this is also consistently seen as an important pedagogic approach. The idea of action orientation has been around for a while: the CEFR, for instance, has promoted an action-oriented approach since 2001, which 'views users and learners of a language primarily as "social agents", i.e. members of society who have tasks (not exclusively language-related) to accomplish in a given set of circumstances, in a specific environment and within a particular field of action' (CoE, 2001: 9). Hufeisen suggests residence abroad experiences, and Passepartout school/student exchange projects, as part of an integrated multilingual curriculum, which would very much be in line with an action orientation. Thus there is an emphasis on practising the language in real-life situations. In a similar vein, albeit with a different emphasis, García and Sylvan (2011) suggest that learning needs to happen both inside and outside school through community-based projects, field trips, etc., as well as regular voluntary work or internships. This also supports the local orientation (see below). Meier and Daniels' (2011) work has shown that experiential learning based on the contribution metaphor (Grabois, 2008), which means making a contribution to the community where the language learning takes place, has been shown to be associated with language learning, social integration and student satisfaction. It follows that the notion of engaging with and making a contribution to society as part of one's learning (e.g. through voluntary work locally or abroad) resonates with a critical paradigm, which is concerned with social change and, in García and Sylvan's words, with social justice, and more widely with social integration and social cohesion, as formulated by Coyle *et al.* (2009).

(9) Evaluation orientation

For the evaluation of multilingual and related competences, portfolios and evaluation based on descriptors are suggested. Passepartout explicitly suggests the evaluation of multilingual competences, namely through the European Language Portfolio. This is based on the CEFR descriptors (CoE, 2001) and is designed for self-evaluation through 'I can' statements. The work with *Mille Feuilles* envisages the evaluation of three aspects in French: communicative action-oriented skills, awareness for languages and cultures, as well as learning strategies (IRDP, 2011). IRDP, who evaluated the work with *Mille Feuilles*, found that teachers found it difficult to evaluate these three competences, and there seems to be no clear guidance on this. It appears that in this case the instrument was not used for self-evaluation, as for instance suggested by Kleppin and Reich and Krumm. Thus, there is an indication that multilingual and related competences should be formatively and perhaps autonomously assessed. Candelier provides a comprehensive descriptor framework (CARAP, 2007b) which is designed for teacher assessment of knowledge (*savoir*, e.g. knows that languages are continuously evolving), attitudes (*savoir-être* or how to be, e.g. sensitivity to linguistic and cultural difference) and skills (*savoir-faire* or how do something, e.g. can perceive lexical proximity). I am not sure 'attitudes' is an appropriate term to translate *savoir-être*, and I would suggest 'self-awareness' in its stead. Be this as it may, there is an overlap with the Swiss model in that the CARAP model suggests formative teacher assessment, based on descriptors. The CARAP approach may indeed provide a good starting point for the evaluation of multilingual learning, based on *savoir* (knowledge), *savoir-être* (self-awareness) and *savoir faire* (skills/strategies). Berg and Weis (2007) mention that summative evaluation alone can in some cases lead to loss of confidence and motivation, so they also suggest a portfolio approach. Thus, formatively assessing multilingual competences that students have acquired might be an important step forward, and might help us move from normalisation of personal multilingualism to recognising it as 'a value, or indeed an added value' (Gajo, this volume). Reich and Krumm argue that portfolios are accepted by teachers as feasible instruments for formative self-evaluation and that there is evidence that they have positive effects on learner motivation.

(10) Local orientation

This orientation was emphasised above by García and Sylvan, while it was also mentioned in Candelier, Reich and Krumm and Weis and Berg. Candelier (2008) argues that *approches plurielles* need to be developed by taking the local situation as a starting point, and Berg and Weis and Reich and Krumm make brief but unclear suggestions for engagement with the local environment. It seems that the European documents are less concerned with making learning locally relevant, or at least they are not explicit about it. García and Sylvan emphasise the importance of situating the learning in the local community. Given that the US school network they examined caters for learners who have migrant histories, this may indeed be of great importance, since many of the learners are likely to be new to the area and need to learn the ropes of negotiating life in the new place. Given the diversity of learners in European countries, I feel this is a consideration that should also form part of any integrated multilingual curriculum, but there is a distinct absence of this orientation in the documents reviewed.

Discussion

I reviewed documents related to integrated multilingual curricula that take into consideration that learners use their entire language repertoires to access language education, and that this requires appropriate pedagogies. The documents reviewed all concern proposals or plans designed in and for mainstream education in European countries (Germany, France, Switzerland, Luxembourg, Austria and neighbouring countries), and took into consideration an article regarding an established, albeit state-independent, programme in the USA. I followed McKernan's (2008) model to consider curricula by asking questions, such as who, when, why and how, and found that the questions that could be answered based on the documentary review were:

- Why? Because of how learners learn, and what competencies they need.
- Who for? For diverse learners who all have unique life stories and language repertoires.
- What? Emphasis on language awareness, content instruction and intercultural understanding.
- How? Through collaborative and action-oriented methods, including formative evaluation.
- Where? In a contextualised and situated learning environment sensitive to local circumstances.

As can be seen from Table 6.1, the orientations found in all reviewed documents were those related to the current understanding of how learners learn languages (language learning orientation), that language awareness and related concepts are important (language awareness orientation), and that this should be embedded in collaborative learning processes (collaborative orientation). Thus these could perhaps be seen as universal orientations that underlie integrated multilingual curricula.

Orientations found in all European documents, but not explicitly in García and Sylvan's (2011) article, are the emphasis on competence development (competence orientation) and that of the development of intercultural understanding (intercultural orientation), and the need for the evaluation of multilingual competences (evaluation orientation). These are interesting points that merit a closer look. Clearly, competence development is what schools are about, and if they cannot demonstrate development of language and content knowledge, as well as skills and strategies, the idea of integrated multilingual curricula is unlikely to be taken seriously. However, as pointed out by Richards (2007), any competences as a basis for curriculum development need to be appropriately described.

As regards the intercultural orientation, drawing on Kymlicka, Cantle (2012: 157) makes the point that there are two types of interculturalism: one is 'global interculturalism, focused on learning about distant/world cultures' and the other is 'local interculturalism', focusing on getting to know diverse local groups. Thus it could be argued that 'foreign' language education relates to the former more cognitively orientated type, and 'language awareness' to the more locally or socioculturally oriented type. The interesting point here is that some integrated multilingual curricula tend to combine the two, providing the opportunity to embrace a holistic view of interculturalism.

Evaluation is important as feedback on an individual's progress and achievements. In conventional education, language competence is usually examined by monolingual formative or summative assessments. However, these cannot make visible any multilingual/plurilingual or related competences that a student has developed. Thus, formative evaluation is proposed in a number of the European documents reviewed, referring to two frameworks of descriptors, namely the CEFR (CoE, 2001) and the CARAP framework (CARAP, 2007b). While the CEFR evaluates language-specific competencies, the CARAP framework is more comprehensive and also includes categories such as *savoir* (knowledge about languages), *savoir-être* (self-awareness) and *savoir-faire* (learning strategies). Thus, there are two very useful instruments at our disposal.

An important point made by Richards (2007) is the evaluation not just of student achievements but also of the curriculum itself. For this he describes two types of evaluation: accountability-oriented (effect of the programme) and development-oriented (programme improvement). Clearly, curricula need to be evaluated, reviewed and adjusted. As McKernan (2008: 13) argues, a curriculum 'is never a finished entity but open to modification'. And the IRDP (2010, 2011) has made a start at evaluating the Swiss programme, as it seems, evaluating both effectiveness and scope for improvement. Additionally, Reich and Krumm (2013) make the very important observation that progression is often overlooked in the literature in this area. While the CEFR (CoE, 2001) makes some suggestions, Reich and Krumm find Sauer and Saudan's (2008) progression sketch useful. This suggests starting with more generally raising awareness (*éveil aux langues*) of locally spoken languages at pre-school stage, through to more systematic recognition of linguistic systems and intercultural communication models at upper primary and secondary stages. Clearly, a curriculum needs to have a clear plan for progression, and this can only be a starting point.

García and Sylvan (2011) emphasise the local orientation, which does not seem to be a priority for the majority of the European authors. This is in line with Richards (2007) who argues that curricula should be guided by a learner and a situational needs analysis. Embedding learning in the local environment (local orientation) and making learning relevant to learners through authentic tasks (action orientation, also found in nearly all documents), may be related and constitute an important part of an integrated multilingual curriculum. Thus, it could be argued that integrated multilingual curricula potentially support the system *and* social integration of young people as described by Hamburger *et al.* (2005), insofar as it enables the young person to integrate not only into the institutional framework (school), but also into their social environment (community). Hamburger maintains that both are required for a successful socialisation of young people. Thus, the overarching perspective of this book, namely ecological models of education (e.g. van Lier, 2004), which emphasise contextualisation, situatedness and social interaction, may be able to inform integrated multilingual curricula in the future.

One of the most important points in García and Sylvan's (2011) article is that of learner heterogeneity, which was shared by some of the European proposals and plans (learner orientation). This is based on the understanding that all learners have different linguistic and life biographies, which require appropriate pedagogies and integrated multilingual curricula, based on a learner needs analysis (Richards, 2007).

In terms of pedagogy, the important orientations that are evident in nearly all documents are that learning should be content based; namely, content should always be a starting point for language learning (content orientation). This is related to local, action and collaborative pedagogic considerations, as discussed above. Thus, from my review, I conclude that CLIL approaches in combination with language awareness approaches could indeed be the core building blocks of an integrated multilingual curriculum. My review, similar to Reich and Krumm's (2013), shows that there seems to be little emphasis on multilingual approaches to CLIL. However, a recent ECML project has started to change this by producing guidelines as to 'how content-based and plurilingual activities can be linked to several subjects of the curriculum' (ECML, 2011).

Theoretically, the models reviewed seem to be based on different positions, including cognitive/constructive, socioconstructive and critical perspectives, or a combination of these. Thus, it could be argued that some types of multilingual education, and multilingual integrated curricula in particular, are based on theoretical pluralism. Larsen-Freeman (2007: 773) explains that it is precisely where two perspectives intersect 'that will prove to be the most productive for future understanding of SLA [second language acquisition], and I believe that there is a new consensus around this point that is emerging'. Thus, I would like to join Larsen-Freeman in inviting researchers to consider examining those intersections when engaging in researching integrated multilingual curricula. This opens interesting paths for researchers, and interdisciplinary teams, given that 'we have only just begun to understand the potential (and the possible limitations) of these educational programs' (García & Sylvan, 2011: 398), and there is much scope for visionary practice and research.

Conclusions

In conclusion, I argue that we may still be a long way from describing our mother tongue as plurilingualism, if indeed that would be desirable, but we have seen that there are a range of proposals for mainstream initiatives that have taken on board current understanding of how people learn, and that may inspire developments elsewhere. The framework of 10 orientations for integrated multilingual curricula, presented in this chapter, is not meant as a template for implementation, but as a framework for reflection on how the multilingual turn could be incorporated into mainstream curricula in different contexts. Thus, I invite teachers, learners, policymakers and other people involved in curriculum development to consider and reflect on this framework and adapt it for their own purposes and circumstances. Time, experimentation, evaluation and much research will have to show what the opportunities and challenges of such integrated multilingual curricula may be for individuals and societies, in different contexts.

Note

(1) This is based on Title (b), page 19 in the Action Plan (Berg & Weis, 2007): 'Le plurilinguisme comme "véritable" langue maternelle des Luxemburgeois' [plurilingualism as the 'real' mother tongue of the Luxembourg people].

References

Bahr, A., Bausch, K.-R., Helbig, B., Kleppin, K. and Tönshoff, W. (1996) Forschungsgegenstand Tertiärsprachenunterricht. Ergebnisse eines empirischen Projekts. Bochum: Brockmeyer.

Baker, C. (2006) Foundations of Bilingual Education and Bilingualism (4th edn). Clevedon: Multilingual Matters.

Bär, M. (2010) Motivation durch Interkomprehensionsunterricht – empirisch geprüft. In P. Doyé and F.-J. Meißner (eds) Lernerautonomie durch Interkomprehension (pp. 281–291). Tübingen: Narr.

Berg, C. and Weis, C. (2007) Réajustement de l'enseignment des langues: Plan d'action 2007–2009. Luxembourg: Éditions du CESIJE.

Bertschy, I., Cavelti, S., Grossenbacher, B., Keller, M., Sauer, E. and Thommen, A. (2010a) Mille feuilles 4 (2): Vachement bien! Bern: Schulverlag plus AG.

Bertschy, I., Cavelti, S., Grossenbacher, B., Keller, M., Sauer, E. and Thommen, A. (2010b) Mille feuilles 4 (2): Vachement bien! Commentaire didactique: Bern: Schulverlag plus AG.

Breidbach, S., Viebrock, B. and Meehisto, P. (eds) (2012) Special issue on CLIL in Germany. International CLIL Research Journal 1 (4).

Candelier, M. (2008) Approches plurielles, didactiques du plurilinguisme: le même et l'autre. Les Cahiers de l'Acedle: Recherches en didactique des langues – L'Alsace au coeur du plurilinguisme 5 (1).

Cantle, T. (2012) Interculturalism. New York: Palgrave Macmillan.

CARAP (2007a) Cadre de référence pour les approches plurielles. FREPA. See http://carap. ecml.at (accessed 30 September 2013).

CARAP (2007b) What Are Descriptors of Resources? FREPA. See http://carap.ecml.at/ Descriptorsofresources/Overview/tabid/2829/language/en-GB/Default.aspx (accessed 20 September 2013).

Carrasco Perea, E. (ed.) (2010) Intercompréhension(s): Repères, interrogations et perspectives. In Synergies Europe 5. Sylvains-les-Moulins: Gerflint.

Cenoz, J. (2012) Third language acquisition. In The Encyclopedia of Applied Linguistics. Oxford: Blackwell.

CoE (Council of Europe) (2001) Common European Framework of Reference for Languages: Learning, Teaching, Assessment (CEFR). Language Policy Unit. Cambridge: Cambridge University Press.

Consejería de Educacíon (2005) Plan de Fomento del Plurlingüismo. Junta de Andalucía: Ministry of Education.

Coyle, D., Holmes, B. and King, L. (2009) Towards an Integrated Curriculum – CLIL National Statements and Guidelines. London: Languages Company. See http://www.languages company.com/images/stories/docs/news/clil_national_statement_and_guidelines.pdf (accessed 22 April 2014).

Cummins, J. (2000) BICS and CALP. In M. Byram (ed.) *Routledge Encyclopedia of Language Teaching and Learning*. London: Routledge.

Cummins, J. (2008) Teaching for transfer: Challenging the two solitudes assumption in bilingual education. In J. Cummins and N.H. Hornberger (eds) *Encyclopedia of Language and Education, Vol. 5 Bilingual Education* (2nd edn). New York: Springer.

Degen, P. and Stadelmann, T. (2007) ELBE: Éveil aux langues/language awareness/Begenung mit Sprachen. Bern: Schulberlag blmv.

Dobson, A., Péréz Murillo, M.D. and Johnstone, R. (2010) *Bilingual Education Project: Evaluation Report*. Manchester: British Council.

ECML (2011) Plurilingualism and pluriculturalism in content teaching. Graz: European Centre for Modern Languages. See http://conbat.ecml.at/ (accessed 28 November 2013).

Elmiger, D1. (2011) *Externe Evaluierung: Praxistest der Lehr- und Lernmittel für Französisch, Schuljahr 2010/2011 (Kurzfassung)*. Institut de recherche et de documentation: Neuchatel.

García, O. (2009) Bilingual education in the 21 century: Global perspectives. Malden, MA: Blackwell.

García, O. and Sylvan, C.E. (2011) Pedagogies and practices in multilingual classrooms: Singularities in pluralities. *Modern Language Journal* 95 (iii), 385–400.

Grabois, H. (2008) Contribution and language learning: Service-learning. In J.P. Lantolf and M.E. Poehner (eds) *Sociocultural Theory and the Teaching of Second Languages* (pp. 382–422). London: Equinox.

Grossenbacher, B., Sauer, E. and Wolff, D. (2012) *Mille feuilles: Neue fremdsprachen-didaktische Konzepte. Ihre Umsetzung in den Lehr- und Lernmaterialien*. Bern: Schulverlag plus AG.

Hamburger, F., Badawia, T. and Hummrich, M. (2005) *Migration und Bildung: über das Verhältnis von Anerkennung und Zumutung in der Einwanderungsgesellschaft*: Wiesbaden: Verlag für Sozialwissenschaften.

Hawkins, E. (1984) *Awareness of Language: An Introduction*. Cambridge: Cambridge University Press.

Hélot, C. and De Mejía, A.-M. (2008) Introduction: Different spaces – different languages. Integrated perspectives on bilingual education in majority and minority settings. In C. Hélot and A.-M. De Mejía (eds) *Forging Multilingual Spaces: Integrated Perspectives on Majority and Minority Bilingual Education* (pp. 1–30). Bristol: Multilingual Matters.

Hudelson, S. (ed.) (1993) *English as a Second Language Curriculum Resource Handbook*. New York: Krause International.

Hufeisen, B. (2003) Muttersprache Französisch – Erste Fremdsprache Englisch – Zweite Fremdsprache Deutsch. Sprachen lernen gegeneinander oder besser miteinander? In F.-J. Meißner and I. Picaper (eds) *Mehrsprachigkeitsdidaktik zwischen Frankreich, Belgien und Deutschland: Beiträge zum Kolloquium zur Mehrsprachigkeit zwischen Rhein und Maas, Goethe-Institut Lille (21/XI/2000)/La didactique du plurilinguisme entre la France, la Belgique et l'Allemagne: contributions au Colloque sur le Plurilinguisme entre le Rhin et la Meuse* (pp. 49–61). Tübingen: Narr.

Hufeisen, B. (2011) Gesamtsprachencurricululm: Weitere Überlegungen zu einem proto-typischen Modell. In R.S. Baur and B. Hufeisen (eds) *'Vieles ist sehr ähnlich'. Individuelle und gesellschaftliche Mehrsprachigkeit als bildungspolitiche Aufgabe* (pp. 265–282). Hohengehren: Schneider.

IRDP (2010) *Externe Evaluierung: Praxistest der Lehr- und Lernmittel für Französisch, Schuljahr 2009/2010 (Kurzfassung)*. Neuchatel: Institut de recherche et de documentation.

IRDP (2011) *Externe Evaluierung: Praxistest der Lehr- und Lernmittel für Französisch, Schuljahr 2010/2011 (Kurzfassung)*. Neuchatel: Institut de recherche et de documentation.

Jessner, U. (2008) A DST model of multilingualism and the role of metalinguistic aware-ness. *Modern Language Journal* 92 (2), 270–283.

Kansanen, P. (2002) Didactics and its relation to educational psychology: Problems in translating a key concept across research communities. *International Review of*

Education/Internationale Zeitschrift für Erziehungswissenschaft/Revue Internationale de l'Education 48 (6), 427–441.

Klein, H.G. (2007) *EuroComprehension*. Europasiegel. See http://www.eurocomprehension. eu/index.htm (accessed 29 July 2013).

Kleppin, K. (2004) Mehrsprachigkeitsdidaktik = Tertiärsprachendidaktik? Zur Verantwortung jeglichen (Fremd-) Sprachenunterrichts für ein Konzept von Mehrsprachigkeit. Paper presented at the Mehrsprachigkeit im Fokus, Arbeitspapiere der 24. Berlin: Frühjahrskonferenz zur Erforschung des Fremdsprachenunterrichts.

Krashen, S.D. (1985) *The Input Hypothesis: Issues and Implications*. New York: Longman.

Labercane, G., Griffith, B. and Feuerverger, G. (1998) Critical language awareness. In W. Tulasiewicz and J.I. Zajda (eds) *Language Awareness in the School Curriculum* (pp. 91–102). Melbourne: James Nicholas Publishers.

Larsen-Freeman, D. (2007) Reflecting on the cognitive-social debate in second language acquisition. *Modern Language Journal (Focus Issue)* 91, 773–787.

Lasagabaster, D. and Sierra, J.M. (2010) Immersion and CLIL in English: More differences than similarities. *ELT Journal* 64, 376–395.

Lüdi, G. (2013) Mesures de gestion des langues et leur impact auprès d'entreprises opérant dans un contexte de diversité linguistique. *Synergies Italie* 9, 59–74.

Lutjeharms, M. (2003) Niederländisch und Deutsch als Tertiärsprachen? In F.-J. Meißner and I. Picaper (eds) *Mehrsprachigkeitsdidaktik zwischen Frankreich, Belgien und Deutschland: Beiträge zum Kolloquium zur Mehrsprachigkeit zwischen Rhein und Maas, Goethe-Institut Lille (21/XI/2000) = La didactique du plurilinguisme entre la France, la Belgique et l'Allemagne: contributions au Colloque sur le Plurilinguisme entre le Rhin et la Meuse* (pp. 92–106). Tübingen: Narr.

McKernan, J. (2008) *Curriulum and Imagination: Process Theory, Pedagogy and Action Research*. London: Routledge.

Mehisto, P., Marsh, D. and Frigols, M.J. (2008) *Uncovering CLIL: Content and Language Integrated Learing in Bilingual and Multilingual Education*. Oxford: Macmillan.

Meier, G. and Daniels, H. (2013) 'Just not being able to make friends': Social interaction during the year abroad in modern language degrees. *Research Papers in Education* 28 (2), 212–238.

Meißner, F.-J. (2003) Grundüberlegungen zur Praxis des Mehrsprachenunterrichts. In F.-J. Meißner and I. Picaper (eds) *Mehrsprachigkeitsdidaktik zwischen Frankreich, Belgien und Deutschland: Beiträge zum Kolloquium zur Mehrsprachigkeit zwischen Rhein und Maas, Goethe-Institut Lille (21/XI/2000) = La didactique du plurilinguisme entre la France, la Belgique et l'Allemagne: contributions au Colloque sur le Plurilinguisme entre le Rhin et la Meuse* (pp. 92–106). Tübingen: Narr.

Meißner, F.-J. (2005) Mehrsprachigkeitsdidaktik revisited: über Interkomprehension-sunterricht zum Gesamtsprachencurriculum. *Fremdsprachen Lehren und Lernen* 34, 125–145.

Meißner, F.-J. and Reinfried, M. (1998) *Mehrsprachigkeitsdidaktik. Konzepte, Analysen, Lehrerfahrungen mit romanischen Fremdsprachen*. Tübingen: Narr.

Moate, J. (2010) The integrated nature of CLIL. A socio-cultural perspective. *International CLIL Research Journal* 3, 38–45.

Moore, D. (1995) *L'éveil aux langues. Notions en Questions 1*. Paris: Didier Erudition.

Norton, B. and Toohey, K. (eds) (2004) *Critical Pedagogies and Language Learning*. Cambridge: Cambridge University Press.

Oomen-Welke, I. and Karagiannakis, E. (1998) Language variety in the classroom. In W. Tulasiewicz and J.I. Zajda (eds) *Language Awareness in the School Curriculum* (pp. 11–20). Melbourne: James Nicholas Publishers.

Passepartout (2007) *Neukonzeption des Fremdsprachenunterrichts im Rahmen er interkantonalen Kooperation zwischen den Kantonen, BL, BE, BS, FR, SO und VS*. Basel: Passepartout.

Passepartout (2008) *Didaktische Grundsätze des Fremdsprachenunterrichts in der Volksschule.* Basel: Passepartout.
Passepartout (2009) *Willkommen . . . bei Passepartout. Fremdsprachen an der Volksschule.* Basel: Passepartout. See http://www.passpartout-sprachen.ch (accessed 29 July 2013).
Reich, H.H. and Krumm, H.J. (2013) *Sprachbildung und Mehrsprachigkeit: Ein Curriculum zur Wahrnehmung und Bewältigung sprachlicher Vielfalt im Unterricht.* Münster: Waxmann.
Richards, J.C. (2007) *Curriculum Devlopment in Language Teaching.* Cambridge: Cambridge University Press.
Sauer, E. and Saudan, V. (2008) Aspects d'une didactique du plurilinguisme: Propositions terminologiques. Basel: Passepartout. See http://www.passpartout-sprachen.ch (accessed 30 September 2013).
Tonnar, C. (2010) *Ouverture aux languages à l'école: Vers des competences plurilingues et pluri-culturelles.* Luxembourg: Government of Luxembourg. See http://www.men.public.lu/publications/syst_educatif_luxbg/langues/100222_ouverture_langues/100222_ouverture_langues.pdf (accessed 10 August 2013).
Truniger, M. (2003) Sprachen der Migration in den Schulen: ein riesiges Poential. *BAK Journal (Zeitschrift des Bundesamters für Kulur).* See http://www.zh.ch/internet/bildungsdirektion/vsa/de/schulbetrieb_und_unterricht/faecher_lehrplaene_lehrmittel0/sprachen/heimatliche_sprache_kultur_hsk0/_jcr_content/contentPar/morethemes/morethemesitems/artikel_potentia_mig.spooler.download.1350312623713.pdf/artikel_hsk-kurse_bak.pdf (accessed 17 September 2013).
van Lier, L. (2004) *The Ecology and Semiotics of Language Learning.* New York: Kluwer Academic Publishers.
von Glasersfeld, E. (1987) *Wissen, Sprache und Wirklichkeit.* Braunschweig: Vieweg.
Watson-Gegeo, K. (2004) Mind, language, and epistemology: Toward a language socialization paradigm for SLA. *Modern Language Journal* 68, 331–350.
Williams, C. (1994) Arfarniad o ddulliau dysgu ac addysgu yng nghyd-destun addysg uwchradd ddwyieithog. PhD thesis, University of Wales, Bangor.

7 Multilingual Teachers' Resources in Three Different Contexts: Empowering Learning

Jean Conteh, Fiona Copland and Angela Creese

Guiding Questions

- What similarities and differences do you notice across the three different teaching contexts described in the chapter?
- What constraints and opportunities are there for the teachers in developing multilingual teaching in their classrooms in each context?
- What points could you take from the chapter to relate to specific settings with which you are familiar?

Introduction

In this chapter, we present three case studies of teachers, focusing on the language resources they bring into their classrooms. Their contexts of teaching and learning are very different from each other and are not usually considered together in the academic literature. Presenting them in this way – we argue – highlights both their commonalities and the distinctive nature of each context. We show how each teacher works with their students to open out multilingual spaces for their learning. Recognising the wider political, cultural and social factors that influence the interactions in each setting, we present detailed data of teaching and learning conversations collected from the three classrooms, as well as interview data which reflect the teachers' own views and voices. The three teachers who are the focus of the chapter are:

- a Greek-Cypriot teacher in a 'frontisteria' school in Cyprus preparing students for the Cambridge upper-intermediate exam (FCE);
- a multilingual, Ethnic Minority Achievement (EMA) teacher in a mainstream primary classroom in the north of England teaching Key Stage 2 (KS2) pupils from a diverse range of backgrounds;
- a complementary school teacher in the English Midlands, teaching GCSE level Panjabi to multilingual students whose families share an inheritance in the language.

Some 'myths' about best practice in language learning and teaching

The teachers who are the focus of this chapter work in very different language teaching and learning contexts. What links them – as we bring out in our analysis – is that they are all bilingual or multilingual and this is directly relevant both to how they teach and how they view themselves as teachers. Using data from their classroom interactions and interviews, we show the range and variety of the ways in which they use language as a pedagogic resource to enhance the learning and teaching experience. We also explore the teachers' own views about this aspect of their work and how they view it as part of their professional identities, reflecting the tensions and uncertainties entailed. In discussing the teachers' approaches and strategies in the way we do, we develop arguments for the pedagogic importance of bi- and multilingualism for empowering learning for all pupils, not just those who bring the same languages as their teachers do to their classrooms. This is an important point: classrooms all over the world are becoming increasingly diverse. Learners, and teachers, are using languages in flexible ways both in classroom settings and in their daily lives. It is becoming more and more difficult – indeed unhelpful – to consider languages as separate at all.

One outcome of our approach is to highlight the shortcomings of some key assumptions about what counts as best practice in language teaching and learning (Cook, 1999; Phillipson, 1992). These often feel like common-sense notions. They are intuitively attractive, but they are unhelpful ideas that are not supported by research, and they need to be challenged. They are reflected in different ways in each setting. We will return briefly to them in our conclusion to the chapter. Here are some of our 'myths' about best practice in language learning and teaching:

- Languages should be kept separate in the classroom, or learners will become confused. Instruction should be carried out exclusively in the target language without recourse to students' L1.

- Translation between L1 and L2 has no place in the teaching of language or literacy.
- The ideal language teacher is a native speaker.
- The more the 'target language' is used in the classroom, the better the results.
- Language diversity is a 'problem', and it is better in multilingual classrooms if children speak English or the target language all the time.

Overview of the theoretical frameworks underpinning the case studies

This section provides a brief overview of what we regard as the key theoretical ideas related to language and learning and how teachers construct their professional identities in their classrooms in terms of language. These ideas also underpin our research methodologies and approaches, which are briefly discussed in the following section.

Languages as resources for users

In considering bilingual and multilingual teachers' language resources in this chapter, we move beyond notions of languages in classrooms as sets of skills, functions or processes to be taught in previously determined ways. In our analysis, we consider first what the teachers are trying to accomplish with their languages, rather than the kinds of language they are using. In doing this, we draw on a range of recent theoretical shifts in conceptualising multilingualism and language diversity, which are referred to in other chapters in the book. Heller (2007), in making a case for a social approach to bilingualism, argues for a view of languages as 'resources called into play by social actors' in order to 'make possible the social reproduction of existing conventions and relations as well as the production of new ones'. García (2009: 45) suggests that such a view entails a radical shift from foregrounding 'the perspective of the language' to considering languages from the 'perspectives of the users themselves'. Blommaert and Backus (2011: 9) invite us to reconsider the long-established sociolinguistic concept of language repertoires, which – they suggest – rather than being associated with notions of fixed 'speech communities', can more helpfully be regarded as 'biographically organized complexes of resources' which 'follow the rhythms of human lives' and which are learnt in a vast range of ways. In addition, researchers are developing concepts that aim to describe the ways in which people use languages, such as 'languaging' (e.g. Makoni & Pennycook, 2007), which they characterise as 'social practices that are actions performed by our meaning-making selves', and García's development of the idea of 'translanguaging' as '... multiple discursive practices in which bilinguals engage in order to make sense of their bilingual worlds ...' (García, 2009: 45). The pedagogic implications of this are indicated in the following section.

Pedagogies for multilingualism

As this book shows, there is a growing body of research in education and applied linguistics that accepts and promotes arguments that pedagogy should develop and work with the full linguistic repertoires of multilingual teachers and students. Exploring the pedagogic implications of translanguaging, García (2009) argues for a dynamic and flexible bilingualism in schools, which centres on the individual teachers' and students' language practices. According to García, the role of educators is to notice learner needs rather than to demarcate lines between particular languages. Meaningful instructional practices support learners' linguistic and cognitive growth. Canagarajah (2009) makes a similar point when he speaks of proficiency in terms of an integrated competence including an intercultural competence, which is a form of social practice appropriate to particular social and linguistic ecologies. García (2010: 524) suggests that language choice in multilingual speakers involves negotiation in every interaction as speakers 'decide who they want to be and choose their language practices accordingly'. Translanguaging, according to García (2009: 7), 'considers multiple language practices in interrelationship'.

Framing this pedagogic model of translanguaging, we take an ecological view of classrooms, seeing them as complex sociocultural contexts where learning is shaped and mediated by a wide and diffuse range of influences: political, ideological, historical, social and cultural. As Creese and Martin (2003: 161) argue, an ecological model of classrooms that includes languages 'requires an exploration of the relationship of languages to each other and to the society in which these languages exist'. In our case studies of the teachers' work, we consider the ideologies and inequalities entailed in the wider society's constructions and discourses of languages and their speakers, and how these impinge on teaching and learning.

Teachers' perspectives

Thinking about languages and learning in the ways we have outlined leads to a recognition that what Cummins and Early (2011) call 'maximum identity investment' is a key factor in learning and educational success. Thus we recognise the powerful links between learning, culture and identity and the importance of understanding the personal and professional identities of students and teachers as part of the processes of teaching and learning. In the case studies, we show how identity negotiation and performance are crucial aspects of educational success for both teachers and learners (Cummins, 2001; García, 2009).

The three teachers who feature in the case studies are all bilingual or multilingual. For at least two of them, it is actually difficult to define which is their 'first' and which their 'second' or additional languages. Their multilingualism is part of their lived reality in societies that are becoming increasingly super-diverse. Research on the ways that languages are used in fluid and creative ways in multilingual communities is extensive (e.g. Blommaert & Backus, 2011; Rampton, 2006), and the implications for how we think about languages have been analysed (Blackledge & Creese, 2010; García, 2009; Heller, 2007; Makoni & Pennycook, 2007). This work constructs a theoretical and methodological framework through which we can develop an understanding of how the teachers' personal and professional experiences of multilingualism provide them with pedagogic resources and at the same time affirm their identities as bilingual/multilingual professionals. The importance of both aspects of diverse teachers' professionalism for promoting transformative teaching and learning, contributing to raising the achievements of pupils who are often marginalised, has been shown (Conteh, 2007a, 2007b). At the same time, Safford and Kelly (2010), among others, have pointed out some of the ways in which such professional resources remain hidden or are ignored in monolingualising systems of education, such as the mainstream system in England.

Likewise in traditional teaching English as a foreign language (TEFL) classrooms, it is still rare for teachers to celebrate their linguistic resources or even to admit to using the learners' first language in class. Communicative language teaching approaches, drawing on notions of comprehensible input (Krashen & Terrell, 1983), learning through interaction (see Larsen-Freeman & Swain, 1991) and total immersion (Swain & Lapkin, 1982), have influenced English language teaching in many countries and in many contexts. In these approaches, the hegemony of target language teaching is largely uncontested. Recent work by Butzkamm (2003), Macaro (2005) and Brookes-Lewis (2009), among others, has, it could be argued, activated a rumbling revolution; however, much of the discontent is in the field of teaching modern foreign languages rather than English, where elite, often government-sponsored, institutions and highly successful international publishing houses continue to promote target language teaching.

Methodological frameworks and processes for researching in multilingual classrooms

To emphasise the methodological commonalities of the case studies, we conclude this introduction with a brief general comment about the research methodologies which frame the case studies and which, we suggest, are those which are best suited to promoting our understanding of the processes of teaching and learning in multilingual classrooms. Case study design is well suited to research in multilingual classrooms as it allows in-depth, iterative data collection and analysis to illuminate the different perspectives of the participants in the processes being studied. It also supports the development of collaborative practices among the researchers, which promote empowerment and allow the sharing of the different kinds of knowledge which underpin interpretation and analysis: linguistic, sociocultural, pedagogic, professional. Both the first and second case studies were small scale, focused on one particular context, while the third was one part of a much larger project (AHRC/HERA, 2010–2011), one of a linked set of studies carried out in different cultural settings across Europe. It employed a 'team ethnography' approach. The research team was comprised of Adrian Blackledge, Jan Blommaert, Angela Creese, Liva Hyttel-Sørensen, Carla Jonsson, Jens Normann Jørgensen, Kasper Juffermans, Martha Sif Karrebæk, Sjaak Kroon, Jarmo Lainio, Jinling Li, Marilyn Martin-Jones, Anu Muhonen, Lamies Nassri and Jaspreet Kaur Takhi. Blackledge and Creese (2010), in detailed descriptions of the day-to-day practices of the co-researchers in other large linguistic ethnographic projects (ESRC, 2003, 2007, 2013), provide a model of team ethnography for researching multilingualism as a pedagogic resource, which empowers researchers and practitioners alike.

In each case study, brief details of the research methods employed, along with the processes of data collection and analysis, are provided. In this way, we maintain the distinctiveness of the studies in order to foreground the voices of the teachers and show something of the particular qualities of their classrooms. To this effect, we retain the different ways in which transcripts were prepared and presented in each study. Reflecting the preferences of the communities involved (and the different nature of the linguistic resources), we also retain the different spellings of Punjabi/Panjabi in the second and third case studies.

The Case Studies

Learning English in a frontisteria

Introduction

In Greece, English is widely studied, both inside and outside school. Schools are generally constrained by the syllabus and examinations system and the level of English children are expected to achieve is relatively low. Greek parents, however, want their children to have good levels of English to improve their employment and education prospects. For this reason, they enrol their teenage children in private language schools to study for the First Certificate Examination (Cambridge ESOL), or equivalent, which is a qualification at upper intermediate level, or Level B2 of the Common European Framework. The private language schools, called 'frontisteria', generally hold classes in the early evenings or at weekends and children attend once, twice or three times a week, often from an early age, until they are ready to take the exam (specific exam preparation is usually 2–3 years).

Working at a frontisteria can be challenging for English language teachers for a number of reasons. For example, the children come to class after school and so can be tired. Many do not understand the importance of learning English as they are too young to be extrinsically motivated by thoughts of better jobs or universities, while others understand its importance but nevertheless look upon learning the language as a chore. In addition, although Cambridge ESOL has recently introduced a FCE examination aimed at teenagers, many frontisteria continue to prepare students for the adult examination, in which neither the content nor the form is always appropriate. Perhaps most significantly, the aim of all stakeholders is for the teenagers to pass the exam: being able to communicate in English is desirable but not imperative.

The data presented here come from a study of four English language teachers who work at four different frontisteria in Greek Cyprus. Data were collected in four classrooms taught by the teachers in two frontisteria in Cyprus. Each class was recorded and observed. Two weeks after each class, which provided space for the data to be listened to, transcribed and for preliminary themes to be identified, the teachers were interviewed in Greek and these interviews were also recorded. A number of themes emerged from the study (for a full description, see Copland & Neokleos, 2011), but here I would like to provide a brief summary of the teachers' translanguaging practices and then discuss the teachers' views of them.

Using two languages

All four teachers used both Greek Cypriot dialect (from here, Greek) and English in the classroom but in different ways and to different extents. Tina (all names are pseudonyms) taught the lesson almost entirely in English, conforming to the belief, overwhelmingly held in EFL contexts, that 'the use of L1 is to be avoided in the FL classroom' (Leibscher & Dailey-O'Cain, 2005: 235). However, while Tina spoke to her students in English, they answered her in Greek, as can be seen in Extract 7.1:

Extract 7.1

Student 1: Τι εν το wasp κυρία;
[*What's a wasp Miss?*]

Tina: Like a bigger bee that stings you
((7 second pause))

Student 1: Δηλαδή;
[*Meaning?*]

Student 2: Ποιος;
[*Who?*]

Tina: It stings you and it hurts (.) It's an insect.

Student 3: Μέλισσα;
[*A bee?*]

Tina: It looks like a bee. It's bigger. They fly too.
Wasp is ακρίδα

Lisa, in contrast, used Greek almost exclusively in the English class as the language of instruction. She used translation a good deal to elucidate meaning (see Cook, 2011, for a reappraisal of translation as pedagogy) and the following extract was typical of her approach:

Extract 7.2

Lisa: Thin εν το λεπτός. Muscular?
                  [Thin *means thin*. Muscular?]
Student 1: Μυώδης.
                  [*Muscular.*]
Lisa: Ωραί well-built?
                  [*Good* well-built?]
Student 2: Γερο
                  [*Strong*]
Student 3: Καλό
                  [*Well*]
Student 2: δεμένος
                  [*Built*]
Lisa: Ναι overweight?
                  [*Yes* overweight?]

The other two teachers, Christina and Maria, used English and Greek much more fluidly in the classroom, with one language 'seeping' (García, 2009) into the other. The extract below provides an example of this fluidity as Maria moves from English into Greek in response to a student's question. All her utterances relate to classroom management issues and it is clear from Student 1's initial question that he has understood the initial instruction. Maria's switch into Greek, then, is neither necessary to ensure understanding nor associated with the function of classroom management:

Extract 7.3

Maria: Please change books with the person sitting next to you and take a pen of different colour.
Student 1: Κυρία με ποιον να αλλάξω εγώ;
                  [*Madam, who shall I change with?*]
Maria: Ποιος εν στο ίδιο θρανίο με σένα;
                  [*Who do you share a desk with?*]
Student 1: Τούτος. ((δείχνει τον διπλανό της))
                  [*With him.* ((points to her classmate))]
Maria: Με τον Πέτρο τότε.
                  [*With Petros then.*]

Although interactional data from only four classrooms are presented here, it is clear that the teachers' languaging practices are varied and pragmatic. Importantly, learners are engaged in learning English, no mean feat given the constraints described above.

Attitudes to two languages

In all cases, the teachers in this study provided affordances for both languages to be used in the classroom to enhance learning. However, only one of the teachers, Maria, valued the practice or saw its benefits. She explained:

> *Extract 7.4*
> What I usually do is say it once in English and then repeat in Greek ... I think it's a good idea if it becomes a habit and they learn to talk in a similar way.

The others, Christina, Tina and Lisa, perceived the practice as deficient. Christina clearly articulates her rejection of Greek in her classroom:

> *Extract 7.5*
> I think one should try to use it as little as possible ... to try to avoid it in every possible way.

Lisa, the teacher who used Greek almost exclusively, was also critical of drawing on the shared L1 of students and teachers:

> *Extract 7.6*
> I do not think that it's the wisest thing to do because you are teaching them a second language ... you should avoid using the mother tongue as much as you can.

The teachers in this study all use two languages – Greek and English – as a resource to teach English. In doing so, they wish to ensure success in the examination: drawing on both languages supports them in this endeavour. As can be seen from the data extracts given here, the students are not confused by the bilingual nature of the classroom discourse and neither is their learning necessarily weakened by the pedagogies of their teachers (all four teachers enjoyed success at exam level). What is more, the teachers' implicit acceptance of the two languages allows them to create a learning environment in which potentially resistant children are drawn in and encouraged to learn. It is unfortunate that one of the main advantages that bilingual teachers have – being able to use, understand and contrast two languages – is not celebrated by all the teachers in this study. Indeed, such is the hegemony of the target language as the sole pedagogic resource that three of them perceive their language skills as disadvantageous to their learners.

It is in the area of TEFL that the ideology of target language teaching has continued to hold most sway, although the rise of content and language integrated learning (CLIL) in modern foreign language teaching is also now flying the flag for target language-only classrooms. It has created such a powerful orthodoxy that many teachers are unwilling even to conceive that a different approach might be possible, never mind in their students' best interests (at recent conference presentations on this topic, TEFL teachers vociferously objected to the arguments presented in this chapter). As discussed above, a number of researchers have recently also turned their lenses on classroom language and the role of the L1 in teaching the L2 (Brooks-Lewis, 2009; Carless, 2008; Liebscher & Dailey-O'Cain, 2005; Macaro, 2005). Nonetheless, few of these studies focus on TEFL and even fewer on English language teaching to children whom, it is argued in this chapter, can benefit in a number of ways from bi- and multilingual teaching.

Teaching multilingually in a mainstream primary school in England

Introduction

The classroom in this case study is different in many ways from those in the Greek frontisteria schools. It is a primary classroom, typical of many in England, where the children speak a range of different languages at home, but at school they are learning English. All their other subjects are taught through the medium of English and the system is overwhelmingly monolingual – the children in this classroom are learning French as a modern foreign language as part of their curriculum, but this is kept totally separate from their other experiences of language learning. The teacher, Meena (a pseudonym) is herself multilingual, and she shares the home languages of many of her pupils. In this, she has some strong similarities with Maria, Christina, Tina and Lisa. But, while this is the norm in Greece, it is unusual in England, where the number of qualified bilingual and multilingual mainstream teachers is still very low. Statistics are collected for ethnicity, not language, so it is very difficult to find out the actual number, but in 2009 the Department for Children, Schools and Families (DCSF) reported that 6% of the teaching workforce were from ethnic minority backgrounds (DCSF, 2009), compared to the National Census figures of 21% for the population as a whole (DfE, 2011a).

Another factor that Meena shares with Maria, but perhaps not so much with the other Greek teachers, is that she recognises the benefits of her own multilingualism, as well as that of the children, for their learning, because of her personal experiences as a pupil in the system in which she now teaches and her professional understandings gained through her studies. Meena is committed to providing opportunities for her pupils to learn multilingually. She tries hard to develop a 'bilingual pedagogy' (NALDIC, 2009), which plays to the strengths of learners and teachers alike. This factor distinguishes her from most other mainstream teachers in England. As part of a small action research project, Meena was observed in her classrooms, and some of her lessons were audio-recorded. Her role in the school at the time was different from that of a typical primary class teacher. As an EMA teacher, Meena was responsible for promoting the English language learning – and the learning more generally – of the children in KS2 (aged 7–11 years) who were 'new to English'.

The data presented in this case study (which have been reported elsewhere; see Conteh, 2007b) were recorded in a Year 4 Geography lesson. There were 25 children altogether, aged 8–9 years. About 15 of them shared their teacher's first language of Punjabi. One or two children spoke Polish, and the remaining children were 'monolinguals'. One 'new to English' child, who had recently come from Denmark, was fluent in both Danish and Punjabi. It was because of this child's presence that Meena had been assigned to the class by the school's senior management. She could have chosen to withdraw the child and provide him with some focused English language teaching, along with other recently arrived pupils. The practice of withdrawal for new arrivals was very common until the mid-1980s, but became frowned on when national policies such as the Swann Report (DES, 1985) began strongly to advocate 'mainstreaming' on the grounds of equality of opportunity. Now, with the lack of any coherent centrally mediated English as an additional language (EAL) policies or practices in mainstream schools and the decline in local authority advisory services in England, schools are beginning to reinstate withdrawal practices on the grounds that their new arrivals need to learn 'survival English' as quickly as possible before being exposed to mainstream classrooms. But instead of this approach, Meena opted to teach the child as part of the whole class.

The lesson was based on the National Curriculum geography curriculum and the theme of *'knowledge and understanding of places, patterns and processes'* (DfE, 2011b). The content centred on the Swat Valley of Pakistan. Meena judged that her own extensive personal and cultural knowledge would help her to present it to the children in a meaningful and interesting way. Also, many of the children knew something about Pakistan from their home backgrounds, and some had been on visits. The lesson time was mostly taken up with the whole class together watching sections of a video, interspersed with questions and discussion. Meena said that her main aim was to raise the children's awareness of the differences and similarities between the community in which they lived and what they saw on the video. In the process of the lesson, she translanguaged between English and Punjabi fairly extensively, mostly while speaking to small groups or to individual children, but sometimes with the whole class.

The lesson was transcribed with the help of Meena and another bilingual teacher. Their comments while listening to the recording have richly informed the analysis. In this case study, one episode from the lesson is discussed, which – we suggest – illustrates more about the teacher's professional identity than her strategies to support the children's learning. Towards the end, the video shows farmers from the Swat Valley bartering the crops they have grown for goods in a nearby town. To explain the idea of bartering, Meena introduces the notion of buying things 'on tick' from the local corner shops, a practice she knows is common in the children's communities. This is where the translanguaging becomes sustained. In this transcript, the words spoken in English are shown in regular font and those in Punjabi in bold, with a gloss in italics afterwards:

Extract 7.7

001 **Meena:** When you ... I know that ... **jilay thusa rai ami thayabba**
001 **janay na dukarnay par paysay ar vacth danay ... dukarn**
003 **daray ... koi ... jraay khusa nay kol**
When your mum and dad go to the 'corner shops' and they pay the shopkeepers, do they pay the shopkeeper there and then ... I mean the shops that are near you

004 **Child 1:** No, they can give ...

005 **Meena:** **Kay karnai?**
What do they give?

006 **Child 2:** **Paysay daynay na**
They give money

007 **Meena:** **Paysay sarai day nay?**
Do they give all the money?

008 **Child 3:** No ... (unintelligible)

009 **Meena:** Who said 'no'? What does your mum do when she goes to the
010 shop? **Paysay daynay ... kai kithabay par liknay saab kithab**
Do they pay (upfront) or do they write it in a book, i.e. 'all your goods'

011 **Child 2:** **Paysay daynay nah**
They pay

012 **Child 3:** **Liknay thay paysay daynay**
They write it and pay

013 **Meena:** I know ... I know ...

Meena is using the funds of knowledge (Gonzalez *et al.*, 2005) of the children to make links between trading carried out in small corner shops in their locality and by the farmers in Pakistan. In the course of this, she uses Punjabi vocabulary that, while transcribing, she said she was surprised she had used. For example, she calls the corner shop 'dukarnay' in line 002, which she and her co-transcriber said was best translated as a 'hut'. They also discussed at length the translation for 'saab kithab' in line 010, and agreed on 'something like a book for all your goods'. They suggested that both these phrases had strong cultural connotations, but that they were not the most commonly used Punjabi terms for the ideas that Meena was trying to communicate. She worried that the Punjabi-speaking children might not have understood the words as they were 'old-fashioned', and that the 'monolingual' children may not have understood anything at all. She felt that she did not achieve her aim of drawing out the commonalities between the Swat Valley and the children's home communities. From my viewpoint as observer, there did not seem to be much to worry about. All the children, not just the Punjabi speakers, seemed to listen intently to what was taking place. I noticed that several of the non-Punjabi speaking children were focusing intently on what was happening and sometimes repeating the Punjabi words to themselves. Perhaps Meena did not totally succeed in achieving her geography objectives, but what she clearly did accomplish at this point in the lesson was to include the whole class in a rich, multilingual discourse. The multilingualism was central to what was happening in the classroom, not just restricted to a small group on the margins, as is usually the case in mainstream classrooms in England.

The transcript clearly shows Meena's confidence in her translanguaging strategies. She believed that her status as a multilingual teacher gave her the right to claim the space in her classroom to place multilingualism in the centre. Research into the professional expertise and identities of diverse mainstream teachers in England (Conteh, 2007a; Conteh & Brock, 2011) is beginning to show the potential for developing our understanding of the ways in which learning can be empowered through multilingualism. But, when this transcript has been presented in academic seminars, questions have been asked as to what the children were actually learning. What did those who could not speak Punjabi learn from the episode, and also was the 'new to English' child ever going to learn English? We suggest that while some of the words may be strange, the lessons offered by Meena's translanguaging in this classroom are powerful, going far beyond the actual language itself. For the 'monolingual' children present, their classmates may speak Punjabi and it may be part of their community contexts, but it is normally marginal to their everyday experiences. Meena's strategies provide an important lesson in language and cultural awareness, important to them personally as well as promoting a more inclusive whole-school ethos, and contributing to wider community cohesion (Conteh, 2003: 120–121). For the 'new to English' child, Meena's approaches foreground the importance of the links between language, social practice, culture and identity, vital for promoting educational success. Knight (1994) argues that all children gain enhanced self-confidence from operating in and between different cultures and languages, a facility she has defined as 'pragmatic biculturalism'. She argues that, if the development of this biculturalism is seen as an important strand in their learning in school, it 'enables pupils to function with greater skill and understanding within the mainstream culture which controls their lives' (Knight, 1994: 102). Such experiences need to be valued and nurtured in schools in order to help all pupils feel that they belong and to open out their full potential for learning.

Complementary school teachers in the Midlands, teaching GCSE level Panjabi to bilingual students whose families share an inheritance in the language

Introduction: A vignette

The following is an interview extract from the project manager of a Birmingham-based Panjabi community language school in which he describes his linguistic history:

Extract 7.7

My mum spoke fluent Swahili, Gujarati, Hindi, Panjabi and Urdu and my dad did the same. But now I can't speak Swahili. I was only two years old when I went to India. Basically I started learning Panjabi first. Because I was in a village. Because our house was in a village and there was no English at the start. Nowadays actually even in smaller schools in India there is a lot of English. In my times it wasn't. So I started learning Panjabi basically. Because my family was from Africa my dad used to speak very fluent English. So I picked it up from there. (Interview with Project Manager)

In South Asia and in many parts of the world, individuals and communities, as the project manager above reminds us, 'are so radically multilingual that it is difficult to identify one's mother tongue or native language' (Canagarajah, 2009: 10). Such intense contact means that languages can no longer be thought of as 'pure' or 'separate' if they ever could (Makoni & Pennycook, 2007). Rather, the notion of 'repertoire' better describes the linguistic and social practices of multilingual people as they make use of various semiotic resources to communicate. Canagarajah (2009: 6) defines repertoire as 'the way the different languages constitute an integrated competence'. Rymes (2010) defines communicative repertoires as 'the collection of ways individuals use language and literacy and other means of communication (gestures, dress, posture, or accessories) to function effectively in the multiple communities in which they participate'. Busch (2014) also speaks of communicative repertoires and argues that pedagogic spaces need to legitimate and recognise young people and teachers' translocal linguistic histories as meaning-making resources. The interview extract above points to the project manager's linguistic repertoire and its complex sociolinguistic biography. Importantly, the programme manager describes how this repertoire is not stable but changes and shifts, sometimes dramatically, during different phases of his life. With migration and other changes brought about by globalisation he records how his transnational and multilingual experiences began in Africa, transferred to India and sedimented in Birmingham. In other words, his transnational journeys fuse the experiences of multilingual

Asia and Africa with contemporary Birmingham through the trajectories and multiple experiences of his individual life.

England, of course, presents a very different picture for discussing plurilingualism to Canagarajah's (2009) description of South Asia. Despite the linguistic diversity of English cities, in media discourse England is often presented as a monolingual nation, at least in institutional and policy terms. Multilingualism is viewed by the state as a personal issue of local and cultural relevance to small segments of English society and is ultimately constructed as not pertinent to majority interests or institutions such as mainstream schools. Where it is relevant to practitioners in different areas of social life, such as education, health and law, multilingualism is either conceptualised as a problem or as a temporary state in a transition to a monolingual English. Rarely is it presented as an asset unless it is manifest in the elite bilingualism of the upper social classes in English private schools and their domains of influence. Even rarer in England are stories of pedagogic innovation which use the complex linguistic histories and repertories of bilingual English citizens in shaping curriculum materials and classroom interaction (but for notable exceptions, see Blackledge & Creese, 2010; Conteh, 2007a, 2007b, 2012; Kenner & Ruby, 2012; Sneddon & Martin, 2012).

The third case study in this chapter presents examples of multilingual approaches which refute the monolingual bias in language teaching with examples of a translanguaging approach to pedagogy. The site of research for making these arguments is complementary schools. I draw on data from our investigations over the last 10 years in multilingual pedagogy, identity performance and discourses of culture and inheritance in Bengali, Chinese, Gujarati, Panjabi and Turkish complementary schools in Birmingham, Manchester, Leicester and London, respectively. Complementary schools are voluntary, community run and outside the state sector. They are also known as supplementary schools, heritage language schools and community language schools in different places in the world. In this case study, I draw on data from our recent project on Panjabi schools which was part of a larger research project on multilingual Europe.

The complementary school

In this case study, one of the bilingual teachers in the Panjabi complementary school is introduced. First her linguistic history is described, before providing one example of a multilingual pedagogy which she has developed in her Saturday Panjabi classes. With her south Asian background and her experiences of education, Hema's professional identity has parallels with Meena's in the case study above. Hema is in her mid-thirties and came to the UK in 1995. She was educated in the Punjab, India and obtained a Masters qualification in economics. After arriving in Birmingham she completed an

ESOL course and began to teach adults at Birmingham's City College. She has worked in a large Birmingham secondary school for over 13 years as a teaching assistant. At the Panjabi complementary school she is seen as a 'senior teacher' because of her long-term commitment to the school and her teaching experience in the different settings of further education (FE) college, secondary school and complementary school. She serves as a mentor not only to her own two classroom assistants but also to the other 14 teachers who work at the complementary school.

Hema is passionate about the necessity of preserving Panjabi and describes the importance of the language in her own life.

Extract 7.8
I think our language is extremely important ... if you don't know your language then what will you do? And secondly if you have your roots, if a tree doesn't have roots then how big will that tree grow? Because you won't have any self-confidence because you won't know who you are. Without an identity then what will you do? (Hema interview)

She has a pragmatic view of language use in the classroom and stresses the importance of drawing on the students' linguistic repertoire as she teaches them Panjabi.

Extract 7.9
... both languages yeah, both languages, we mix them yes when they don't understand and we don't have words in Panjabi to describe to them me we then describe them in English. (Interview with Hema)

In the extract above, Hema refers to a multilingual approach to language teaching which has been described as common in complementary school classrooms (Kenner *et al.*, 2008). The importance of not keeping the languages separate in the teaching of Panjabi is mentioned by Hema in her interview extract above. One language can serve as a resource for another language in the teaching of a language. Hema also points to the porous boundaries between the two languages. At times 'English' can be used when 'Panjabi' is not available for various reasons. In other words, translation is not always possible and at that point an English word becomes a Panjabi word and vice versa.

In the classroom transcript below, we see an example of this. Hema, rather unusually, addresses the class directly about the integration and separation of languages. She asks them to reflect on the kinds of decisions bilinguals are asked to make in life beyond the classroom. Hema has just been doing a pronunciation and translation exercise with the students which prompts questions about borrowings from English into Panjabi and how to translate them. From the field notes we record:

Extract 7.10
She talks about how she was doing a translation and she gave the Panjabi word for community but nobody recognised it and so she translated 'community' as 'community'. Some words she explains are easier to say in English. (Field notes)

Below is the full classroom recording of this narrative.

Extract 7.11
And erm, will share one thing with you. Last week I was doing a translation for somebody. Er, it was a Gurdwara {*Sikh temple*} and there was a leaflet. Couple of lines only I had to translate for some, er Babaji {*grandfather*}, like bazurgh {*elderly person*} yeah? Elderly person. Er and the word was community yeah? And, I was doing the translation and I said Samhudai {*community*} yeah? Community means Samhudai. Couldn't understand! Ah then I tried to make this word more easier. No! Then I was thinking 'hunh mein ehnoo ki dasaa?' {*'what shall I tell him now?'*}

'what shall I tell him now?' Then I said shall I say the word 'community'? I said 'community'.

It was fine! [laughter] [He] did understand because some words like, they are so familiar right? (.) The people, the people living with those words right? He easily understood what I'm talking about. Community 'haa puth, tu community kehna si, community kehna si menoo!' {*yes child, you should have said community, should have said community to me!*} I said ok. I was 'uncleji {*uncle*} I was doing word to word translation'. Ok? Some words they are more easier to understand if you say them in English.

Hema's multilingualism is at the heart of her story. She points to its relevance beyond the classroom. Her anecdote to the students serves as a pedagogic curriculum and also as a model of translanguaging as she moves between her languages to convey the drama of the story. One of Hema's skills as a teacher is her communicative repertoire, which she refers to as linking many communities and contexts beyond the classroom. This repertoire needs to be sensitive and nuanced depending on communicative function. Rymes (2010: 531) argues that '"correctness" is a construction that functions secondarily to communicative goals'. In Hema's narrative the message to the students appears to explicitly agree with this line. Speaking 'textbook' Panjabi causes Hema problems within the interaction and she must adjust her language use and make it more appropriate to the context. In pointing this out, Hema provides a lesson in critical language awareness.

The narrative anecdote told by Hema here is an example of social accommodation in process. Hema must accommodate her language use in order for her interlocutor and herself to reach an understanding. The directionality of the accommodation is towards the elder. Hema's narrative addresses issues of social and language change in communities in Birmingham. She uses her bilingualism to make connections to different timescales, social practices and communities. She makes a point of endorsing older people's contributions within the community and family. Importantly, she addresses the questions about language use that the young people themselves bring to the classroom. Through a process of identification she constructs them as facing the same dilemmas she herself must resolve as a bilingual person in Birmingham. She assumes a shared Panjabi heritage with her students while constructing their affiliation beyond the classroom (Leung *et al.*, 1999).

Concluding comments

In this case study, one teacher's pedagogic practices have been discussed. We have looked at how she draws on her own rich linguistic and cultural heritage as well as her more recent experience and participation in Birmingham's multiple communities to enrich her students' learning experience. Translanguaging or flexible bilingualism is a common practice for creating a multilingual ideological space in complementary schools. We argue this is an effective pedagogy which values student, teacher and community multilingualism.

Conclusions

This chapter presents data from three different multilingual classrooms, complementary, mainstream and private language school, which we analyse to show the teachers' translanguaging practices, that is, teachers using the full range of their language resources in interaction with their learners. We show how translanguaging is a feature of these teachers' normal, everyday pedagogic practices. It is a feature which has tended to be ignored in many classrooms where the 'target language' is seen as the sole pedagogic resource. We argue that translanguaging opens multilingual spaces which provide affordances for effective teaching and learning. We also suggest that translanguaging can provide a bridge between the everyday social worlds of multilingual members of society and the teaching and learning of languages in formal settings. What is more, it has the potential for reducing dissonance between home and school, for recognising the voices of many of our young people and for challenging the monolingual norm.

From the teachers' viewpoints, we show how translanguaging is important to them in performing their identities as bi- and multilingual teachers, and how this at times can bring uncertainty and tension. In each case study, there are points at which the teachers question their own professional multilingual identities. The ways in which these are mediated show something of the importance of integrating research and practice. The monolingualising ideologies underpinning the 'myths' we alluded to at the start of this chapter are still prevalent, leading to many misconceptions in languages teaching. A powerful one is that there is only one ideal way to teach and anything else must fall short in some way. This leads to the assumption – particularly in TEFL classrooms – that it is only the 'ideal native speaker' who can model the target language in the best ways for students to learn. In a world where multilingualism is increasingly the norm and languages are taught and learnt in so many contexts, it is surely unhealthy to continue to believe in a one-size-fits-all approach or that one variety of a language is superior to another. We need contextualised pedagogies that are 'particular, practical and possible' (Kumaravadivelu, 2001). We need now to focus on the role of languages in these pedagogies in order to decisively reject the notion that there is only one particular, practical and possible language for learning and teaching.

For the three teachers whose work we present, to become an 'idealised native speaker' is clearly an impossible goal and indeed one which does not recognise their distinctive strengths and expertise. For their multilingual students, translanguaging has importance in promoting affordances for learning in ways that allow them to use their full repertoires of language resources. For their 'monolingual' students, as reflected most clearly in the second case study, it promotes affordances for learning, not just about the content of the lesson or the language mediated in the classroom, but about the multilingual societies of which they are members. Thus, it combats the prevailing, restrictive monolingualising ideologies in mainstream education policy and practice, and offers great positive potential for our multilingual futures in the wider society.

Acknowledgments

We would like to thank Georgios Neokleos for permission to use the data gathered at the four different frontisteria in Greek Cyprus for this chapter. We also wish to acknowledge the invaluable contributions of Safina Hussain and Ishrat Dad to the writing of this chapter.

References

AHRC/HERA (2010–2011) *Investigating Discourses of Inheritance and Identity in Four Multilingual European Settings* (HERA-JRP-CD-FP-051). HERA. See http://heranet.info/idi4mes/index (accessed 20 August 2014).

Blackledge, A. and Creese, A. (2010) *Multilingualism: A Critical Perspective*. London: Continuum.

Blommaert, J. and Backus, A. (2011) Repertoires revisited: 'Knowing language' in superdiversity. Working Papers in Urban Language and Literacies No. 67. London: King's College London. See http://www.kcl.ac.uk/innovation/groups/ldc/publications/workingpapers/download.aspx.

Brooks-Lewis, K.A. (2009) Adult learners' perceptions of the incorporation of their L1 in foreign language teaching and learning. *Applied Linguistics* 30 (2), 216–235.

Busch, B. (2014) Building on heteroglossia and heterogeneity: The experience of a multi-lingual classroom. In A. Creese and A. Blackledge (eds) *Heteroglossia as Practice and Pedagogy*. New York: Springer.

Butzkamm, W. (2003) 'We only learn language once'. The role of the mother tongue in FL classrooms: Death of a dogma. *Language Learning Journal* 28 (1), 29–39.

Canagarajah, S. (2009) The plurilingual tradition and the English language in South Asia. In L. Lim and E.-L. Low (eds) *Multilingual, Globalizing Asia: Implications for Policy and Education. Aila Review* 22, 5–23.

Carless, D. (2008) Student use of the mother tongue in the task-based classroom. *English Language Teaching Journal* 62 (4), 331–338.

Conteh, J. (2003) *Succeeding in Diversity: Culture, Language and Learning in Primary Classrooms*. Stoke-on-Trent: Trentham.

Conteh, J. (2007a) Opening doors to success in multilingual classrooms: Bilingualism, codeswitching and the professional identities of 'ethnic minority' primary teachers. *Language and Education* 21 (6), 457–472.

Conteh, J. (2007b) Bilingualism in mainstream primary classrooms in England. In Z. Hua, P. Seedhouse, L. Wei and V. Cook (eds) *Language Learning and Teaching as Social Interaction* (pp. 185–198). Basingstoke: Palgrave Macmillan.

Conteh, J. (2012) Families, teachers and pupils learning together in a multilingual British city. *Journal of Multilingual and Multicultural Development (Special Issue: Language Policy and Practice in Multilingual, Transnational Families and Beyond)* 33 (1), 101–116.

Conteh, J. and Brock, A. (2011) Safe spaces? Sites of bilingualism for young learners in home, school and community. *International Journal of Bilingual Education and Bilingualism* 14, 347–360.

Cook, G. (2011) *Translation in Language Teaching*. London: Oxford University Press.

Cook, V. (1999) Going beyond the native speaker in language teaching. *TESOL Quarterly* 33 (2), 185–209.

Copland, F. and Neokleos, G. (2011) L1 to teach L2: Complexities and contradictions. *ELT Journal* 65 (3), 270–280.

Creese, A. and Martin, P. (2003) Multilingual classroom ecologies: Inter-relationships, interactions and ideologies. *International Journal of Bilingual Education and Bilingualism* 6 (3&4), 161–167.

Cummins, J. (2001) *Negotiating Identities: Education for Empowerment in a Diverse Society* (2nd edn). Ontario, CA: California Association for Bilingual Education.

Cummins, J. and Early, M. (eds) (2011) *Identity Texts: The Collaboration of Power in Multilingual Schools*. Stoke-on-Trent: Trentham Books.

DCSF (2009) *School Workforce in England (Including Local Authority Level Figures), January 2009* (Revised). London: Department for Children, Schools and Families. See http://www.education.gov.uk/researchandstatistics/statistics/allstatistics/a00196163/school-workforce.

DES (Department of Education and Science) (1985) *Education for All: The Report of the Committee of Inquiry into the Education of Children from Ethnic Minority Groups* (The Swann Report). London: HMSO.

DfE (2011a) *Schools, Children and their Characteristics: January 2011*. London: Department for Education. See http://www.education.gov.uk/rsgateway/DB/SFR/s000925/index.shtml.

DfE (2011b) *The National Curriculum: Geography at Key Stage Two*. London: Department for Education. See http://www.education.gov.uk/schools/teachingandlearning/curriculum/primary/b00199002/geography/ks2.

ESRC (2003) *Complementary Schools and their Communities in Leicester* (ESRC R000223949). Swindon: Economic and Social Research Council.

ESRC (2007) *Investigating Multilingualism in Complementary Schools in Four Communities* (ESRC RES-000-23-1180). Swindon: Economic and Social Research Council.

ESRC (2013) *Researching Multilingualism, Multilingualism in Research Practice* (ESRC RES-046-25-0004). ESRC Researcher Development Initiative. Swindon: Economic and Social Research Council.

García, O. (2009) *Bilingual Education in the 21st Century*. Oxford: Wiley-Blackwell.

García, O. (2010) Languaging and ethnifying. In J.A. Fishman and O. García (eds) *Handbook of Language and Ethnic Identity. Disciplinary and Regional Perspectives, Vol. 1* (2nd edn) (pp. 519–534). Oxford: Oxford University Press.

González, N., Moll, L. and Amanti, C. (eds) (2005) *Funds of Knowledge: Theorizing Practices in Households, Communities and Classrooms*. New York: Routledge.

Heller, M. (ed.) (2007) *Bilingualism: A Social Approach*. Basingstoke: Palgrave Macmillan.

Kenner, C. and Ruby, M. (2012) Co-constructing bilingual learning: An equal exchange of strategies between complementary and mainstream teachers. *Language and Education* 26 (6), 517–535.

Kenner, C., Creese, A. and Francis, B. (2008) Language, identity and learning in complementary schools. *CILT Community Languages Bulletin* 22, 2–4.

Knight, A. (1994) Pragmatic biculturalism and the primary school teacher. In A. Blackledge (ed.) *Teaching Bilingual Children* (pp. 101–111). Stoke-on-Trent: Trentham Books.

Krashen, S.D. and Terrell, T.D. (1983) *The Natural Approach: Language Acquisition in the Classroom*. London: Prentice Hall.

Kumaravadivelu, B. (2001) Towards a post-method pedagogy. *TESOL Quarterly* 35 (4), 537–560.

Larsen-Freeman, D. and Swain, M. (1991) *An Introduction to Second Language Acquisition Research (Applied Linguistics and Language Study)*. London: Longman.

Leung, C., Harris, R. and Rampton, B. (1999) The idealized native speaker, reified ethnicities and classroom realities. *TESOL Quarterly* 31 (3), 543–560.

Liebscher, G. and Dailey-O'Cain, J. (2005) Learner code-switching in the content-based foreign language journal. *Modern Language Journal* 89 (2), 234–247.

Macaro, E. (2005) Codeswitching in the L2 classroom: A communication and learning strategy. In E. Llurda (ed.) *Non-Native Language Teachers: Perceptions, Challenges and Contributions to the Profession* (pp. 63–84). New York: Springer.

Makoni, S. and Pennycook, A. (2007) Disinventing and reconstituting languages. In S. Makoni and A. Pennycook (eds) *Disinventing and Reconstituting Languages* (pp. 1–41). Clevedon: Multilingual Matters.

NALDIC (2009) *Developing a Bilingual Pedagogy for UK Schools*. Working Paper No. 9. Reading: National Association for Language Development in the Curriculum. See http://www.naldic.org.uk/eal-publications-resources/Shop/shop-products/wp9.

Phillipson, R. (1992) *Linguistic Imperialism*. Oxford: Oxford University Press.

Rampton, B. (2006) *Language in Late Modernity*. Cambridge: Cambridge University Press.

Rymes, B.R. (2010) Classroom discourse analysis: a focus on communicative repertoires. In N. Hornberger and S.L. McKay (eds) *Sociolinguistics and Language Education* (pp. 528–546). Bristol: Multilingual Matters.

Safford, K. and Kelly, A. (2010) Linguistic capital of trainee teachers: Knowledge worth having? *Language and Education* 24 (5), 401–414.

Sneddon R. and Martin, P. (2012) Alternative spaces of learning in east London: Opportunities and challenges. *Diaspora, Indigenous, and Minority Education* 6 (1), 34–49.

Swain, M.I. and Lapkin, S. (1982) *Evaluating Bilingual Education: A Canadian Case Study*. Clevedon: Multilingual Matters.

8 Multilingualism and Social Cohesion: Two-way Immersion Education Meets Diverse Needs

Gabriela Meier

Guiding Questions

- What is unique about the model in Berlin?
- To what extent can schools promote social cohesion?
- What are the opportunities and challenges of two-way immersion education?

Introduction

This chapter contributes to the topic of this book insofar as it presents a pedagogic model that strives to offer equal opportunities and is likely to meet the varied linguistic and social needs of multilingual societies. It argues that two-way immersion (TWI) education, which recognises and promotes at least two locally spoken languages in school, can play an important role in the promotion of social cohesion.

There is increasing agreement that the languages children bring to school should be recognised and promoted, while all children should also study one or more 'foreign' or 'modern' language at school (CoE, 2001; Maalouf, 2008). This creates a situation where schools have to meet varied linguistic needs. Thus, schools face various challenges, for instance: how to deal with the multitude of languages present in many schools; how to explain to children who are already bilingual why they need to learn a third modern or foreign language and potentially forget their first; and how to make learning a modern or foreign language relevant to the everyday lives of the learners.

My interest in the TWI model is based on the fact that, as Genesee (2008) indicates, TWI is a model that combines bilingual immersion education for majority and minority language learners, and thus it offers a way of reconciling the language learning needs of all these groups.

Historically, language education in Europe, and in other parts of the world, was based on the one-nation-one-language doctrine promoted as part of the nation-building project of early 20th century Europe (Wright, 2004). Thus, schools in many Western nations have operated on a monolingual assumption, while local populations have become increasingly multilingual in recent decades. Gogolin describes this in her book as 'the monolingual habitus in multilingual schools' (Gogolin, 1994, my translation). Based on Bourdieu (1979: 167ff), Gogolin presents 'habitus' as a useful concept to understand why people do what they do in everyday life. She argues that the 'monolingual habitus' is 'common to the classical European nation states as an example of a linguistic habitus', based on the belief that 'monolingualism is the universal norm for an individual and for a society' (Gogolin, 2006). According to Gogolin this no longer reflected reality in 1994, and it is even less the case at the time of writing, 20 years later. This chapter argues that TWI challenges our understanding of social integration in two ways. First it challenges the monolingual habitus in school by using at least two languages as regular languages of instruction, and second it challenges prevalent social integration discourses, which are based on the idea that it is the minority population that has to adapt while the majority population can largely continue as before. According to Crowley and Hickmann (2008), it depends on how we see society, whether or not we think that one or the other has to make an effort to adapt. Their study in the UK found that local contexts that recognise that society is diverse or heterogeneous see social cohesion more as a shared responsibility, while local contexts in which heterogeneity is ignored tend to consider social cohesion as the responsibility of the minority population. Thus, if schools recognise, rather than ignore, linguistic diversity it may be a step towards understanding integration as a shared responsibility.

Clearly, the reasons why different linguistic groups share a space can be complex: it can be based on economic, political, educational reasons (e.g. Wales, Macedonia), based on more recent migration (e.g. Berlin, New York), or on language contact in border areas where languages and their speakers meet. Often it is a combination of these.

TWI programmes are indeed a way of recognising that children in school speak two or more languages. Thus these programmes integrate learners of two different first languages (e.g. German and Portuguese in Berlin) in one classroom and use these two languages for instruction. While there are different practices in terms of allocating time to languages, in Europe the 50:50 model seems to predominate, while in the USA other proportions are also common. In Berlin, for instance, this means that half the lessons are in a dominant or official language (e.g. German in Germany) and the other half in another locally spoken language (e.g. Portuguese in Germany). Thus schools include the home languages of children with a non-dominant language background, making these a valuable asset and a useful skill when they start school, rather than a deficit. At the same time, this model teaches children with a dominant-language background another locally relevant language, which recognises their peers' linguistic background as a resource for learning. Thus it offers children the opportunity to learn two languages from and with each other. There are various models, with various language combinations depending on the context. In Berlin, for instance, it addresses the linguistic backgrounds of autochthonous (majority German) and allochthonous (minority or migrant) children in schools (Sukopp, 2005).

The aims of these programmes usually are threefold, 'to promote bilingualism and biliteracy, grade-level academic achievement, and positive cross-cultural attitudes and behaviors in all students' (CAL, 2012). Indeed, research confirms that TWI can benefit first of all bilingualism and biliteracy (Baker, 2006; Cummins, 1981) and secondly grade-level cognitive development or learning in other subjects (Cummins, 1996). In terms of this chapter, the third aim, namely socially relevant outcomes and processes, are of particular interest, such as the development of identities (Cummins, 1996), and any social benefits (Freeman, 1998; Lindholm-Leary, 2001). Some of these schools were specifically set up to foster social integration in the USA (Ahlgren, 1993; Peterson, 2007), and to serve as peace-building instruments in areas of conflict, for instance in Israel/Palestine (Bekerman & Horenczyk, 2004; Feuerverger, 2001) and Macedonia (Tankersley, 2001).

I have written this chapter from a UK perspective, looking at a programme in Germany which, as I argue in this chapter, could serve as a model for England, and other multilingual regions, where the monolingual habitus may predominate in schools. Clearly my own multilingual background and migratory biography as a multilingual person of Swiss origin, currently residing in the UK, has influenced my interest in the questions discussed in this chapter.

As to the structure of this chapter, I will define and evaluate TWI education as a model for schooling in multilingual environments in the next section. Then I will define social cohesion and the role of schools in promoting social cohesion and establish an analytical framework. This will be followed by an introduction to the quasi-experimental study in Berlin and the hypothesis to be tested. Then I will discuss the findings based on the dimensions established in the third section. The conclusion will highlight the main findings and discuss them in terms of the wider scope of the book.

Two-way Immersion Education

In English-language literature, the school model under discussion is often referred to as *two-way immersion* (Craig, 1996; Lindholm-Leary &

Howard, 2008) or as *dual-language education* (Collier & Thomas, 2004; Freeman, 1996). In German, I tend to use the term *Zweiwegimmersion* (Meier, 2012a) and at other times *paritätisch zweisprachiges Programm*, which reflects the reciprocal character of this model. Elsewhere, I have started to compile a multilingual list of the term (Meier, 2012b). In French it is referred to as *education bilingue reciproque*, which refers to the fact that children and young people are given the opportunity to learn two languages with and from one another, making both groups linguistic experts in lessons that use different languages for instruction. This makes the languages studied at school relevant not only for the future but for everyday school life. To what extent the languages are also relevant outside school depends largely on the opportunities learners have to meet speakers of the other languages in the neighbourhoods where they live.

Evaluation of TWI

As with all educational initiatives, it is important that certain criteria are met for TWI programmes to be successful. In the following, I combine Howard and Christian's (2002) and Lindholm-Leary's (2001) criteria for success with my insights from Berlin (Meier, 2010) and London (Meier, 2012c). The most important criteria for success are:

Structure of the programme
(1) Length: a minimum of 4–6 years of bilingual instruction.
(2) Additive bilingualism: all students have the opportunity to develop two languages, including their first language.
(3) Learners: there are balanced proportions of first-language speakers of both languages and learners with bilingual backgrounds.
(4) Staff: principals, teachers and support staff are open and interested in learning about different ways of doing things.
(5) Authority: support from authorities is crucial.

In the classroom
(6) Language exposure and use: comprehensible, interesting and sufficient exposure to both languages, and opportunities for language use.
(7) Content and language integration: all lessons are language lessons, which focus on subject content and linguistic form.
(8) Learner interaction: learners should be given the opportunity for meaningful interaction, e.g. through group work.

Research has shown that the added value of TWI programmes that largely comply with the above criteria is that they offer opportunities to all children to learn to read and write in two languages to a relatively high standard (Genesee & Gándara, 1999; Gräfe-Bentzien, 2001; Greene, 1998; Kielhöfer, 2004; Reich & Roth, 2002; Söhn, 2005; Willig, 1985). Furthermore, 'the development of additive bilingual and biliteracy skills entails no negative consequences for children's academic, linguistic, or intellectual development' (Cummins, 1996: 109) and it can also bring cognitive (Baker, 2006), as well as social and intercultural benefits (Bekerman & Horenczyk, 2004; Freeman, 1998; Meier, 2010). For instance, TWI research has established a positive link between TWI classes and group cohesion and conflict-resolution skills. Indeed, in terms of teaching children an additional (foreign) language, it is often seen as the most effective model of school-based language education (Fäcke, 2007; Reich & Roth, 2002), and it has been argued that this could well serve as a model for education in multilingual regions (Zydatiß, 1998).

As to the limitations, many authors warn that TWI programmes cannot be seen as a panacea to resolve all social and structural inequalities from which children with diverse backgrounds may suffer (Cummins, 2001; Rösch, 2001; Söhn, 2005). Thus, school programmes can only have a limited effect on structural inequalities, especially in areas of segregated communities such as in Israel (Bekerman & Horenczyk, 2004). Challenges identified have further related to the recruitment of a balanced number of pupils speaking either language (Meier, 2010), employment conditions of teachers specifically in Germany (Gleeson & Hertz, 1998), as well as to political and societal attitudes to TWI projects, which have caused controversies chiefly in the USA (Cummins, 2001). This takes us back to the question of who has to adapt to whom. In the USA, campaigns against TWI education have led to TWI being banned in several states (presumably by those who see the USA as a monolingual country). Lindholm-Leary (2001) associates such developments with racist movements, and Edwards (2004) makes the link between language education policy and nationalist movements. Thus, we have to understand that the integration of different linguistic groups and additive bilingualism in schools may be seen as a threat to some. As Edwards (2004: 216) argues, such 'debates which on the surface focus on language are actually about culture, identity, power and control'. Clearly, for some people, 'pluralism, biculturalism and multilingualism are a desirable outcome' (Baker, 2006: 282), probably for those who accept that their country is a multilingual place, as Crowley and Hickmann (2008) have argued. This debate can probably only be resolved if we can show that all children and the wider society can benefit from this model, and this chapter aims to make a contribution to this. A further challenge observed in TWI models is the fact that TWI students themselves may speak more than two languages, and the local environment may well host further languages, which are often ignored in the TWI streams (Meier, forthcoming). Thus, TWI models could be enriched through language awareness activities (see, for example, Chapter 12 by Anderson & Chung, this volume), or multilingual approaches to learning (see Chapter 6 by Meier, this volume). Another point that stakeholders should be aware of is that research shows that TWI programmes should run for at least 4–6 years (Howard & Christian, 2002), or six years (Gogolin *et al.*, 2007), since students develop more slowly in the first few years and catch up with their peers later.

TWI programmes for multilingual neighbourhoods

In English-speaking regions two languages are usually combined in one programme, enabling the development of bilingual competencies. However, TWI programmes in Germany, where two languages are used for content instruction and normally English is added as a third language, offering opportunities to develop 1+2, namely the mother tongue, a locally relevant language, and an international language, as suggested in Maalouf's (2008) report based on work by a high-level EU group. In this way, in Berlin for instance, 10 languages are used in different neighbourhood schools as languages of instruction, as is described below.

In the USA, for instance, where TWI programmes have been implemented from the 1960s, and currently there are over 400 programmes (CAL, 2012), these mostly combine English and Spanish as languages of instruction, but other languages spoken by local communities are also used as languages for learning in TWI projects, such as Cantonese, French, German, Italian, Japanese, Korean and Mandarin (CAL, 2012). Similarly in Europe, there has been interest in TWI programmes since the 1960s, which accelerated in the 1990s. However, it is less clear how many programmes there are. In Germany there have been programmes in many cities, together combining at least 10 locally spoken languages with German. These are Czech, English, French, Greek, Italian, Polish, Portuguese, Russian, Spanish and Turkish (Meier, 2012a). A themed multilingual journal (Meier, 2012d) presents articles regarding TWI in Europe, covering pre-school, primary, secondary and higher education, as well as teacher education, and including 17 languages in combination with another.

As noted above, TWI education cannot be seen as a panacea to solve all problems. It is nevertheless encouraging to see it being given increasing consideration as an alternative programme to the monolingual, assimilationist model that prevails in Europe and in other parts of the world.

Social Cohesion

Given my interest in TWI education and integration, I will now turn to social cohesion and how this is understood and measured with the aim of bringing the two together. Sometimes the term social cohesion is used synonymously with social inclusion, social integration, community cohesion or social capital. Community cohesion and social cohesion are especially contested and ambiguous terms that are used interchangeably, including in government publications (see Worley, 2005). *Community cohesion* seems to have been adopted for political purposes, especially in England (iCoCo, 2009), while in academic literature *social cohesion* seems to be more common (Green *et al.*, 2006). In this chapter I use the term *social cohesion*, following the tradition established by other academics (Dagenais *et al.,* 2008). While the definition is unclear, the idea itself is perhaps less contested.

> [F]or most people, in most societies, social cohesion is probably a desirable state, so long as it is based on equality, or at least relative equality, of access to goods, opportunities and power. But such situations have rarely been achieved, historically, without social conflicts and struggle. Such is the paradox of social cohesion. (Green *et al.*, 2006: 10)

Some have argued that the notions of community cohesion and social capital are attractive to politicians as they enable them to shift attention away from structural inequalities and focus more on the perceived deficiencies of individuals or minority groups (Hope Cheong *et al.*, 2007).

The term community cohesion was first used in the UK context in the

Along similar lines, a number of researchers criticise current political discourse for representing migrants as potential threats to social cohesion and national security (Crowley & Hickman, 2008; McKenna, 2003). Furthermore, dominant discourses (such as the 'monolingual habitus in multilingual schools' – Gogolin, 2001), assume that integration requires the settled population to make no changes – or at most only changes of attitude – while migrants are expected to change their behaviour and values (Crowley & Hickman, 2008), and assimilate linguistically. By placing the responsibility for lack of social cohesion on people from minority groups, official discourse deflects attention from the discrimination and social exclusion which they experience from 'mainstream' groups, and which may force them to turn inwards to their own group for support (Dwyer, 2000; Reynolds, 2007).

The term community cohesion was first used in the UK context in the aftermath of the social unrest in Bradford, Burnley and Oldham in 2001 (Cantle, 2006). It is argued that this unrest was associated with exclusion, discrimination or xenophobia based on a lack of understanding of migrant cultures and their plight, which may lead to perceiving migrant cultures, their members and their languages as a threat (see Cantle, 2006). It has also been connected with lack of English, among other explanations (see Anne Cryer's speech analysed in Blackledge, 2004). The continued interest in community cohesion in the UK is reflected in several events as outlined on the Institute of Community Cohesion website. These include the Cantle (2001, 2006) and Denham (2002) reports, the foundation of the Institute for Community Cohesion (iCoCo) in 2005, and the Government Commission for Integration and Cohesion (CIC), as well as the introduction of a duty to promote community cohesion in schools in England (DCSF, 2007). There is no consensus on this duty, however, since this was introduced by the Labour government in 2007 and rescinded by the coalition government (Conservatives and Liberal Democrats) in 2010.

Thus, community cohesion has attracted interest from policy makers, since experts observed that in some UK cities ethnic groups lead separate lives and there is hardly any or no contact between the different groups (Cantle, 2006; Olssen et al., 2006). The definition of community cohesion has since been criticised because it is based on the assumption that communities are fixed, bounded entities, tied to particular places and ethnicities, whereas this does not match the reality of people's everyday lives (see, for instance, James, 2009).

The main issue relating to both community and social cohesion appears to be the emphasis on commonalities, belonging, opportunities and relationships while differences must be respected, but perhaps not emphasised. The dimensions associated with social cohesion, as described here, largely overlap with developing social capital as is discussed below, but first I turn to the opposite of social cohesion: social segregation.

The view that segregation leads to lack of social cohesion is based on the assumption that greater contact between different groups will result in greater openness and tolerance. However, some writers have suggested that greater contact can lead to increased tension, particularly when different groups perceive themselves as competing with each other for scarce resources (Amin, 2002). The nature of the intergroup contact is therefore important. Building on Allport's (1954) much-cited intergroup contact theory, Amin (2002) argues that co-presence alone is insufficient to create meaningful interaction, and recommends fostering 'cultural transgression', which comes about when people from different backgrounds are placed in 'new settings where engagement with strangers in common activity disrupts easy labelling of the stranger as enemy and initiates new attachments' (Amin, 2002: 970).

Social cohesion and the role of schools

Schools are widely viewed as crucial sites for the development of social cohesion (see, for example, Green et al., 2006; McKenna, 2003; Oder, 2005), particularly through citizenship education (Golmohamad, 2009; Jansen et al., 2006) and religious education (Jackson, 2004; Panjwani, 2005), and increasingly through language education, specifically bilingual education, which is discussed in this chapter. Conversely, segregation – particularly ethnic segregation – in schools and neighbourhoods is assumed to be a barrier to social cohesion (Crowley & Hickman, 2008).

If schools have indeed a role to play in social cohesion, we have to question to what extent we create equal and socially just structures on the one hand and opportunities to develop social cohesion on the other. I argue that TWI can address both to a certain extent. However, we must also be aware that schools are given increasing responsibilities to level out what are effectively societal inequalities. Thus, schools can perhaps make an important contribution, but only as part of a broader programme to address societal inequalities.

Conceptualisation of social cohesion in schools

Some writers do not differentiate between social cohesion and social capital (Crowley & Hickman, 2008). Thus I draw on literature of both social cohesion and on social capital. In general, social capital is understood as 'traits of individual trust, tolerance, and civic participation which are said to underpin the relations of reciprocity in well-functioning participative communities' (Green *et al.*, 2006: 3). Holland (2009) proposes a definition which was formulated by the ESRC Families and Social Capital Research Group: 'The values people hold and the resources that they can access, which both result in and are the result of collective and socially negotiated ties and relationships'.

Social capital is often seen as a 'cure' for lack of social/community cohesion. One of the main proponents of this argument is Putnam, who defines social capital as the 'features of social life – networks, norms and trust – that enable participants to act together more effectively to pursue shared objectives' (Putnam, 2004). In his book 'Bowling Alone', Putnam (2000) proposes the concepts of 'bonding' social capital (to describe within-group ties) and 'bridging' social capital (to describe cross-group ties). Other authors also used metaphors, indicating cohesion between groups or individuals, namely 'weak ties' (Granovetter, 1973, 1983), based on networks of acquaintances that enable access to resources, mostly employment, and 'strong ties' (Lin, 2001) based on intimate and frequent contacts within a close-knit group. Hope Cheong *et al.* (2007: 29) note that: 'as a refinement to Putnam's work, a third form of "linking" social capital has also been proposed. Linking social capital refers to the vertical relations that help individuals gain access to resources from formal institutions for social and economic development.'

There is some agreement that there are two main strands of social capital theory. One focuses on issues of collective action and integration (Bole & Gordon, 2009; Putnam, 2000). In the UK context, Fahmy (2006) focuses on this aspect in a study which investigates the links between young people's social capital and their civic participation. The other strand emphasises questions of social justice and inequality (Holland *et al.*, 2007). Green *et al.* (2006) note that policy thinking in the UK and US has linked social capital with 'traits of individual trust, tolerance, and civic participation which are said to underpin the relations of reciprocity in well-functioning participative communities'.

As regards research, there is debate about the level at which social cohesion, or social capital, should be analysed. Chan *et al.* (2006) criticise researchers who have only analysed social cohesion at the systemic level with little explicit reference to individual-level empirical data. They claim that such research is flawed because it does not provide insight into how social cohesion can be defined and operationalised. Their response to such limitations is to formulate the following definition: 'Social cohesion is a state of affairs concerning both the vertical and the horizontal interactions among members of society as characterised by a set of attitudes and norms that includes trust, a sense of belonging and the willingness to participate and help, as well as their behavioural manifestations' (Chan et al., 2006: 290). Chan et al. state that 'members of society' include groups, organisations and institutions, as well as individuals. In contrast, Green et al. (2006), who examined social capital, argue that 'relationships between education and social cohesion cannot be adequately analysed at the individual level because such analyses ignore the effects of powerful contextual influences, such as the nature of the state and its re-distributive and welfare systems, which are not visible at the individual level' (Green et al., 2006: 14). Indeed, Le Pape Racine and Buser (interviewed by Meier, 2012e) suggest that TWI programmes should be examined at the macro, meso, micro and nano level. Thus, individual agency as well as contextual variables are important and both should form part of the relevant analysis.

Criticism has been levelled at social capital theory from various perspectives. It has been criticised for having a US orientation (Bassani, 2007), as well as being normative and functionalist (Hope Cheong et al., 2007: 30), and being based on the notion of the nation state (Crowley & Hickman, 2008; Dooly & Unamuno, 2009). Further, it is accused of reflecting ideologies of individualism and of neo-classical economists (Green et al., 2006: 4), as well as for being considered a static and atemporal, rather than a dynamic and fluid construct (Dagenais et al., 2008: 87; Holland, 2009). Additionally, researchers claim that children's or young people's agency to build their own social capital has been underestimated and under-researched (Holland, 2009; Morrow, 2005).

Social cohesion related to young people or schools has been examined by a number of people; however, not many have taken the language dimension into consideration.

A conceptual framework

Despite the criticism levelled at attempts to conceptualise social cohesion, I argue that it is important to examine the role of schools in relation to social cohesion, but I agree that we need a more dynamic and fluid conceptualisation, based on the understanding that young people socially negotiate vertical and horizontal networks in the context of their changing environments, and we need to understand that this in turn is connected to social capital and behavioural manifestations.

Based on the above, I propose a model for the examination of social cohesion that emphasises the role of the context (macro/societal, meso/institutional, micro/school, nano/group), the individual (knowledge, skills and attitudes), social capital (belonging, relationships, shared values, resources and trust), behaviour manifestations (e.g. group cohesion/fragmentation, violence, discrimination), and processes (social interactions, individual roles,

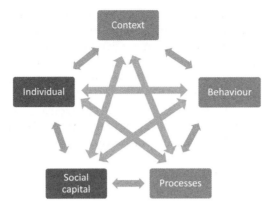

Figure 8.1 Framework to examine social cohesion in schools

peer learning). We need to recognise the legitimate existence of a number of flexible and fluid communities which permanently or temporarily overlap through common interests and values, and co-exist side by side while transgressing cultural and linguistic difference. The fluidity and dynamic nature of social cohesion thus conceptualised is represented by the arrows in Figure 8.1. This will serve as a conceptual framework for the examination of data collected in the Berlin TWI programme, presented below.

In this chapter, I examine all of these aspects apart from 'processes', since this requires a different, more qualitative research design, as discussed in Meier (forthcoming).

Example: Staatliche Europa-Schule Berlin

The TWI model that I am presenting here is a well-established and extensive state-run programme in the multilingual context of Berlin. I first outline the need for the study, and then I describe the context, the participants and methods before I report research findings.

The study

To date, there seems to be no systematic, quantitative study of social cohesion or social capital related to TWI education besides my initial study (Meier, 2010) on which this chapter is based. However, there is research by Nicht (2012), who has used network analytical methods to examine social relationships between linguistic groups in TWI settings in another part of Germany. And finally, after more than 20 years, a wider study has been initiated (Europa-Studie, 2014) to evaluate the Berlin TWI project, including linguistic, subject-specific and intercultural competences.

Initially, my plan was to collect qualitative and quantitative data, but access to schools was limited, so only the quantitative part was realised, which clearly limits the depth of the findings. Given that social cohesion is highly political, one of my aims was to produce 'hard' evidence that is often required by policy makers, the more so given that hardly any quantitative research exists relating social cohesion and TWI education. The study presented in this chapter measured constructs relating to social cohesion as laid out in Table 8.2, and used these to test the following hypothesis: **there is better social cohesion in groups of TWI students compared to groups of similar mainstream students**. Thus, it compared TWI and mainstream (MS) students, using a quasi-experimental design.

Context

Staatliche Europa-Schule Berlin (SESB) or Berlin State Europe School (official English translation), using 10 locally spoken languages, must be the largest state-run TWI programme in Europe. It is a fully integrated programme that runs from primary school to university access at the age of 19 years old. About 6000 students are enrolled at any one time (SENBJS, 2008). SESB was founded after the fall of the Berlin Wall with high-prestige languages of the postwar allied forces, and other migrant languages followed. Six state schools started bilingual streams in 1992, offering TWI education in German, in combination with English, French and Russian. In 1996 combinations with Spanish, Italian, Portuguese, Greek and Turkish and, more recently, Polish were added (Sukopp, 2005).

SESB classes are run as streams alongside MS classes in Berlin schools. This means that in certain Berlin schools and colleges one school class in each year is a TWI class. Currently there are 30 SESB locations, of which 17 provide TWI education at primary and 13 at secondary level.

Participants

A total of 603 students between 14 and 18 years old participated in the study. They were from seven schools in different parts of Berlin, and 272 were enrolled in TWI classes, while 331 were enrolled in MS classes. All classes were multilingual, on average 63% had a bilingual or non-German background, and the students had 38 different home languages. In order to categorise their language backgrounds, parental first languages were used to establish three subgroups, see Table 8.1: German, bilingual (German and one or more other languages), and non-German (languages other than German).

The students were enrolled in two different school types: Comprehensive school (*Gesamtschule*): SESB = 166; MS = 187) and an academically focused school type, preparing students for the German *Abitur* or type of baccalaureate (Gymnasium: SESB = 106; MS = 144). Thus, research participants were not just recruited from academically focused streams, but from a cross-section.

Table 8.1 Language backgrounds of participants

Language category	TWI		MS		Total	
	n	%	n	%	n	%
German	56	21	169	51	225	37
Bilingual	90	33	52	16	142	24
Non-German	126	46	108	33	234	39
Total	272	100	329	100	601	100
Missing	0		2		2	

Method

Data were collected in classrooms through questionnaires (return rate 83% – published in Meier, 2010). The design consisted of multivariate and bivariate analyses, and compared TWI and MS groups in terms of dimensions related to social cohesion. For the purpose of this chapter, I used the framework established above to analyse these data. The dimensions considered are represented in Table 8.2.

In this section, I build on the (perhaps overambitious) peace-linguistic framework that I established for the study of social cohesion in multilingual schools (Meier, 2010, 2012a). This was based on social capital theory, peace education and critical applied linguistics. In the following, I describe how I revisited the data from that project and re-examined them from the above – more

Table 8.2 Dimensions examined in Berlin study

Level	Dimension	Based on research by
Context	TWI model	Meier (2010)
Individual factors	Conflict resolution skills	Martin Luther King's steps of conflict resolution (Harris & Morrison, 2003)
	Empathy	Maes et al. (1995)
	Critical thinking skills	Haas (2006)
	Attitude towards integration	Torney-Purta et al. (2001)
Social capital	Sense of belonging	Li et al. (2003)
	Resources	Li et al. (2003)
	Trust	Linssen et al. (2002)
Behaviour manifestation	Perceived sense of inclusion	Bovier (1997)
	Perceived frequency of violence	Bovier (1997)
	Perceived discrimination	Marplan (1996)

user friendly – perspective. The origins of the dimensions in Table 8.2 are described in detail in Meier (2010). The multi-item scales consisted of between three and eight items and had good Cronbach Alpha values, which indicates that their internal reliability was satisfactory, and the results were based on multivariate scale and bivariate item analyses.

Social Cohesion and TWI Classrooms

In this section, I discuss the data in terms of the social cohesion framework set up in the second section. The following discussion is based on data, where appropriate, to illustrate findings (for details see Meier, 2010) and compares the findings with literature established above. The four dimensions (Table 8.2) serve as headings.

Context

Green *et al.* (2006: 14) stressed the importance of contextual factors in relation to social cohesion. The most important finding in terms of context for the Berlin study was that there is indeed a difference between a TWI and a MS learning context, namely that TWI seems to be associated with all four social cohesion dimensions examined by this study to a lesser or greater extent. While the wider political, demographic and educational context of the Berlin school model is discussed in Meier (2010), here I only take the institutional variable of TWI or MS into consideration.

Behaviour manifestation

A clear pattern becomes visible (Table 8.3), when examining the three sub-dimensions, using multivariate methods: all beta coefficients[1] are positive in terms of inclusion (TWI scored higher than MS, see Figure 8.2 for items), and negative in terms of perceived discrimination (Figure 8.4) and violence (Figure 8.3) (TWI scored lower than MS), and some of these differences were statistically significant.

This means that TWI students above all perceived *greater inclusion/less group fragmentation* in their class than MS students, which allows the conclusion that TWI class-groups were more socially cohesive than those in MS education. As can be seen in Figure 8.2, TWI groups score higher on positively worded items (16.2, 16.4) and lower on negatively worded items (16.5, 16.1, 16.3).

This means that a perceived sense of inclusion or lack of a fragmented class community seems to be related to TWI. This resonates with findings from several other contexts (Bekerman & Horenczyk, 2004; Freeman, 1998; Genesee & Gándara, 1999; Lindholm-Leary, 2001; Torres-Guzmán, 2002). Thus this points to a finding that is consistent with existing relevant research.

Table 8.3 Behaviour manifestation: Differences between TWI and MS (beta coefficients)

Sub-dimensions measured		Entire sample	Subgroups		
			German	Bilingual	Non-German
Inclusion in class	B	1.172**	1.452**	2.151**	0.553
(5 items, α 0.693)	β	0.161	0.172	0.309	0.075
	R²	0.020	0.024	0.071	
Perceived discrimination	B	−0.358	−0.185	−0.213	−0.595
(5 items, α 0.790)	β	−0.046	−0.025	−0.027	−0.067
	R²				
Perceived violence	B	−0.685*	0.194	−0.711	−1.083*
(3 items, α 0.794)	β	0.102	0.025	−0.104	−0.160
	R²	0.008			0.019

Notes: **$p \leq 0.010$; *$p \leq 0.050$.

Furthermore, and this may be related, TWI students perceived *less violence* (threats of violence, physical violence) in their school than the MS students. In the subgroups, the greatest difference was between the subgroups with a non-German background. While this effect was found in the multi-item scale, I illustrate this by the one item where this was most strongly visible: perceived frequency of physical violence in class.

In terms of perceived frequency of physical violence (Figure 8.3), there is a distinct difference between the TWI (between hardly ever and a few times a year) and the MS group (nearer the mark of a few times a year). The starkest difference is between the subgroups with a non-German background. As can be seen below, this TWI subgroup also had a greater interest in peaceful conflict resolution (Figure 8.5).

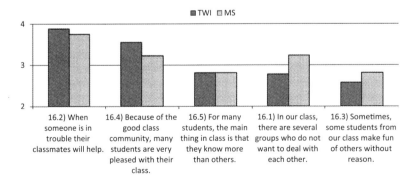

Figure 8.2 Sense of inclusion
Notes: mean per item: 1, strongly disagree; 2, disagree; 3, tend to disagree; 4, tend to agree; 5, agree; 6, strongly agree.

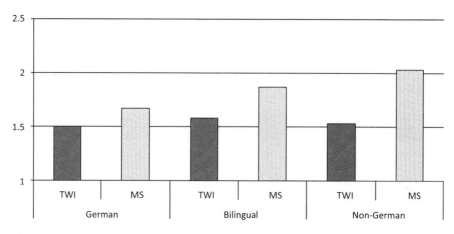

Figure 8.3 Perceived frequency of physical violence in class
Notes: mean per item: 1, never/hardly ever; 2, a few times a year; 3, about once a month; 4, several times a month; 5, several times a week.

The third sub-dimension examined was perceived discrimination (see Figure 8.4). This was not related to discrimination perceived in the class, but in the wider society. Interestingly, the school model did not have an effect on this, but there was a difference between the three subgroups.

As can be seen from Figure 8.4, there is hardly any difference in terms of discrimination perceived on the basis of gender and appearance, but in terms of nationality, religion and mother tongue there is a clear pattern. This is in line with studies that show that young people with migrant backgrounds may be disadvantaged by society and the system (Gomolla & Radtke, 2007). The encouraging finding is that in relative terms discrimination is perceived

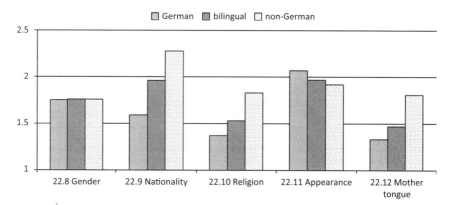

Figure 8.4 Perceived discrimination
Notes: mean per item: 1, never; 2, rarely; 3, sometimes; 4, often; 5, always.

to happen infrequently, namely between never and rarely, with a couple of subgroups scoring slightly above these.

Thus, the TWI factor seems to be able to positively affect perceived behaviour in classrooms, but perhaps not beyond. However, the evidence on which this is based is rather limited and further research would have to examine any TWI effects beyond the classroom.

Individual factors

An analysis related to relevant dimensions showed again a clear TWI effect, with some statistically significant differences (Table 8.4). Again all directions (Beta coefficients) point towards a positive TWI effect, apart from Empathy in the non-German group which showed the opposite. Thus, the statistically significant differences show that the TWI group scores higher in the entire sample (conflict resolution skills) and also in the subgroups (critical thinking, conflict resolution and attitudes towards integration). This analysis confirms Bekerman and Horenzcyk's (2004) findings that TWI students seem to have greater **conflict resolution skills** compared to their mainstream peers. The main difference occurred in the item about interest in learning more about conflict resolution skills (Figure 8.5).

It is particularly the TWI group with a bilingual, but also the one with a non-German background, where a difference can be found between TWI and MS. Indeed these TWI subgroups were more likely to agree that they would like to learn more about peaceful conflict resolution than the MS

Table 8.4 Individual dimensions: Differences between TWI and MS (beta coefficients)

Sub-dimensions measured		Entire sample	Subgroups		
			German	Bilingual	Non-German
Critical thinking	B	0.463	0.867*	0.639	0.170
(5 items, α 0.681)	β	0.078	0.138	0.107	0.027
	R²		0.016		
Conflict resolution	B	0.724**	0.000	1.609**	0.847
(4 items, α 0.678)	β	0.109	0.000	0.229	0.115
	R²	0.009		0.040	
Empathy	B	0.166	0.924	1.239	−0.574
(7 items, α 0.799)	β	0.014	0.071	0.106	−0.046
	R²				
Attitudes towards integration	B	0.114	1.463**	1.040	0.755
(5 items, α 0.769)	β	0.015	0.189	0.137	0.106
	R²		0.029		

Notes: **$p \leq 0.010$; *$p \leq 0.050$.

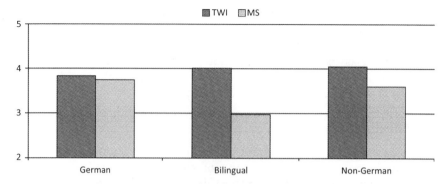

Figure 8.5 Interest in learning more about conflict resolution
Notes: mean per item: 1, strongly disagree; 2, disagree; 3, tend to disagree; 4, tend to agree;
5, agree; 6, strongly agree.

subgroups. Thus, as it seems, the TWI effect is particularly strong in the group with varied allochthonous backgrounds. This is an important finding, since sometimes the migrant population is seen as problematic in terms of social cohesion (Crowley & Hickman, 2008; McKenna, 2003), but my findings indicate that TWI education may turn this group into a positive force. Indeed, Angelova *et al.* (2006: 187) found that especially the TWI learners with bilingual family backgrounds 'played a very important role as not only language mediators but also as social mediators in the process of learning'. From their study it seems that especially bilingual children play an important role in creating social cohesion in the group by offering help to others.

As can be seen from the above, the TWI effect was pronounced in the bilingual and non-German subgroups, but TWI also had an effect on the German subgroup. This was the case regarding **greater critical thinking skills** (Figure 8.6). Interestingly, it was also in this subgroup where TWI students had more open **attitudes towards rights of 'immigrants'** (Figure 8.7). The most important TWI effect in the subgroup with a German background was with regard to language. The young TWI learners in this subgroup were more likely to agree that immigrants should have the opportunity to maintain their languages. While this is the largest difference, there is a very clear pattern overall for these items. This may mean that TWI students are more likely to listen to different opinions, which may make them more open-minded towards people with an allochthonous background. This question was related to the society at large rather than just to the school context. Thus, TWI may have an effect beyond the school context.

On one of the sub-dimensions measured, the TWI model seemed to have no effect: the ability to feel **empathy** with others. Looking at the overall mean of the entire sample, according to the data (Figure 8.8), the students in both streams see themselves as rather empathetic towards other people. They score highly (between 'tend to agree' and 'agree') on positively worded

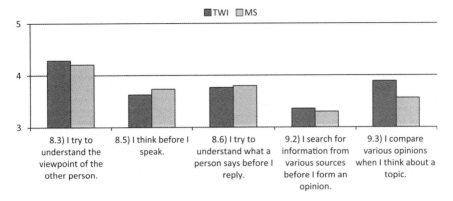

Figure 8.6 Critical thinking skills in the German subgroup
Notes: mean per item: 1, strongly disagree; 2, disagree; 3, tend to disagree; 4, tend to agree; 5, agree;
6, strongly agree.

items and low (between 'tend to disagree' and 'disagree') on negatively worded items. This indicates that the TWI factor can be associated with the individual dimension, since there are clear effects in terms of conflict resolutions skills, critical thinking and attitudes towards 'foreigners'; some are more general effects and some are more pronounced in the autochthonous or in the allochthonous groups.

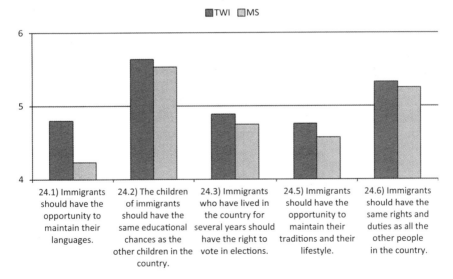

Figure 8.7 Attitudes to 'foreigners' in the German subgroup
Notes: mean per item: 1, strongly disagree; 2, disagree; 3, tend to disagree; 4, tend to agree;
5, agree; 6, strongly agree.

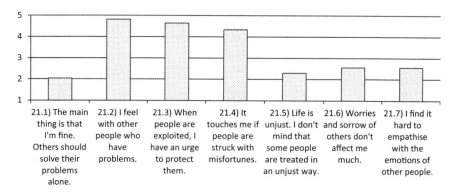

Figure 8.8 Ability to empathise with others – entire sample

Notes: mean per item: 1, strongly disagree; 2, disagree; 3, tend to disagree; 4, tend to agree; 5, agree; 6, strongly agree.

Social capital

An interesting finding in terms of 'weak ties' (acquaintances rather than friendships), which according to Granovetter (1983) is associated with perceived similarities between groups, was the difference between TWI and MS groups regarding the **sense of belonging**. In the study described here, this dimension was the only social-capital dimension that was suitable for multivariate analysis (since the data were continuous), and this showed that again all directions indicate a positive TWI effect. This was particularly pronounced in the bilingual group (Table 8.5). Further dimensions (resources and trust) were analysed using bivariate methods and are discussed below. As can be seen in Figure 8.9, there is a very consistent pattern, which supports the argument that students with bilingual backgrounds develop strong ties in their class.

Thus, it could be argued that young people with bilingual backgrounds feel particularly 'at home' in bilingual programmes, since they incorporate the programme aims of being bilingual, and perhaps relate to all peers and both their teachers. Their peers in mainstream education may find it harder

Table 8.5 Social capital dimension: Differences between TWI and MS (beta coefficients)

Dimensions measured		Entire sample	Subgroups		
			German	Bilingual	Non-German
Belonging (8 items, α 0.871)	B	0.958	1.369	3.410**	0.030
	β	0.069	0.079	0.256	0.002
	R²			0.048	

Notes: **$p \leq 0.010$; *$p \leq 0.050$.

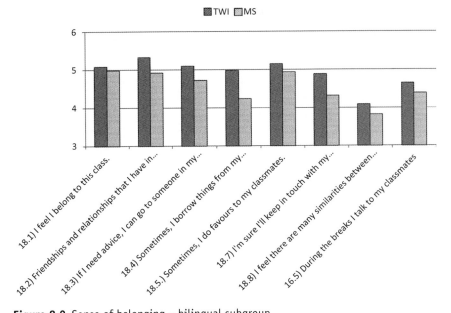

Figure 8.9 Sense of belonging – bilingual subgroup
Notes: mean per item: 1, strongly disagree; 2, disagree; 3, tend to disagree; 4, tend to agree;
5, agree; 6, strongly agree.

to develop this sense of belonging, when their second language is not recognised in school. It is interesting, however, that in the non-German subgroup there was virtually no difference between TWI and MS. Intuitively, I expected the non-German group in the TWI stream to be associated with a greater sense of belonging. Clearly, the integration of non-German groups into schools has to be seen with reference to the complexity of wider societal structures. This study, thus, confirms other studies that found that TWI can make a difference within school, but have not found that it can address entrenched inequalities in wider society (Bekerman & Horenczyk, 2004; Freeman, 1998).

There was no overall effect in terms of access to **resources**. It is perhaps interesting to see that it was TWI students again in the bilingual subgroup that were more likely to feel that they could ask someone in their class for money compared to the same subgroup in mainstream education. Looking at this together with the items related to sense of belonging, this confirms that the classroom networks of bilingual TWI learners seem to be based on strong bonds. However, more research is required to establish potential strong bonds between individuals in schools and beyond.

TWI again did not make an overall difference in terms of **trust** in other people. An interesting finding is that TWI seems to have an effect on the German subgroup, but not on the bilingual and the non-German. In fact the

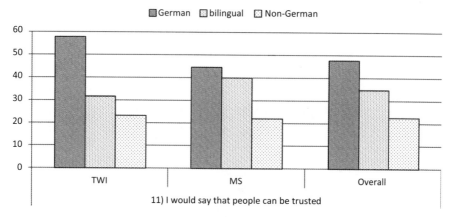

Figure 8.10 Trust in other people (percentage of participants who said 'yes')

MS bilingual group seems to trust people more than the TWI group. The important finding here is that there was a clear pattern between the subgroups when looked at together (TWI and MS): students with a German background trusted other people most, while bilingual students trusted other people less and non-German students least (Figure 8.10). This dimension asked whether people in general can be trusted, rather than peers in school. Therefore, further research would have to establish whether there might be a difference between trust in people in school and trust in people outside school.

Further dimensions that should be examined are vertical and horizontal relationships, namely **social networks**, as well as **shared values** to gain an understanding of actual friendships (strong ties) and the wider circle (weak ties). This was not analysed in this study, since I was not able to conduct interviews.

Summary of the Berlin study

The study presented here shows that there is a consistent TWI effect in that all statistically significant differences either pointed to a positive TWI effect, or to no effect. These effects are found when comparing all TWI with all MS students (violence, sense of inclusion, conflict resolution skills); some of these effects were particularly pronounced when comparing linguistic subgroups in TWI with those in mainstream education (e.g. belonging in the bilingual group). Additionally, some effects were found only in subgroups (critical thinking skills, attitudes towards 'foreigners', sense of belonging, resources). This indicates that the TWI model has an overall effect, and affects subgroups in different ways. These effects are summarised and illustrated in Figure 8.11.

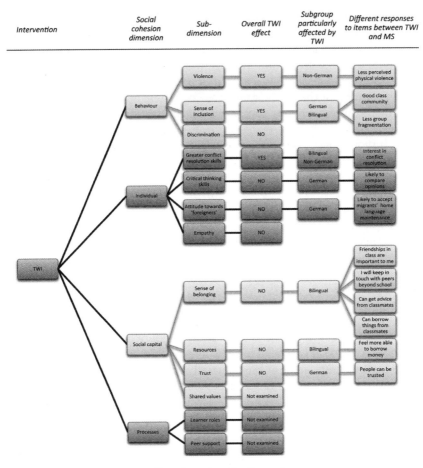

Figure 8.11 Summary of TWI effect based on Berlin study

Limitations and further questions

The Berlin study provided a snapshot of the views of the participants at a given point in time; clearly this is expected to change over time, and longitudinal studies could illuminate to what extent social cohesion dimensions are indeed fluid. Furthermore, the study was not based on a true experiment, since the parents choose to send their children to TWI streams. There may, of course, be some antecedent family variable that influences the result. However, I did control for the participants' perceived parental involvement in their educational and social development, based on a multi-item scale, and no difference could be shown between TWI and MS participants. There are two additional and important questions that arise from this study: to what extent does the TWI education affect young people's life outside the classroom, namely in school and the wider society; and can the TWI effect be sustained into the future, and if so in what way does this manifest itself with a view to social cohesion dimensions. This is likely to depend on the individual and the structural and agential parameters found in the wider society, and more research is required in this area.

A limitation of the Berlin study presented here is that it did not look into the dimension of processes such as social interaction and cooperation that may lead to, or may help explain, group or individual outcomes. Further research would need to include this aspect of the social cohesion matrix in order to gain a clearer picture of social cohesion, and how it can be promoted or hindered in schools and the stakeholders involved. Indeed, through a pilot study in an English–French programme in London I have identified a series of processes that may be associated with such outcomes: these are changing learner roles and use of distributed expertise, as well as sensitivity to peers' learning needs and linguistic scaffolding by peers (Meier, forthcoming).

Conclusions

In this chapter I show that TWI education can make a contribution to social cohesion based on the examination of context, individual attributes, behaviour and social capital. Thus the hypothesis, introduced in the section on the Berlin study, can be at least partially confirmed. While not all relevant dimensions have been examined, the evidence produced points to some very clear positive TWI effects. While the TWI effect seems to be evident in the school context to a greater or lesser degree in terms of all the social cohesion dimensions, it is not clear to what extent TWI might also affect individuals' attitudes and behaviours in the wider society, or to what extent TWI might affect social integration discourse more widely.

This study confirms that schools can play a role in promoting social cohesion and that in all likelihood the status of languages plays a role in this. Based on this, I argue that TWI education may, on the one hand, reduce institutionalised, linguistic discrimination and recognise the existence and legitimacy of migrant groups associated with these languages. On the other hand, TWI education does not expect the allochthonous population to adapt and change while the autochthonous population stays the same; on the contrary, TWI invites the resident population to engage with the language and culture that a part of the population brings to school. Thus, it creates opportunities to meet on a more level playing field and makes social integration more of a two-way process, and thus a shared responsibility as discussed by Crowley and Hickmann (2008).

Clearly, languages can play a uniting or divisive role in schools, and school policies have to satisfy different social integration ideologies. Despite the fact that TWI faces a series of challenges and cannot provide easy answers to discriminatory societal practices, evidence increasingly points to positive outcomes linguistically and socially, not just for young people with minority backgrounds but also – and this is a compelling argument – for the so-called majority resident population.

I conclude that educational practice in the form of well-implemented TWI programmes (see above for criteria) can promote greater societal multi-lingualism and personal plurilingualism, while it brings additional benefits in terms of social cohesion, at least in the classroom. At this point we can only speculate to what extent it may also influence wider social integration discourses, and challenge the monolingual habitus prevalent in many societies. Drawing this chapter to a close, I argue that there is sufficient evidence to recommend TWI programmes, such as the one in Berlin, as a useful and more holistic educational model for other linguistically diverse settings that may well benefit learners, and potentially societies, with varied language needs. Thus, TWI could be a response to Cantle's (2012: 208) recent plea for 'more general internationally oriented educational and experiential learning opportunities' and a curriculum that reflects this. I would like to close with a quotation from Cantle's latest book:

> Segregation and integration have to be given new and more nuanced understandings. Breaking down segregation, or promoting integration can be advanced in many different ways and at different levels, without endangering existing conceptions of ourselves. This enables new identities to be added to existing ones, creating layers and multifaceted forms which will also continue to change and evolve over time and in different contexts. (Cantle, 2012: 206)

While Cantle (2012: 208) feels that schools do have a role to play in turning 'singular identities into [. . .] multiple ones', he does not explicitly mention multilingualism in relation to this. However, I have shown in this chapter that it may well be necessary to take the languages children speak at home seriously when we talk about social cohesion and schools; in many respects, the TWI programme in Berlin demonstrates that the multilingual turn can be implemented more widely and could serve as one possible model for this.

Note

(1) The unstandardised Beta (B) indicates how much difference occurred in the entire score. A positive result means SESB scored higher; a negative B means SESB scored lower than the CG. The standardised Beta (β) is a standardised value that can be compared across dimensions.

References

Ahlgren, P. (1993) La Escuela Fratney: Reflections on a bilingual, anti-bias, multicultural elementary school. *Teaching Tolerance* 2 (2), 26–31.

Allport, G. (1954) *The Nature of Prejudice*. Reading, MA: Addison-Wesley.

Amin, A. (2002) Ethnicity and the multicultural city: Living with diversity. *Environment and Planning* 34 (6), 959–980.

Angelova, M., Gunawardena, D. and Volk, D. (2006) Peer teaching and learning: Co-constructing language in a dual language first grade. *Language and Education* 20 (3), 173–190.

Baker, C. (2006) *Foundations of Bilingual Education and Bilingualism* (4th edn). Clevedon: Multilingual Matters.

Bassani, C. (2007) Five dimensions of social capital theory as they pertain to youth studies. *Journal of Youth Studies* 10 (1), 17–34.

Bekerman, Z. and Horenczyk, G. (2004) Arab-Jewish bilingual coeducation in Israel: A long-term approach to intergroup conflict resolution. *Journal of Social Issues* 60 (2), 389–404.

Blackledge, A. (2004) Constructions of identity in political discourse in multilingual Britain. In A. Pavlenko and A. Blackledge (eds) *Negotiations of Identities in Multilingual Contexts* (pp. 68–92). Clevedon: Multilingual Matters.

Bole, B. and Gordon, M. (2009) E pluribus unum: Fostering a new era of citizenship by teaching civic engagement and healthy civic discourse. *Journal of Public Affairs* 9 (4), 273–287.

Bourdieu, P. (1979) *Distinction: A Social Critique of the Judgment of Taste* (Richard Nice trans.). Harvard University Press.

Bovier, E. (1997) Emanzipatorische Erziehung und Gewalt an Schulen: Linke Lehrer zwischen pädagogischem Anspruch und Burnout. Doctoral thesis, Technische Universität Chemnitz-Zwickau.

CAL (2012) *Directory of Two-Way Bilingual Immersion Programs in the US*. Washington, DC: Center for Applied Linguistics. See http://www.cal.org/twi/directory/index.html (accessed 19 October 2012).

Cantle, T. (2001) *Community Cohesion: A Report of the Independent Review Team*. London: Home Office.

Cantle, T. (2006) *Review of Community Cohesion in Oldham: Challenging Local Communities to Change Oldham*. Coventry: Institute for Community Cohesion, Coventry University.

Cantle, T. (2012) *Interculturalism: The New Era of Cohesion and Diversity*. Basingstoke: Palgrave Macmillan.

Chan, J., To, H.P. and Chan, E. (2006) Reconsidering social cohesion: Developing a definition and analytical framework for empirical research. *Social Indicators Research* 75, 273–302.

CoE (Council of Europe) (2001) *Common European Framework of Reference for Languages: Learning, Teaching, Assessment (CEFR)*. Language Policy Unit. Cambridge: Cambridge University Press.

Collier, V.P. and Thomas, W.P. (2004) The astounding effectiveness of dual language education for all. *NABE Journal of Research and Practice* 2 (1), 1–20.

Craig, B.A. (1996) Parental attitudes toward bilingualism in a local two-way immersion program. *Bilingual Research Journal* 20 (3/4), 383–410.

Crowley, H. and Hickman, M. (2008) Migration, postindustrialism and the globalized nation state: Social capital and social cohesion re-examined. *Ethnic and Racial Studies* 31 (7), 1222–1244.

Cummins, J. (1981) The role of primary language development in promoting educational success for language minority students. *Schooling and Language Minority Students: A Theoretical Framework* (pp. 3–50). Sacramento, CA: California Department of Education.

Cummins, J. (1996) *Negotiating Identities: Education for Empowerment in a Diverse Society*. Covina, CA: California Association for Bilingual Education.

Cummins, J. (2001) *Language, Power and Pedagogy: Bilingual Children in the Crossfire*. Clevedon: Multilingual Matters.

Dagenais, D., Beynon, D. and Mathis, N. (2008) Intersections of social cohesion, education, and identity in teachers, discourses, and practices. *Pedagogies* 3 (2), 85–108.

DCSF (2007) *Guidance on the Duty to Promote Community Cohesion.* London: Department for Children, Schools and Families. See http://www.education.gov.uk/publications/eOrderingDownload/DCSF-00598-2007.pdf (accessed 22 April 2014).

Denham, J. (2002) *Building Cohesive Communities: A Report of the Ministerial Group on Public Order and Community Cohesion.* London: Home Office.

Dooly, M. and Unamuno, V. (2009) Multiple languages in one society: Categorisations of language and social cohesion in policy and practice. *Journal of Education Policy* 24 (3), 217–236.

Dwyer, C. (2000) Negotiating diasporic identities: Young British South Asian Muslim women. *Women's Studies International Forum* 23, 475–486.

Edwards, V. (2004) *Multilingualism in the English-speaking World: Pedigree of Nations.* Oxford: Blackwell Publishing Ltd.

Europa-Studie (2014) Europa-Studie: Evaluation der Staatlichen Europa-Schule Berlin (SESB). See http://www.europa-studie.uni-kiel.de/de/ueber-die-studie (accessed 29 May 2014).

Fäcke, C. (2007) Sprachliche Bildung und zweisprachige Erziehung. Überlegungen zum Partnersprachenmodell der Staatlichen Europa-Schule Berlin (SESB). In D. Elsner, L. Küster and B. Viebrock (eds) *Fremdsprachenkompetenzen für ein wachsendes Europa: Das Leitziel Multiliteralität, Vol. 31* (pp. 241–256). Frankfurt: KFU, Peter Lang.

Fahmy, E. (2006) Social capital and civic action: A study of youth in the United Kingdom. *Young* 14 (2), 101–118.

Feuerverger, G. (2001) *Oasis of Dreams: Teaching and Learning Peace in a Jewish-Palestinian Village in Israel.* New York: Routledge.

Freeman, R.D. (1996) Dual language planning at Oyster bilingual school: It's much more than language. *TESOL Quarterly* 30 (3), 557–582.

Freeman, R.D. (1998) *Bilingual Education and Social Change.* Clevedon: Multilingual Matters.

Genesee, F. (2008) Dual language in the global village. In T. Williams Fortune and D.J. Tedick (eds) *Pathways to Multilingualism: Evolving Perspectives on Immersion Education* (pp. 22–45). Clevedon: Multilingual Matters.

Genesee, F. and Gándara, P. (1999) Bilingual education programs: A cross-national perspective. *Journal of Social Issues* 55 (4), 665–685.

Gleeson, F. and Hertz, G. (1998) Interkulturelle Lehrerkooperation als Voraussetzung bilingualen Unterrichts. In M. Göhlich (ed.) *Beiträge zur Schulentwicklung: Europaschule – Das Berliner Modell* (pp. 66–76). Neuwied, Kriftel: Hermann Luchterhand Verlag.

Gogolin, I. (1994) *Der monolinguale Habitus der multilingualen Schule.* Münster and New York: Waxman.

Gogolin, I. (2001) *Sprachenvielfalt durch Zuwanderung – ein verschenkter Reichtum in der (Arbeits-)Welt?* Förderung von MigrantInnen in der beruflichen Bildung durch sprachbezogene Angebote. Bonn (Germany): Good Practice Center. See http://www.good-practice.de/1_Gogolin.pdf (retrieved 25 April 2014).

Gogolin, I. (2006) Linguistic habitus. In J.L. May (ed.) *Concise Encyclopedia of Pragmatics.* Oxford: Elsevier.

Gogolin, I., Neumann, U. and Roth, H.-J. (2007) *Schulversuch bilinguale Grundschulklassen in Hamburg: Wissenschaftliche Begleitung – Bericht 2007. Abschlussbericht über die italienisch-deutschen, portugiesisch-deutschen und spanisch-deutschen Modellklassen.* See http://www.epb.uni-hamburg.de/files/Bericht2009.pdf (retrieved 25 April 2014).

Golmohamad, M. (2009) Education for world citizenship: Beyond national allegiance. *Educational Philosophy and Theory* 41 (4), 466–486.

Gomolla, M. and Radtke, F.-O. (2007) *Instiutionelle Diskriminierung: Die Herstellung ethnischer Differenz in der Schule* (2nd edn). Wiesbaden: VS Verlag für Sozialwissenschaften.

Gräfe-Bentzien, S. (2001) Evaluierung bilingualer Kompetenzen. Eine Pilotstudie zur Entwicklung der deutschen und italienischen Sprachfähigkeiten in der Primarstufe beim Schulversuch der staatlichen Europa-Schule Berlin (SESB). Doctoral thesis, Freie Universität Berlin.

Granovetter, M. (1973) The strength of weak ties. *American Journal of Sociology* 78, 1360–1380.

Granovetter, M. (1983) The strength of weak ties: A network theory revisited. *Sociological Theory* 1, 201–233.

Green, A., Preston, J. and Janmaat, J.G. (2006) *Education, Equality and Social Cohesion.* Basingstoke: Palgrave Macmillan.

Greene, J. (1998) *A Meta-Analysis of the Effectiveness of Bilingual Education.* Claremont, CA: Tomas Rivera Policy Insitute.

Haas, B.E. (2006) *Youth Life Skills Evaluation.* See http://www.humanserviceresearch.com/youthlifeskillsevaluation/ (accessed 22 April 2014).

Harris, I.M. and Morrison, M.L. (2003) *Peace Education* (2nd edn). Jefferson, NC: McFarland.

Holland, J. (2009) Young people and social capital: Uses and abuses? *Young* 17 (4), 331–350.

Holland, J., Reynolds, T. and Weller, S. (2007) Transitions, networks and communities: The significance of social capital in the lives of children and young people. *Journal of Youth Studies* 10 (1), 97–116.

Hope Cheong, P., Edwards, R., Goulbourne, H. and Solomos, J. (2007) Immigration, social cohesion and social capital: A critical review. *Critical Social Policy* 27 (1), 24–49.

Howard, E.R. and Christian, D. (2002) Two-way immersion 101: Designing and implementing a two-way immersion education program at the elementary level. Educational Practice Report No. 9. Washington, DC: Center for Applied Linguistics. See http://www.cal.org/crede/pdfs/epr9.pdf (accessed 4 March 2009).

iCoCo (2009) Building community cohesion in Britain: Lessons from iCoCo local reviews. Coventry: Institute of Community Cohesion. See http://resources.cohesioninstitute. org.uk/Publications/Documents/Document/DownloadDocumentsFile.aspx?record-Id=108&file=Wordversion (accessed 15 September 2010).

Jackson, R. (2004) Intercultural education and recent European pedagogies of religious education. *Intercultural Education* 15 (1), 3–14.

James, M. (2009) Interculturalism: Social policy and grassroots work. London: Baring Foundation.

Jansen, T., Chioncel, N. and Dekkers, H. (2006) Social cohesion and integration: Learning active citizenship. *British Journal of Sociology of Education* 27 (2), 189–205.

Kielhöfer, B. (2004) Strukturen und Enwicklungen in der zweisprachigen Grundschule – eine Evaluation an der Berliner Europa-Schule Judith Kerr. *Neusprachliche Mitteilungen* 57 (3), 168–176.

Li, Y., Pickles, A. and Savage, M. (2003) *Conceptualising and Measuring Social Capital: A New Approach.* Manchester: Centre for Census and Survey Research.

Lin, N. (2001) *Social Capital.* Cambridge: Cambridge University Press.

Lindholm-Leary, K.J. (2001) *Dual Language Education.* Clevedon: Multilingual Matters.

Lindholm-Leary, K. and Howard, E.R. (2008) Language development and academic achievement in two-way immersion programs. In T. Williams Fortune and D.J. Tedick (eds) *Pathways to Multilingualism: Evolving Perspectives on Immersion Education* (pp. 177–200). Clevedon: Multilingual Matters.

Linssen, I., Leven, R. and Hurrelmann, K. (2002) *Jugend 2002. Zwischen pragmatischem Idealismus und robustem Materialismus.* Frankfurt: Fischer Taschenbuch Verlag.

Maalouf, A. (2008) A rewarding challenge: How the multiplicity of languages could strengthen Europe. Brussels: European Commission. See http://www.poliglotti4.eu/docs/a_rewarding_challenge.pdf (accessed 22 April 2014).

Maes, J., Schmitt, M. and Schmal, A. (1995) *Gerechtigkeit als innerdeutsches Problem: Werthaltungen, Kontrollüberzeugungen, Freiheitsüberzeugungen, Drakonität, Soziale Einstellungen, Empathie und Protestantische Arbeitsethik als Kovariate.* Trier: Fachbereich I – Psychologie, University of Trier.

Marplan (1996) *Untersuchung über die Lebensbedingungen ausländischer Jugendlicher in Deutschland: Fragebogen für griechische jugendliche Frauen (18–25 Jahre).* Offenbach: Technische Universität Chemnitz-Zwickau, Deutsches Jugendinstitut.

McKenna, N. (2003) Myths and realities. *Education Review* 17 (1), 119–124.

Meier, G. (2010) *Social and Intercultural Benefits of Bilingual Education: A Peace-linguistic Evaluation of Staatliche Europa-Schule Berlin, Vol. 12.* Frankfurt: Peter Lang.

Meier, G. (2012a) Zweiwegintegration durch zweisprachige Bildung? Ergebnisse aus der Staatlichen Europa-Schule Berlin. *International Review of Education* 3 (58), 335–352.

Meier, G. (2012b) Introduction (Traduit par Katharine Pipe). In G. Meier (ed.) *Éducation bilingue en Europe et ailleurs: Statu quo et itinéraires de recherche possibles. Synergies Europe 7* (pp. 5–16). Sylvains-les-Moulins: Gerflint.

Meier, G. (2012c) Enseignement bilingue et amélioration scolaires: Les conclusions de l'expérience Wix Primary School/École de Wix à Londres (Traduit par Laurent Battut). In G. Meier (ed.) *Éducation bilingue en Europe et ailleurs: Statu quo et itinéraires de recherche possibles. Synergies Europe 7* (pp. 53–76). Sylvains-les-Moulins: Gerflint.

Meier, G. (2012d) *Éducation bilingue en Europe et ailleurs: Statu quo et itinéraires de recherche possibles. Synergies 7.* Sylvains-les-Moulins: Gerflint.

Meier, G. (2012e) Entretien avec Christine Le Pape Racine et Mélanie Buser (Propos recueillis par Gabriela Meier). In G. Meier (ed.) *Éducation bilingue en Europe et ailleurs: Statu quo et itinéraires de recherche possibles. Synergies Europe 7* (pp. 25–31). Sylvains-les-Moulins: Gerflint.

Meier, G. (forthcoming) "Cette entraide et ce tutorat naturel qui s'organise entre eux" – A research framework for two-way bilingual immersion programmes. In N. Morys, C. Kirsch, I. de Saint-Georges and G. Gretsch (eds) *Lernen und Lehren in multilingualen Kontexten: Zum Umgang mit sprachlich-kultureller Diversität im Klassenraum/Learning and Teaching in Multilingual contexts: Dealing with Linguistic and Cultural Diversity in the Classroom.* Frankfurt: Peter Lang.

Morrow, V. (2005) Conceptualising social capital in relation to the well-being of children and young people. In H. Hendrick (ed.) *Child Welfare and Social Policy: An Essential Reader* (pp. 143–156). Bristol: The Policy Press.

Nicht, J. (2012) Netzwerkanalytische Perspektiven auf binational-bilinguale Schulklassen: Peer-Beziehungen in einem deutsch-polnischen und einem deutsch-tschechischen Schulprojekt. In G. Meier (ed.) *Éducation bilingue en Europe et ailleurs: Statu Quo et itinéraires de recherche possibles. Synergies Europe 7* (pp. 105–118). Sylvains-les-Moulins: Gerflint.

Oder, E. (2005) The social cohesion role of educational organizations: Primary and secondary schools. *PJE. Peabody Journal of Education* 80 (4), 78–88.

Olssen, M., Codd, J. and Anne-Marie, O.N. (2006) *Education Policy: Globalization, Citizenship and Democracy.* London: Sage.

Panjwani, F. (2005) Agreed syllabi and un-agreed values: Religious education and missed opportunities for fostering social coheison. *British Journal of Educational Studies* 53 (3), 375–393.

Peterson, B. (2007) La Escuela Fratney: A journey towards democracy. In W. Apple and J. Beane (eds) *Democratic Schools: Lessons in Powerful Education* (pp. 30–61). Portsmouth, NH: Heinemann.

Putnam, R. (2000) *Bowling Alone: The Collapse and Revival of American Community.* New York: Simon & Schuster.

Putnam, R. (2004) Tuning in, tuning out: The strange disappearance of social capital in America. In T. Donovan and K. Hoover (eds) *The Elements of Social Scientific Thinking* (8th edn; pp. 161–190). Belmong, CA: Thomson/Wadsworth.

Reich, H.H. and Roth, H.-J. (2002) *Spracherwerb zweisprachig aufwachsender Kinder und Jugendlicher: Ein Überblick über den Stand der nationalen und internationalen Forschung.* Hamburg: Local Government Authority for Education and Sport.

Reynolds, T. (2007) Friendship networks, social capital and ethnic identity: Researching the perspectives of Caribbean young people in Britain. *Journal of Youth Studies* 10 (4), 383–398.

Rösch, H. (2001) Zweisprachige Erziehung in Berlin im Elementar- und Primarbereich. *EliSe, Essener linguistische Skripte* 1, 1. See http://www.uni-due.de/imperia/md/content/elise/ausgabe_1_2001_roesch.pdf (accessed 22 January 2009).

SENBJS (2008) *Staatliche Europa-Schule Berlin.* See http://www.berlin.de/sen/bildung/besondere_angebote/staatl_europaschule/ (accessed 12 November 2008).

Söhn, J. (2005) *Zweisprachiger Schulunterricht für Migrantenkinder: Ergebnisse der Evaluationsforschung zu seinen Auswirkungen auf Zweitspracherwerb und Schulerfolg.* Berlin: WZB. See http://skylla.wzb.eu/pdf/2005/iv05-akibilanz2.pdf (accessed 3 September 2009).

Sukopp, I. (2005) *Bilinguales Lernen: Konzeption, Sprachen, Unterricht.* Berlin: LISUM, SENBJS.

Tankersley, D. (2001) Bombs or bilingual programmes? Dual language immersion, transformative education and community building in Macedonia. *International Journal for Bilingual Education and Bilingualism* 4 (2), 107–124.

Torney-Purta, J., Lehmann, R., Oswald, H. and Schulz, W. (2001) *Citizenhsip and Education in Twenty-eight Countries: Civic Knowledge and Engagement at Age Fourteen.* Amsterdam: International Association for the Evaluation of Educational Achievement.

Torres-Guzmán, M.E. (2002) Dual language programs: Key features and results. *Directions in Language and Education* 14. National Clearinghouse for Bilingual Education, Washington, DC.

Willig, A.C. (1985) A meta-analysis of selected studies on the effectiveness of bilingual education. *Review of Educational Research* 55, 269–317.

Worley, C. (2005) 'It's not about race. It's about the community': New Labour and 'community cohesion'. *Critical Social Policy* 25 (4), 483–496.

Wright, S. (2004) *Language Policy and Language Planning: From Nationalism to Globalisation.* Basingstoke: Palgrave Macmillan.

Zydatiß, W. (1998) Ein Spracherwerbskonzept für die Staatliche Europa-Schule Berlin. In M. Göhlich (ed.) *Beiträge zur Schulentwicklung: Europaschule – Das Berliner Modell* (pp. 66–76). Neuwied, Kriftel: Hermann Luchterhand Verlag.

Part 3

Visions of the Multilingual Turn in Pedagogy and Practice

Jean Conteh and Gabriela Meier

In the final part of the book, we present examples from classrooms of what could be seen as the multilingual turn in practice. Together, these classrooms constitute a wide range of teaching and learning contexts, from complementary to mainstream, populated by teachers representing a rich diversity of professional backgrounds, experience, and personal and social knowledge, and pupils of all ages from a similarly wide range of language and cultural backgrounds. Each chapter provides a description of specific classroom practice, situated in a particular sociocultural and historical context and theorised by the authors using frameworks, many of which have already been referred to in Parts 1 and 2 of the book. As in the previous parts, the chapters raise issues about the implications of the multilingual turn for all members of society, not just those categorised as 'multilingual'. Readers are invited to consider their relevance and implications for the educational contexts that are most familiar to them, including possibly for their own practices as teachers.

The four chapters offer different perspectives on learning and how it can be defined (see the introduction to the whole book for a fuller discussion). **Chapter 9** (Conteh, Begum & Riasat) emphasises learning as a cultural process and the importance of family and community contributions; **Chapter 10** (Piccardo & Aden) provides convincing arguments and evidence for recognising the emotional aspects of learning in promoting plurilingualism; **Chapter 11** (García & Kano) describes the translanguaging strategies employed by bilingual students in developing academic writing; and **Chapter 12** (Anderson & Yu-Chiao) links creativity and identity in presenting a range of arts-based activities in different classroom settings.

While they represent different research methodologies and data collection strategies, a significant common feature of the chapters in this part is that they all, in different ways, show the importance of collaborative research in understanding classroom practices. All of the chapters report small-scale, often longitudinal projects, some of them externally funded but not all. They illustrate how researchers and practitioners can – indeed, we argue, need to – collaborate as equal partners in research in order to generate authentic data, which reveal the complexity of classroom activity, situated in richly described contexts. The activities described in **Chapter 9** have been developed over several years by a university-based teacher educator and two teachers working together in a complementary learning setting. **Chapter 10** demonstrates how researchers worked over an extended period with a skilled teacher and an actress to document and analyse drama-based language lessons. In **Chapter 11**, a PhD student and her supervisor present a case study where high school students actively engage in analysing their own dynamic bilingual writing practices. Finally, in **Chapter 12**, university-based teacher educators work with teachers in a range of contexts to develop and document children's learning in creative projects. A key message of this part of the book is of the need for more research of this type, where practitioners are empowered to engage in analysing their own practices, developing the professional knowledge and self-confidence to construct their own pedagogies to promote their pupils' success.

Generic questions for Part 3

- What changes might be needed in the traditional roles and relationships between teachers and learners, and in the development of policy and curricula to facilitate the changes suggested in this part of the book?
- How might some of the ideas developed in the chapters be interpreted in practice in classrooms with which you are familiar?

9 Multilingual Pedagogy in Primary Settings: From the Margins to the Mainstream

Jean Conteh, Shila Begum and Saiqa Riasat

Guiding Questions

- What ideas could you take from the chapter to develop teaching activities in a context with which you are familiar?
- What issues might 'monolingual' teachers face in developing pedagogies similar to those illustrated in the chapter?
- How might the 'funds of knowledge' model of learning help in developing pedagogies that benefit all learners, not just those who are 'multilingual'?

Introduction

Over recent years in England there have been a number of small-scale research studies which link multilingual primary children's learning across the different contexts of family, community and mainstream school (e.g. Conteh *et al.*, 2007; Gregory *et al.*, 2004; Kenner & Ruby, 2012; Lytra & Martin, 2010). Despite the hopeful signs they reveal of the benefits of home languages for children's learning and achievement in mainstream school, language diversity is still widely regarded as a 'problem' (Safford & Drury, 2013) by teachers and policy makers in mainstream settings. This chapter aims to move the debate forward by illustrating some of the classroom practices that have been developed over the past 10 years in a complementary Saturday class with primary-aged pupils in a post-industrial, multilingual city in the north of England. This is contextualised in the theoretical frameworks of language and learning that underpin the multilingual turn as developed in this book, and in the local and national political, historical, cultural and social contexts in which the class is situated. Our intention is to offer to mainstream practitioners a different and more positive perspective from which to consider the 'problem' that Safford and Drury identify, as well as some starting points for developing their own 'multilingual pedagogies' in ways that could benefit all their pupils, not just those who may be categorised as learning English as an additional language (EAL). In addition, we hope that researchers may gain insights from our work into ways of developing research approaches and strategies that will enhance our understandings of the complex issues that surround the multilingual turn in languages education in primary settings.

This chapter has four main sections. In the first, we indicate the theoretical frameworks related to language and learning that underpin the chapter. The second section provides contextual information about language diversity in primary education in England, focusing on the curriculum, and the perspectives of mainstream teachers and of ethnic minority parents and families. Following this, the third section introduces the complementary class and the activities that form the main substance of the chapter, and finally we provide a discussion of the activities and the implications for mainstream teachers and then draw some general conclusions.

Theoretical Contexts of Learning and Language

As discussed in the Introduction to this volume (pp. 1–14), ecological perspectives on learning (Bronfenbrenner, 1979) and the 'funds of knowledge' (Gonzalez et al., 2005) concept offer helpful frameworks for understanding learning in multilingual contexts, particularly for younger pupils. Both foreground the importance of reciprocity between teacher and learners, and thus the importance of understanding the role of identity, which is 'produced and legitimised in discourse and social interaction' (Blackledge & Creese, 2010) in learning. We – along with many others – argue that 'maximum identity investment' (Cummins & Early, 2011) is vital for educational success. Classrooms and schools need to be constructed as communities of practice with dialogically constructed cultures in which identity negotiation and performance take on vital roles in learning (Cummins, 2001; García, 2009). Learning in such classrooms is not just cognitive, but social, affective and cultural, enriched by the resources brought to the classroom by all the participants, both teachers and learners. Such a view clearly has important implications for pedagogy in multilingual classrooms, and the work reported in the third section of this chapter provides examples of the kinds of activities that could contribute to such an approach. Other examples, taken from mainstream classroom contexts, can be found in Conteh (2012: Chapters 4 and 5).

Language plays a central role in learning. The multilingual turn, funds of knowledge and ecological perspectives on learning all have clear implications for the ways we think and talk about language. As Moll (2005: 276) asserts, the language and cultural experiences of students are 'their most important tools for thinking'. From the perspective of the users, languages need to be understood as sets of social and cultural processes that contribute to identity construction and allow us to get things done in every social situation, rather than as discrete sets of systems of sounds, words and texts, understood through the 'neutral' disciplines of phonology, lexis and semantics. Linked with the funds of knowledge model of learning as joint culture creation between teacher and pupil, notions such as translanguaging (see the Introduction and Chapters 7, 8 and 11 in this volume) offer more appropriate ways of understanding how young learners use their language resources to make links between home and school and construct their own understandings of the new knowledge. For many children in England, as we see below, translanguaging is a normal aspect of their home and community experiences.

The language repertoires of the participants in many English mainstream primary classrooms are hugely diverse. While some may bring different languages to the classroom context, others bring variety in dialects and accents of English. As we show in discussing the teachers' (especially Meena's) strategies in Chapter 7, this opens out pedagogic possibilities for all pupils. Instead of focusing on the problems of language diversity, we need to explore the ways in which the potential for learning is enriched by the repertoires of linguistic and cultural resources that both teachers and learners bring to the context. Learning can become a transformative process in which learners draw upon diverse resources, both familiar and new ... 'syncretising languages, literacies, narrative styles' to 'transform the languages and cultures to create new forms ...' (Gregory, 2005). But, as we see below in the section on 'Teachers in mainstream schools – caught in the middle', this creates many tensions and uncertainties for mainstream primary teachers in England.

Language Diversity and Primary Education in England: An Ecological Overview

In this section we present a brief overview of the contexts of multilingualism in primary schools in England, beginning with the national language, social and cultural contexts and the particular local contexts of the city where the Saturday class takes place. Following this, we outline the ways in which languages and language diversity are and have historically been constructed and mediated in the primary curriculum and by primary teachers and teaching assistants in the multilingual classrooms they work in. The final strand in this contextual framing is a summary of some of the issues surrounding the ways in which parental involvement is mediated, related to families from some minority ethnic backgrounds.

National and local contexts

Currently, about 16.8% of pupils in primary and 12.3% in secondary schools in England are multilingual, in that they speak other languages but English at home (DfE, 2011a). The term most commonly used in policy to categorise them is 'EAL' (English as an additional language). This term is sometimes contested and often misunderstood, reflecting the complex history of language diversity and its constructions in the education system in England. It is frequently used to refer only to pupils who are new to English and who are actually more specifically defined in policy as 'new arrivals' (DfES, 2006: 2). These are often children whose families decided to move to the UK to find work or to join relatives following the changes to the European Union in 2004, including the accession of the so-called A8 countries. This has led to a marked increase in the range of languages represented in primary classrooms in England: it is not easy to establish an accurate figure, but around 360 is normally quoted. It is not uncommon to find primary schools where the pupils between them speak more than 40 languages at home. While London is still home to the majority of pupils from migrant backgrounds, there is no longer any part of England that can be regarded as linguistically homogeneous (DfE, 2011a). England has, without doubt, become a 'superdiverse' society (Vertovec, 2007).

But language diversity in schools in England has a much longer history than these recent and much publicised changes. Diversity has been a feature of British society for centuries. Large, postcolonial migrations from the 1940s onwards led to the formation in most English cities of settled, multilingual communities, originating from the Indian subcontinent, Africa, the Caribbean and other former colonies. Children from these communities, now second- or third-generation British citizens, form the largest group among EAL learners, sometimes defined as 'advanced bilingual learners' (DfES, 2006: 2). The city of Bradford, where the class discussed in this chapter takes place, is part of one of the most diverse areas in England outside London. Its largest minority ethnic community is of Pakistani heritage, descended from the young men who began arriving from the Mirpur region in the 1950s to work in the huge and profitable woollen mills. A slightly smaller migration began arriving from Bangladesh from the 1970s. Over a third of pupils overall in primary schools in Bradford are now of south Asian heritage. These pupils are all multilingual, but English is often their dominant language, so EAL, as it is currently defined and perceived, is not a helpful way to describe their language repertoires.

The maintenance of strong family links with 'back home' (Bolognani, 2007: 60) feeds a two-way traffic between Bradford and Pakistan and

Bradford and Bangladesh. Thus, as well as English, children may speak and write some of several south Asian languages. A study carried out in Bradford (Aitsiselmi, 2004) reveals the wide and complex array of languages and dialects that south Asian-heritage families have at their disposal from their heritage countries. And these languages are not disappearing as time goes on. Aitsiselmi (2004: 3) comments on how 'their ... multiple layers of identities ... may be expressed through each of the various languages used for the purposes of spoken or written communication'. As Leung *et al.* (1997: 544) argue, the children 'actively construct their own patterns of language use, ethnicity, and social identity', often in 'strong contradiction to the fixed patterns and the reified ethnicities attributed' to them, attributed – it can be added – mainly through the language education policies that construct their classroom experiences, mediated by their mainstream teachers.

The primary curriculum

Responses to multilingualism in the primary curriculum in England, as in mainstream education in general, reflect the tensions of attempting to recognise the diversity of the pupil population while meeting the requirements of a 'universal model of language development and assessment' (Safford, 2003: 8). In addition, the 'equality of opportunity' goals of the National Curriculum entail the entitlement to standard English for all (Cameron & Bourne, 1988), and so – we argue – through conflating 'equal opportunity' with 'doing the same thing with every child', promote an overall 'monolingualising' ethos (Heller, 2007). A subtractive view of multilingualism prevails, which can be tracked through key national policies over many years. Central to this is the influential Swann Report (DES, 1985), which concluded that supporting the teaching of the so-called 'community languages' was beyond the remit of mainstream education and was 'best achieved within the ethnic minority communities themselves' (DES, 1985: 406). Thus, the maintenance of multilingualism and the promotion of bilingualism were implicitly not recognised as worthwhile aims for mainstream education. Indeed, the underlying assumption, as the Curriculum 2000 statement on inclusion 'including all learners' reinforces, is that speaking other languages than English can lead to deficit, (DfE, 2011b):

> A minority of pupils will have particular learning and assessment requirements which ... if not addressed, could create barriers to learning. These requirements ... may be linked to a pupil's progress in learning English as an additional language.

Provision for languages teaching in the primary curriculum reflects the monolingualising ethos, constructing languages as atomised, separate 'boxes' of content with no apparent connections between them. This promotes a 'sequential monolingualism' in languages education, which has been embedded in the curriculum for many years. Various changes since 2010, designed to 'raise standards' (DfE, 2010) have reinforced it. At the Foundation Stage (for children aged 3–5 years and not compulsory in England), the former six areas of learning (DfE, 2013a), which included communication, language and literacy development (CLLD) have been reconfigured as seven. CLLD has become CLD and 'literacy' has been separated out, largely taken up with early training in sound recognition and discrimination as preparation for discrete phonics teaching by the age of five. Children at Key Stage 1 (KS1, for pupils aged 5–7 years) begin the National Curriculum, in which the Programme of Study for English, now packaged as literacy, remains the only statutory requirement for language teaching (DfE, 2013b). As Alexander (2004: 24) tellingly points out, the political control is total: 'literacy is standards, not curriculum'. For the past few years, a central feature of this has been rigorous, discrete training in 'systematic synthetic phonics' (SSP), with the notorious 'phonic screening check' at the end of Year 1 (DfE, 2013c), purporting to assess children's abilities in phonically decoding regular clusters of letters. Alongside this, children follow a tightly structured, text-based approach to literacy and their reading and writing attainments are summatively assessed at the end of Year 2. In Key Stage 2 (KS2, 7–11 years), the teaching of literacy continues and is assessed by the newly introduced and externally marked 'SPAG' (spelling, punctuation and grammar) test (DfE, 2013d).

Other languages besides English are severely under-represented in the primary curriculum – indeed, in the mainstream curriculum generally. Currently many students leave mainstream school at 16 or 18 with no systematic knowledge at all of any other language but English – and a significant number, of course, go on to become teachers. Primary modern foreign languages (PMFL) were reintroduced into the curriculum at KS2 from 2005. The KS2 languages framework (DfES, 2005), as well as covering the standard oracy and literacy in learning a new language, offered a potentially interesting approach to developing language awareness, knowledge about language, language learning strategies and intercultural understanding (Cable et al., 2012). Cable et al. (2012: 368) also point out how language learning contributed to 'a school ethos which valued diversity and increased tolerance and understanding of other people'. The KS2 framework did not specify which languages should be taught. While the most popular language choices were French and Spanish, a small number of primary schools took advantage of resources within their communities to introduce into their mainstream teaching languages such as Arabic and Urdu. A key benefit of this approach was that, in schools where there were knowledgeable and interested staff, innovative and exciting pedagogies for primary languages teaching began to develop, and publishers began to cash in on the market with lively and effective resources (Cable et al., 2012; Kirsch, 2012). Sometimes, this had a spin-off into EAL as obvious connections were made and the benefits of learning new languages began to be perceived (Conteh & Begum, 2008; Kirsch, 2012). But, as with all other areas of the curriculum, PMFL has been the object of a review since the change of government in 2010 (DfE, 2012a). A clear intention of this is to bring PMFL in line with MFL in secondary schools:

> Secondary schools have expressed a desire for consistency in the primary curriculum to provide some assurance of what language teaching pupils entering secondary school have received. ... Some schools argue that they have little choice but to start again or spend considerable time unpicking things which they consider have been incorrectly taught. (DfE, 2012a: para 2.8)

The new primary curriculum, which becomes statutory in September 2014, allows for schools to choose among the same languages as those offered in their feeder secondary schools, including Latin and Ancient Greek. The beginnings of the development of a primary pedagogy for languages have thus been stopped in their tracks. Despite this, it is significant that a substantial proportion of the respondents to the consultation felt that the proposed list was too limited and pupils should have '... the opportunity to learn community languages and a language or languages of their own culture ...', and that 'schools should be free to choose a language that would reflect the needs and strengths of their communities'. Comments such as these are perhaps indicative of recognition, outside government policymaking, of the importance of the funds of knowledge of families and communities for learning in mainstream school.

Teachers in mainstream schools – caught in the middle

Even before Safford and Drury (2013) pointed out the 'problem' of language diversity, it had been well documented that mainstream primary teachers in England, in general, have professional and personal concerns about promoting multilingualism through, for example, allowing their pupils to use their home languages in their learning (Conteh, 2003, 2007; Kenner & Ruby, 2012; Pearce, 2012; Wardman et al., 2012). Pearce (2012: 460) argues that, 'it is because the dominant, white, group is monolingual that multilingualism is seen as problematic'. Through no fault of their own, many mainstream primary teachers lack the personal experience and theoretical knowledge about bilingualism and language diversity that would help allay their fears. As suggested below, they get very little support in this in their initial training. A quote from one (monolingual) mainstream teacher illustrates these issues.[1] This teacher has worked for several years with multilingual, EAL pupils, and has taught children from the Saturday class. She shows great empathy for her pupils and strong support for the idea that the children need to maintain their home languages, but when asked about using home languages in her classroom, she responded:

> ... that would be interesting ... I can't pick up any languages at all ... they tell me words, we do some of that sometimes, but I don't pick any of it up at all, I can't remember it ... it's good the majority of the time, but then somebody uses a rude word, and I can't understand it all and the class is in uproar ...

As well as revealing her deep uncertainties about her own personal and professional capabilities, this teacher's words seem to suggest, almost, a fear of not fulfilling one of her basic responsibilities as a class teacher, that of keeping the children under control. They hint at the risk of 'disruption' to 'the institutionally constructed discourses and classroom routines of mainstream teachers' practice' that Bourne (2001: 256) argues reflect historically constructed models of 'good practice' in primary classrooms.

Following the introduction of new 'Teachers' Standards' (DfE, 2012b), EAL is even less a recognised aspect of initial teacher education than it was previously, despite the fact that anxiety about working with 'EAL learners' has for years figured prominently in surveys of newly qualified teachers (NALDIC, 2013). Mainstream teachers such as Meena (see Chapter 7) are indeed rare, not just because of her confidence and effectiveness in using multilingualism as a teaching strategy in her mainstream classroom, but because she is herself a multilingual qualified teacher. As Bourne (2001) and others (e.g. Biggs & Edwards, 1994; Martin-Jones & Saxena, 1995, 1996, 2003) have long argued, in primary classrooms in England, the prevalence of bilingual assistants rather than teachers (an outcome of the transitional bilingualism constructed in the Swann Report), means that 'monolingual definitions of "bilingual support" remain dominant' (Bourne, 2001: 256). And this is despite the fact that in some schools the assistants outnumber the teachers. Multilingualism is firmly contained within the 'clear power asymmetry in the roles constructed ... between the class teacher who controls the classroom space' (Bourne, 2001: 256) and the bilingual assistant, who is inevitably lower in the hierarchy. Indeed, as Bourne (2001: 254) points out, this power imbalance has led to some bilingual teachers refusing to apply for designated bilingual posts, fearing that this could lead to 'marginalisation, low status and poor career prospects'.

At the same time, the more recent studies cited at the start of the chapter, while pointing out the reservations, also show how many mainstream teachers are quick to realise the potential of a pedagogy that recognises the full language repertoires of their pupils, and of bilingual teachers themselves. Kenner and Ruby's (2012) work bringing together teachers from complementary and mainstream settings offers many hopeful signs, and indicates the kinds of classroom activities that make children's (and teachers') language and cultural resources the starting point of teaching. Similarly, Wardman's (2012) collaboration with Judith Bell and Karen Sharp, two mainstream teachers, shows the possibilities of such an approach. It also demonstrates the great value of continuing professional development of a sustained, principled nature – something sorely lacking in the system in England in relation to EAL. Other studies (e.g. Conteh, 2007, 2010; Chapter 7 in this volume) are beginning to show the ways in which the distinctive skills and professional knowledge of multilingual teachers can contribute to the success of EAL learners and offer powerful lessons about multilingualism to 'monolingual' pupils too.

Parental involvement

The importance of parental involvement in their children's learning has for long been a politically significant feature in mainstream education in England. As an implication of the funds of knowledge concept, this should be a positive thing. But, in many ways, the model of involvement promoted in policy is a narrow and exclusive one (Crozier & Davies, 2007), which does not recognise the diversity of ways in which children both learn at home and are supported by their families, and the funds of knowledge they bring to their learning in mainstream school. As has been suggested above, the monolingualising nature of the curriculum and of primary classroom contexts means that multilingualism is simply not recognised as a matter of any interest. Indeed, in the rigid assessment and attainment regime that prevails in the mainstream system, only a very limited range of knowledge is valued. Children belonging to some minority ethnic groups are thus regarded as 'underachieving' and their families sometimes categorised as 'hard to reach' or 'vulnerable' (Kendall et al., 2008: 53) and so in need of extra support in order to become the kinds of parents that fit the school's ideal model. Researchers such as Drury (2007) and Bligh (2011) reveal how differing cultural practices in families in relation to language and learning can create dissonance with accepted school practices, particularly in the early years.

But the evidence of family and community learning presented by researchers such as Gonzalez et al. (2005) offers a wealth of reasons to rebut this deficit view of parents. As Crozier and Davies (2007) argue, it is often the schools, with their fixed and inflexible models of parental involvement that are 'hard to reach', not the families. Conteh (2003: 57–64) shows something of the tensions that minority ethnic parents can face in attempting to develop conversations with their children's teachers, despite the many positive ways in which families do and can enhance their children's learning at home (e.g. Jessel et al., 2004; Gregory et al., 2004). From working with the parents whose children attend the class, we have gained an understanding of some of the ways they can make links between their children's learning in different contexts. One parent, for example,[2] who was keen to support her four sons in any way possible, was led to realise the value in involving them in cooking activities at home through her participation in such activities at the class. Thus her own self-confidence and sense of agency grew:

> He loved the cooking classes . . . he wants me to teach him how to do atta [i.e. measure flour to make chapattis] at home. . . . I have noticed I would overlook opportunities, but now I try and motivate myself and my children. I've learnt that understanding my family is very important.

The importance of this is in the way it opened out the possibilities for this parent of what was entailed in learning, and so of her awareness of the importance of doing things with her children at home that she was easily able to do. Rather than feeling disempowered and deskilled because she felt she lacked the kind of 'academic' knowledge that could help her children to succeed, she found confidence in her own ability and identity. Thus, what may be necessary, sometimes, is not that parents be 'educated' by schools in ways to support their children's learning at home, but that they are affirmed in what they already do. As Hensley (2005: 143) suggests, 'being an ethnographer' with parents and attempting to understand things from their viewpoints develops a rapport and opens access to the funds of knowledge that parents have.

The Class and the Activities

This section has three subsections: in the first, we outline the history and aims of the complementary Saturday class where the activities we present took place; in the second subsection we explain how the pedagogy employed in the class was developed; and in the final subsection we present examples from two sets of learning activities from the Saturday class. This subsection is further subdivided to incorporate two kinds of activity: the first is a project about family and community histories and the second is a set of ongoing activities to consolidate knowledge about time and numbers.

The Bilingual Teaching and Learning Association

The Bilingual Learning and Teaching Association (BLTA; see http://www.blta.co.uk/) is a charity, run by two qualified bilingual primary teachers, who are the co-authors of this chapter. Established in 2002, its work has been funded from 2012 to 2014 by the Paul Hamlyn Foundation. The BLTA aims to:

- Promote a 'bilingual pedagogy' to enhance children's achievements in mainstream school.

- Address misconceptions about the role and value of ethnic minority children's home languages both in school and at home among parents, children, teachers and the wider community.
- Provide a 'safe space' to promote children's identities as bilingual learners and their self-confidence in taking control of their own learning.
- Contribute to dialogue with policy makers regarding 'bilingual pedagogies'.

The BLTA works with families from some of the so-called 'hard to reach' groups referred to above, in the section on 'Parental involvement'. The complementary Saturday class is the most established part of the association's work, having run more or less continuously since 2003. It is for children aged 5–11 from minority ethnic backgrounds and is open to any family in the vicinity of the mainstream school where it is held, no matter what their language and cultural background. The teachers work collaboratively with the children and their parents to develop a pedagogy that uses their funds of knowledge as a positive resource for learning. Learning activities draw on the personal and cultural, as well as the professional knowledge of the teachers. The children who currently attend the class all come from Pakistani- and Bangladeshi-heritage backgrounds and speak a range of south Asian languages, including Punjabi, Urdu, Bengali and Pashto. Most of them are also learning Arabic through religious teaching in their local mosques or at home. It is important to emphasise that it is not a heritage language class: the teachers are not teaching the home languages. Rather, they are using the languages to open out and enhance the children's understandings of what they are learning.

Developing a 'bilingual pedagogy' in the Saturday class

The funds of knowledge philosophy includes a processual approach to developing pedagogy in which teacher-led collaborative research into community practices is followed by their integration into mainstream classroom activities (see Part Two of González et al., 2005). We develop teaching and learning in the Saturday class in similar ways. One of our aims is to integrate theory and practice, using a transformative Action Research (AR) methodology (Conteh et al., 2008; Somekh, 2006; Wells, 2011). In planning topics in the class, we have developed similar processes to those described by Sandoval-Taylor (2005: 155), in her 'thematic cycle approach to curriculum construction'. Teachers and parents take on collaborative roles, identifying a theme and specific plans for the initiation of the project, along with a list of possible related activities to follow on. This promotes 'maximum identity investment' (Cummins & Early, 2011) in creative ways, based on the personal and cultural knowledge of the families, as well as the professional knowledge of the teachers. Connections are made to new learning through a continuing process of formative assessment and more detailed planning with both the children and their families as the project develops. To facilitate this, activities involve a strong focus on conversations among the children and between children and teachers as part of collaborative, participatory activities. Thus, the learning centred on the topic grows from week to week, following the children's interests and engagement, usually over half a term but sometimes longer. As Sandoval-Taylor (2005: 159) points out, this leads to a different kind of learning from that which can be assessed by the more common, individualised types of high-stakes assessment that are embedded in mainstream systems.

A second type of activity which we employ in the class is work of a more ongoing nature, involving games, role plays, dialogues and other activities of the type which are also used in PMFL and mainstream school literacy lessons. The difference here is that home languages and funds of knowledge are brought dialogically into the learning to consolidate the children's knowledge about generic themes, usually related to literacy and maths. Such themes include number work, arithmetic and times tables, telling the time, reading and writing stories, developing systematic grammatical knowledge in various ways and so on. Through these activities, the teachers reinforce concepts directly relevant to the children's learning in their mainstream settings. They take opportunities to promote knowledge about language by actively comparing the ways that things are said and written in different languages and in English and by comparing ways of doing activities in different languages and at home and school.

As well as in the type of activity developed, the 'bilingual pedagogy' referred to above in the BLTA's aims is developed in the nature of the interactions that take place among all the participants in the classroom. A good proportion of the interaction takes place in English, as this tends to be the children's strongest language and the lingua franca. The teachers do not understand all the languages that the children speak, so at times they are learning from the children. We have written about different aspects of the class elsewhere (Conteh, 2007, 2010, 2012; Conteh & Begum, 2008), arguing in different ways for its potential for influencing practice in the mainstream system. Here, our main intention is to describe some of the activities we do in the class, and suggest how they may contribute to a multilingual pedagogy for mainstream classrooms.

The classroom activities

Family heritage-related activities

This project, led by Begum, began with the book *Here to Stay* (BHRU, 1994), which tells the history of south Asian immigrants in Bradford with wonderful images of family portraits taken by a professional photography studio in Bradford from the 1950s to the 1970s. This book was chosen because some of the photos showed people actually known to the children's families. The children were asked to discuss the photos with each other and feed back to the teachers. They were particularly surprised to discover that after the photos were taken they were edited so that the participants were made to look paler, and interested in the use of props such as pens, banknotes and cameras to help to create an image of wealth and prosperity. Their responses illustrate what was significant to them in the photos, as well as the ways they translanguaged to express their meanings:

Fizah: Ay photo olden days which san, boo old kapray thay old clothes laanay san.
These photos were taken in the olden days, they used to wear really old clothes then.

Lubnah: Suit laanay san photo chiknay san, aping precious cheez naal karma san
They would wear suits to get the photos taken and would take their precious belongings with them.

Ismailah: Ay thray para oosan. Unna nay zaroori cheeza unna naal san
These three will be brothers. Their important things will be with them.

The nature of the children's talk here is very different from their usual, everyday conversations. They use wider vocabulary and more complex grammar in both English and their home languages. Following this, some children brought in their own family photographs from home, which we shared and talked about their family members: who they were? What was their relationship with these people? To continue the visual theme, we had some practice in observational drawing, using shading and dots rather than line to replicate the effect of the black-and-white photos. The children quickly got down to work. They were surprised at their ability to create artwork with just a pen, and without a rubber. Some of them soon came and said, 'Miss I have finished'. We said, 'Look at the photograph more carefully. Find more light and dark, some parts are darker, some are lighter and others are in between.' With this encouragement, some children produced very carefully observed portraits, which took a great deal of time and care.

The children discussed the use of using additional props to enhance the photos as in the *Here to Stay* book and liked the idea of posing for photos. This interest led to the next major activity; we invited a small enterprise called Desi Portraits, who take professional photos using traditional south Asian props, to our class. They set up a scene so that the children could be taken in family groups along with their parents. Everyone really enjoyed the occasion, and there were some lovely photos to keep. Afterwards some of the children's written comments (written in Punjabi but in Roman script) surprised us in the extent and sophistication of their use of home languages.

Shahid: May hush saa because unna dithay san like fans thay props wee. Photo kar kharnay saa.

I was happy because they gave us fans and props. We took the photos home.

Anais: Hush ooya sa mari ami ni ami san asa naal photo chickya see. May flute lapray see thay moo naal rakhya saa.
I was happy, my mum's mum was with us and took a photo with us. I held a flute and put it against my mouth.

Family interviews

One of the things we knew from previous activities with the children, which also emerged in our conversations about the photos, was their detailed understanding of their extended families. They were always very eager to share knowledge and discuss their families. They were particularly keen to talk about their grandparents, and it transpired that not all children felt that they could converse well in their home languages with grandparents. So we decided to give them the opportunity to conduct an interview with their grandparents in the class. They got very excited by this prospect and drafted some interview questions, writing the questions in English first and then translating them into their home languages. One grandmother arrived, who had nine of her grandchildren at the class. The children took it in turns to ask questions, and we encouraged them to use their home languages. They felt a little awkward at first, but soon got used to it and became very enthusiastic about the activity. Here is a section of the interview, which shows the richness of the cultural exchange between the grandmother and the children at the class.[3]

Zahida: Jaylay thusa paylay ithay ai so thusa ki kisra laga si?
How did you first feel when you came to the UK?
Grandma: Payna praa wee ithi san, thay dil lagi gaya see saalay chay meenay baad. Ithay sardi ay, damp ay . . . uthay apnay mulkay khuli waa lagni see, thup lagni see, kam karnay saa baarya wich. Manja rakya san, dud chonay sa, taalay baanay sa.
My brothers and sisters were here, I got used to being here after six months to a year. It is cold here, damp here . . . there in our own country we got plenty of fresh air, sun, we worked in the fields. We had cows there; we milked them and fed them.
Riyadh: Thusa sawaylay sawaylay kiya utnay so?
Why did you wake up early in the morning?
Grandma: Sawaylay manji gathawa baanay sa, manji chownay sa, paa satnay sa, cha mananay sa, roti pakanay sa . . . bariya taakiya maarnay sa.
In the morning I fed the cows, milked the cows, cleared the cow dung, made tea and cooked chappati . . . brushed up and did the cleaning.
Lubnah: Bay bili bili karo!
Grandma do cat cat!

Grandma: Ithay bili manj badi, ithay bili katta bada, ithay bili andi chaari ay, ithay bili roti pakai ay, ithay bili khat dai ay, ithay bili sai gai ay! *Here the cat tied the cow, here the cat tied the calf, here the cat did the cooking, here the cat made the chappati, here the cat put the bed out and here the cat fell asleep!* [Grandma touches each finger on child's hand while saying each part of the poem before tickling him under arm on the last part of the poem]

We videoed the interview and watched it later with the children. They were all very interested and enjoyed watching the interview in which they had participated. They loved listening to the nursery rhyme that the grandmother shared. We listened carefully to the rhyme several times and developed a slightly different version of it, along with actions. Some children produced illustrated written versions in transliterated Punjabi of the rhyme for their parents.

Ik Bili rotu khani see,
Ik Bili Ithay khat dai yay see,
Ik Bili Andi pakani see,
Ik Bili Ithay sai gayee see,
Ik Bili Ithay khai gai (Tickle under arm)

One cat was eating chapatti,
One cat was sat on the bed,
One cat was making dinner,
One cat was sleeping,
One cat went over here to eat (Tickle under arm)

Time- and number-related activities
Learning the days of the week – time and tenses

In teaching new vocabulary, Riasat has developed a socioconstructive approach, beginning by trying to draw out from the children what understanding they already have about the concept and what vocabulary they have in their home languages. We realised that the children knew some words for the days of the week in their home languages, but did not necessarily know which days the words related to. A lot of the KS2 children were familiar with the day *'Jumma'* (Friday), because of its significance for Muslims in terms of the Friday prayers, but for many of them, it was the first time they made the connection that the word has dual meanings, referring to a day of the week as well as the act of praying. We did a range of activities related to the days of the week, with the names displayed in Punjabi, Bangla and English (all in Roman script). The children then had to do either pictorial or written diary entries for each day of the week, following our modelling of things we do on certain days.

Samaray mai apnay bachaya naal naashthay alay club jaaneya
On Monday I go with my children to breakfast club.

Children had to share their work with the whole class, using full sentences, if possible in the home languages. Moving on, we discussed words for 'yesterday' and 'tomorrow', using grammatical vocabulary, as this is interesting in Punjabi: there is only one word for both and that is *'Kal'*. The way they are distinguished is by the auxiliary words used.

> Kal mai baar jaasa (Jaasa is future tense)
> *Tomorrow I will go out*
> Kal mai baar geesa (Geesa is past tense)
> *Yesterday I went out*

Telling the time – comparing languages

Using a big clock, we once again began by checking the children's understanding of the concept of telling the time and whether they could do so in their home language. The majority of the children had heard the words in Punjabi such as *'baachay'* (o'clock) and *'saday'* (half past) but, as is often the case, in our Saturday class we helped them to see them in a meaningful context for the first time. The KS2 children were introduced to *'quarter to'* and *'quarter past'*. In Punjabi, there is a shift in meaning. The *'quarter past'* has the same meaning, *'sava'*, but *'quarter to'* in Punjabi becomes *'ponay'*, which means *'three-quarters'*. Some children commented that they had heard this word a lot and Hibah remembered that her mum used it in a clothes shop. She commented that she now knew why her mum used it there, and what she meant.

Humah: Miki ponay kaaz thayo
Give me three quarters of a yard

The younger children drew the correct time, given in home languages, on blank clock faces and the more able children were invited to write word problems for each other using different vocabulary for telling the time and answering each other's questions. Then we went back to the days of the week and the diaries (see previous section), and the children all had to add times to their entries. In this way, they slowly build up more vocabulary and can gradually talk about things in more detail, as well as reinforcing generic concepts.

Reinforcement of the language is very important. Once the children have done activities such as the above, we move onto doing role plays, which requires them to use the vocabulary we have been focusing on. They really enjoy role play and often give back in their dialogues more than we actually thought they knew. They are creative and colourful with language and demonstrate a very good understanding of cultural jokes. When the parents collect their children, we remind them to use at home what we have been learning in the Saturday class in order for it to become embedded. Some children will come the following week and tell us of conversations they had with grandparents or parents and how they felt more confident in constructing their sentences.

In the Saturday class we often discuss funny rules of the home language and English when we encounter them. For example in Punjabi, if you said *'half past one'* as *'saday ik'* the users of that language would probably laugh at you (as I [Saiqa] know from personal experience in my teenage years). For some peculiar reason, you need to say it is *'daid'*. The same applies to *'half past two'*, which is not *'saday dou'* but is *'tie'*.

Consolidating counting – dice games

We noticed that the younger children did not confidently know their numbers beyond 10, and the older ones beyond 20, in their home languages. We often count from zero to 30 in different languages with our children and then throw them random numbers in their home language to convert into English or vice versa. This is an area we have encouraged parents to be more proactive in by reinforcing the numbers at home with their children. We often shock parents by saying that if your child was nine years old and did not know their numbers beyond 20 in English we would be deeply concerned, yet in the home language such little progress is acceptable!

We have also introduced the children to a variety of games involving dice, which required them to use the four number operations and provided them with lots of opportunities to count and use numbers in their home languages. In the *'jamma'* game, the children were told to think what would be the highest and lowest number they could get if they threw two dice and added the numbers that came up. Most children understood it was two and 12, but some needed to be shown by counting the dots on the two dice. After this, the children paired up or played in groups of three. They had to choose any four numbers between two and 12 and then each child threw the two dice together and added the total. If the total of the two dice was any of the four chosen numbers, they crossed that number out. The child who crossed all their numbers out first was the winner. While playing, we go around the room observing children's use of the languages and encourage them to count and use the operational words in the home languages. Often, their main concern is to win, so they do not realise that this activity is helping them embed the numbers in their home language. Even the children who are not using home languages much are having it reinforced through their peers' responses.

Discussion and Conclusions

It would be impossible to package activities such as those described in the previous section and turn them into materials that teachers could take off the shelf to use in their own classrooms. It is not the intention of this chapter to do this. Rather, it is to illuminate the implications of the multi-lingual turn for primary classrooms, showing the kinds of approaches to pedagogy that can open out learning and provide the rich conversations which empower teachers and through which in turn children are empowered as learners. The teachers in the Saturday class have deep knowledge of the children and their family contexts, and of the theoretical background of multilingualism, and this is clearly very important in their work. Most mainstream teachers do not share this advantage, and their opportunities to develop such professional knowledge are – as discussed in the section above on 'Teachers in mainstream schools – caught in the middle' – currently very sparse in teacher education and continuing professional development in England. But confidence can be gained from other sources. As a mainstream teacher using the funds of knowledge approach, Sandoval-Taylor (2005: 162) explains how she had initial concerns about the outcomes in terms of the quality of her pupils' production of English. But she was pleasantly surprised when what they wrote was of a higher level than they had previously achieved. She argues that this was because 'what they brought from home surrounded and supported their learning'. Although she did not share the language and cultural backgrounds of her pupils, she was able to appreciate the importance of their home and community learning experiences for their success in mainstream school.

The teaching approaches that we have developed in the BLTA class reveal some of the fallacies of the 'myths' about best practice in learning and teaching languages (see Conteh, Copland & Creese, this volume). For example, they promote the kinds of translanguaging practices that could be condemned for leading to poor models of language. Yet, in the class, they promote the children's active engagement and the use of language in more sophisticated ways than could otherwise be expected of them. The Saturday class activities revolve around talk, but it is very different from the fast-paced, teacher-directed dialogues in current recommended approaches in literacy work (e.g. DfE, 2011c). The reciprocal discussions that teachers and pupils generate together relate much more closely to the model of dialogic teaching developed by Wolfe and Alexander (2008) (and see Conteh & Meier, Introduction, p. 8). Some of their distinctive features are:

- Their richness in affordances for using language in different ways, particularly through talk.
- Their dialogic qualities, in the full sense of the term.
- Their emergent, iterative nature, where future activities are based on responses to earlier ones.
- Their responsiveness to the developing interests of the children

The teachers have developed an approach to classroom interaction with their pupils, which – it could be argued – constitutes genuinely dialogic classroom conversations. Their approach is remarkably similar to guidelines suggested over 20 years ago by Wells and Chang-Wells (1992), which they categorised as 'leading from behind'. Conteh (2003: 145) summarises the main features, which include:

- Take what children say seriously and treat it as evidence of their best efforts to solve the problem in hand.
- Listen carefully to what children say and ask questions to help you correctly and fully understand the points they want to make.
- Modify your contribution to what you know of each individual child's ability as well as your pedagogical intentions.

We suggest that these features of dialogic classroom activities could be taken as principles by mainstream teachers to plan their own activities related to a wide range of topics and language learning goals. The approach clearly entails a shift in the relationship between teacher and learner, from one of the teacher being in charge to one of mutual empowerment. As Sandoval-Taylor warns (2005: 162), this 'letting go of the reins of teacher-directed instruction' can be difficult for mainstream teachers, working within the constraints of an assessment-driven system. It needs flexibility and open-endedness, which requires professional confidence and the space for teachers to make their own decisions. But, as García (2009: 313) argues, it is teachers who implement policies, and who have the power to 'create, contest, change and transform policies, as they enact their pedagogy'. Her 'two basic principles of bilingual pedagogy' – both 'social justice' and 'social practice' (García, 2009: 318 ff.) – offer principled ways forward, and strategies such as dialogic teaching offer rich possibilities for practice.

We suggest that a clear need that emerges from the evidence and arguments we present in this chapter is for a recognised pedagogy for multilingualism in mainstream schools in England. While this may be a long way off when, as Alexander (2004) emphatically points out, we really have no principled pedagogy at all for primary education, perhaps languages education is the area of the curriculum that can lead the way. As Safford and Drury (2013: 75) point out, we already have 'vantage points' from which to begin in the studies already done in languages learning in both early years and complementary learning contexts, and it is hoped that this chapter can offer another vantage point from which to begin.

Notes

(1) This quote is taken from an interview conducted as part of a set of case studies of 12 children from the class (funded by the Paul Hamlyn Foundation; see Conteh *et al.*, 2013).
(2) Taken from an interview conducted as part of a set of case studies (see Note 1).
(3) With thanks to Najma Mafuz for the translation.

References

Aitsiselmi, F. (2004) *Linguistic Diversity and the Use of English in the Home Environment: A Bradford Case Study*. Bradford: Department of Languages and European Studies, School of Social and International Studies, University of Bradford.

Alexander, R. (2004) Still no pedagogy? Principle, pragmatism and compliance in primary education. *Cambridge Journal of Education* 34 (1), 7–23.

BHRU (Bradford Heritage Recording Unit) (1994) *Here to Stay: Bradford's South Asian Communities*. Bradford: Arts, Museums and Libraries Service.

Biggs, A.P. and Edwards, V. (1994) I treat them all the same: Teacher-pupil talk in multi-ethnic classrooms. In D. Graddol, J. Maybin and B. Stierer (eds) *Researching Language and Literacy in Social Context* (pp. 82–99). Clevedon: Multilingual Matters.

Blackledge, A. and Creese, A. (2010) *Multilingualism: Critical Perspectives*. London: Continuum.

Bligh, C. (2011) Rights in early years settings and a young child's rights to silence In P. Jones and G. Walker (eds) *Children's Rights in Practice* (pp. 95–108). London: Sage.

Bolognani, M. (2007) The myth of return: Dismissal, survival or revival? A Bradford example of transnationalism as a political instrument. *Journal of Ethnic and Migration Studies* 33 (1), 59–76.

Bourne, J. (2001) Doing 'what comes naturally': How the discourses and routines of teachers' practice constrain opportunities for bilingual support in UK primary schools. *Language and Education* 15 (4), 250–268.

Bronfenbrenner, U. (1979) *The Ecology of Human Development*. Cambridge, MA: Harvard University Press.

Cable, C., Driscoll, P., Mitchell, R., Sing, S., Cremin, T., Earl, J. Eyres, I., Holmes, B., Martin, C. and Heins, B. (2012) Language learning at Key Stage 2: Findings from a longitudinal study. *Education 3–13 (Special Issue: What Can Primary Languages Offer the Curriculum?)* 40 (4), 363–378.

Cameron, D. and Bourne, J. (1988) No common ground: Kingman, grammar and nation. *Language and Education* 2 (3), 147–160.

Conteh, J. (2003) *Succeeding in Diversity: Culture, Language and Learning in Primary Classrooms*. Stoke-on-Trent: Trentham Books.

Conteh, J. (2007) Culture, languages and learning: Mediating a bilingual approach in complementary Saturday classes. In J. Conteh, P. Martin and L. Helavaara Robertson (eds) *Multilingual Learning Stories in Schools and Communities in Britain* (pp. 119–134). Stoke-on-Trent: Trentham Books.

Conteh, J. (2010) Making links across complementary and mainstream classrooms for primary children and their teachers. In V. Lytra and P. Martin (eds) *Sites of Multilingualism, Complementary schools in Britain Today* (pp. 149–160). Stoke-on-Trent: Trentham Books.

Conteh, J. (2012) Families, teachers and pupils learning together in a multilingual British city. *Journal of Multilingual and Multicultural Development* 33 (1), 101–116.

Conteh, J. and Begum, S. (2008) Bilingual teachers as agents of social change: Linking the community and the mainstream. In C. Kenner and T. Hickey (eds) *Multilingual Europe: Diversity and Learning* (pp. 104–110). Stoke-on-Trent: Trentham Books.

Conteh, J., Martin, P. and Helavaara, R.L. (eds) (2007) *Multilingual Learning Stories in Schools and Communities in Britain*. Stoke-on-Trent: Trentham Books.

Conteh, J., Beddow, D. and Kumar, R. (2008) Investigating pupil talk in multilingual contexts: Sociocultural learning, teaching and researching. *Education 3–13* 36 (3), 223–235.

Conteh, J., with Riasat, S. and Begum, S. (2013) Children learning multilingually in home, community and school contexts in Britain. In M. Schwartz and A. Verschik (eds) *Successful Family Language Policy: Parents, Children and Educators in Interaction*. Dordrecht: Springer.

Crozier, G. and Davies, J. (2007) Hard to reach parents or hard to reach schools? A discussion of home-school relations with particular reference to Bangladeshi and Pakistani parents. *British Educational Research Journal* 33 (3), 295–313.

Cummins, J. (2001) *Negotiating Identities: Education for Empowerment in a Diverse Society* (2nd edn). Ontario, CA: California Association for Bilingual Education.

Cummins, J. and Early, M. (eds) (2011) *Identity Texts: The Collaboration of Power in Multilingual Schools*. Stoke-on-Trent: Trentham Books.

DES (Department of Education and Science) (1985) *Education for All: The Report of the Committee of Inquiry into the Education of Children from Ethnic Minority Groups* (The Swann Report). London: HMSO.

DfE (2010) *The Importance of Teaching: Schools' White Paper*. London: Department for Education. See http://www.education.gov.uk/schools/toolsandinitiatives/schoolswhitepaper/b0068570/the-importance-of-teaching/school-improvement/incentivise-to-raise-standards.

DfE (2011a) *Statistical First Release: Schools, Pupils and their Characteristics*, January 2011. London: Department for Education (DfE). See http://www.education.gov.uk/rsgateway/DB/SFR/s001012/sfr12-2011.pdf.

DfE (2011b) *The School Curriculum: Including All Learners: Potential Barriers*. London: Department for Education. See http://www.education.gov.uk/schools/teachingand learning/curriculum/b00199686/inclusion/barriers.

DfE (2011c) *Focus on Talk*. London: Department for Education. See http://webarchive.nationalarchives.gov.uk/20110809091832/http://teachingandlearningresources.org.uk/node/22849.

DfE (2012a) *Making Foreign Languages Compulsory at Key Stage 2*. London: Department for Education. See https://www.education.gov.uk/aboutdfe/departmentalinformation/consultations.

DfE (2012b) *Teachers' Standards*. London: Department for Education. See https://www.education.gov.uk/publications/eOrderingDownload/teachers%20standards.pdf.

DfE (2013a) *Early Years Foundation Stage (EYFS)*. London: Department for Education. See http://www.education.gov.uk/schools/teachingandlearning/curriculum/a0068102/early-years-foundation-stage-eyfs.

DfE (2013b) *Primary National Curriculum until 2014*. London: Department for Education. See http://www.education.gov.uk/schools/teachingandlearning/curriculum/primary?page=1.

DfE (2013c) *Phonics Screening Check*. London: Department for Education. See http://www.education.gov.uk/schools/teachingandlearning/pedagogy/a00198207/faqs-year-1-phonics-screening-check.

DfE (2013d) *KS2 English Grammar, Punctuation and Spelling Samples: Levels 3–5 Materials*. London: Department for Education. See http://www.education.gov.uk/schools/teachingandlearning/assessment/keystage2/b00218030/gps-sample-materials/gps-3-5-sample-materials.

DfES (2005) *The Key Stage 2 Framework for Languages*. London: Department for Education and Skills. See https://www.education.gov.uk/publications/standard/publicationDetail/Page1/DFES%201721%202005.

DfES (Department for Education and Skills) (2006) *Excellence and Enjoyment: Learning and Teaching for Bilingual Children in the Primary Years (Primary National Strategy)*. See http://www.naldic.org.uk/Resources/NALDIC/Teaching%20and%20Learning/Introductory guide.pdf

Drury, R. (2007) *Young Bilingual Learners at Home and at School: Researching Multilingual Voices*. Stoke-on-Trent: Trentham Books.

García, O. (2009) *Bilingual Education in the 21st Century: A Global Perspective*. London: Wiley-Blackwell.

Gonzalez, N., Moll, L. and Amanti, C. (eds) (2005) *Funds of Knowledge: Theorising Practices in Households, Communities and Classrooms*. New York: Routledge.

Gregory, E. (2005) Playful talk: The interspace between home and school discourse. *Early Years* 25 (3), 223–235.

Gregory, E., Long, S. and Volk, D. (eds) (2004) *Many Pathways to Literacy: Young Children Learning with Siblings, Grandparents, Peers and Communities*. London: Routledge.

Heller, M. (ed.) (2007) *Bilingualism: A Social Approach*. Basingstoke: Palgrave Macmillan.

Hensley, M. (2005) Empowering parents of multicultural backgrounds. In N. Gonzalez, L. Moll and C. Amanti (eds) *Funds of Knowledge: Theorising Practices in Households, Communities and Classrooms* (pp. 143–152). New York: Routledge.

Jessel, J., Arju, T., Gregory, E., Kenner K. and Ruby, M. (2004) Children and their grandparents at home: A mutually supportive context for learning and linguistic development. *English Quarterly/Canadian Journal of English in Education* 36 (4), 16–23.

Kendall, S., Straw, S., Jones, M., Springate, I. and Grayson, H. (2008) *Narrowing the Gap in Outcomes for Vulnerable Groups: A Review of the Research Evidence*. Slough: National Federation for Education Research (NFER). See http://www.nfer.ac.uk/nfer/research/projects/narrowing-the-gap/narrowing-the-gap_home.cfm.

Kenner, C. and Ruby, M. (2012) *Interconnecting Worlds: Teacher Partnerships for Bilingual Learning*. Stoke-on-Trent: Trentham Books.

Kirsch, C. (2012) Developing children's language learner strategies at primary school. *Education 3–13 (Special Issue: What Can Primary Languages Offer the Curriculum?)* 40 (4), 379–399.

Leung, C., Harris, R. and Rampton, B. (1997) The idealised native speaker, reified ethnicities, and classroom realities. *TESOL Quarterly* 31 (3), 543–560.

Lytra, V. and Martin, P. (eds) (2010) *Sites of Multilingualism: Complementary Schools in Britain Today*. Stoke-on-Trent: Trentham Books.

Martin-Jones, M. and Saxena, M. (1995) Supporting or containing bilingualism? Policies, power assymetries and pedagogic practices in mainstream primary schools. In J. Tollefson (ed.) *Power and Inequality in Language Education* (pp. 73–90). Cambridge: Cambridge University Press.

Martin-Jones, M. and Saxena, M. (1996) Turn-taking, power asymmetries, and the positioning of bilingual participants in classroom discourse. *Linguistics and Education* 8, 105–123.

Martin-Jones, M. and Saxena, M. (2003) Bilingual resources and 'funds of knowledge' for teaching and learning in multi-ethnic classrooms in Britain. *International Journal of Bilingual Education and Bilingualism* 6 (3/4), 267–281.

Moll, L. (2005) Reflections and possibilities. In N. Gonzalez, L. Moll and C. Amanti (eds) (2005) *Funds of Knowledge: Theorising Practices in Households, Communities and Classrooms* (pp. 275–287). New York: Routledge.

NALDIC (2013) *EAL and the Initial Training of Teachers*. Watford: National Association for Language Development in the Curriculum. See http://www.naldic.org.uk/eal-initial-teacher-education/ite-programmes.

Pearce, S. (2012) Confronting dominant whiteness in the primary classroom: Progressive student teachers' dilemmas and constraints. *Oxford Review of Education* 38 (4), 455–472.

Safford, K. (2003) *Teachers and Pupils in the Big Picture: Seeing Real Children in Routinised Assessment*. Watford: National Association for Language Development in the Curriculum.

Safford, K. and Drury, R. (2013) The 'problem' of bilingual children in education settings: Policy and research in England. *Language and Education* 27 (1), 70–81.

Sandoval-Taylor, P. (2005) Home is where the heart is: A funds of knowledge-based curriculum module. In N. Gonzalez, L. Moll and C. Amanti (eds) (2005) *Funds of Knowledge: Theorising Practices in Households, Communities and Classrooms* (pp. 153–166). New York: Routledge.

Somekh, B. (2006) *Action Research: A Methodology for Change and Development.* Milton Keynes: Open University Press.

Vertovec, S. (2007) Super-diversity and its implications. *Ethnic and Racial Studies* 30 (6), 1024–1054.

Wardman, C., Bell, J. and Sharp, E. (2012) Valuing home languages. In D. Mallows (ed.) *Innovations in English Language Teaching for Migrants and Refugees* (pp. 37–48). London: British Council.

Wells, G. (2011) Integrating CHAT and Action Research. *Mind, Culture, and Activity* 18 (2), 161–180.

Wells, G. and Chang-Wells, G.L. (1992) *Constructing Knowledge Together: Classrooms as Centers of Inquiry and Literacy.* Portsmouth, NH: Heinemann.

Wolfe, S. and Alexander, R.J. (2008) *Argumentation and Dialogic Teaching: Alternative Pedagogies for a Changing World.* London: Futurelab. See http://www.beyond currenthorizons.org.uk/?s=wolfe+and+alexander&x=7&y=7.

10 Plurilingualism and Empathy: Beyond Instrumental Language Learning

Enrica Piccardo and Joëlle Aden

Guiding Questions

- Why do the links between languages and emotions deserve special attention in language education?
- What are the implications of empathy and plurilingualism for language acquisition and intercultural awareness?
- How do theatre techniques contribute to language proficiency?

> It is when the desires and aims, the interests and modes of response of another become an expansion of our own being that we understand him. We learn to see with his eyes, hear with his ears, and their results give true instruction, for they are built into our own structure.
>
> John Dewey (1934: 350)

> The human capacity to injure other people has always been much greater than its capacity to imagine other people. Or perhaps we should say, 'the human capacity to injure other people is very great precisely because our capacity to imagine other people is very small'.
>
> Elaine Scarry (2002: 102)

Introduction

Faced with more and more linguistically and culturally diverse classes, teachers and educators are in need of new ways of helping learners to become aware of their own linguistic, cultural and emotional potential so that they can enhance their language level and attain effective intercultural communication. Language proficiency is not something neutral that can easily be measured through standardized discrete items. It is a complex endeavour that involves individuals at a deep personal level and is strongly culturally and emotionally connoted. To cope with such complexity a shift in the way language is viewed is needed. Recent developments in neuroscience, particularly research on empathy, are to play a significant role in addressing this crucial matter as they offer new ways of understanding the connections between physicality, imagination, emotion, language and reason.

After presenting the reasons why the link between languages and emotions deserves special attention, we discuss the notions of plurilingualism and empathy and try to analyze their implications for language acquisition and intercultural awareness. Finally, we investigate the role of theatre and its potential contribution to effective language learning. In particular, we present two categories of mechanisms on which we rely to train empathy through theatre as a starting point for a more dynamic complex and plurilingual attitude towards languages: the emotional channel based on synchrony, mimicry and emotional contagion and the cognitive channel which uses perspective taking and self-other distinction. We exemplify this by presenting some techniques that incorporate both physical and emotional simulation, able to help students to put themselves in somebody else's shoes, thus supporting them in the process of acquiring an open-minded attitude, which is critical for effective language learning.

Between Standardization and Complexification: Actual Tendencies in Language Education

The social and linguistic landscape of the global village has been deeply modified by mobility and contact and by transcendence of time and space boundaries, resulting in a radically multilingual world society (Aronin & Singleton, 2010) and a shift towards 'liquid modernity' (Bauman, 2000), 'institutionalized pluralism, variety, contingency and ambivalence' (Bauman, 1992: 187). Diversity has become omnipresent, and proposes itself as the other face of unifying trends commonly associated with globalization. In this magmatic landscape, language education is undergoing the influence of two opposite forces: standardization and complexification.

The first one can be observed in the proliferation of standard-setting tools (Huver & Springer, 2011), and in the underlying philosophy which stresses the need for analytical reporting, comparability and transferability beyond specific geopolitical contexts; the second is characterized by a reconsideration of language learning as a dynamic complex phenomenon, following a non-linear systemic perspective (Larsen-Freeman, 1997, 2002; Piccardo, 2005, 2010; van Lier, 2004).

Since the early 2000s conceptual frameworks for second/foreign language education like the Common European Framework of Reference for Languages (CEFR) (CoE, 2001) have been introduced, which tend to be used exclusively as product-oriented standard-setting tools, even when they can potentially care for the multidimensionality of language acquisition. For instance, only some aspects of the CEFR, i.e. the description of the functional dimension of the language together with proficiency standard setting, seem to be given high priority in textbook instruction, curricula and official documents. We refer in particular to the Council of Ministers of Education of Canada (CMEC, 2010) *Working with the Common European Framework of References (CEFR) in the Canadian Context. Guide for Policy Makers and Curriculum Designers*. A similar tendency can be observed outside the school context where other assessment tools for linguistic competencies are used, such as the Canadian Language Benchmarks (CLB, 2012), or the American Council on the Teaching of Foreign Languages (ACTFL, 2013) *Proficiency Guidelines in the United States*.

Even though the two tendencies, standardization and complexification, were not meant to be incompatible, but rather playing two different – and possibly complementary – functions, the first is taking precedence as it appears more straightforward. As a consequence, we can observe that, while on the one hand, new theoretical frameworks like complexity and sociocultural theory are increasingly being used for investigating the process of second language acquisition (Lantolf, 2000; Larsen-Freeman, 2002; Swain *et al.*, 2011; van Lier, 2004, among others), on the other hand the idea that language proficiency can be described exclusively as a series of separate competences and organized in the form of lists of discrete items one can tick on a grid is more and more widespread, as shown by the multiplications of frameworks in all domains (above all in assessment but also competence specification, curriculum planning and quality assurance). This oversimplification is extended to all language features, including the cultural ones. Despite growing current discourse on intercultural communication in fact, the use of discrete items for measuring (and assessing) all components of language proficiency results in a superficial consideration of intercultural awareness as a simple polarized vision of 'us' versus 'the others'. Even worse, intercultural awareness is sometimes reduced to a more efficient communication in different cultural settings or contexts, at the service of a purely functional vision of language.

Although the CEFR (CoE, 2001) proposes that *savoir-être* (existential competence) and the 'mental context of the language user' be taken into account, these dimensions are still not given adequate consideration in curricula and in teaching practices (Aden, 2008, 2009a; Carrasco Perea & Piccardo, 2009). Unfortunately, only one dimension prevails, the vertical one of standard setting (Little, 2006; Piccardo, 2012b). The horizontal one, which encompasses a complex and potentially innovative vision of language education rooted in the notion of *savoir-être* is still neglected.

Cognition, Socialization and Emotions in Language Learning: An Emerging Paradigm

Learning a language is a much deeper process than learning a somehow 'neutral' linguistic phenomenon enriched by some anecdotal cultural knowledge. It is something that involves the whole person: 'Nobody acquires a language as he/she would do for any other subject: language guides and filters our relationships, deeply questions what we have achieved but also our affective, symbolic and imaginary references, as well as our values' (Coïaniz, 2001: 248, our translation). Language is an extremely powerful phenomenon. 'Each of the languages we speak adds its unique dimension to our signifying self' (Coïaniz, 2001: 248, our translation); it modifies what the CEFR refers to as *savoir-être*, which goes well beyond a series of attitudes related to identity, confidence and positioning vis-à-vis languages and cultures.

Language implies a tension between real and symbolic, between objective and subjective meaning, between historical and imagined dimension (Kramsch, 2009), and 'both the historical and the imagined one are real, as they get inscribed in the flesh-and-blood reality of the language user's embodied minds' (Kramsch, 2009: 44).

Broader and more systemic theories like the sociocultural theory based on Vygotsky's (1978) work help us overcome a fragmented and reductive vision of language learning and are able to encompass its complexity. In order to overcome the idea of language as a collection of isolated and disconnected elements, still so widespread, van Lier (2002), for instance, proposes what he calls an ecological semiotic vision of second language acquisition, a vision where language learning is seen as a semiotic, non-linear activity. He emphasises that rather than simply providing 'inputs' to learners, it is important to expose them to *affordances*, a term borrowed from Gibson which defines them as 'meaningful ways of relating to the environment through perception-in-action' (Gibson, 1977: 147). Affordances are opportunities, possibilities of action offered to individuals (Swain *et al.*, 2011: 149). Precisely, affordances enable individuals to acquire the language, as the meaning of words is not limited to what is written in the dictionary but encompasses all psychological facts that appear to the conscience, everything that is linked to the personal experiences of an individual. Thinking in terms of affordances allows us to take into consideration all aspects and dimensions of human communication and of language use, the cognitive and emotional one, the physical and the intellectual one. Emotions are in fact 'socially constructed dimensions of human experience' (Benesch, 2012: 36).

The individual who uses (and learns) languages is engaged in a two-way process, as he/she is acting on his/her environment, which is acting in return. The notion of actor–environment mutuality is encapsulated in the affordance perspective (Aronin & Singleton, 2010).

[T]he symbolic power that comes from being able to use several symbolic systems is not only a declarative power, that is the power to represent the world in different linguistic codes, but a performative power that can create different symbolic realities in different languages and, by changing others' perceptions of social reality, can change that reality. (Kramsch, 2009: 188)

Thinking in terms of affordances helps us get out of language nomination (Aronin & Singleton, 2010), of thinking in terms of mother tongue, first, second and foreign language, which automatically implies separation and hierarchy and where all the terms have a strong connotation, both cultural and emotional. The role of languages in human trajectories is more volatile and changeable, as studies on emotions and emotion-related words in the mental lexicon show (Pavlenko, 2005). Adopting a vision where the first language is the sole language of emotions 'is to oversimplify the relationship between languages, emotions and identities in bi- and multilingualism' (Pavlenko, 2005: 236).

Some new emerging concepts are particularly effective in casting light onto the complex process of language learning. We are referring in particular to *languaging, translanguaging* and *mediation. Languaging* (Becker, 1991; Swain, 2006) 'serves as vehicle through which thinking is articulated and transformed into an artifactual form' (Swain, 2006: 97) and refers to the process of 'making meaning and shaping knowledge and experience through words' (Swain, 2006: 98). Languaging is a two-way process: on one hand, that of putting concepts into words and on the other, that of shaping those same concepts through the very action of articulating them. Translanguaging (Baker, 2001; García, 2009) refers to the process of shaping experiences, gaining understanding and knowledge through the use of two languages (Baker, 2011: 288). In comparison to languaging, translanguaging focuses more on the bilingual and multilingual perspective as it refers to hybrid language use, a process of meaning making that is 'systematic, strategic and affiliative' (Gutierrez *et al.*, 2001). Translanguaging is what bilinguals naturally do when accessing meaning. It includes, but is not limited to, code-switching as it is an approach that does not consider languages as autonomous, fixed entities (García, 2009) but rather focuses on the dynamic and changing process of communication and language construction.

Finally, mediation is the pivotal concept of a new philosophy of language pedagogy, the key element around which we can 'reconceptualise language as an activity' (Thorne & Lantolf, 2007: 171), as 'a series of communicative resources that are formed and reformed in the very activity in which they are used' (Thorne & Lantolf, 2007: 177), as 'une dynamique émergente de sens partagé qui s'autoproduit et se transforme dans les interactions du sujet avec son environnement' ('*An emergent dynamic process of shared meaning, which creates and transforms itself through interactions of individuals with their environment'*, Aden, 2012: 275, our translation). Mediation is critical to mean-ing making and it is essential both at the individual and at the social level (Piccardo, 2012a). It is precisely what connects the social with the individual (Swain *et al.*, 2011). Language as a symbolic tool is directly influencing our psychological self. Besides, language is culturally constructed, as are all human-made mediational means (Swain *et al.*, 2011: 152).

According to Vygotsky, different forms of social and cultural mediation precede the formation of concepts (Lantolf, 2000) and the entire psychic activity is mediated, (Vygotsky, 1978). With tools we act on nature, through signs we act on ourselves and other individuals, and language is the privi-leged sign system for controlling others and ourselves (Schneuwly, 2008). Language can be considered as 'socialization into communities of practice through the mediation of material signs' (Kramsch, 2002: 6).

Vygotsky totally rejects the cognitive theory according to which concept formation happens at the level of individual first and only later is transferred to social context. On the contrary, individuals reconstruct in their minds mediated social interactions they have experienced, and this mediation hap-pens through the senses and by means of all sorts of signs: acoustic, linguis-tic and visual ones. Language is produced through social experiences and later undergoes a process of reflection. Individuals can thus reconstruct and interiorize psychological processes like thinking and learning. According to such a vision, 'language can be studied in its social context, but language itself is seen as a system of arbitrary signs or symbols that are given social existence through their reference to a context which is itself outside of lan-guage' (Kramsch, 2002: 133). This goes clearly against the common vision where learning is seen as an individual cognitive process first, which is later tested and used within the social context, a process which implies strict separation between the language and the language user.

Through mediation it is possible to overcome such a dichotomy. Because mediation is primarily a process that bridges the gaps, it overcomes the sepa-ration between individuals on one side and culture and society on the other (Engeström, 1999).

Such a complex vision of language learning stresses how languages and language users are not separate entities and how languages do not exist per se but only in connection to individuals and the way these individuals use, shape and transform the language(s). An increasingly diverse global village witnesses all forms of contact of languages and cultures, of hybridity of lan-guage use, and complex combinations of languages and cultures within each individual. The emerging notion of plurilingualism is particularly important, where languages are not seen as separate fixed entities that are piling up, but rather as elements coming into a dynamic and ever-changing combination characterized by reciprocal influence and synergies.

In a plurilingual individual, the experience of affordances, where the cul-tural dimension plays a fundamental role, becomes critical, as well as the need to cope with complex and diverse emotional experiences. Through different affordances individual's *savoir-être* is structured, both cognitively and emotionally.

Plurilingualism and Complexification: The Need for Further Investigation

The study of emotions and their characteristics opens new perspectives and provides a new lens for approaching language learning. It helps us understand the depth of personal and cultural implication involved in language use and in the process of language learning. Adopting a plurilingual vision also implies the need for a dynamic attitude, for dealing with the unpredictable and for increased awareness of the potential contribution of different codes. Let us consider the notion of plurilingualism in more detail in order to cast light on the links between plurilingualism and emotions.

Even though in the English-speaking world the term multilingualism is still preferred to plurilingualism and is used as an umbrella term under which several concepts are investigated, which focus on the contact of languages and hybridity, we share with colleagues the belief that it is important to distinguish the two terms (Canagarajah & Liyanage, 2012; Piccardo, 2013) as suggested by the CEFR (CoE, 2001). We certainly acknowledge that scholars working in the English-speaking world and researching language plurality use the term multilingualism as an overarching term for investigating such notions as translanguaging, and in general all phenomena of language contacts and mixing; nevertheless, we prefer using the notion of plurilingualism, as distinct from multilingualism, as a lens to investigate the present linguistic landscape and its implications on language education. According to the CEFR, while multilingualism keeps languages distinct both at the societal level and at the level of the individual, stressing the separate, advanced mastery of each language a person speaks, plurilingualism stresses the dynamic process of language acquisition and use, in contrast with equal mastery of each language and co-existence of isolated languages. The notion of plurilingualism, stressing non-compartmentalization of languages and linguistic and cultural competences, and underlying linguistic proficiency and cultural awareness as a dynamic process, provides a more effective theoretical framework and enables a new attitude towards the language acquisition process.

Whereas only some decades ago separation and purity of languages represented an unquestioned value, in recent years plurality of languages has started to be seen as a source of positive features for learners, such as higher cognitive flexibility, the ability to operate linguistic and cultural and conceptual transfer, and enhanced capacity of abstract, divergent and creative thinking (Boekmann *et al.*, 2011). The new and potentially revolutionary vision of plurilingualism appears in line with changes that are being observed in different domains. Firstly, in the psycho-cognitive theoretical domain, neuroscientific research increasingly supports a new connectionist paradigm in describing the functioning of the brain (Bickes, 2004: 38); in particular, the brains of individuals speaking more than one language is considered as a complex and unique system rather than the sum of monolingual brains (Bialystok, 2001; Perani *et al.*, 2003). Secondly, sociocultural theory supports consideration of individuals as social actors and stresses how language acquisition is intrinsically linked to interaction and mediation between different individuals. Each individual in turn represents a unique linguistic and cultural system within a larger linguistically, culturally and sociologically defined configuration (Lantolf, 2011). Finally, language pedagogy has also adopted a broader and more complex vision supported by the post-method movement (Bell, 2003; Kumaravadivelu, 2001), where methodologies are no longer seen as something neutral and external to be implemented in language classes, but rather as a dynamic, mediated and idiosyncratic process. Educational practices 'must be extended to reflect the complex multilingual and multimodal communicative networks of the twenty-first century' (García, 2009: 5).

What is proposed here is a 'paradigm shift' – a refusal of compartmentalization, of considering learning languages as separated from each other and separated from culture(s) – a rather strong statement, but in line with a complex and systemic view of reality, where plurality concerns languages but also identity negotiation, crossing borders and the shared illusion of effective communication (Kramsch *et al.*, 2008: 15).

Plurilingual competence is seen as a non-fixed entity, something capable of changing with time, of evolving both vertically in the scale of competences – going up and down, i.e. progressing or regressing – but also horizontally by constructing the language with a back and forth movement between languages and within the same language. Profiles of both linguistic and cultural biographies are transitory and dependent on a wealth of different factors such as personal or professional trajectories, tastes and choices of individuals. As imbalance is characterized by change and movement, it is possible to draw upon both linguistic and general competences to convey a message; it is allowed to combine and alternate languages in different ways, to overcome the straitjacket of an exclusive use of one single (target) language, to use a wealth of codes, to code-switch, -mix and -mesh, all being possible expressions of a plurilingual/pluricultural identity. It is the entire language acquisition process by the individual that is at stake.

Plurilingualism is uneven and partial and is idiosyncratically based on the learners' experiences with all language affordances both at the social and at the individual level. Finally, the notion of imbalance is linked to the idea that competences are not stored in neatly separated drawers. As we mentioned before, the cognitive system of individuals is nowadays considered in terms of connectionism and of a complex ecosystem (dynamic systems)

(Bickes, 2004; Murray Thomas, 2001), where the modification of each variable implies modifications in other variables and, in the end, has an impact on the whole system. In cognitive psychology, interactionist theories, in contrast to modular theories, underline how 'information processing involves pooling multiple, interacting sources of information, and that "partial products" of processing at one level can influence processing at other levels' (Whitaker, 2010).

Considering sociopolitical developments and advances in linguistic, psychological and neuroscientific research, it is logical to view plurilingualism as an asset for an individual, certainly not as a handicap. Nevertheless, despite the advances in research and theorization, in everyday practice the impact of the implicit shift heralded in by plurilingualism is still marginal and a monolingual ideology is widely applied. Unfortunately, separation of languages is still perceived as a value and is still common in school practice (Cummins, 2007). 'Multilinguals throughout the world translanguage in order to make sense of their world. It is only when they get to school that their language complexity becomes stigmatized' (García, 2009: 384). Every code-mixing is perceived as a transgression to the norm or, in the best of cases, as an inevitable choice due to a lack of other, more effective, means – and this in spite of what research shows (Ferguson, 2009). The actual organization of curricula usually separates languages, not only different languages but also, particularly, additional languages and the mother tongue(s), as these are believed not to have any common feature. In primary language acquisition two interrelated processes take place: one of *conceptual development*, where words and phrases acquire denotative meaning', (Pavlenko, 2005: 154) [and one of] *affective linguistic conditioning*, where words and phrases acquire affective connotations and personal meanings through association and integration with emotionally charged memories and experiences' (Pavlenko, 2005: 155) and '[b]oth processes contribute to the perception of *language embodiment*, whereby words invoke both sensory images and physiological reactions' (Pavlenko, 2005: 155). In the case of additional languages, they are hardly ever taught in a way that enables the activation of both processes, at least in mainstream education. The emotional and affective dimension of language is not given any space or importance (Piccardo, 2007, 2010); it is neither developed nor evaluated in the second language educational context (Kramsch, 2009; Piccardo, 2005, 2007). What is worse, the dimension of desire is totally removed from the class where often the only feeling accompanying language production is anxiety (Pavlenko, 2005: 155; Scott Brewer, 2010).

Nowadays, though, teachers are more and more faced with learners 'with embodied memories of various languages acquired in various circumstances and with varying degrees of proficiency' (Kramsch, 2009: 190). Teaching such multilingual learners implies a shift and calls 'for an ecologically oriented pedagogy that approaches language learning and language use not just

as an instrumental activity for getting things done but as a subjective experience' (Kramsch, 2009: 190) as language is a living thing, a blood-and-flesh
experience, a form of emotionally and bodily mediated knowledge.

Body and Emotions in Language Education

The physical and the emotional dimensions of language, even when mentioned, are not given any specific attention in existing curricula.

Indeed, the emotional dimension of the language requires new consideration in the present sociopolitical context, characterized by increasing linguistic and cultural diversity (Pavlenko, 2002, 2005, 2012). An exclusively
linguistic-driven vision of the language as a tool useful for engaging in functional exchanges in fact is detrimental to a balanced development of a multicultural society where individuals should be encouraged to develop a
flexible and open attitude towards diversity of languages and cultures in the
community, to recognize and value their own plurilingual competence and
plural identity (Cummins, 2001; Moore & Gajo, 2009; Pavlenko, 2011;
Piccardo, 2012b) and finally to engage in developing intercultural competences and attitudes, essential features for pacific co-existence in multicultural societies (Byram & Fleming, 1998).

Reality is an individual and social construct that both divides and links
people, and the filters that hinder social understanding in another language
are, first and foremost, cultural (Grèzes, 2010; Grèzes & de Gelder, 2009) and
emotional (Mayer et al., 2004). In the case of another linguistic system, learning implies that individuals are capable of grasping what is real in a different
way, and therefore can change their system of reference. Learning is an interactive process in which learners perceive situations and build up meaning
through: (i) the filter of their own cultural references, experience and knowledge; (ii) emotions they perceive, which act as cognitive strategies, as they
influence the way we learn, make decisions and act (Damasio, 1994, 1999;
Frijda, 1986; LeDoux, 2003; Wells-Jopling & Oatley, 2012); and (iii) empathy,
which is the capacity to put oneself in someone else's shoes while distancing
oneself through fictional make-believe (Aden, 2010b). Mayer and Salovey's
(1995) broad framework of emotional intelligence highlights a wide range of
emotional skills that profoundly affect thinking and action, namely the ability to perceive emotion, to communicate feelings, to understand and to
appreciate emotional meanings. This emotional scale offers useful scaffolding for developing an empathetic attitude. To understand the cultural aspects
of a situation in a second language, one relies on complementary strategies
which involve predicting, remembering and imagining, and which all interrelate with emotion.

As early as 1987, in their Tree of Knowledge, Maturana and Varela had
already established a crucial link between bodily experience and abstract

knowledge by arguing that cognition is embodied. Recent neuroscientific research has enriched our understanding of mental processes, which will lead to new insights into the relationships between language, bodily action and emotional experience (Lowerse, 2008; Nadel & Decety, 2002; Rizzolatti & Arbib, 1998). The discovery of mirror neurons which revealed that, when we watch or imagine someone perform an action, the same neurons are fired in our brains as if we ourselves were doing the action (di Pellegrino *et al.*, 1992) has brought with it a realization that we are equipped with a neuronal system, the mirror neuron system (MNS), whose primary function is to enable us to understand and be understood through emotional and motor resonance. Motor resonance underlies both kinaesthetic and emotional empathy through automatic imitation and simulation of the expressions of emotions. Motor resonance and emotional resonance seem to be connected, even if, strictly speaking, the former only refers to movements.

The discovery of mirror neurons has triggered experimental research, which has found neural evidence for the interplay between language, gesture and action (Willems & Hagoort, 2007). The study of motor resonance in comprehension shows that verbal comprehension involves traces of perceptual and physical experience (Zwaan & Taylor, 2006). These theories are also in keeping with the 'embodied' approach to language taken by cognitive linguists such as Lakoff, Johnson, Kovecses and Deane (Shanahan, 2007). Kovecses (2000), in particular, demonstrates to what extent metaphors for emotions rely on the body. In turn, the model for generation of consciousness offered by Damasio (1999) supports the embodied nature of symbols, which posits that we conceptualize through the filter of our senses. Cognitive linguists, who argue that conceptual knowledge is mapped within the sensory motor system (Gallese & Lakoff, 2005), hypothesize that understanding requires sensory motor simulation. All those points of view offer a new perspective on the role of imitation, simulation, empathy and intention in communication and provide sufficient argument for exploring new methods in second language education.

Empathy, the capacity to take on another person's viewpoint, yet remaining conscious of your own self-referenced point of view (Thirioux & Berthoz, 2010), is partly based on low-level mechanisms – mimicry and physical resonance – which facilitate embodied cognition, thus allowing one to perceive meaning and intention through physical simulation and emotional contagion (Berthoz, 2004; Hatfield *et al.*, 1994; Lamm *et al.*, 2009). These mechanisms progressively make way for high-level processes like perspective taking and reading other people's intentions. We posit that both low- and high-level mechanisms can be used in second language education in order to facilitate learners' comprehension of others and of pragmatic situations.

The language of theatre is a very efficient means to develop empathy as it is based on those very mechanisms. Actors rely on empathy to engage with the audience when they deliver a believable performance. It has been shown that using drama techniques in language classrooms enhances students' capacity to reconcile verbal and bodily and emotional languages (Aden, 2010b) as acting requires remembering cues and lines together with emotions, body postures and expressions. Most importantly, when student-actors seek ways of engaging with other actors or the audience they need to learn how to become aware of their emotional states and to recognize and share the emotional states of others in make-believe situations (Aden, 2008). They learn how to switch between realities, thus practising multiple changes of perspective (Aden, 2010a). We will see now how these mechanisms operate.

Resonance and Emotional Contagion: Low-level Mechanisms

Instinctively, when an infant interacts with someone, s/he observes, copies and gesticulates. This is a basic means of communicating referred to as 'resonance behaviour', in which one reproduces, overtly or internally, movements or actions made by another individual. Miming and imitating enable one to unconsciously 'feel inside' the other person, thus reaching an experiential level of understanding of the other. Rizzolatti and Arbib (1998) distinguish another type of resonance behaviour in which the observation of an action triggers a neural pattern, which determines the making of the observed action. According to them, this second type of resonance behaviour is at the basis of the understanding of actions made by others. We are therefore capable of understanding, without the use of words, the actions, and even the intentions and feelings of others through the MNS. This is the first system of communication, which steadily and rapidly gives way to verbal communication. Communicating with words and structures involves classifying the world by symbolic systems, giving access to abstraction. But the development of verbal language does not abolish or replace low-level mechanisms.

In 1959, in his book *The Silent Language*, the American anthropologist E.T. Hall had already understood that 'people also speak without words' and that 'the relationship between language and gesture is much closer than between language and other cultural systems' (Hall, 1959: 12). Later, Jacques Lecoq (1997), in his international theatre school, used the same insight, so we hypothesize that this 'parallel' system of resonance could enhance the understanding of actions and intentions and in turn facilitate the access to verbal language without the need for a systematic interpretation process or extended translation.

One of the techniques that can be used in building the understanding of a narrative or a situation in a foreign language is to use the very powerful mechanism of imitation and mimicry, which is based on the combination of action/perception. Children primarily communicate in this way until the age of four when the verbal language usually takes over. For Nadel and Decety (2002), whose considerations help us to understand why imitation plays such a central role in language learning, mimesis helps children distinguish their actions from those of others. Miming is thus the basis for empathy. There are of course different degrees of imitation; however, Nadel suggests they be considered as a continuum going from the unconscious reproduction of gestures, facial expressions and attitudes (particularly in the phenomena of motor, followed by emotional, contagion in the newborn) to the reproduction of new and more complex conscious actions (such as playing a character). When students are engaged to work silently in drama workshops in second or foreign languages, they very quickly realize that 'they are able to interact and understand through kinaesthetic and emotional resonance without resorting to a systematic verbal interpretation or extended translation. They can be presented with verbal elements later, when pragmatic embodied meaning has been constructed' (Aden, 2010a).

We know that the emotional impact of mime is equal in both its perception and its realization: taking up a position, seeing someone take up this position or imagine taking it ourselves, all trigger a realization of the intention embedded in the action and of its consequences. So, reproducing the action is – in some way – understanding it. The notion of interaction is also irrevocably linked to the concept of bridging a gap: between one and the other, between the familiar and the foreign, between the subjective and the objective, between the internal world (being formed) and the external world (established), or even between the body and language. Managing distance is crucial in intercultural communication and can also easily be trained through drama exercises. In some cases, the 'space between' oneself and the other may seem so wide as to appear as an unbridgeable gap or, on the contrary, it may seem to disappear through phenomena of emotional fusion (a football game, a rock concert or a religious ceremony).

> Theatre allows for an exploration of the space between people by offering different variations on these distances, through multiple sensory experiences. This is a crucial step in a process where it is impossible to verbally address the subject of cultural differences, and where the common denominator is the spatial experience of the body. (Aden, 2010a: 106)

Empathy and Changing Viewpoints: High-level Mechanisms

In multicultural and multilingual classrooms, learning a new language requires a capacity to adapt to a variety of social behaviours, which allows us to adequately navigate between multiple identities without those identities becoming contradictory. One cannot simply 'be plural' and find a way between cultures and languages without any support or scaffolding. Translanguaging and moving back and forth between cultures is a process acquired through the acceptance of others, the capacity to see oneself as another, and it requires the ability to change points of view about situations, the others and oneself. Changing a point of view leads to empathy, as we must put ourselves in someone else's place. Whether we arrive in a foreign country or meet a foreigner in our own country, there are numerous ways misunderstandings can happen. Some are explicit: for example, when I offer my hand as a greeting sign and the other does not respond. Some are implicit: for example, when I feel I behaved quite normally but the other perceives me to be careless or insincere. To develop an attitude of empathy during a break-down in communication, one must put oneself in the place of the other, essentially taking control of one's emotions. The case where I offer my hand and the other does not respond generates an emotional sequence (Frijda, 1986; Stein & Trabasso, 1992). This lack of response triggers an assessment of the situation (what's going on?), I am overwhelmed by an emotion (embarrassment, anger, shame) that will lead to a series of responses, at first physiological (I blush, my throat tightens in anger), behavioural (I withdraw or advance my hand) and finally verbal (either to myself: he doesn't want to say hello, who does he think he is? or directly to the person or to those around me). Empathizing assumes the ability to analyze a situation by accepting another's point of view, at the moment when this point of view is experienced or considered, which in turn may change one's reaction to the situation. Instead of feeling aggrieved or attacked, for example, I can put myself in the other person's place and understand what he/she feels. Berthoz (2004: 266) called this displacement 'a change in point of feeling' through which one is capable of posing questions which are not geared towards oneself but towards others. His theory is that 'in order to feel empathy, or to leave the mental path traced by egocentric conditioning and the isolating nature of a world shaped by fanaticism, the child must undergo a de-centring operation similar to that which is required to pass from an egocentric geometry to an allocentric geometry' (Berthoz, 2004, translated in Aden, 2010a: 261). Based on Berthoz's theories of 'change in point of feeling', it accordingly seems relevant to focus on empathy as a skill in itself, one that underpins inter- and intracultural communication (Aden, 2010a). 'Empathy involves controlling emotions and the body in space, in view of liberating the individual from the emotional contagion that may distort both his judgments and actions' (Thirioux & Berthoz, 2010).

An experiment (Aden, 2010a) has shown that actors can run plurilingual workshops relying almost exclusively on low-level mechanisms and non-verbal communication. In the study we are referring to, 54 young people aged between 12 and 18, speaking 27 different languages, who had immigrated with their families to six European countries involved in the project (Germany, UK, France, Greece, Italy and the Netherlands) all met in France for an intercultural encounter through theatre. They were split into four plurilingual groups run throughout a whole week by two artists who did not share the same languages and had different artistic backgrounds. The study of the interactions in each group shows that artists training young people with whom they share no common language, instinctively 'organize their workshops on a continuum that goes from motor resonance to cognitive empathy, passing by the differentiation between oneself and another'. Their selection of activities is 'standard' in terms of drama techniques; however, it is in their improvised organization and in the mediation that we can find the beginning of a unique intercultural approach. In this approach, emotional and cognitive empathy are interwoven and can be observed on a continuum spanning from lower to higher levels: 'observing/miming, managing distance, perceiving intentions, acting/reacting towards others, empathizing, imagining and, eventually, communicating' and translanguaging (Aden, 2012: 100).

Acting and Re-acting in the Foreign Language: Using Theatrical Situations for Developing Language Strategies

Theatrical situations can also enhance language learning strategies by anchoring the new language(s) on emotional and non-verbal strategies. In this case, the theatrical situation can be seen as a 'rich space' (*espace de potentialisation*) (Aden, 2008), which offers affordances for the new language to be understood. A protocol that aimed at understanding the impact of acting on the acquisition of linguistic and emotional competences (Aden, 2009b) has shown that, in this 'rich space', students can associate elements of the new language to what is already known in other languages.

The research was conducted over six months (December–May 2007) with a group of high school students in a southwestern suburb of Paris. The English teacher who organized a theatre project every year had selected a contemporary play, *Two*, by Jim Cartwright. The play, which was created in London in 1990, stages a series of scenes that picture all kinds of different couples meeting in an English pub. The play was studied both in class with the language teacher and with a professional Australian actress in an 18-hour workshop outside school hours. Qualitative data were collected through class observation, video recording of four lessons, eight drama workshops and of the final performance, video-recorded student interviews, and audio-recording of the teacher and the facilitator while they were commenting on the different aspects of the students' progress and strategies. We will focus in particular on the actress interview as she offered a particularly relevant account of how the students used the affordances of the performance to improvise new suitable language strategies in the foreign language.

The analysis of the process the students underwent to build their characters highlights the cognitive dimension of emotional processes: to play a character in another language jointly develops emotional, linguistic and physical competences. In acting, the language used in a very precise context emerges from a network of possibilities that the students explore, starting from their knowledge base, their strategies and their personal beliefs.

It was observed that students had progressed in two domains: linguistic and strategic. The first one, which was reported by the teacher, represents the most predictable one and was visible through clues on the micro-performances of the students (such as, for instance, better placement of stresses in sentences they had learned by heart or respect for the intonations) but, most importantly, the actress who had guided the students in the workshops and the rehearsal of the performance reported less predictable elements which were systematically analyzed. They confirm the impact theatre work can have in triggering emotional reactions and gestures from language learners and in enhancing their ability to rely on emotions and gestures for conveying messages, for interacting efficiently with the audience despite possible linguistic issues and for acquiring the capacity to deal effectively with unforeseen situations. In particular, the actress was struck by improvisations that some students had made during the final performance. According to her, they had unconsciously implemented the strategies that professional actors use: they had improvised elements of the play, restored ruptures in dialogues that no one had noticed, and used body memory as well as verbal memory. As these observable features belong precisely to the strategies for interaction that we chose to analyze, a detailed study of the students' improvisation in the final performance was carried out which highlighted the fact that the students used gestures, words or strategies that had never been discussed, suggested or negotiated in the rehearsal workshops. Twelve significant students' improvisations were analyzed from the point of view of the study of empathy and emotional relevance.

The analysis of the students' interviews shows that their choices and strategies are closely linked to their different layers of identities and episodic memories (Aden, 2008). One of the students who played an old man who lives in an imaginary world in which he can meet and talk with his deceased wife was expected, in a monologue, to suggest the presence of his wife by spreading his arms wide open, like a reunion. This is how the actress comments on this referential gesture:

Actress: When He says 'oh!' *(20:04) (She refers to his attitude and the way he folds his arms)*. It works…It used to be: 'oh!' *(She throws her arms open towards the sky)* but on stage, he really gets that feeling of that … When I saw him do that, I remember thinking 'wow!'

Interviewer: What you say is that suddenly, something emerges, the gesture or attitude which is the right feeling... The feeling that matches the text.

Actress: Yes, absolutely! (Aden, 2009b: 87)

The gestural dialectics that emerged in the performance indicated a heuristic access to the 'deeper' meaning of the character. We made the assumption that it is perhaps necessary to repress stereotypical gestures at first, in order to find the correct gesture. Finding the right gesture is the praxis of the actor, a path towards the listening of the other in oneself, and therefore a path towards empathy.

It should be noted that the student who played the old man hardly respected tonic accents and deformed the pronunciation of various phonemes, which made his verbal discourse virtually impossible to understand. However, the actress gave a very positive appreciation of his play as, according to her, the character released 'a true dramatic intensity', and triggered a sort of emotional contagion, which proved very moving. Everything happened in this scene as if the semiotics of the gesture and the attitude of the student had priority over the text for the comprehension of this scene. The right gesture seemed to emerge from the meaning of the dramatic situation; the approval of the audience acted as a pillar, a support that reinforced the gesture.

In another occurrence, a student playing the wife of the pub owner forgot, in her soliloquy, large parts of her cue. As she realized that she had partly forgotten her text, she did not stop but rearranged the sentences she remembered with new connecting words so that the audience did not realize what she had missed. The syntax of the sentences was correct and she respected exactly the style of her character.

This improvisation showed the student's ability to avoid the interruption of her thought by manipulating the cues of her character, rather than only reciting it, using gestures and attitudes as 'operational elements that establish a link between thoughts and speech' (Colletta, 2004: 186).

Another student who played the submissive Mr Iger forgot half of a long cue. He chose to make a gloss on his text while reconstructing the logical order of the sequence. He understood the intentions of his character so well that he was able to invent cues that matched his character's personality. The drama coach remarked:

He forgets 'short ones and long ones', instead he says, 'Come on! Come on!' He uses the right expressions and everything. (Aden, 2009b: 92)

This student managed to use an episode of forgetfulness or lack of concentration to improve his play. This may have been made possible through all the work on introspection made in the rehearsals; his mistake thus became a real theatrical find, a find that he would use with great success in the second performance.

Here is what another student said about his role approximately one month before the final performance, when asked about his personal work:

> At first, I was always in the same kind of register. I ah ... couldn't ... ah ... reproduce this ... ah ... kind of natural attitude of ... ah ... violence. But then I really tried to ah ... to interpret him my way ... I haven't finished working on that yet, and I haven't learned everything by heart either, but now try to ... change the rhythm in the scene and to ... well it's really not regular ... I think I'm trying to create surprise ... but I'm not sure ... in the audience with an attitude that can seem nice at the beginning, and then all this violence that he has inside him ... stress ... stress comes out all of a sudden, a bit like the calm before the storm ... well, like in a book I read called the silence of the sea ... so, basically what I'm trying to do is ... I'm trying to modulate the different aspects of this character. (Aden, 2009b: 95)

As the students' interviews reveal, improvisations on stage did not emerge out of nothing, but seemed to be the consequence of, and to have matured through, the long process students had undergone before the performance, a maturation that prepared 'a network of virtual actions' (Masciotra *et al.*, 2008: 49). According to these authors, who model the enactive approach of Francisco Varela in the field of pedagogy, any person working towards a definite goal does not take part in only one action, but rather in a series of actions, each action standing out from a network of possibilities. Thus, the 'improvisations' that we found are 'linguistic emergences', enactions that came out of a network of interiorized situations.

The moments of improvisation that we described are particularly useful to language teaching in the sense that the repairing of interactions is in itself a fundamental skill used to manage comprehension between people, since it allows the maintaining of comprehension between the different interactants.

In everyday life, communication and speech create norms of expectations for the co-speakers, and depend on the understanding of the previous utterance. Sequentiality is established through prospective and retrospective links throughout the conversation (Mondada & Pekarek-Doehler, 2000: 12). The processes used to control the interaction thus form a part of the interactional skill – to attract attention, start, continue, or interrupt a conversation, etc. which, according to Coulter (1974: 117) can only be learned in the action: this is what is called 'known-only-in-doing'.

Speaking of the emotional involvement, the student does not personally take part in the interaction, because he/she plays the role of someone else. He/she is de facto free from the burden of self-image or moral involvement that causes some speakers to create an image of themselves that will preserve their social role.

In addition, it should be noted that verbal and non-verbal behaviours create additional relations in interactions. Words, voice and body are inseparable in language and gestures, and gestures and attitudes are also indicators of semantic operations. This opens an array of pedagogic perspectives that will help to create better methods of teaching in order to develop interactional skills.

Acting thus offers optimal situational conditions for students, encouraging them to use their capacity for adaptation in a real communication situation that they are building themselves. These first observations still need to be confirmed, but they already show that the development of these strategies can only be achieved through situations in which intentionality is a feature of the action. It is not about delivering a text without making mistakes. It is about recreating the situation physically by displacing one's point of view to fully embody the character's, which is made possible by the work on empathy.

Conclusions and Opening a New Vision

The dominating notion of languages as statically codified entities, as clearly defined spaces following conventions monolingual speakers had agreed upon (Piccardo, 2013), proves more and more unrealistic and invented (Makoni & Pennycook, 2007). Language education has been, and still is, largely dominated by a functional vision where language uses are mainly referential and instrumental, and where intercultural awareness is reduced at its worst to knowledge of 'the other', and at its best to acceptance of or interest in 'the other'. Global sociological changes and the emergence of super-diversity on a societal level and increased plurilingualism at the level of the individual are showing how such a vision is reductive, precisely because it assumes a monolingual perspective which does not care for the plurality of languages and cultures that shapes individuals' identities. The idea of separation of languages and cultures also underestimates the emotional and symbolic dimension of languages, and does not incorporate it in the teaching of additional languages. Language education has neglected for too long the symbolic power of words and the embodied dimension of meaning.

We put forward the idea that adopting a more holistic and flexible attitude towards language learning, where instrumental use of languages is complemented by the cognitive and emotional components, will help learners become more aware of the dynamic nature of the learning process and therefore enhance their sense of agency in the construction of their own language proficiency. In turn, awareness of the multidimensionality of communication and of the role played by emotions in the process of learning and using languages can reinforce students' agency and awareness of the plurality of their linguistic and cultural experiences, and eventually lead to a more effective language learning process and development of intercultural skills.

Considering that empathy in language learning implies taking into account the biological basis of communication, theatre workshops offer opportunities to use the physiological resources that we all have, namely motor and emotional resonance.

Because theatre explores the physical and symbolic distance between people, it is a powerful tool to train perspective taking, mediating and empathy in intercultural situations and to restore the emotional, physical and affective dimension in language education. Neurosciences open a wide field of exploration, and it is high time to investigate further by adopting a multidisciplinary perspective (Shanahan, 1997).

Training students to develop an empathetic attitude may result in a deeper interpersonal understanding and an enhanced capacity to acquire cultural and metacultural awareness. Dealing with cultural diversity can stop being seen as an issue, and rather become part of a natural, ordinary, nonthreatening way of doing and of being. 'Local citizens who possess metacultural awareness can selectively filter, and creatively – as Dewey might say, artistically – "translate" global forces in ways that develop their culture while protecting the elements that are essential to its overall integrity' (Rolbin & Della Chiesa, 2010: 204).

References

ACTFL (2013) *Proficiency Guidelines in the United States.* Alexandria, VA: American Council on the Teaching of Foreign Languages. See http://www-01.sil.org/lingualinks/languagelearning/OtherResources/ACTFLProficiencyGuidelines/contents.htm.

Aden, J. (2008) Compétences interculturelles en didactique des langues. Développer l'empathie par la théâtralisation. In J. Aden (ed.) *Apprentissage des langues et pratiques artistiques* (pp. 67–101). Paris: Éditions Le Manuscrit.

Aden, J. (2009a) La créativité artistique à l'école: Refonder l'acte d'apprendre. In J. Aden and E. Piccardo (eds) *La créativité dans tous ses états: enjeux et potentialités en éducation. Synergies Europe* 4 (pp. 173–180). Sylvains-les-Moulins: Gerflint.

Aden, J. (2009b) Improvisation dans le jeu théâtral et acquisition de stratégies d'interaction. In J. Aden (ed.) *Didactique des langues-cultures: Univers de croyance et contextes* (pp. 77–99). Paris: Éditions Le Manuscrit.

Aden, J. (2010a) *Rencontre interculturelle autour de pratiques théâtrales.* Compte rendu de recherche, traduit en allemand et en anglais (p. 106). Berlin: Schibri-Verlag.

Aden, J. (2010b) L'empathie, socle de la reliance en didactique des langues-cultures. In J. Aden, T. Grimshaw and H. Penz (eds) *Enseigner les langues-cultures à l'ère de la complexité: Approches interdisciplinaires pour un monde en reliance* (pp. 23–44). Brussels: Peter Lang.

Aden, J. (2012) La médiation linguistique au fondement du sens partagé: vers un paradigme de l'enaction en didactique des langues. In J. Aden and D. Weissmann (eds) *La médiation linguistique: Entre traduction et enseignement des langues vivantes.* Études de linguistique appliquée (ELA) No. 167 (pp. 267–284). Paris: Cairn.Info.

Aronin, L. and Singleton, D. (2010) Affordances and the diversity of multilingualism. *International Journal of the Sociology of Language* 205, 105–129.

Baker, C. (2001) *Foundations of Bilingual Education and Bilingualism* (3rd edn). Clevedon: Multilingual Matters.

Baker, C. (2011) *Foundations of Bilingual Education and Bilingualism* (5th edn). Bristol: Multilingual Matters.

Bauman, Z. (1992) *Intimations of Postmodernity*. New York and London: Routledge.

Bauman, Z. (2000) *Liquid Modernity*. Cambridge: Polity.

Becker, A.L. (1991) A short essay on languaging. In F. Steier (ed.) *Reflexivity: Knowing as Systemic Social Construction* (pp. 226–234). Newbury Park, CA: Sage.

Bell, D.M. (2003) Method and postmethod: Are they really so incompatible? *TESOL Quarterly* 37 (2), 325–336.

Benesch, S. (2012) *Considering Emotions in Critical English Language Teaching. Theories and Praxis*. New York: Routledge.

Berthoz, A. (2004) Physiologie du changement de point de vue. In A. Berthoz and G. Jorland (eds) *L'Empathie* (pp. 251–275). Paris: Odile Jacob.

Bialystok, E. (2001) *Bilingualism in Development: Language, Literacy, and Cognition*. Cambridge: Cambridge University Press.

Bickes, H. (2004) Bilingualismus, Mehrsprachigkeit und mentales Lexikon – Evolutionsbiologische, soziokulturelle und kognitionswissenschaftliche Perspektiven. *Fremdsprachen lehren und lernen* 33, 27–51.

Boekmann, K.-B., Aalto, A., Atanasoska, T. and Lamb, T. (2011) *Promoting Plurilingualism – Majority Language in Multilingual Settings*. Strasbourg: Council of Europe. See http://www.ecml.at/tabid/277/PublicationID/75/Default.aspx.

Byram, M. and Fleming, M. (eds) (1998) *Language Learning in Intercultural Perspective: Approaches through Drama and Ethnography*. Cambridge: Cambridge University Press.

Canagarajah, S. and Liyanage, I. (2012) Lessons from pre-colonial multilingualism. In M. Martin-Jones, A. Blackledge and A. Creese (eds) *The Routledge Handbook of Multilingualism* (pp. 49–65). London and New York: Routledge.

Carrasco Perea, E. and Piccardo E. (2009) Plurilinguisme, cultures et identités: la construction du savoir-être chez l'enseignant. *Revue de linguistique et de didactique des langues (LIDIL)* 39, 19–41.

CLB (2012) Centre for Canadian Language Benchmarks website. See http://www.language.ca.

CoE (2001) *Common European Framework of Reference for Languages: Learning, Teaching, Assessment (CEFR)*. Language Policy Unit, Council of Europe. Cambridge: Cambridge University Press. See http://www.coe.int/t/dg4/linguistic/cadre_en.asp.

Coïaniz, A. (2001) *Apprentissage des langues et subjectivité*. Paris: L'Harmattan.

Colletta, J-M. (2004) *Le développement de la parole chez l'enfant âgé de 6 à 11 ans: corps, langage et cognition*. Sprimont: Mardaga.

Coulter, J. (1974) The ethnomethodological programme in contemporary sociology. *Human Context* 6 (1), 103–122.

CMEC (2010) *Working with the Common European Framework of References (CEFR) in the Canadian context. Guide for Policy Makers and Curriculum Designers*. Ottawa: Council of Ministers of Education of Canada. See http://www.cmec.ca/docs/assessment/CEFR-canadian-context.pdf (accessed 4 October 2012).

Cummins, J. (2001) *Negotiating Identities: Education for Empowerment in a Diverse Society* (2nd edn). Los Angeles, CA: Association for Bilingual Education.

Cummins, J. (2007) Rethinking monolingual instructional strategies in multilingual classrooms. *Canadian Journal of Applied Linguistics* (Special issue) 10, 221–240.

Damasio, A. (1994) *Descartes' Error. Emotion, Reason and the Human Brain*. New York: Avon Books.

Damasio, A. (1999) *The Feeling of What Happens, Body and Emotion in the Making of Consciousness*. New York: Harcourt Brace.

Dewey, J. (1934) *Art as Experience*. New York: Putnam. Reprinted Perigee Trade paperback edition 2005.

di Pellegrino, G., Fadiga, L., Fogassi, L., Gallese, V. and Rizzolatti, G. (1992) Understanding motor events: A neurophysiological study. *Experimental Brain Research* 91, 176–180.

Engeström, Y. (1999) Innovative learning in work teams: Analyzing cycles of knowledge création in practice. In Y. Engeström, R. Miettinen and R.-L. Punamaki (eds) *Perspectives on Activity Theory*. Cambridge: Cambridge University Press.

Ferguson, G. (2009) What next? Towards an agenda for classroom codeswitching research. *International Journal of Bilingual Education and Bilingualism* 12 (2), 231–241.

Frijda, N. (1986) *The Emotions*. Cambridge: Cambridge University Press.

Gallese, V. and Lakoff, G. (2005) The brain's concepts: The role of the sensory-motor system in conceptual knowledge. *Cognitive Neuropsychology* 22, 455–479.

García, O. (2009) *Bilingual Education in the 21st Century: A Global Perspective*. Malden, MA: Wiley-Blackwell.

Gibson J.J. (1977) The theory of affordances. In R. Shaw and J. Bransford (eds) *Perceiving, Acting, and Knowing* (pp. 67–82). Hillsdale, NJ: Lawrence Erlbaum.

Grèzes, J. (2010) Comprendre les actions, émotions et états mentaux d'autrui: psychologie et neurosciences. In A. Berthoz, C. Ossola and B. Stock (eds) *La pluralité interprétative: Fondements cognitifs*. Paris: Les conférences du Collège de France.

Grèzes, J. and de Gelder, B. (2009) Social perception: Understanding other people's intentions and emotions through their actions. In T. Striano and V. Reid (eds) *Social Cognition: Development, Neuroscience and Autism* (pp. 67–78). Oxford: Blackwell.

Gutiérrez, K., Baquedano-López, P. and Alvarez, H. (2001) Literacy as hybridity: Moving beyond bilingualism in urban classrooms. In M. de la Luz Reyes and J. Halcón (eds) *The Best for our Children: Critical Perspectives on Literacy for Latino Students* (pp. 122–141). New York: Teachers College.

Hall, E.T. (1959) *The Silent Language*. New-York: Garden City.

Hatfield, E., Cacioppo, T. and Rapson, R.L. (1994) *Emotional Contagion*. Cambridge: Cambridge University Press.

Huver, E. and Springer, C. (2011) *L'évaluation en langues*. Paris: Didier.

Kovecses, Z. (2000) *Metaphor and Emotion: Language, Culture and Body in Human Feeling*. Cambridge: Cambridge University Press.

Kramsch, C. (2002) *Language Acquisition and Language Socialization. Ecological Perspectives*. New York: Continuum.

Kramsch, C. (2009) *The Multilingual Subject*. Oxford: Oxford University Press.

Kramsch, C., Levy, D. and Zarate, G. (2008) Introduction générale. In G. Zarate, D. Levy and C. Kramsch (eds) *Précis du plurilinguisme et du pluriculturalisme* (pp. 15–23). Paris: Édition des archives contemporaines.

Kumaravadivelu, B. (2001) Toward a postmethod pedagogy. *TESOL Quarterly* 35 (4), 537–560.

Lamm, C., Meltzoff, A.N. and Decety, J. (2009) How do we empathize with someone who is not like us? Insights from event-related and effective connectivity measurements. *Journal of Cognitive Neuroscience* 22, 362–376.

Lantolf, J. (ed.) (2000) *Sociocultural Theory and Second Language Learning*. Oxford: Oxford University Press.

Lantolf, J. (2011) The sociocultural approach to second language acquisition: Sociocultural theory, second language acquisition, and artificial L2 development. In D. Atkinson (ed.) *Alternative Approaches to Second Language Acquisition* (pp. 24–47). New York: Routledge.

Larsen-Freeman, D. (1997) Chaos/complexity science and second language acquisition. *Applied Linguistics* 18 (2), 141–165.

Larsen-Freeman, D. (2002) Language acquisition and language use from a chaos/complexity theory perspective. In C. Kramsch (ed.) *Language Acquisition and Language Socialisation* (pp. 33–36). London and New York: Continuum.

Lecoq, J. (1997) *Le corps poétique: Un enseignement de la création théâtrale.* Paris: Actes Sud-Papiers.

LeDoux, J. (2003) *Neurobiologie de la personnalité.* Paris: Odile Jacob.

Little, D. (2006) The Common European Framework of Reference for Languages: Content, purpose, origin, reception and impact. *Language Teaching* 39, 167–190.

Lowerse, M. (2008) Embodied relations are encoded in language. *Psychonomic Bulletin & Review* 15 (4), 838–844.

Makoni, S. and Pennycook, A. (2007) *Disinventing and Reconstituting Languages.* Clevedon: Multilingual Matters.

Masciotra, D., Roth, W.-M. and Morel, D. (2008) *Enaction: Apprendre et enseigner en situation.* Brussels: DeBoeck.

Maturana, H.R. and Varela, F.J. (1987) *The Tree of Knowledge: The Biological Roots of Human Understanding.* Boston: Shambhala Publications.

Mayer, J.D. and Salovey P. (1995) The intelligence of emotional intelligence. *Intelligence* 17, 433–442.

Mayer, J.D., Salovey, P. and Caruso, D.R. (2004) Emotional intelligence: Theory, findings, and implications. *Psychological Inquiry* 15, 197–215.

Mondada, L. and Pekarek-Doehler, S. (2000) Interaction sociale et cognition située: quels modèles pour la recherche sur l'acquisition des langues? *AILE (Acquisition et Interaction en Langue Etrangère)* 12, 147–174. See http://aile.revues.org/document947.html

Moore, D. and Gajo, L. (2009) Introduction. French voices on plurilingualism and pluriculturalism: theory, significance and perspectives. *International Journal of Multilingualism and Multiculturalism* 6 (2), 137–153.

Murray Thomas, R. (2001) *Recent Theories of Human Development.* Thousand Oaks, CA: Sage.

Nadel, J. and Decety, J. (eds) (2002) *Imiter pour découvrir l'humain: Psychologie, neurobiologie, robotique et philosophie de l'esprit.* Paris: PUF.

Pavlenko, A. (2002) Bilingualism and emotions. *Multilingua* 21, 45–78.

Pavlenko, A. (2005) *Emotions and Multilingualism.* Cambridge: Cambridge University Press.

Pavlenko, A. (2011) *Thinking and Speaking in Two Languages.* Bristol: Multilingual Matters.

Pavlenko, A. (2012) Multilingualism and emotions. In M. Martin-Jones, A. Blackledge and A. Creese (eds) *The Routledge Handbook of Multilingualism* (pp. 454–469). New York: Routledge.

Perani, D., Abutalebi, J., Paulesu, E., Brambati, S., Scifo, P., Cappa, S.F. and Fazio, F. (2003) The role of age of acquisition and language usage in early, high-proficient bilinguals: an fMRI study during verbal fluency. *Human Brain Mapping* 19, 170–182.

Piccardo, E. (2005) Complessità e insegnamento delle lingue straniere: Ripensare un paradigma. *RILA* 2–3 (37), 75–92.

Piccardo, E. (2007) 'Humain, trop humain' – une approche pour esprits libres: de la nécessité d'une dimension humaniste dans la didactique des langues. *Les cahiers de l'ASDIFLE* 19, 21–49.

Piccardo, E. (2010) L'enseignant un stratège de la complexité: quelles perspectives pour la formation? In G. Baillat, D. Niclot and D. Ulma (eds) *La formation des enseignants en Europe: Approche comparative* (pp. 79–98). Brussels: de Boeck.

Piccardo, E. (2012a) La médiation linguistique: entre traduction et enseignement des langues vivantes. *Études de linguistique appliquée (ELA)* 167, 285–294.

Piccardo, E. (2012b) Multidimensionality of assessment in the Common European Framework of Reference for Languages (CEFR). Cahiers de l'ILOB/OLBI Working Papers No. 4 (pp. 37–54). See http://www.olbi.uottawa.ca/ CCERBAL/files/pdf/vol4-piccardo.pdf.

Piccardo, E. (2013) Plurilingualism and curriculum design: Towards a synergic vision. *TESOL Quarterly* 47 (3), 600–514.

Rizzolatti, G. and Arbib, M.A. (1998) Language within our grasp. *Trends in Neurosciences* 21 (5), 188–194.

Rolbin, C. and Della Chiesa, B. (2010) 'We share the same biology…' Cultivating cross-cultural empathy and global ethics through multilingualism. *Mind, Brain, and Education* 4 (4), 196–207.

Scarry, E. (2002) The difficulty of imagining other people. In M.C. Nussbaum (ed.) *For Love of Country?* (pp. 98–110). Originally published: Cohen, J. (ed.) (1996) *For Love of Country? Debating the Limits of Patriotism*. Boston: Beacon Press.

Schneuwly, B. (2008) *Vygotski, l'école et l'écriture*. Cahiers des Sciences de l'éducation No. 118. Geneva: Pratiques Theorie.

Scott Brewer, S. (2010) Un regard agentique sur l'anxiété langagière. In J. Aden, T. Grimshaw and H. Penz (eds) *Enseigner les langues-cultures à l'ère de la complexité: Approches interdisciplinaires pour un monde en reliance* (pp. 75–88) Brussels: Peter Lang.

Shanahan, D. (1997) Articulating the relationship between language, literature, and culture: Toward a new agenda for foreign language teaching and research. *Modern Language Journal* 81 (2), 164–174.

Shanahan, D. (2007) *Language, Feeling and the Brain*. New Brunswick: Transaction Publishers.

Stein, N.L. and Trabasso, T. (1992) The organization of emotional experience: Creating links among emotion, thinking, language, and intentional action. *Cognition & Emotion* 6 (3–4), 225–244.

Swain, M. (2006) Languaging, agency and collaboration in advanced second language proficiency. In H. Byrnes (ed.) *Advanced Language Learning. The Contribution of Halliday and Vygotski* (pp. 95–108). London: Continuum.

Swain, M., Kinnear, P. and Steinman, L. (2011) *Sociocultural Theory in Second Language Education*. Bristol: Multilingual Matters.

Thirioux, B. and Berthoz, A. (2010) Phenomenology and physiology of empathy and sympathy: How intersubjectivity is the correlate of empathy. In J. Aden, T. Grimshaw and H. Penz (eds) *Teaching Language and Culture in an Era of Complexity: Interdisciplinary Approaches for an Interrelated World* (pp. 41–57). Brussels: Peter Lang.

Thorne, S.L. and Lantolf J.P. (2007) A linguistics of communicative activity. In A. Pennycook and S. Makoni (eds) *Disinventing and Reconstituting Language* (pp. 170–195). Clevedon: Multilingual Matters.

van Lier L. (2002) An ecological-semiotic perspective on language and linguistics. In C. Kramsch (ed.) *Language Acquisition and Language Socialization. Ecological Perspectives* (pp. 140–164). New York: Continuum.

van Lier, L. (2004) *The Ecology and Semiotics of Language Learning*. Boston, MA: Kluwer Academic Publishers.

Vygotsky, L. (1978) *Mind and Society: The Development of Higher Psychological Processes*. Cambridge, MA: Harvard University Press.

Wells-Jopling, R. and Oatley, K. (2012) Metonymy and intimacy. *Journal of Literary Theory* 6, 235–251.

Whitaker, H. (2010) *Concise Encyclopedia of Brain and Language*. Oxford: Elsevier.

Willems, R.M. and Hagoort, P. (2007) Neural evidence for the interplay between language, gesture, and action: A review. *Brain and Language* 101 (3), 278–289.

Zwaan, R.A. and Taylor, L.J. (2006) Seeing, acting, understanding: Motor resonance in language comprehension. *Journal of Experimental Psychology* 135 (1), 1–11.

11 Translanguaging as Process and Pedagogy: Developing the English Writing of Japanese Students in the US

Ofelia García and Naomi Kano

Guiding Questions

- What are the characteristics of the translanguaging pedagogy used by Kano that distinguish it from much traditional second language and bilingual pedagogy?
- What understandings about bilingual acquisition do you gather from the perspectives expressed by the bilingual learners in this chapter that may be different from the traditional second language acquisition literature?
- What are the advantages of a translanguaging pedagogy for both bilingual and monolingual learners? What may be the difficulties in enacting it?

Introduction

The multilingual turn experienced in the 21st century has greatly impacted national school systems, many of which have been unwilling to use the language diversity of their students as a resource to learn. But despite the resistance of many, multilingualism has in itself 'turned' schools and pedagogical practices, as educational systems try to catch up with their sociolinguistic realities.

The United States has always been a nation of immigrants, but schools have focused on encouraging the language shift to English, which has characterized the US in the past. But the multilingual turn experienced globally in

258

the 21st century has not escaped the US or its students. Despite its limitations, the US Census reports that 22% of students aged 5–17 years old in US schools speak languages other than English at home (US Census Bureau, 2011). The percentage of bilingual students in schools financed by the government, known in the US as public schools, is even greater. It is also now common in the US for students to be 'bi-schooled' (Nagaoka, 1998); that is, many US students go to public American schools, and at the same time attend educational programs in languages other than English and following curricula established by other national systems (see García *et al.*, 2012b). That is, these 'bi-schooled' students are not only being educated bilingually, but are also following different national curricula delivered by educators with different nationalities and through pedagogies grounded in different sociocultural frameworks. This is the case of the Japanese American students who are the subject of this chapter. Bilingual Japanese American students have remarkable language and literacy abilities, able to read and write using two different scripts and discourse traditions, and expecting to achieve the same national standards in Japanese as those of their peers in Japan, and in English as those of their American peers in the US. To do that, they attend both English public day schools and Japanese supplementary schools either at weekends or after school. But the separateness of their educational spaces – one solely in English and the other solely in Japanese – means that they are never asked to use their bilingual abilities to make sense of what they are learning. This chapter describes an exception, the construction of an instructional space where these bilingual students' complex bilingual practices, which we call here their translanguaging, were used as a resource to develop their academic writing in English. We start by discussing the concept of dynamic bilingualism and translanguaging, before we turn to the translanguaging instructional space in which the study was conducted, and to what we learned about the translanguaging process from the students.

Dynamic Bilingualism and Translanguaging

Motivated by a desire to better understand what happens when all language practices are used to develop a specific practice that is linked to a specific discourse, one of the authors of this chapter, Naomi Kano, designed an English essay writing class for Japanese students in which the students' bilingual practices were used dynamically to teach and learn. In the 21st century, an additive view of bilingualism as two linear wholes, which has been called the monolingual view of multilingualism (Grosjean, 1982), no longer holds. Different linguistic features are not bound by geographical territories, national spaces or speech communities, but rather they represent complex local practices of interactions that are dynamically enacted by human beings in communication (Mignolo, 2000; Pennycook, 2010) and that are linked to broader sociopolitical systems, creating possibilities for both agency and resistance (Irvine & Gal, 2000).

Many have argued that bilingualism can be better seen as *dynamic* (De Bot *et al.*, 2005; García, 2009; Larsen-Freeman & Cameron, 2008). Herdina and Jessner (2002) have proposed a dynamic model of multilingualism based on dynamic systems theory, which posits that there is an interplay between language systems and that there is no simple addition of these systems. They argue that there are no separate language systems, and bi-/multilingualism produces a change in the systems involved, as well as in the degree of meta-linguistic and metacognitive awareness of the speaker (Jessner, 2006).

This dynamic bilingualism goes beyond the descriptive models of additive and subtractive bilingualism of the past or even the plurilingualism espoused by the Council of Europe (CoE, 2001) today as 'the ability to use several languages to varying degrees and for distinct purposes', and instead acknowledges the complexity of the language practices of bilingual and multilingual people. Dynamic bilingualism is enacted through fluid languaging practices that scholars have called by different terms, meaning slightly different things. Jørgensen (2008) refers to the combination of features that are not discrete and complete 'languages' in themselves as *polylingualism*. Jacquemet (2005) speaks of *transidiomatic practices* to refer to the communicative practices of transnational groups that interact using different communicative codes, simultaneously present in a range of local and distant communicative channels. Otsuji and Pennycook (2010) refer to fluid practices in urban contexts as *metrolingualism*, rejecting the fact that there are discrete languages or codes. Canagarajah (2011) uses *codemeshing* to refer to the shuttle between repertoires in writing for rhetorical effectiveness, and refers to *translingual practices* (Canagarajah, 2013).

Perhaps the term that has had the most traction in the literature to refer to these flexible language practices is that of *translanguaging*. The term translanguaging comes from the Welsh (*trawsieithu*) coined by Cen Williams (1994). In its original use, it referred to a pedagogical practice where students are asked to alternate languages for the purposes of receptive or productive use; for example, students might be asked to read in English and write in Welsh and vice versa (Baker, 2011). Since then, the term has been extended by many scholars (Blackledge & Creese, 2010; Canagarajah, 2011; Creese & Blackledge, 2010; García, 2009, 2011, 2013; García & Sylvan, 2011; Hornberger & Link, 2012; Lewis *et al.*, 2012a, 2012b) to refer to both the complex discursive practices of bilinguals, as well as to pedagogical approaches that use those complex practices.

We use translanguaging in this chapter to refer not to the use of two separate languages or even the shift of one language or code to the other. Rather, translanguaging is rooted on the principle that bilingual speakers select language features from a repertoire and 'soft assemble' their language practices in ways that fit their communicative situations (García, 2009,

2013). That is, bilinguals call upon different social *features* in a seamless and complex network of multiple semiotic signs, as they adapt their languaging to suit the immediate task. Translanguaging, as a soft-assembled mechanism, emerges with enaction, with each action being locally situated and unique to satisfy contextual constraints, and creating an interdependence among all components of the system (Kloss & Van Orden, 2009; Turvey & Carello, 1981). Translanguaging can be defined as a process by which students and teachers engage in complex discursive practices that include *all* the language practices of students in order to develop new language practices and sustain old ones, communicate appropriate knowledge, and give voice to new sociopolitical realities by interrogating linguistic inequality. We argue that in today's globalized world what is needed is the ability to engage in fluid language practices and to soft assemble features that can 'travel' across geographic spaces to enable us to participate fully as global citizens.

Language education programs, and even bilingual education programs, often insist that the two languages be kept separate (García, 2009). The philosophy has been that the students' home language practices can never be used, and that the teacher should exclusively use the additional language. Even in bilingual education programs, the two languages are most often strictly allocated according to different teachers, different subjects, different time of day or different places. This is what Cummins (2007) refers to as 'the two solitudes'. Very early on, Cummins (1981) posited the interdependence hypothesis. Cummins explains that the surface features of the different languages may be distinct, but there is a 'common underlying proficiency' that enables bilinguals to transfer cognitive and/or academic abilities from one language to the other. Cummins now explains that educators have not used his interdependence and common underlying proficiency to develop programmatic structures and pedagogies that would truly support this interdependence.

In the US, the only educational programs that give students the possibility of developing bilingualism are 'dual language' bilingual education programs that are based on the principle that the languages should be kept separate. The common assumption that only the 'target' language is to be used in language education programs has become increasingly questioned (Cummins, 2007; Fitts, 2006; García, 2009, 2013; García *et al.*, 2012a). Fu (2003) writes about the ways in which she uses what she calls a 'bilingual process approach' to develop Chinese students' writing abilities in English:

> I believe thinking (reasoning and imagination) and the ability to organize ideas are equally, or even more, important than language skills in learning to write. If we let our students express themselves and present their ideas in their primary language, we give them opportunities to continue the development of their thinking. With this development uninterrupted, they are able to write well in a second language once they develop proficiency in it. (Fu, 2003: 74)

Translanguaging as a pedagogic practice is increasingly being used to sustain the dynamic languaging of students and to enable them to learn (Creese & Blackledge, 2010; for a pedagogical guide on translanguaging, see Celic & Seltzer, 2012).

Although most language education programs are set up to separate language practices into two neat systems, in practice students and teachers language flexibly in classrooms (see chapter by Conteh, Copland & Creese, this volume). If used strategically, the flexible use of different language practices, translanguaging, has an important purpose in language education. This was precisely the goal of the special private class designed for a group of Japanese American students and taught by Naomi Kano, which we discuss in the next section.

A Transcultural/Translanguaging Class

The purpose of the class taught by Kano was to prepare Japanese students, ranging from 12 to 16 years of age, for the Scholastic Achievement Test (SAT) that American universities use for admissions. The course, taught privately to 10 students in one of the students' homes, targeted as product the kind of English academic essay that the US values, such as clear organization, critical thinking, unity and coherence, point of view supported by appropriate evidence and examples, and skilful use of language and grammar. To develop the Japanese students' essay writing abilities, Kano focused on two issues: (1) the organization of the text; and (2) the quality of the ideas that were formulated in writing.

For the most part, the organization of written texts in Japanese schools and American schools differs. English texts follow what Kano (2012) calls 'a bento-box' deductive organization; that is, the discrete paragraphing of English essays is like having compartments in a bento box, a Japanese compartmentalized lunch box to-go, in which one can immediately tell what the main dish is. It also allows one to get what one wants at a glance. In contrast, Japanese texts generally follow an inductive organization (Hinds, 1990; Kaplan, 1966). The tendency of Japanese writers is to write inductively, which results in an argument that has not been fully developed, and an expectation on the reader to infer the point being made. Writing deductively has to be taught explicitly to meet the expectation of American readers. For Japanese students, it is often not the language itself (vocabulary, grammar, etc.) that prevents them from getting high scores in the SAT essays, but the ways in which they organize their ideas. Additionally, Japanese students are often hampered by their inability to express ideas on themes with which they are not familiar. This was the focus of the other strand of Kano's teaching activities.

The teacher, Kano, conducted a thematic analysis of all SAT prompts since 2005 and divided the topics into those which were more foreign to

Japanese culture, such as those having to do with independence, democracy and individuality, and those that were very much part of Japanese culture, such as harmony and cooperation. Japanese students' scores are often low because of the quality of ideas having to do with themes with which they are not familiar.

What makes it challenging for Japanese student writers to produce English texts, besides the linguistic differences, is the different emphasis in text organization and the expectation of familiarity with ideas that are culturally laden. But to explicitly develop text organization and quality of ideas requires that the teacher acknowledges what students already know and know how to do – their own ideas and the ways they organize ideas in Japanese written texts. That is, teaching has to be responsive to students who know other ways of languaging, other discourses, and other ways of writing, the result of their being bi-schooled. What bilingual students already know in other languages and have learned in other schools is hardly ever recognized in American public schools.

In thinking about how to develop the abilities of Japanese students to expand and organize their ideas, Kano developed a curriculum that used translanguaging pedagogically (see Kano, 2012). This translanguaging pedagogy rested on the ability of the students to use their entire linguistic repertoire (even though an English essay was expected as a product), while giving students agency to use their language practices flexibly in order to construct their own meaning and develop strong English essays. The translanguaging pedagogy followed three steps:

(1) Students read bilingual texts on the topic about which they were assigned to write. These bilingual texts were presented side-by-side, or there was an English text coupled with a parallel translation in Japanese, or a set of English and Japanese texts about the same subject, but not parallel translations.
(2) Students discussed the bilingual readings mostly in Japanese.
(3) Students wrote an essay in English on the topic of the bilingual reading and the discussion in Japanese about the readings.

The English essay writing curriculum was carried out over a period of six months in 21 weekly lessons of 90 minutes each. Throughout the six-month period, students were given reading material in both English and Japanese to use in constructing their English essays.

The bilingual students

The 10 Japanese students in the class consisted of seven girls and three boys of middle-school and high-school age whose parents wanted them to do well in English essay writing for the SAT. However, the parents also wanted a Japanese teacher, able to understand the gaps in language and discourse norms between the two social contexts, and able to be especially sensitive to cultural and social differences. Intuitively, these parents understood that their children had a resource that had hereto not been tapped – their dynamic bilingual practices. They also assumed that only a teacher able to understand the two trans-discursive cultural styles would be able to negotiate the differences. All the students spoke Japanese at home, although, as we said before, they attended American public schools during the day and Japanese schools at weekends. Not all students were at the same points of the bilingual continuum (García, 2009; Grosjean, 2010); that is, some students spoke, read or wrote with different degrees of proficiency in one language or the other. Five students were *emergent bilinguals* (García & Kleifgen, 2010); that is, they were developing academic English, and were receiving English as a second language instruction in their public schools. The other five students were *experienced bilinguals*, able to use English and Japanese well to read and write academic texts. Table 11.1 displays the characteristics of the 10 students in the study.

What is striking about these students is that these are transnational Japanese American youth. Only one of the 10 was born in the US and has lived in the US since then. Of the five emergent bilinguals, three were born in Japan and came to the US at the age of 12. But the other two had moved frequently. One was born in Japan, went to Singapore at the age of two, to Hong Kong at the age of six, to Japan at the age of nine, and came to New York at the age of 14. The other emergent bilingual was born in the Netherlands; at six she moved to the UK, three years later she went back to Japan, and at 12 she came to the US. Among those who are experienced

Table 11.1 Students in the study

Emergent bilinguals

Emi	F	13	Netherlands → UK (6*) → Japan (9) → US (12)
Haruka	F	15	Japan → Singapore (2) → Hong Kong (6) → Japan (9) → US (14)
Masato	M	14	Japan → US (12)
Nozomi	F	16	Japan → US (12)
Satomi	F	13	Japan → US (12)

Experienced bilinguals

Chihiro	F	12	Japan → US (2)
Daiki	M	13	US → Japan (1) → US (5)
Kei	F	12	Japan → Canada (2) → US (7)
Risa	F	12	US
Yuji	M	14	Canada → US (4)

Notes: Numbers in parentheses refer to the ages of the students when they arrived in that country. The first country that appears is the country of birth.

bilinguals, two were born in the US, one was born in Canada and two were born in Japan but had moved to the US and Canada at the age of two. Of the two born in the US, one had moved to Japan when he was one, and returned at the age of five. Clearly these students have led transnational as well as transcultural lives, picking up different linguistic and cultural practices from all the social contexts and schooling systems they have experienced. And yet, both their American and their Japanese schooling only take into consideration a small part of their linguistic, cultural and schooling practices.

Research Methodology and General Findings

The purpose of this study was to better understand the students' perceptions of translanguaging as pedagogy and as a learning strategy. To do so, a *stimulated recall technique* was used in which portions of translanguaging-enriched instruction were videotaped and then played back to individual students involved in the task. These interviews took place twice during the six-month period and were conducted in Japanese.

Introspective studies of multilingualism have been used in the past to disclose the experiences of participants in solving tasks (Faerch & Kasper, 1986). These studies usually consist of *self-reports* of what the participants are doing, of *self-observations* in which participants are asked to inspect their language behavior, and of *self-revelation* in which participants disclose their thought process (Cohen, 1996). This study asked the participants to reveal what they were thinking as they inspected their language behavior and to report what they were doing during the translanguaging-enriched task that was videotaped. Despite the fact that some participants were able to say much more than others, the stimulated recall technique enabled the students to focus especially on their thought process as they were engaged in the translanguaging task.

The analyses of the interviews confirmed the fact that translanguaging played an important role in how the students processed their English essay writing. As we will see, translanguaging as a pedagogy made students more aware of their language use; that is, their metalinguistic awareness became more developed. Learners were making choices according to social and motivational factors, as Clyne (2003) has shown. In addition, their anxiety about writing English essays was lowered. However, it also became clear that translanguaging was used differently by the experienced bilinguals and the emergent bilinguals. Whereas the experienced bilinguals used translanguaging seamlessly for their own *enhancement*, the emergent bilinguals used translanguaging as *support*, and sometimes to *expand* their understandings. As we will see, emergent bilinguals had a *dependent translanguaging* pattern, whereas experienced bilinguals had an *independent translanguaging* pattern. In all cases, however, both languages seemed to be continuously activated, but to different degrees (Green, 1986; Thierry & Wu, 2007). That is, although the goal of the lesson was to produce an English language text, the students could not achieve this without working with, and through, Japanese. As we will see, the translanguaging pedagogy, focusing on the dynamic nature of the interaction between the components of the bilingual system, led to the emergence and development of metalinguistic and metacognitive awareness (Herdina & Jessner, 2002), abilities which can facilitate self-regulation in learning.

Translanguaging in Action

The interviews revealed that all students, regardless of where they were positioned in the bilingual continuum, translanguaged frequently in order to make sense of the lesson being taught, as well as in the process of writing their English essays. All students used the readings provided in both Japanese and English, although they used them selectively and differently. They demonstrated much linguistic awareness of their own needs and were cognizant of their strengths and weaknesses. Beyond that, the students demonstrated much autonomy and control in languaging appropriately for the task in which they were involved. Nevertheless, whereas the emergent bilinguals often translanguaged because they were dependent on their expertise with other language practices in order to complete the task, the experienced bilinguals translanguaged only to enhance the task, demonstrating their greater autonomy and ability to self-regulate. We first look at what the emergent bilinguals said about their reading of bilingual texts in order to build their background knowledge and develop the quality of their ideas, and then discuss how the experienced bilinguals handled the same exposure to bilingual texts.

Emergent bilinguals translanguaging for support

Satomi, Masato and Nozomi were all born in Japan and came to the US at the age of 12. Thus, they have been in the US for one to four years and are at the beginning points of the bilingual continuum. All three benefited greatly from the bilingual reading texts that the teacher prepared, but they each used them differently.

Satomi shows her ability to zoom in on the language that she needs for a particular task. She is shown a video clip in which she is engaged in reading the bilingual texts. When asked in what language she was reading, she answers:

英語で、わかんないところだけ、日本語を見てました。

[*In English, I was reading corresponding passages in the Japanese language whenever I didn't understand it in English.*]

This says much about Satomi's self-regulating process of learning. She knows she is going to write in English, and thus prefers to read in English.

However, whenever she does not fully understand the English language, she goes back to the Japanese. In a way, Satomi is doing what all good readers do – they use all their semiotic resources to negotiate meaning with the text. This is a strategy used by many of the students, and certainly by another two emergent bilingual students, Masato and Nozomi.

When shown the video clip of his reading and asked what language he first read in, Masato says:

日本語。で必要な部分を見て、そこを英語で見て、アウトラインを書きました。

[*The Japanese one. Then, I picked relevant parts and switched to the English text for writing the outline.*]

Masato's strategy is different from the one used by Satomi in that the order of the language in which he enters the reading texts is different. Satomi first reads the English text, knowing that she would have to write in English, and only relies on Japanese when she does not understand. Masato goes straight for full comprehension of the reading and thus reads the Japanese text first, going back to the English text only when he has to write. Satomi and Masato's different approaches to the process of translanguaging reveal something about their different learning styles. Satomi is interested in doing well in English, and uses Japanese as a resource when she does not understand English. Masato, on the other hand, really wants to understand and gain deep content knowledge. Although some might understand his reading of Japanese first as 'taking the easy way out', in reality he reads in Japanese first because it gives him the most depth in comprehension. That is, the Japanese text is used as a resource to understand deeply. Masato understands that writing is about rendering in written words a thought, an idea, a feeling, and that the more one understands, the easier it is to develop it in writing.

There is much more going on in Masato's language use than just an alternate use of his different language resources. Masato also reveals how he uses his linguistic resources purposefully and simultaneously. He describes what he was doing in the video clip as he was getting ready to write:

アウトラインに書く文章は頭の中で英語にして考えて、日本語で読んだのの要点とかを考えるときは、日本語になってると思います。

[*I was thinking in English about what I was going to write in English; for summing up the main points of the text I read in Japanese, I was thinking in Japanese.*]

Masato has at his disposal a range of language resources, which are not in any way the same. Just as Japanese and English have different scripts, in a class to develop English academic writing the languages have different purposes. Masato thinks in English if he is planning to write in English, but he uses Japanese to better comprehend the text that will be the springboard for his writing in English. In other words, through the translanguaging pedagogy used in this class, Masato is made aware of the advantages of using his bilingualism dynamically to learn and to show what he knows. He self-regulates the construction of his knowledge and uses Japanese for *knowledge input*, and English for *language input*.

Another of the emergent bilinguals was Nozomi, a 16-year-old who has been in the US for four years. Nozomi was also asked to comment on a video-clip where she is shown working with the bilingual texts. Her strategy was different again from that of Satomi and Masato, for she read in both Japanese and English. She explains:

日本語のほうを最初に読んで、それで使いたい所を見て英語のその部分だけ読んだりしてます.... 日本語でそのまま訳すと変になっちゃうんで、英語のを見て見本にして書いたほうがまだわかりやすいかな、って。

[*I read the Japanese text first, and then I decided the area that is relevant to my essay, and read the equivalent part in English. . . . If I translate directly from the Japanese I've written, the product [in English] may seem odd. Referring to the English text makes my English essay easier to understand for the readers.*]

Nozomi's strategy is similar to Masato in that she reads the Japanese text first, but then quickly identifies the equivalent part in English, which she then uses to write her English essay. Whereas Masato is interested in the deep meaning that the Japanese text provides, Nozomi is looking for ways to use Japanese to complete the academic task, which is the English essay.

Nozomi was the least bilingual in the bilingual continua of all the students in the study. She has learned to write English by finding her words in what she reads, and as she says above, refers to the English written text to produce her own English written text. However, Nozomi also reveals in her interview what is not readily seen, which is, as we have explained above, crucial to the delivery of a good English essay – what happens as she constructs her ideas and organizes them. She explains:

だいたい考えておいて、どんなことを書くか決めて、そのあと日本語で考えながら、英語にします。

[*Before I start writing, I roughly organize my thoughts, and decide on what I'm gonna write, and while thinking in Japanese, I write in English.*]

Thinking internally in Japanese, alongside the external English written product, allows Nozomi to write an English essay.

The three emergent bilingual students introduced in this section have the least proficiency in English, and yet they translanguage differently and show a great deal of autonomy and control over the task they are performing.

They are knowledgeable translanguagers, able to translanguage to support their learning and the production of an English essay. The following section portrays how the two other emergent bilinguals who are further along the bilingual continuum use translanguaging.

Emergent bilinguals translanguaging for expansion

Emergent bilinguals who are further along the bilingual continuum seldom rely on the Japanese written texts to make meaning of the English texts. But this does not mean that they do not also use translanguaging actively. Emi and Haruka are the two other emergent bilingual students; however, because they have lived in many other international contexts, they arrived with very good receptive ability in English.

Emi is shown the video clip in which she is engaged in pre-writing the English essay. She explains what she's doing:

英語でメモ取ってるときでも、たまにわからなかったりしたときはそれをその部分だけちょっと日本語でまとめて、書いてやってます。

[*While taking notes in English, when I come across things I don't get, I quickly jot it down in Japanese instead.*]

Emi uses all her linguistic resources to expand her understanding, to speed up her learning, to save cognitive space and time. For example, Emi annotates her own notes in English with Japanese, to ensure that she understands, remembers and appropriates the meanings, and that she speeds up the process of making meaning. Her annotations in Japanese expand her ability to make meaning. This is the same process used in glosses – marginal or interlinear annotations of texts – used since medieval times to enlighten the comprehension of texts written in Classical languages.

Haruka, who had lived in Singapore, Hong Kong and Japan before arriving in the US, is shown a video clip of herself working on an English vocabulary exercise in which she has to come up with synonyms. She is asked what language process she used to accomplish the task. Her answer reveals her use of translanguaging not simply as a support, but as an expander. She says:

そのときは日本語で考えてました. . . あの、思いつかなくて、やっぱり日本語でどんどんことばが出てきちゃったので。それに関しては日本語でした。[同義語練習問題の例]‘use up’っていうことばがあって、それ、’消費’って思い出したら、‘consume’が出て来たんで。そういうふうに日本語を使ってました。

[*I was thinking in Japanese at the time. . . . I couldn't think of synonyms in English because Japanese words kept shooting through my mind one after*]

*another. So, I depended on my Japanese. [For example], we had 'use up' among
the list. When I understood the word in Japanese ('消費'), an English word
'consume' came through my mind. This way, I used the Japanese language for
the task.]*

For this emergent bilingual student, translanguaging enables her to complete
the academic task in English, as she uses her entire linguistic repertoire,
which includes lexicon from Japanese, to generate lexicon in English. Emi
and Haruka, the two emergent bilinguals who are further along the bilingual
continuum, are using translanguaging to expand their cognitive and linguistic experiences, and not simply as support. How experienced bilinguals use
translanguaging is the topic of the next section.

Experienced bilinguals translanguaging for strategic expediency and enhancement

Experienced bilinguals use their entire linguistic repertoire in seamless
ways and translanguage for strategic expediency, as well as to enhance their
learning. Yuji, an experienced bilingual student, is asked to explain his process of thinking when writing in Japanese or English. He communicates his
facility with matching up his thinking process with his reading and writing
process:

> 英語で書いていれば、たぶん英語で考えてますけど、英語の本読みながら日
> 本語で話していたら英語で考えてます. . .（このクラスでは）英語で書い
> てない限りは日本語で考えてます。

> *[If I were to write in English, I would most likely think in English. When I am
> reading a book in English and having a discussion in Japanese, my brain would
> be working in English. . . . [in this class] If I'm not writing in English, I'd most
> likely be thinking in Japanese.]*

Yuji seems to be saying that his performance of academic language in reading
and writing is matched by his thinking ability in that particular language,
and especially by his self-regulation and awareness of the appropriate
response in that case. However, he also reveals that it is possible for him to
have a discussion in Japanese, while thinking in English in ways that permit
him to expand the meaning of the reading in English. Yuji has only had
experience with a *separation approach* to biliteracy where students and teachers are expected to match the language in which they are communicating
around writing to the language of the text (García, 2009). But in the translanguaging space of this special class, Yuji is beginning to move away from
this separation approach to biliteracy, moving towards what has been termed
pluriliteracies (García *et al.*, 2007), that is, a recognition that written-linguistic

modes of meaning are intricately bound up with all kinds of visual, audio and spatial semiotic systems (Cope & Kalantzis, 2000; Kress, 2003). Pluriliteracies give agency to the person involved in the literacy act to use different literacy practices to capitalize on the meaning of the text that is being received or produced.

What makes the concept of pluriliteracies important is the emphasis on having bilingual students develop the agency to use their entire language repertoire to make meaning, regardless of the language of the text or the language of instruction. The idea is that literacy practices are about making meaning from texts and in texts; thus, the communication that takes place in or around writing has to draw on the entire semiotic and bilingual continua, including the continua between receptive and productive language, oral and written, and home-school language practices (Hornberger, 1989).

Hornberger and Skilton-Sylvester (2003) emphasize that biliteracy is better obtained when learners can draw on all points on the continua of biliteracy, especially those aspects that have less power in the school system, such as oral language and home language practices. A flexible dynamic translanguaging approach towards the development of literacy can indeed situate students in in-between border spaces. In these spaces, as Mignolo (2000) makes clear, alternative representations and buried histories of linguistic subjugation are released; that is, ideologies about language and identity, constrained by nation states, are allowed expression, thus also freeing different ways of speaking and being. Yuji is starting to find that place where he translanguages not for support, not even for expansion, but for enhancement.

Yuji also recounts how he made the best use of his bilingual abilities, using both languages to research because he wanted to get the best information. He recalls how he used different texts in both languages to prepare an essay:

今年の作文なんですけど、携帯電話が良いか悪いか、でリサーチをしたとき、日本語のものも英語のものも両方使いました. . . 携帯電話が有益かどうか、日本語でやってみて、で日本語のリサーチを取って、英語でも、って英語のやつも取って、でそれを二つ使いました. . . 両方のことばで調べてみて、一番良いのを使おうと思って。

[*This year, when I was doing research on the pros and cons about cell phones, I used materials both in Japanese and English. . . . I searched for the articles in Japanese on whether cell phones were beneficial, and I took some of them. Then I did the same thing in English. I ended up using the materials in both languages. . . . I searched in both languages in order to get the best ones available.*]

Yuji is an active translanguager, using every opportunity he has to develop his bilingual abilities. Yuji was born in Canada, moved to the US at the age of four, and has never lived in Japan, and yet he speaks Japanese confidently and fluently. Yuji reveals his strategy to develop his Japanese:

> 英語ではこう言う、で、日本語ではこう言う、っていうのは時々考えてます ．．授業中とか、たまに先生のいうことばを日本語に変えてみたりすること はあります。
>
> [*Sometimes, I think of a word in English and another word in Japanese that has the same meaning. ... I sometimes translate what the teacher says in English into Japanese.*]

It turns out that Yuji consciously uses translanguaging as a self-regulating strategy to develop his bilingual skills. Not only does he take every chance to use his full linguistic repertoire, but he also spontaneously creates opportunities to augment such chances, and to enhance his linguistic abilities.

Yuji is not the only one who uses translanguaging to bolster and enhance his bilingual abilities. An advantage of a translanguaging pedagogy, even when applied to an English essay class, is that by making use of the full linguistic repertoire available to students, it also allows students to self-regulate their development of either language. Chihiro is another experienced bilingual who uses the English texts to develop her understanding of Japanese. In expressing her support for the translanguaging approach of the classroom, she says:

> 自分では日本語のほうがボキャブラリーがちょっと少ない気がするんで、あ と漢字が不得意なんで、それで英語で一回読んで、それにそのあとに日本語 であてはめれば少しずつことばとかわかるので、結構それは好きです。
>
> [*I think my vocabulary range is more limited in Japanese than in English. And I'm not good at Chinese characters. If I read an English text once, then I apply what I understood there to reading the Japanese text. I can understand the Japanese words little by little. So I like it.*]

It turns out that, although the translanguaging pedagogy used in this special class was specifically to teach English essay writing, experienced bilinguals also use it actively and fruitfully to sustain and develop their Japanese literacy abilities, a by-product of this teaching.

All the experienced bilinguals used their language resources fluidly and flexibly in order to participate in class discussion, mostly in Japanese, read the bilingual texts and write in English. Chihiro watched a video clip of herself preparing to participate in class discussion in Japanese, and tried to explain what she was doing:

> （英語の）テキストは日本語に訳さないでそのまま読んでました。でも日本 語でディスカッションしてたので、発言したりする前にはある程度日本語に 直してました。

[I was reading the text [in English] without translating it. But before stating my opinion, I was putting what I was getting from the text into Japanese, as we were talking in Japanese.]

This statement by Chihiro demonstrates her awareness of how she uses her linguistic repertoire flexibly in order to communicate appropriately and expediently. All the experienced bilingual students translanguaged to potentialize effective communication for strategic expediency but also for enhancement. Translanguaging enabled them to enrich their languaging and academic experiences.

The experienced bilinguals also acknowledge their frequent use of translanguaging as a strategic expedient resource to complete the academic task. Risa, born in the US, says, for example:

前のクラスでやったときに日本語で考えたことは（今回も）日本語で考えてて、（前回）英語で考えてたことは（今回も）英語で考えてて、そういうふうに書いたのを見ながらやってたから、そのまま、日本語（でとったノート）を読んで日本語で考えて、英語（でとったノート）を読んで英語で考えて、みたいな。

[If I thought about something in Japanese in the last lesson, I would think about it again in Japanese in this lesson. If I thought about something in English in the last lesson, I would think about it again in English this lesson. I would write my notes down in Japanese if what I was thinking about was in Japanese. If my notes were in Japanese, I would think about what I was reading in Japanese. It's the same case if this happened in English.]

And she continues:

エッセーが英語のときは英語で書いて、エッセーが日本語のときは日本語で書きます．．．何かを（英語で書いたものに）足したいとき、日本語で説明とか入れたりします。

[When the essay is in English, I write them in English, and when the essay is in Japanese, I do it in Japanese. ... If I want to add something (to the notes in English), I may add notes in Japanese.]

Experienced bilinguals are able to use their entire linguistic repertoire for their own enrichment. They seem to have an enhanced multilingual monitor that activates different language use when they have to perform certain academic tasks with specific language practices (Jessner, 2006), but privately, it is their translanguaging that enables them to produce the specific language for the academic task. It is also their ability to translanguage and the opportunities to translanguage in this class that develops their dynamic bilingualism as they self-regulate as learners.

In many ways what the interviews with the experienced bilinguals reveal is precisely the common underlying proficiency that Cummins (1981) posited so long ago. What we see, the surface features, are indeed what may be deemed as two languages socially. But if we capture the thinking and self-talk process that students use to produce academic tasks in one or the other language – in Vygotskyan terms, their private speech (Antón & Di Camilla, 1998) – it is translanguaging practices that are the motor of the process which may result in products in one or the other language.

Conclusions

The students' reflections on their linguistic behavior demonstrated much metalinguistic and metacognitive awareness – essential abilities to develop as bilinguals and learners because they facilitate self-regulation in learning. The translanguaging pedagogy used in this experimental class enabled Japanese students to become more aware of the differences in the construction of Japanese and English written texts, to develop expertise in using their own translanguaging strategies to construct academic texts in English, and to build their biliteracy practices. It turned out that a translanguaging pedagogy which took into account the entire linguistic and discursive repertoire of Japanese students produced better written texts in one language, English. And although this was not the purpose of our study, in some cases evidence was provided through the interviews that students' greater awareness of language differences also had repercussions for their understanding and construction of Japanese written texts. The translanguaging pedagogy, enabling students to move back and forth along their entire linguistic repertoire, actually overcame the differences in language, discourse and idea inventory, of Japanese American students writing in English. That is, their English essay repertoire was enriched through the inclusion and attention paid to their translanguaging practices.

Students at different points of the bilingual continuum, however, used translanguaging to construct written texts in English differently. Some of the emergent bilinguals translanguaged, with autonomy and control, to support their learning. Other emergent bilinguals who were further along the bilingual continuum used translanguaging even more actively to expand their cognitive and linguistic performance. In general, the use of translanguaging by emergent bilinguals falls under what we call a dependent translanguaging pattern where new language practices emerge in interrelationship with old ones. Experienced bilinguals, on the other hand, used their entire linguistic repertoire seamlessly and translanguaged only for strategic expediency, as well as to enhance their learning. We refer to this as an independent translanguaging pattern, pointing to the flexible use of language practices by experienced bilinguals to respond to different languaging situations within an integrated dynamic system of language practices.

In a translanguaging classroom, by rejecting the subjugation of one language to the other and giving agency to bilingual students to self-regulate their language practices in learning, diverse linguistic and cultural repertoires are harnessed to their fullest extent. Through those experiences, bilingual students can construct truly bilingual identities and enrich their languaging and academic experiences.

Although in this chapter the translanguaging pedagogy was used with bilingual students, one can imagine that this pedagogy would also be effective with monolingual students who are learning an additional language. For monolingual students to 'catch up' to the multilingual turn would require that all schools engender opportunities for translanguaging, available through families, students and media in all classrooms. What are needed in the 21st century are more classroom spaces where translanguaging is not seen as an illegitimate practice, or solely understood as scaffold for those learning a new language, but as a resource for all students to learn and be part of the dynamic multilingual turn.

Acknowledgments

The authors would like to thank Kate Seltzer for her careful reading of this chapter.

References

Antón, M. and Di Camilla, F. (1998) Socio-cognitive functions of L1 collaborative interaction in the L2 classroom. *Canadian Modern Language Review/La Revue canadienne des langues vivantes* 54 (3), 314–342.

Baker, C. (2011) *Foundations of Bilingual Education and Bilingualism* (5th edn). Bristol: Multilingual Matters.

Blackledge, A. and Creese, A. (2010) *Multilingualism: A Critical Perspective*. London: Continuum.

Canagarajah, A.S. (2011) Codemeshing in academic writing: Identifying teachable strategies of translanguaging. *Modern Language Journal* 95 (iii), 401–417.

Canagarajah, A.S. (2013) *Translingual Practice. Global Englishes and Cosmopolitan Relations*. London and New York: Routledge.

Celic, C. and Seltzer, K. (2012) *Translanguaging: A CUNY-NYSIEB Guide for Educators*. New York: CUNY-NYSIEB. See http://www.cuny-nysieb.org.

Clyne, M. (2003) *Dynamics of Language Contact*. Cambridge: Cambridge University Press.

CoE (2001) *Common European Framework of Reference for Languages: Learning, Teaching, Assessment (CEFR)*. Language Policy Unit, Council of Europe. Cambridge: Cambridge University Press.

Cohen, A. (1996) Verbal reports as a source of insights into second language learner strategies. *Applied Language Learning* 7 (1), 5–24.

Cope, B. and Kalantzis, M. (2000) *Multiliteracies: Literacy Learning and Design of Social Futures*. London: Routledge.

Creese, A. and Blackledge, A. (2010) Translanguaging in the bilingual classroom: A pedagogy for learning and teaching? *Modern Language Journal* 94 (i), 103–115.

Cummins, J. (1981) The role of primary language development in promoting educational success for language minority students. In California State Department of Education (ed.) *Schooling and Language Minority Students: A Theoretical Framework.* Los Angeles, CA: Evaluation, Dissemination and Assessment Center.

Cummins, J. (2007) Rethinking monolingual instructional strategies in multilingual classrooms. *Canadian Journal of Applied Linguistics* 10 (2), 221–240.

De Bot, K., Lowie, W. and Verspoor, M. (2005) *Second Language Acquisition: An Advanced Resource Book.* London and New York: Routledge.

Faerch, C. and Kasper, G. (1986) One learner – two languages: Investigating types of interlanguage knowledge. In J. House and S. Blum-Kulka (eds) *Interlingual and Intercultural Communication Discourse and Cognition in Translation and Second Language Acquisition Studies* (pp. 211–227). Tübingen: Narr.

Fitts, S. (2006) Reconstructing the status quo: Linguistic interaction in a dual-language school. *Bilingual Research Journal* 29 (2), 337–365.

Fu, D. (2003) *An Island of English.* Portsmouth, NH: Heinemann.

García, O. (2009) *Bilingual Education in the 21st Century: A Global Perspective.* Malden, MA and Oxford: Wiley-Blackwell.

García, O. (2011) From language garden to sustainable languaging: Bilingual education in a global world. *Perspective. A Publication of the National Association for Bilingual Education* September/October, 5–10.

García, O. (2013) Theorizing and enacting translanguaging for social justice. In A. Creese and A. Blackledge (eds) *Heteroglossia as Practice and Pedagogy* (pp. 1–30). London and New York: Springer.

García, O. and Kleifgen, J.A. (2010) *Educating Emergent Bilinguals. Policies, Programs and Practices for English Language Learners.* New York: Teachers College Press.

García, O. and Sylvan, C. (2011) Pedagogies and practices in multilingual classrooms: Singularities in pluralities. *Modern Language Journal* 95 (iii), 385–400.

García, O., Bartlett, L. and Kleifgen, J. (2007) From biliteracy to pluriliteracies. In P. Auer and W. Li (eds) *Handbooks of Applied Linguistics, Vol. 5: Multilingualism* (pp. 207–228). Berlin: Mouton de Gruyter.

García, O., Flores, N. and Woodley, H.H. (2012a) Transgressing monolingualism and bilingual dualities: Translanguaging pedagogies. In A. Yiakoumetti (ed.) *Harnessing Linguistic Variation for Better Education* (pp. 45–76). Berne: Peter Lang.

García, O., Zakharia, Z. and Otcu, B. (eds) (2012b) *Bilingual Community Education and Multilingualism: Beyond Heritage Languages in a Global City.* Bristol: Multilingual Matters.

Green, D. (1986) Control, activation and resource: A framework and a model for the control of speech in bilinguals. *Brain and Language* 27, 210–223.

Grosjean, F. (1982) *Life with Two Languages.* Cambridge, MA: Harvard University Press.

Grosjean, F. (2010) *Bilingual Life and Reality.* Cambridge, MA: Harvard University Press.

Herdina, P. and Jessner, U. (2002) *A Dynamic Model of Multilingualism.* Clevedon: Multilingual Matters.

Hinds, J. (1990) Inductive, deductive, quasi-inductive: Expository writing in Japanese, Korean, Chinese, and Thai. In U.M. Connor and A. Johns (eds) *Coherence in Writing: Research and Pedagogical Perspectives* (pp. 87–109). Alexandria, VA: TESOL.

Hornberger, N. (1989) Continua of biliteracy. *Review of Educational Research* 59, 271–296.

Hornberger, N. and Link, H. (2012) Translanguaging and transnational literacies in multilingual classrooms: A bilingual lens. *International Journal of Bilingual Education and Bilingualism* 15 (3), 261–278.

Hornberger, N. and Skilton-Sylvester, E. (2003) Revisiting the continua of biliteracy: International and critical perspectives. In N. Hornberger (ed.) *Continua of Biliteracy. An Ecological Framework for Educational Policy, Research, and Practices in Multilingual Settings* (pp. 35–70). Clevedon: Multilingual Matters.

Irvine, J. and Gal, S. (2000) Language ideology and linguistic differentiation. In P. Kroskrity (ed.) *Regimes of Language: Ideologies, Polities and Identities* (pp. 34–38). Santa Fe, NM: School of American Research Press.

Jacquemet, M. (2005) Transidiomatic practices: Language and power in the age of globalization. *Language and Communication* 25, 257–277.

Jessner, U. (2006) *Linguistic Awareness in Multilinguals: English as a Third Language.* Edinburgh: Edinburgh University Press.

Jørgensen, J.N. (2008) Polylingual languaging around and among children and adolescents. *International Journal of Multilingualism* 5 (3), 161–176.

Kano, N. (2012) Translanguaging as a process and a pedagogical tool for Japanese students in an English writing course in New York. Doctoral dissertation, Teachers College, Columbia University.

Kaplan, R. (1966) Cultural thought patterns in intercultural education. *Language Learning* 16 (1), 1–20.

Kloss, H. and Van Orden, G. (2009) Soft-assembled mechanisms for the grand theory. In J.P. Spencer, M. Thomas and J. McClelland (eds) *Toward a New Grand Theory of Development? Connectionism and Dynamics Systems Theory Reconsidered* (pp. 253–267). Oxford: Oxford University Press.

Kress, G. (2003) *Literacy in the New Media Age.* London and New York: Routledge.

Larsen-Freeman, D. and Cameron, L. (2008) *Complex Systems and Applied Linguistics.* Cambridge: Cambridge University Press.

Lewis, G., Jones, B. and Baker, C. (2012a) Translanguaging: Developing its conceptualisation and contextualisation. *Educational Research and Evaluation: An International Journal on Theory and Practice* 18 (7), 655–670.

Lewis, G., Jones, B. and Baker, C. (2012b) Translanguaging: Origins and development from school to street and beyond. *Educational Research and Evaluation: An International Journal on Theory and Practice* 18 (7), 641–654.

Mignolo, W. (2000) *Local Histories/Global Designs.* Princeton, NJ: Princeton University Press.

Nagaoka, Y. (1998) A descriptive study of Japanese biliterate students in the United States: Bilingualism, language-minority education, and teachers' role. Doctoral dissertation, University of Massachusetts-Amherst.

Otsuji, E. and Pennycook, A. (2010) Metrolingualism: Fixity, fluidity and language in flux. *International Journal of Multilingualism* 7 (3), 240–254.

Pennycook, A. (2010) *Language as a Local Practice.* London and New York: Routledge.

Thierry, G. and Wu Y.J. (2007) Brain potentials reveal unconscious translation during foreign-language comprehension. *Proceedings of the National Academy of Sciences* 104 (30), 12530–12535.

Turvey, M.T. and Carello, C. (1981) Cognition: The view from ecological realism. *Cognition* 10 (1–3), 313–321.

US Census Bureau (2011) *American Community Survey.* B16004. See http://factfinder2. census.gov/faces/tableservices/jsf/pages/productview.xhtml?pid=ACS_11_1YR_ B16004&prodType=.

Williams, C. (1994) Arfarniad o ddulliau dysgu ac addysgu yng nghyd-destun addysg uwchradd ddwyieithog. PhD thesis, University of Wales, Bangor.

12 Transforming Learning, Building Identities: Arts-based Creativity in the Community Languages Classroom

Jim Anderson and Yu-Chiao Chung

Guiding Questions

- How can engagement with arts-based projects provide a richer context for language learning in general and for the study of community/heritage languages in particular?
- What strategies did teachers use to stimulate learner creativity in the project described in this chapter?
- In what ways has work carried out in the project helped to promote social cohesion and social action?

Background

The multilingual turn witnessed over the past decade in Britain and elsewhere reflects a realisation that we are living in an increasingly interconnected and interdependent world and one in which an ability to navigate different cultural and linguistic realities has become a core skill. One consequence of this has been a growing recognition of the languages spoken within our communities and how these need to be supported for the benefit of our bilingual students, but also because of the potential to enhance literacy and citizenship education for all learners (DfES, 2002, 2007; Ofsted, 2008).

While some teaching of community languages, also referred to as 'heritage' languages in the United States and Canada, has taken place in mainstream schools, the main provision has been in the voluntary community-based complementary schools, which are also referred to as 'supplementary', 'mother tongue' and 'weekend' schools. Many thousands of children across the country attend these schools, and a substantial body of recent research (Blackledge & Creese, 2010; Conteh *et al.*, 2007; Francis *et al.*, 2009; Kenner & Ruby, 2012) has highlighted their importance both in terms of academic achievement and of a positive bilingual-bicultural identity construction. We have also seen renewed attempts to build links between the mainstream and complementary sectors, not least through the government-sponsored Our Languages project (CILT, 2007–2009).

A major issue affecting community language teaching has been the failure to develop a pedagogy distinct from mother tongue and foreign language models which recognises the background and needs of bilingual learners (Anderson, 2008, 2011). However, there have been important efforts internationally to begin to address this issue, leading to the recognition of community/heritage language education as 'a new field emerging' (Brinton *et al.*, 2008). In this chapter we look at the potential of arts-based creativity to contribute to developments in this area, drawing on recent research with school students learning Arabic, Mandarin, Panjabi and Tamil in London schools. (For a detailed report on this research as well as information on a range of related resources on the project, please visit Goldsmiths, University of London, Multilingual Learning website.)

For some time now there has been growing interest in the creative dimension to learning, stimulated in part by the need for more flexible and innovative thinking in the workplace and in part by the realisation that a too highly regimented and performance-oriented school culture can easily lead to student disengagement (Claxton, 2008; Robinson, 2011). The landmark government-sponsored report, *All our Futures: Creativity, Culture and Education* (NACCCE, 1999), grounded in democratic and universalised understandings of creativity, defined it as 'Imaginative activity fashioned so as to produce outcomes that are original and of value'. There are close links between this perspective on creativity and a sociocultural view of learning (Craft, 2005). Such a view prioritises process over production, emphasises the importance of social and cultural context and seeks to establish links to learners' prior knowledge and experience. This is a holistic approach, which accommodates cognitive and affective factors and recognises the importance of learner agency in heightening levels of engagement and building confidence. The importance of the arts in this context is seen to lie in the way they allow young people to 'experiment with and try to articulate their deepest feelings and their own sense of cultural identity and belonging' (NACCCE, 1999: 79).

As far as foreign language teaching is concerned, there has been growing recognition that thematic, arts-related work can provide much greater stimulus for learning than the narrow topic-based approach that remains widespread in schools (Anderson, 2009; Brown & Brown, 1996; Coyle *et al.*, 2010; Grenfell, 2002). This applies to an even greater extent in relation to community languages classrooms where students come with a background in the language and culture, albeit highly varied in terms of competence levels, and an opportunity to use it in their everyday lives. Such students are typically more linguistically aware and, since they are used to shifting between different linguistic and cultural frames in their daily lives, they commonly display greater mental flexibility. Within a social and mainstream educational context which may not always be supportive of diversity, they also have an emotional need to develop a harmonious sense of identity, which resists essentialised views of culture and opens up a dynamic space for the development of critical perspectives (Conteh *et al.*, 2007; Cummins, 2006; Datta, 2007). Thus there are strong grounds for believing that arts-based creativity might have a valuable part to play in the development of content and pedagogy suited to the community languages classroom.

It should be remembered, however, that teacher creativity is not the same as learner creativity and that introducing creative work, whether this be in the form of stories, paintings or drama, may or may not lead to learner creativity (Craft, 2005). This understanding and the shift towards transformative pedagogy arising from it was reflected in the four dimensions identified as central to the way creativity was understood within this project. These four dimensions were:

(1) Seeing new or other possibilities – including different linguistic/cultural perspectives.
(2) Active participation in a collaborative process of generating, shaping and evaluating ideas – drawing on prior knowledge and experience as well as 'funds of knowledge' at home and in the community.
(3) Personal investment and self-expression – taking ownership.
(4) Pursuing meaningful goals and presenting to others – affirming identity and challenging the marginalised status of community languages.

Research Design

The ethnographic study upon which this chapter is based took place between 2007 and 2010. It was collaborative and participatory in nature, involving a team of researchers at Goldsmiths, University of London, working with teachers of Arabic, Mandarin, Panjabi and Tamil in four London schools – two mainstream and two complementary. Our two key questions were:

(1) What contribution can arts-based creative work make to the learning and teaching of community languages in mainstream and complementary

school contexts? More specifically, can such work help meet the intellectual and emotional needs of children from bilingual/bicultural backgrounds?

(2) What are the implications for pedagogy, i.e. what opportunities are opened up? What conditions are required for learner creativity to develop?

Data were collected on a series of three arts-based tasks carried out in each of the four settings. This included field notes, video recordings of lessons, and semi-structured interviews with selected students, teachers and parents, as well as outcomes of students' work and teaching plans and resources. Background on the four schools, including the tasks carried out in each, is provided in Table 12.1.

Striking here is the range of arts-based work that teachers incorporated into languages lessons, covering painting, story, song, dance, drama, puppetry and film-making. The choice of which art forms to work with reflected the strengths of the teachers, but also the interests of the students. Worth noting too is the range of student ages and attainment levels involved. In spite of the differences in settings, student profiles and the types of arts-based work, data analysis revealed clear patterns clustering around language and literacy, cognition, intercultural understanding and personal and social development; these are reflected in the vignettes below. It also provided important insights in relation to pedagogy and teacher professional development.

Vignettes

To give a flavour of the work carried out and the impact it had on learners as well as teachers and parents, we have chosen to focus mainly on one task in each of the four schools, progressing from primary to secondary levels:

- the scrapbook activity at London Mandarin School;
- the song stories and South Indian dance at Downderry Primary School;
- the development and performance of a drama focusing on a community issue at Rathmore Asian Community School;
- the creation of artworks reflecting the Arab world, but also children's own identities, at Sarah Bonnell School.

Since it is not possible here to capture fully the work carried out in the project, we would urge readers to refer also to the 'Creativity' area on Goldsmiths' Multilingual Learning website (see References for address) where a range of resources, including photographic data, are housed.

Table 12.1 School background data

School	Task A	Task B	Task C
Sarah Bonnell School (SBS) (Mainstream secondary girls' school in Newham) Class: Year 7–8 (students from diverse backgrounds, but mainly beginners in Arabic) (Age 11–12)	Artwork integrating images and text (Exhibition)	Dual-language storybooks (Presentation in local primary school)	Puppet show (Performance in class)
Downderry Primary School (DPS) (Mainstream mixed primary school in Lewisham) Class: Year 3–6 (after school) (Age 6–10, mainly 2nd generation) (Tamil)	South Indian dance based on song stories; complementary work carried out in language and dance lessons	South Indian dance based on song stories (Performance in school assembly and local Tamil community event)	Drama and digital film-making based on song stories (Presentation in class)
London Mandarin School (LMS) (Mixed primary–secondary complementary school in Hackney) Class: Year 1–3 (Age 5–7, mainly 2nd–3rd generation) (Mandarin)	'Four Season Song' based on traditional three-word chant	Scrapbook: pages made up of drawings, natural garden material as well as Chinese characters representing spring and summer (Slide-show posted on school website)	Drama adaptation of the Chinese classic 'Journey to the West' (Performance in school talent show)
Rathmore Asian Community Project (RACP) (Mixed primary–secondary complementary school in Greenwich) Class: Year 3–12 (Age 6–17, mainly 3rd–4th generation) (Panjabi)	Family drama conceived, scripted and performed by students with support of teachers and parents (Performance for school and community members)	Wedding scene from drama expanded to incorporate traditional and modern dance (Performed for school and community members)	Dual language comic book based on the family drama (Presented to school and community members)

The scrapbook task at London Mandarin School

The idea behind this task developed out of work that the teacher had been doing with the young children in her class on the seasons. When initiating work on this theme, the teacher had introduced the 'Four Season Song', based on a traditional Chinese three-word chant. At a meeting of researchers and teachers at Goldsmiths it was suggested that the children might take this work forward by producing artwork on the seasons, adding labels in Chinese characters. As the class teacher was reluctant to give up precious class time for this task, it was agreed that this should be set as a homework activity. Thus children were asked to create a page for what might become a class scrapbook using any material they could find and to write the characters next to items if they knew them. They were also encouraged to ask parents or other family members for help.

As this was the first time the class had been set this kind of homework task, there was scepticism about how the children might respond to it. As it turned out, however, the task was taken very seriously. Children used plants from their own gardens or from parks and also personalised their work by drawing what they did and what they could see in spring or summer, incorporating elements from Chinese painting and adding labels written in basic Chinese characters with which they were familiar.

Describing how the scrapbook task at London Mandarin School helped relate learning to real life for her young child, one mother explained:

> This project connects the books with practical things. Before, they only learnt these in the textbook. But now, those are in the real world for them. When they go out sometimes, they cannot stop looking for the things they want for the work. They kept on asking me what things are in Mandarin as well. (Mother, LMS)

Other parents commented that, while welcoming their interest and support, children were adamant that this was their work and they didn't want anyone else to do things for them. As one mother put it:

> I helped them when they didn't know how to write some words. They are full of their own ideas and they want the work to be in the way they like. They didn't even allow me to write the Chinese characters on their paper. I have to write them on another piece of paper and then they tried to copy them to their work. (Mother, LMS)

Another compromise struck in one case was a joint composition, where the child wrote as much as she could using characters she knew how to write and then asked her mother to complete what she wanted to say, but using a different colour pen.

When children handed in their scrapbook pages, the teacher was impressed by the range and quality of work produced and the effort that had gone into it. She also mentioned how she had received very positive feedback from parents about the task set. In order to celebrate and share the children's work, she created a slideshow made up of photos of the scrapbook pages and posted this on the school blog. In class she then went on to compare the seasons in England and China using the children's work as a stimulus and noted a high level of learner engagement. She also noted the longer term impact on overall motivation, commenting that:

> The students who did this project are very confident in learning Mandarin now. They like to come to school. I also continue to do the scrapbook work. (Mandarin teacher, LMS)

The song stories and South Indian dance at Downderry Primary School

Before this project, Downderry Primary School had been running after-school classes in Tamil language and South Indian dance (Bharatha Natyam) for some years with the support of a local complementary school, the Tamil Academy of Language and Arts. Although working with the same group of children, the two classes had operated independently with little collaboration between the specialist teachers. Through becoming involved in the project, the question was raised as to whether a cross-curricular unit of work could be developed by means of collaboration between the language and dance teachers with support from the school and from the Goldsmiths research team.

A key link was established through the fact that South Indian dance is based on dramatised versions of song stories which often draw on cultural or moral themes. It was suggested, therefore, that in languages lessons the main aim could be to develop understanding of the song stories and the messages underlying them, while in dance lessons the focus could shift to expressing the meaning of the stories through the medium of dance.

During a series of meetings between colleagues, detailed plans were created to support the integrated approach with an emphasis on ways to encourage the active engagement of learners through pair and group work including peer assessment. A range of resources was also created to scaffold learning processes. These included posters, PowerPoint presentations containing a wealth of colourful images, worksheets and research tasks to be set for homework. (See Goldsmiths Multilingual Learning website, at http://www.gold.ac.uk/clcl/multilingual-learning/.) It was also planned that the work should lead up to a performance at a school assembly.

The integrated approach began with the Tamil language teacher telling the simplified story to the class in Tamil, drawing on visuals to convey the meaning of key words. She then introduced the song with a musical recording modelling a number of gestures and facial expressions suited to the Bharatha Natyam dance style. Next she had pupils sing the song, copying gestures and facial expressions. It was found that the incorporation of these kinaesthetic and musical elements supported language development and led to greater enjoyment and better retention of new vocabulary.

> All of the children are very happy. I can tell. They always like stories but this time, they learn more than just stories. They do movements and songs. They really like that. (Tamil language teacher, DPS)

This work was built on in dance lessons, drawing on students' increased awareness of how combinations of words, music and gesture can combine to enhance communication, leading naturally into more extended expression through dance movement. The dance teacher, teaching almost entirely through the medium of Tamil, found that students were more confident in their dance lessons because they had a better understanding of the story elements which translated into a greater sense of purpose when it came to expressing themselves through dance. In spite of limited rehearsal time, knowing that they were working towards a performance to schoolmates, parents and teachers served to focus students' minds.

Commenting on the assembly performance, the head teacher noted not only the sense of achievement and pride felt by those involved, but also the concentration and interest of the children in the audience who were seeing their classmates and another culture in a new light. She was also clear how the work connected with wider school priorities:

> The cross-curricular dance-language project is such a great idea ... It's a very exciting and useful way of actually learning the language. We are trying to do that as a school with our broader curriculum, for instance we are trying to link in literacy with other subjects including dance. (Head teacher, DPS)

As with the task set at the London Mandarin School, parental involvement was encouraged and important bridges built between school and home:

> Parents are very involved and very supportive. They work with me and Navaraj all the time. They help the students do the homework and printed out things for the students from the Internet. They helped make invitation cards and sort out the costumes. (Tamil language teacher, DPS)

Also similar to London Mandarin school, developing this more integrated approach with an emphasis on active learning and creative expression was found to provide a more stimulating and supportive context in which to develop both linguistic and dance skills.

> This project inspired us how we can teach in a different way, such as the language teacher can work with the dance teacher. Previously the language and dance classes were separate, so children didn't make connections. The teachers have also learnt different teaching styles and teaching techniques. We tried different things in classrooms. We also learnt to use ICT in our classes. (Tamil language teacher, DPS)

The development and performance of a drama focusing on a community issue at Rathmore Asian Community School

Although students attending this Panjabi complementary school covered a wide range of ages and proficiency levels, the head teacher was clear that all should be involved in the project and that students should take the main responsibility for leading it. Thus the decision to create and perform a drama came from the students themselves. Encouraged to choose a theme which they considered important for their community, they decided that the drama should focus on the situation of young women when they marry and in particular the unfair treatment they may receive from their mothers-in-law. Discussion about plot, characters and scenes took place among the students themselves and a drama was built up in which there was serious engagement with issues taking different standpoints into account, but also reflecting an awareness of tradition and the need to find solutions that allow family unity to be preserved. A script was then drafted by two of the older students in Panjabi script as well as in a transliterated version and in English.

Students explained that in order to give an accurate picture of traditional family practices around weddings they researched on the web and in the local library as well as consulting teachers and members of their own families. Once roles had been assigned – and it was agreed that all students as well as several mothers should participate – the rehearsal process began. Here again the strong emphasis placed on teamwork and collaboration revealed itself particularly in the way the older students supported the younger ones in remembering their lines and in bringing expression to their acting. In fact, as the project developed and students took more and more ownership of it, the head teacher noticed a change of attitude towards coming to classes:

> They are keen to come to school and don't want to miss any lesson. I remember X missed one day and he phoned me twice and he sent me some paper work about the task. This means they have got the sense of responsibility. Before, they didn't even inform me when they were going to miss classes. (Head teacher, RACP)

While the emphasis was on the process more than the outcome, the fact that work was building up to a performance meant that the audience had to be taken into account, as well as the most effective means of maximising interest while respecting cultural norms and conveying important moral messages. It also gave students the impetus to work on their speaking skills, in particular to improve pronunciation and fluency and to learn to project their voices. Indeed the teacher leading the project was eager to point out that:

> X, one of the boys, who was in charge of the dance, used to hesitate to speak Panjabi. I always ask him to be brave and speak. But now he is confident in speaking Panjabi because of the drama. He also said that he cannot believe that he could speak proper Panjabi and even acted in a drama. (Head teacher, RACP)

Following a performance of the drama to family, teachers and other community members, the students decided to follow up by expanding a wedding scene and performing it as a musical. They were clearly proud of what they had achieved collaboratively and also realised the benefits that the project had both for their learning and motivation. As one student put it:

> I think the task has made learning Panjabi a lot more interesting. When you learn Panjabi, you usually sit there and prepare for tests. It seems a bit boring ... but then this, you get the chance to learn words from the lyrics; you get the chance to learn about your culture. I am sure the other children also enjoyed this activity and have learnt a lot from it. It helps us to learn a lot more culture than we could when sitting in the classroom. (Student, RACP)

The creation of artworks reflecting the Arab world, but also children's own identities, at Sarah Bonnell School

The students in the Year 7 Arabic class involved in this project were mainly from a Muslim faith background and, although only a few spoke Arabic at home, there was great interest in the language for religious reasons and some had gained an insight into aspects of it through attending Quranic classes at the mosque. The teacher was working on the Arab world with the class and decided to have students create artworks reflecting particular Arab countries, but also their own diverse backgrounds. In the tradition of Islamic art it was expected that some text would be incorporated into these artworks and the teacher began by showing a PowerPoint presentation with examples of this, where the calligraphic representation was integral to the overall concept and design of the artwork. Students then worked in groups, planning, researching and then drafting and redrafting their artworks, drawing on symbolic use of colour and national emblems and incorporating text in Arabic. Such learner-directed projects with their multicultural and multimodal dimensions are an example of what Cummins (2006: 60) refers to as 'identity texts', because they involve cognitive engagement and identity investment and 'hold a mirror up to students in which their identities are reflected back in a positive light'.

The final works were framed and exhibited and students talked about them proudly with visitors, revealing an appreciation of the way in which cultural meanings are communicated through different media. For the Head of Languages at the school the value of the work in terms of intercultural understanding as well as language development was clear to see:

> It is the bridge between the language and the culture that people don't often see. So when you come along today, you are not just hearing the language but you are also seeing the meanings to the students. The students apparently chose the things that mean a lot to them. The other thing I love about it is bring it together with cultures. Here you can see Mauritius, Egypt, Kenya, all together. I think it is a wonderful way to bridge the students. (Head of Languages, SBS)

The effect on the class teacher was dramatic in terms of understanding how giving students greater control can lead to much greater levels of engagement and creativity, improve motivation and promote deeper learning:

> The students have learnt more profoundly because of this project. If you don't put the languages into a live context, which is I am learning and so I can use it. If you don't put them into this context, I don't think they can understand that why are they learning. (Teacher, SBS)

Transformative Pedagogy, Citizenship and Identity

Through these snapshots of work carried out in the four project schools, we have seen how arts-based creativity enabled a dynamic and cognitively challenging interaction with heritage and culture, how it can support and extend children's linguistic and multiliteracy development, how it can empower learners and develop a pride in mixed identities, and how it can provide an effective means of drawing on funds of knowledge in the home. Much of this resonates with studies by Edwards (1998), Datta (2007) and Sneddon (2009) and the manifestation in their work of the benefits of an inclusive approach to language and literacy. Alongside these key findings from our research, there also emerged a clearer understanding of the shift in pedagogy required to bring about the positive outcomes identified. There are a number of important aspects to this.

Firstly, teachers and curriculum managers need to be willing to step across curriculum boundaries, to explore connections, to plan in an integrated way and to utilise the range of scaffolding strategies required to support the development of content and creative skills at the same time as supporting language use. Part of this interdisciplinary emphasis should be an understanding the way in which this kind of work extends notions of literacy beyond the bounds of English and contributes to active citizenship. Indeed we have seen in the two mainstream schools how senior colleagues made these connections to broader perspectives on the curriculum and recognised how this enriched the learning experience for all students.

Secondly, there needs to be a re-conceptualisation of teacher and learner roles. While providing context, structure and resources to stimulate thinking, teachers need to be willing to stand back at times and encourage collaboration between learners so that a sense of agency, responsibility and ownership can be experienced. This can be disconcerting at first for teachers used to more traditional approaches, especially when initially progress may appear slow. As one teacher put it:

> Until you see the end of it and then you feel ohh they did something. It is hard because you get used to the way that you stand in front of the whiteboard and give them instructions. Then, listen, repeat and write. This is the way we used to learn and the way we used to teach. And to shift from this to that, it is a little bit that you are not sure ... It is a good feeling that they want to learn! It is not that I want to teach them and want them to learn. They want to learn! (Teacher, SBS)

Thirdly, instead of imposing fixed, essentialised notions of culture related to the past, it is important to create a space in which learners can construct understandings based on their own lived experience and the need to reconcile different cultural frames. It is not enough to introduce famous traditional stories or poems or artworks. Learners must be given the opportunity to interact with these works in their own terms, to reinvent and reinterpret them for themselves. Here the links between personal investment, learning and pride in identity (Cummins, 2006) become transparent.

Fourthly, a process orientation is essential, allowing students to try out ideas, make connections, take risks, make mistakes, review and refine their work. Having said this, establishing a clear end goal in the form of a presentation, performance or exhibition is also important because thinking about audience helps give a sense of direction and builds positive energy. It is also a means of recognising and celebrating achievement and building confidence.

Fifthly, the value of involving parents and drawing on funds of knowledge in the home and community needs to be recognised from the beginning. The contribution of parents in each of the schools in this project was significant and created a new basis for dialogue and mutual support. At the same time it reinforced links between schools and communities.

Conclusions

In this chapter we have sought to highlight the potential of arts-based creativity to contribute to the building of a pedagogical approach attuned to the needs of community/heritage language learners in mainstream and complementary school contexts. We see this as being crucial for our bilingual students, but also as important in building an inclusive and inter-culturally oriented curriculum for all learners. The multilingual turn has brought an increased awareness of the linguistic and cultural capital present within our communities. This should support us all in making links across the curriculum, between school and home and between mainstream and complementary sectors.

Acknowledgments

The authors would like to express their sincere gratitude to the head teachers of the four schools involved for their support: Tracey Lewis (Downderry School, Lewisham), Iqbal Sanghara (Rathmore Asian Community Project), Cauthar Tooley (Sarah Bonnell School, Newham) and Xiu Qin Liao (London Mandarin School, Hackney). Very warm thanks also go to the five teachers who took part in the project: Luma Hameed (Sarah Bonnell School), Xiu Qin Liao (also head teacher at London Mandarin School), Kristhuraja Nithiya and Muthusamy Navaraj (Downderry School) and Iqbal Sanghara (also head teacher at Rathmore Asian Community Project). They are also grateful for the invaluable support and advice given by colleagues at Goldsmiths, University of London (Yangguang Chen, Eve Gregory, Charmian Kenner, Clare Kelly, Claudine Kirsch, Siva Pillai, Ana Souza) as well as by Maggie Gravelle (University of Greenwich). Finally the authors wish to thank the Nuffield Foundation for funding the project.

References

Anderson, J. (2008) Towards integrated second language teaching pedagogy for foreign and community/heritage languages in multilingual Britain. *Language Learning Journal* 36 (1), 79–89.
Anderson, J. (2009) Relevance of CLIL in developing pedagogies for minority language teaching. In D. Marsh, P. Meehisto, D. Wolff, R. Aliaga, T. Asiakinen, M.J. Frigols-Martin, S. Hughes and G. Lange (eds) *CLIL Practice: Perspectives from the Field* (pp. 124–132). Jyväskylä: CCN, University of Jyväskylä. See http://www.icpj.eu/.
Anderson, J. (2011) Reshaping pedagogies for a plurilingual agenda. *Language Learning Journal* 39 (2), 135–147.
Blackledge, A. and Creese, A. (2010) *Multilingualism: A Critical Perspective*. London: Continuum.

Brinton, D., Kagan, O. and Bauckus, S. (eds) (2008) *Heritage Language Education: A New Field Emerging*. New York: Routledge.

Brown, K. and Brown, M. (1996) *New Contexts for Modern Language Learning: Cross-curricular Approaches*. London: CILT.

CILT (2007–2009) *Our Languages Project*. CILT, the National Centre for Languages, National Resource Centre for Supplementary Education, Specialist Schools and Academies Trust and School Development Support Agency. *See* http://www.our languages.org.uk/.

Claxton, G. (2008) *What's the Point of School? Rediscovering the Heart of Education*. London: Oneworld Publications.

Conteh, J., Martin, P. and Robertson, L. (eds) (2007) *Multilingual Learning: Stories from Schools and Communities in Britain*. Stoke-on-Trent: Trentham Books.

Coyle, D., Hood, P. and Marsh, D. (2010) *CLIL: Content and Language Integrated Learning*. Cambridge: Cambridge University Press.

Craft, A. (2005) *Creativity in Schools: Tensions and Dilemmas*. Oxford: Routledge.

Cummins, J. (2006) Identity texts: The imaginative construction of self through multi-literacies pedagogy. In O. García, T. Skutnabb-Kangas and M. Torres-Guzmán (eds) *Imagined Multilingual Schools: Languages in Education and Glocalization* (pp. 51–68). Clevedon: Multilingual Matters.

Datta, M. (ed.) (2007) *Bilinguality and Literacy: Principles and Practice* (2nd edn). London: Continuum.

DfES (2002) *Languages for All: Languages for Life*. London: Department for Education and Science. See https://www.education.gov.uk/publications/eOrderingDownload/DfESLanguagesStrategy.pdf.

DfES (2007) *Languages Review*. London: Department for Education and Science. See https://www.education.gov.uk/publications/standard/publicationDetail/Page1/DFES-00212-2007.

Edwards, V. (1998) *The Power of Babel*. Stoke-on-Trent: Trentham Books (in association with Reading: Reading and Language Information Centre).

Francis, B., Archer, L. and Mau, A. (2009) Language as capital, or language as identity? Chinese complementary school pupils' perspectives on the purposes and benefits of complementary schools. *British Educational Research Journal* 35 (3), 519–538.

Grenfell, M. (2002) *Modern Languages Across The Curriculum*. London: Routledge-Falmer.

Kenner, C. and Ruby, M. (2012) *Interconnecting Worlds: Teacher Partnerships for Bilingual Learning*. Stoke-on-Trent: Trentham Books.

NACCCE (1999) *All Our Futures: Creativity, Culture and Education*. London: National Advisory Committee on Creative and Cultural Education. See http://sirkenrobinson.com/skr/pdf/allourfutures.pdf.

Ofsted (2008) *Every Language Matters*. Manchester: Ofsted. See http://www.ofsted.gov.uk/.

Robinson, K. (2011) *Out of Our Minds: Learning to be Creative*. Chichester: Wiley.

Sneddon, R. (2009) *Bilingual Books – Biliterate Children: Learning to Read Through Dual Language Books*. Stoke-on-Trent: Trentham Books.

Conclusion: The Multilingual Turn in Languages Education

Gabriela Meier and Jean Conteh

The appearance of the second book on the multilingual turn (see May, 2014) within a short period of time confirms that the multilingual turn in languages education is indeed a reality. It is evident in the work of an increasing number of researchers and practitioners and in some important current developments in relation to language, learning and pedagogy, as discussed in the three parts of this book. We outlined these in our introduction and summarise them here, indicating what we see as the main implications for languages education:

- Scholarly understanding (at least in some fields) and research are moving away from the monolingual conception of language to develop understandings of the nature of multilingualism and the multilingual mind. This is linked with notions about the ways in which languages (including language varieties) are integrated within an individual's linguistic repertoire – they do not exist as separate entities.
- Learners use their entire language repertoires, and draw on their previous learning, to construct new knowledge. This means that we need to question the usefulness of any separation of languages in teaching and learning. An ecological, socioconstructive model seems to offer a promising lens in order to understand the processes of learning which recognise the diversity of language and cultural knowledge brought to the context by teachers and learners.
- Based on the above, pedagogies are beginning to emerge that are grounded in ecologically informed, multilingual approaches to teaching and learning. This entails a move away from conceptualising as bi/multilingual only those learners who grew up with more than one language, towards an understanding that all learners are capable of developing language awareness, and competence in additional languages.

As can be seen from the chapters, these perspectives are still not often recognised by policy makers and practitioners. The long-established mono-lingual 'target language' approaches to pedagogy are still widespread and are often seen intuitively as the right way to proceed. One of our key aims in this book is to contribute to the growing number of studies that question these approaches, and to reveal the opportunities and challenges of those afforded by the multilingual turn.

As you may have noted, there is a particular emphasis in this book on equality and inclusion. This is clearly connected with a model of pedagogy that views learning as a collaborative process between learners and teachers, based on two important notions:

- that learners bring diverse linguistic, cultural and other knowledge to their learning processes;
- that peers can learn much from one another and that teachers, learners and peers are all partners in learning.

One of the main motivations behind this book is to present the argument that the multilingual turn is based not only on a new understanding of how learners learn, but also on a wider discourse of enabling equal opportunities for learning in a globalised and diverse world.

Based on the above and on the ideas that all the authors have presented in their different ways in this book, we return to the title and offer some conclusions. In the following two sections, we have attempted to synthesise the main ideas in the book, developed through the chapters, and indicate their implications for the future of languages education. Thus, we present what we consider are the opportunities and the challenges for practice, research and policy entailed in the multilingual turn.

Opportunities for Individuals and Societies

Inviting different languages and knowledges into the classroom

In this book we have developed a model of learning as collaborative, dialogic, participatory, reciprocal and based on empowerment for teachers and learners. Learners build new knowledge in interaction with others, grounded in their existing knowledge and experience. We need to recognise, value and activate this as an important resource for learning. One way is through multilingual activities that value all languages, language varieties and knowledges. This legitimises diverse identities so that learners – and, in many cases, teachers – are not required to leave important parts of them-selves at the school gate. Inviting their fuller identities to unfold in school may have important implications for learning and socialisation in schools.

From monolingual to emergent multilinguals

A number of chapters in this book show how our language repertoires are dynamic, changing over our life courses through our experiences in the globalised world. Thus, we argue that we should move away from feeding a binary discourse, which describes individuals as either monolingual or bi/multilingual, and move towards considering all human beings as users of language in diverse ways, and as potential and emergent multilinguals. This entails the assumption that we all have at least some awareness and knowledge of other languages, and can be expected to master more than one language in our lifetimes, which is in line with CEFR's vision of the plurilingual repertoire (CoE, 2001), conceived more than a decade ago.

Multi-layered identities and social cohesion

Similar to our language repertoires, our identities are dynamically constructed and changing over time. Group identities, which are important categories in the construction of self, can act as a barrier to linking with other groups if the identity is constructed as essentialist and unchanging. Cantle (2012: 206) writes in his latest book about 'interculturalism':

> Segregation and integration have to be given new and more nuanced understandings. Breaking down segregation, or promoting integration can be advanced in many different ways and at different levels, without endangering existing conceptions of ourselves. This enables new identities to be added to existing ones, creating layers and multifaceted forms which will also continue to change and evolve over time and in different contexts.

He goes on to say that we need to develop ways of understanding ourselves in a 'new global context in which transnational [and we argue intergroup] connectivity will begin to describe global values' (Cantle, 2012: 206), working towards a 'common world future' based on a shared world history and culture (Cantle, 2012: 208). Building on Cantle's argument, the chapters in this book illustrate that language forms an essential part of constructing identities that are multi-layered, and which are in turn indexed by different languages or language varieties. Our argument also builds on that promoted by Cantle (2012: 208), that schools have indeed a role to play in turning 'singular identities into those of multiple ones'. Clearly, this depends on what identities are allowed, fostered and encouraged, and which ones are ignored, denigrated or rejected at school. In this book we have shown that nearly all educational models and all teachers have the potential to foster multi-layered and multilingual identities, at least to a certain extent. Thus the multilingual turn does not pose a threat to our understanding of self; on the contrary, it may allow multi-layered and shared identities with different and changing groups to strengthen social links, which is a dimension of social capital and thus an important indicator of social cohesion.

Multilingual pedagogies and achievement

As we have indicated above, one of the key themes running through the book is the need to construct models of learning that recognise and value diversity in all its forms, in order to widen affordances for all learners, opening out their potential for success. As the authors of several chapters show, the multilingual turn does seem to offer the possibility of enhancements in the quality of learning and achievement for all. Teachers who find spaces in their classrooms to promote such approaches are often surprised and pleased with the benefits they see for their students. Research is beginning to show the enriched quality of classroom interaction and the growth in individual learners' motivation, self-confidence and positive identities, factors shown in the chapters to be connected with richer learning. However, the pressures of universal, externally imposed assessment and inspection regimes need to be taken into account, and there is work to be done in documenting and promoting the positive outcomes of the multilingual turn for the kinds of learning that, we, along with many authors of the book, advocate.

Working in multilingual research teams

Much of the content of this book is based on collaborative partnerships between researchers, teacher educators and practitioners and between speakers of different languages. This book is co-edited and many of the chapters are co-written; sometimes the co-authors are peer academics, but in other cases they are representatives of different groups in the academic hierarchy, such as supervisor and student, researcher and teacher, and principal and co-researcher. Several chapters are also the result of partnerships between speakers and writers of different languages, revealing the ways in which language and cultural expertise and different knowledges can be shared in mutually enriching ways. Thus, this volume demonstrates ways forward in breaking down the normalised power relationships which can sometimes mean that diverse voices are not heard in the academic discourses and debates around the multilingual turn.

Challenges for Individuals and Societies

Biases of Western English-speaking discourses

The multilingual turn in languages education, as we have traced it in this book, describes a development that is partly grounded in an English language dominated academic discourse, but by no means exclusively. Those who have the ability to work in other languages might unearth further evidence of multilingual turns elsewhere. For example, in different parts of the world such as India, Africa or southeast Asia, many school systems are multilingual. It could be argued that some non-Western contexts are ahead of the West: there have been calls in Africa to adopt mother-tongue based multilingual education (Ouane & Glanz, 2007; Pinnock, 2009), which recognises that the widespread practice of banning the mother tongue as a medium of instruction can have detrimental effects on the education of individuals. Moreover, language policy in India has prescribed the teaching of three languages at school since the 1950s, often including Hindi and English as well as a regional language or the mother tongue (Annamalai, 1995). Clearly, policy adoption alone is but one step towards multilingual practice; we need to remember that some policy formulations 'have mostly remained political and ideological statements far removed from actual practices' (García *et al.*, 2006: 275). It follows that even where policy reflects understanding of multilingual approaches and their benefits, these may not be translated into practice for many different reasons.

Teacher education and professional development

As is shown in a number of chapters, some teachers are already embracing the possibilities of developing multilingual pedagogies. But many teachers struggle with the idea of legitimising multilingualism in their classrooms. Often, this is because they have had little opportunity to reflect on this during their teacher education, and to develop appropriate teaching strategies. Even if sympathetic to the idea, they often do not feel empowered or qualified to bring a more multilingually informed approach to their classrooms. While teacher education increasingly includes some discussion on these topics, we argue that they should have more official status, especially in the knowledge, skills and understandings required by newly qualified teachers. All teachers need to begin their careers with positive attitudes to language diversity, some understanding of the broader issues of multilingualism in society, and a basic toolkit of strategies for developing multilingual practices in their classrooms. As their careers progress, they need opportunities to develop more principled, theoretical knowledge of multilingualism in order to grow and develop as teachers in multilingual societies. We hope that this book may be one of the resources that could be used for this purpose.

Unrealistic expectations of schools and teachers

In this book we have shown that schools and teachers can make an important contribution to the positive construction of identity, socialisation and even to social integration, by adopting more ecologically informed multilingual approaches to learning and teaching. Clearly, teachers and teacher educators should be aware of this important opportunity. However, there is a danger of overloading and expecting too much from schools and teachers. They are increasingly given parental, societal and economic responsibilities that they cannot tackle alone. Often, the pressures are worsened by the imposition of top-down policy, which demands one-size-fits-all responses to the problems they face. Policy development needs to become a conversation between policy makers and practitioners, informed by the kinds of research that reveal the complexities of daily life in schools. Positive identity development and the socialisation of children as well as social integration are tasks for the whole of society – family, community and institution – and should not be left to schools alone.

Final Words: Implications for Pedagogy, Policy and Research

We hope that this book will give classroom practitioners confidence and some ideas, as well as points of reflection and theoretical underpinning for their work in their local classrooms. As illustrated in the chapters, every classroom and learning context is different; thus, multilingual approaches need to be well thought out and sensitive to local needs and circumstances. To return to the ecological metaphor, what is needed is an ecologically informed approach to incorporating the multilingual turn in the local environment, taking into account all its biodiversity and its social, economic, historic and political climate.

We have repeatedly referred to our view that the multilingual turn in languages education already is a theoretical reality, but needs to be more widely translated into mainstream practice. To make this happen, we need to keep building a sound research base that legitimises diverse knowledges in classrooms and informs policy, teacher education and classroom practice. We call for research which values the perspectives of all participants in particular settings, and which is imbued with openness to different epistemological positions and understandings of the world. For this we advocate Greene's approach to research (2007: 14), which suggests that researchers need to:

> ... set a large table, to invite diverse ways of thinking and valuing to have a seat at the table, and to dialogue across such differences respectfully and generatively toward deeper and enhanced understanding.

Greene argues that is a question of 'active engagement with difference', challenging the normalised binaries of much academic research, including so-called 'soft' and 'hard' science. This is likely to have greater potential to inform our understanding and contribute to policy making. Thus, this active engagement with difference, which is the main thread running through our book, can be enacted at all levels through the education system in practice, research and policy. To conclude, we offer a number of questions that we invite readers to consider for their own future research.

Language ideology and socialisation

(1) The reciprocal links between what happens in the classroom and the outside world have been demonstrated by a number of authors in this book. We need to know more, however, about the ways in which empowered and multi-layered learner and teacher identities may or may not contribute to wider social cohesion or wellbeing.

(2) We need a better understanding of what effects the recognition and use of locally spoken and other languages in classrooms has on individuals in schools and societies more widely, and how all learners can benefit from all the languages they encounter in their lives.

Language learning

(3) We need more research on how learners can use their linguistic repertoires in peer-learning situations or in multilingual interactional spaces, and how teachers can encourage constructive multilingual peer support.

(4) Some authors have shown how creativity, empathy and funds of knowledge, as part of the multilingual turn, enable learning in more holistic and multi-modal ways. More research is required into the processes and outcomes of these and related approaches to learning.

Language pedagogies and curricula

(5) While in this book authors have questioned the usefulness of separating languages, we need research that shows to what extent and in what situations it may or may not be useful to integrate or separate languages and what the respective processes and outcomes might be.

(6) There have been calls that every lesson should integrate content and language learning. Authors in this book have shown that accessing and constructing content knowledge on the basis of multilingual repertoires can have positive outcomes, but more research is required into pedagogic approaches to content and language integrated learning in different subjects, through the development of multilingualism/plurilingualism and multiliteracies across the curriculum.

Ultimate Word

Finally, we have to recognise that any enactment of the multilingual turn in languages education, or in any other sphere for that matter, can only ever be a series of compromises. For instance, the European Union has pledged to recognise all official languages, but effectively operates in English and French; the book you are holding in your hand is written in English to reach the widest possible audience which, in the end, is a pragmatic as well as a commercial decision. Thus, we are working towards enactment of the multilingual turn, but we must not be too harsh on ourselves. We need to avoid dogmatic stances, as we can, in all likelihood, only ever partially implement our ideas in our diverse practices and, as with all educational initiatives, what may work in one context may not work in another. The multilingual turn necessarily describes a journey and not a final destination, for which collaborative, reciprocal and mutually empowering ways of working in research and practice can guide the way.

References

Annamalai, E. (1995) Multilingualism for all: An Indian perspective. In T. Skutnabb-Kangas (ed.) *Multilingualism for All* (pp. 215–219). Lisse: Swets & Zeitlinger.

Cantle, T. (2012) *Interculturalism: The New Era of Cohesion and Diversity*. Basingstoke: Palgrave Macmillan.

CoE (2001) *Common European Framework of Reference for Languages: Learning, Teaching, Assessment (CEFR)*. Language Policy Unit, Council of Europe. Cambridge: Cambridge University Press.

García, O., Skutnabb-Kangas, T. and Torres-Guzman, M.E. (2006) *Imagining Multilingual Schools: Languages in Education and Glocalization*. Clevedon: Multilingual Matters.

Greene, J.C. (2007) *Mixed Methods in Social Inquiry*. San Francisco, CA: Jossey-Bass.

May, S. (2014) (ed.) *The Multilingual Turn – Implications for SLA, TESOL and Bilingual Education*. New York: Routledge.

Ouane, A. and Glanz, C. (2007) *Why and How Africa Should Invest in African Languages and Multilingual Education: An Evidence- and Practice-based Policy Advocacy Brief*. Hamburg. UNESCO Institute for Lifelong Learning.

Pinnock, H. (2009) *Reflecting Language Diversity in Children's Schooling: Moving from 'Why Multilingual Education' to 'How?'*. Reading: CfBT Education Trust and Save the Children.

Author Index

This list contains authors whose works are cited in more than one chapter in the book

Subject Index